LIBERATING PAUL

The Bible & Liberation

An Orbis Series in Biblical Studies

Norman K. Gottwald and Richard A. Horsley, General Editors

The Bible & Liberation Series focuses on the emerging range of political, social, and contextual hermeneutics that are changing the face of biblical interpretation today. It brings to light the social struggles behind the biblical texts. At the same time it explores the ways that a "liberated Bible" may offer resources in the contemporary struggle for a more human world.

Already published:

The Bible and Liberation: Political and Social Hermeneutics (Revised edition), Norman K. Gottwald and Richard A. Horsley, Editors

Josiah's Passover: Sociology and the Liberating Bible, Shigeyuki Nakanose

The Psalms: Songs of Tragedy, Hope, and Justice, J. David Pleins

Women and Jesus in Mark: A Japanese Feminist Perspective, Hisako Kinukawa

Becoming Children of God: John's Gospel and Radical Discipleship, Wes Howard-Brook

LIBERATING PAUL

*The Justice of God and the Politics
of the Apostle*

Neil Elliott

ORBIS BOOKS

Maryknoll, New York 10545

The Catholic Foreign Mission Society of America (Maryknoll) recruits and trains people for overseas missionary service. Through Orbis Books, Maryknoll aims to foster the international dialogue that is essential to mission. The books published, however, reflect the opinions of their authors and are not meant to represent the official position of the society.

Copyright © 1994 by Neil Elliott

Published by Orbis Books, Maryknoll, NY 10545-0308

Manufactured in the United States of America

Library of Congress Cataloging-in Publication Data

Elliott, Neil.
    Liberating Paul : the justice of God and the politics of the apostle / Neil Elliott.
       p.   cm. — (the Bible & liberation series)
    Includes bibliographical references and index.
    ISBN 0-88344-981-1
    1. Bible. N.T. Epistles of Paul—Theology. 2. Paul, the Apostle, Saint—Political and social views. 3. Liberation theology. 4. Justice—Biblical teaching. I. Title. II. Series.
    BS2651.E49 1994
    227'.06—dc20   94-3540
                                              CIP

Contents

v

Preface

In August 1991, George Bush was basking in the glow of the highest approval ratings of his presidency in the wake of the Persian Gulf war. As a result, the peace activists, ministers, social workers, teachers, and other friends of the Sojourners community who gathered that month in Grand Rapids, Michigan, to celebrate the twentieth anniversary of *Sojourners* magazine needed more than a morale boost. In one workshop, Ched Myers of the American Friends Service Committee compared the war's emotional toll on the peacemaking community with the trauma of ongoing domestic violence: The fatigue and depression felt by many of the workshop's participants corresponded to the response of abuse victims who go on living in a family that denies the abuse.

As I attended different workshops over that three-day celebration, I was struck by one question asked over and over again, with real anguish, by Christians committed to peacemaking in a violent society: "But what do we do with the Bible?" Further discussion usually revealed that the heart of that question was "What do we do with Paul?" For it was Paul's voice that we heard most often when our churches debated war, or when they discussed domestic violence, or economic injustice, or a number of other "peace and justice" concerns.

This book was conceived during that celebration, as an attempt to answer the question, "What do we do with Paul?"

My title, *Liberating Paul*, is deliberately ambiguous, and audacious in either of its possible meanings. Given a history in which the apostle's voice has again and again rung out like iron to enforce the will of slaveholders or to legitimate violence against women, Jews, homosexuals, or pacifists, proposing to describe a "liberating Paul" may sound like a joke in bad taste. The phrase will ring especially hollow to those who have encountered the oppressive face of the apostle personally, whether on protest lines, in courtrooms, in church board meetings, or in the intimacy of their own bedrooms.

It is just because the voice we have learned to accept as Paul's is the voice of the sanctified status quo that continued efforts to reclaim Paul's genuine voice are necessary. For centuries the apostle's legacy has been systematically manipulated by human structures of domination and oppression, from the conservative interpreters of Paul who found their way into the New Testament itself, down to the legitimation of the "New World Order" or the sonorous waves of antifeminist backlash in our own time.

The task is an urgent one. Much more is at stake here than pointing out differences among current interpretations of the Bible. Long before our century, the voice of Paul was taken over as one of the ideological weapons in the arsenal of Death. Paul's readers today thus find themselves on a terrible battleground between spiritual forces. I believe that our struggle to liberate human beings from the power of Death requires "liberating Paul" from his enthrallment to that power.

This book is written, first of all, for those who have found Paul a stumbling block in their attempt to follow Jesus on the way of justice and peace. I am convinced that what many people experience as the scandal of Paul is the unfortunate consequence of the way Paul has usually been read, or rather misread, in the churches. One of my aims throughout the book is to give the reader an impression of the extent to which traditional assumptions about Paul are hotly debated by interpreters today. Another is to show how a new understanding of Paul, drawn from recent studies by a number of scholars, can help to remove this obstacle and allow another, deeper scandal—the scandal of the cross of Christ (1 Cor. 1:18–25)—to manifest itself more clearly.

It will be evident that I have kept another audience in mind as well: my colleagues in professional biblical studies. Although this book is intended for any reader interested in Paul, I have deliberately engaged current debates in scholarship, and particularly questions about the contours of Paul's theology, along the way. I am convinced that the way forward for all of us, interested lay readers and scholars alike, lies in recognizing that Paul's legacy to us is more expressly liberative than we have previously been led to think.

I can imagine that some of my academic colleagues may be surprised by so explicitly political an agenda as "liberating Paul." Although avowing such an agenda is still unusual in academic biblical study, it is not unknown. In her 1987 presidential address before the Society of Biblical Literature, Elisabeth Schüssler Fiorenza advocated a new understanding of "the public-political responsibility of biblical scholarship" and called for "decentering the dominant scientist ethos of biblical scholarship by recentering it in a critical interpretive praxis for liberation." While Schüssler Fiorenza has elaborated this proposal and applied it to the history of early Christianity in a number of books, including *Bread Not Stone: The Challenge of Feminist Biblical Interpretation* (1984) and *In Memory of Her: A Feminist Theological Reconstruction of*

Christian Origins (1988), it is her public appeal to biblical scholars to engage their professional activities in a broader political struggle for justice that informs the approach I take here. This book is an attempt to apply such politically engaged interpretation to the legacy of Paul.

Given the ways Paul has been misrepresented, by his admirers and his enemies alike, through the centuries, and given the magnitude of the social, political, and economic interests that continue to benefit from that misrepresentation, we should hardly expect to arrive at a new understanding of Paul until we grapple with the interpretive tradition very seriously. For that reason, I have postponed an examination of Paul's action as an apostle in "evangelizing" and guiding Christian congregations, what I term his "apostolic praxis," to part 2 of this book. I begin in part 1 with a sampling of the ways in which Paul has been appropriated by the powerful to perpetuate their own privileges, at the expense of their victims, and proceed to analyze the exegetical and theological mechanisms of that distortion. These chapters provide the context in which I turn in part 2 to examine the political dimensions of Paul's theology of the cross and of his own apostolate.

I am grateful for the constant encouragement of colleagues at the College of St. Catherine, where this project was supported with a faculty development grant. Father George and Mary Metcalf extended to me their warm hospitality at the Oratory of St. Mary, where chapter 4 was written. Special gratitude is due to Robert Ellsberg, editor-in-chief at Orbis, whose confidence and support have proven invaluable, and to Ched Myers, who very generously read and commented on the manuscript. Above all I give thanks for Holly's dear companionship and theological acumen throughout the journey.

I

PAUL IN THE SERVICE OF DEATH

"The history of Pauline interpretation is the history of the apostle's ecclesiastical domestication."

Ernst Käsemann

1

Paul in the Service of Death

In a letter to his ecclesiastical superiors, the Reverend Francis Le Jau, a French Huguenot missionary toiling in the fields of the Lord, or more prosaically, in the tobacco plantations of colonial South Carolina, described his customary practice when baptizing African slaves.

He felt a responsibility "to remove all pretense from the Adult Slaves I shall baptize of their being free upon that account" and required the slave's consent to a formal declaration before baptism: "You declare in the Presence of God and before this Congregation that you do not ask for the holy baptism out of any design to free yourself from the Duty and Obedience you owe to your Master while you live, but merely for the good of Your Soul and to partake of the Graces and Blessings promised to the Members of the Church of Jesus Christ."

A sensitive man, the Reverend Le Jau agonized privately in later mission reports that his parishioners routinely tortured and mutilated their slaves in punishment for "the slightest fault." One of the more popular tortures—forcing a difficult slave into a coffin, then loading rocks onto the coffin lid—had in fact killed several slaves. Le Jau was also incensed when his neighbors set out on armed expeditions to capture slaves from Spanish settlements to the south. A progressive, he preached against the "barbarous using of the Slaves" and urged that newly captured slaves "be used with Christian Charity." His preaching was clear enough to earn him the suspicion of some local slaveholders, though apparently not so harsh as to prevent them from attending his services.

The minister's more vigorous educational efforts were reserved for the slaves. He instituted a catechetical program after the Sunday liturgy for Africans and Native Americans. White planters also frequented these sessions, clearly suspicious of his intentions. They need not have worried. The content of Le Jau's "catechism," by his own account, was that "the Slaves shall be fed and provided for by the Masters, and the whole time of the Slaves shall be their Masters'; this is what I have continually urged; knowing how idly and criminally the Slaves spent the time given to them to work for themselves. I bless God for having at last rendered the Masters sensible of their own Advantage in this respect." The Reverend Le Jau considered this part of his ministry an unqualified success: "those Slaves behave themselves very well, and do better for their Masters' profit than formerly, for they are taught to serve out of Christian Love and Duty."[1]

The allusion to Scripture is unmistakable. The basis for the slaves' catechism is the biblical injunction to slaves to give obedience to their masters "as to the Lord," an injunction that appears in the New Testament under the name of Paul.

THE MASSACHUSETTS BAY COLONY, 1637

It was not immediately clear to women among the Puritan dissenters who colonized New England whether, and how, the bold experiments in Calvinist theocracy would affect their own liberties. A number of more independent-minded women and men in Boston were drawn to the home of Anne Hutchinson, a remarkably erudite and devout Puritan, the mother of thirteen children, whom the colony's governor, John Winthrop, described as "a woman of a haughty and fierce carriage, of a nimble wit and active spirit, and a very voluble tongue, more bold than a man; though in understanding and judgement," he felt compelled to continue, "inferior to many women." The conversations in Hutchinson's home centered around learned discussions of the preaching in local pulpits.

The ministers of the Bay Colony did not appreciate such unsolicited reviews of their sermons. The General Court of the Colony arraigned Anne Hutchinson on charges of "troubling the peace of the commonwealth and the churches," citing her defiance of previous admonitions to desist from promoting such of her opinions as were "prejudicial to the honour of the churches and ministers thereof."

The transcript of the trial includes a tortuous exchange between Anne Hutchinson, who insisted she had violated none of the colony's regulations, nor done anything beyond what was customary for any of the men assembled in the courtroom, and Governor Winthrop, whose eagerness to declare her guilty and pronounce a sentence of banishment was scarcely restrained. Their exchange revolved around two passages from Paul's letters. Winthrop pressed the accused woman to admit to having taught in the presence of men in her house, in clear violation of 1 Tim. 2:12 ("I permit no woman to teach or hold authority over a man"); she repeatedly denied that any but women were present in the meetings she led, on the authority of Titus 2:3–5 (older women are to "train the younger women").

Frustrated when this straightforward line of prosecution failed, Winthrop and his deputy governor fell back upon weaker and weaker arguments. An attempt to find fault with Hutchinson's theology was doomed: The transcript shows her dancing circles around her clerical accusers. Clergymen called to testify that Hutchinson had slandered the Bay Colony ministers could not agree on any incriminating remarks.

At last the deputy governor challenged Anne Hutchinson's right to speak her mind at variance with the ordained ministers of the community. She confessed to speaking "what in my conscience I know to be truth"; pressed to explain, she replied, "by an immediate revelation." The court promptly condemned her, despite the repeated protests of the Reverend John Cotton, one of the ministers Hutchinson was accused of slandering, that her views were not theologically objectionable. The deputy governor declared her "deluded by the devil." The governor labeled her "the principal cause of all our trouble" and banished her from the colony on the strength of a majority vote, the Reverend Cotton apparently assenting.

Hutchinson left for Rhode Island in 1638, accompanied by thirty-five other families. When she moved her family to the island of Aquidneck, later Long Island, Narragansetts who had been defrauded of their land thought she was one of their enemies; they killed her and her family.

Back in Boston, neither the agitation by women in the churches nor the fury of the male oligarchy was spent. A few months after Hutchinson's banishment, Katherine Finch was ordered whipped for "speaking against the magistrates, against the churches, and against the elders." In the next year, Philipa Hammond was excommunicated from her Boston church for publicly declaring that Anne Hutchinson had not deserved her sentence. In 1640 Hutchinson's friend and associate Jane Hawkins was convicted of witchcraft and banished from the colony: She and Hutchinson had served as midwives when their friend Mary Dyer gave birth to a deformed child. Twenty years later Dyer, the only woman who had spoken up for Hutchinson at her trial, was hanged along with two other Quakers for "rebellion, sedition, and presumptuous obtruding themselves." Sarak Keayne was punished in 1646 for "irregular prophesying in mixed assemblies"; Joan Hogg, for "disorderly singing and idleness" and for "saying she was commanded of Christ so to do." Mary Oliver, who refused to testify regarding her conversion experience as a prerequisite for being admitted to communion, was subjected to public torture in 1651 and died soon after in England.[2]

The brutal suppression of activist religious women found justification in a flurry of sermons from Puritan pulpits. Anne Hutchinson's condemnation became an immediate precedent. In Puritan sermons preached over the next twenty years, the cherished Pauline admonition to wifely subordination to the husband (Eph. 5:22) was now supplemented by warnings against the "notorious" example of Mrs. Hutchinson. Even in England, the rise of agitation by independent women in the churches was suppressed by reference to the sentence in the colonies. "Henceforth," inveighed the Reverend John Brinsley in Yarmouth, England, in 1645, "no more Women Preachers!"

The infamous witch trials of Salem were still decades away.

KULMHOF, "GREATER GERMANY" (CHELMNO, POLAND), 1941–1945

The citizens of Chelmno remember Simon Srebnik as the youth with the sweet, clear voice singing love ballads and soldiers' songs as he rowed SS officers down the Narew River.

Srebnik has other memories of Chelmno. After watching his father die in the Lodz ghetto, Simon and his mother were deported to the Nazi death camp at Chelmno, where his mother was murdered in a gas van. A boy of thirteen, Simon was put to work on a *Sonderkommando*, a "special detail," pulling gold teeth from the skulls of Jews who had been gassed to death in the vans before the corpses were loaded into the crematorium.

On one occasion, Srebnik recalls, another Jewish boy working on the *Sonderkommando* recognized his sister's body. In his sudden terror, the boy managed to wrench his ankle free from the iron chain that held him; somehow he made his way out of the camp and reached the Narew, where a Polish peasant offered to ferry him across the river. But the Pole betrayed the boy to a German soldier, who shot him and took his body back to the death camp, where it was put on display in the *Sonderkommando* hut. An SS captain ordered fifteen Jews outside and shot them, then warned Srebnik and the others, "If any of you tries to run away I will kill you all."

Beginning on December 7, 1941, over the next four years the Nazis killed 360,000 Jews at Chelmno.

As Soviet troops approached the camp in January 1945, the Nazis set about killing the surviving Jews in the *Sonderkommando*. Srebnik was among the first five marched out of the barracks, ordered to lie down on the frozen ground, and shot in the back of the head. But Srebnik did not die. Though shot through the neck, he managed over the next hours to crawl through the woods to a Polish farm, where he hid in the pigsty. The Polish farmer, a Gentile, hid Srebnik until the Soviets overran the position. The Soviet physician who examined the gunshot wound to Srebnik's spine gave him less than twenty-four hours to live.

In fact Srebnik survived—one of only two Jews to survive the Chelmno death camp—to testify at the trial of Adolf Eichmann in

Jerusalem in 1961 and to be reunited years later with some of the citizens of Chelmno for the filming of Claude Lanzmann's documentary, *Shoah*.[3]

In a chilling scene in that film, smiling Poles surround Srebnik outside their Roman Catholic church, following a festival Mass. Srebnik listens in glassy silence as the Christians reminisce about the routine roundups of Jews in the church courtyard and the sorting of Jewish property within the church building some forty years earlier. The Christians appear as untormented by the memory of the fate awaiting those Jews as they are oblivious to the survivor's physical presence among them. They consistently refer to "the Jews" in the past tense. They engulf Srebnik as they edge closer to the camera in their cheerful enthusiasm. It is as though this Jew does not exist: as though he has become the theological abstraction to which these Catholics give their terrible, smiling assent, the abstraction that rises up from the Gospel texts to form a perversely fantastic reminiscence in their minds. A Jewish rabbi, they assure the camera, encouraged his synagogue to submit to murder because "around two thousand years ago the Jews condemned the innocent Christ to death." A Polish Christian smiles into the camera: "That's all; now you know!"

An abyss of horror yawns before these calm, happy faces, an abyss opened up by the Gospels and by the words that appear in 1 Thess. 2:14–15: "The Jews . . . killed both the Lord Jesus and the prophets, and drove us out, and displease God. . . . But God's wrath has come upon them at last!"

THE "NEW WORLD ORDER": GUATEMALA, 1982

The 1954 CIA coup against the progressive Arbenz government ushered in a series of right-wing dictatorships in Guatemala, each propped up by U.S. military aid. Energized by Ronald Reagan's inauguration, the Guatemalan military launched a massive campaign of death-squad-style political murders and, in rural areas, scorched-earth warfare that wiped out whole villages of Indians. By 1982 Guatemala was convulsed by U.S.-sponsored civil war.

Reenter General Efraín Ríos Montt, a popular Evangelical who had lost his presidency in a 1974 army coup. Ríos Montt enjoyed considerable moral and financial support from the Reagan administration, who saw in this pious soldier its brightest prospect for continuing the oppression in Guatemala without jeopardizing congressional funding, and from "The Word," a fringe Pentecostal church in southern California that had given the general solace after the 1974 coup. (This Pentecostal connection would make it easier for Fundamentalist televangelists like Pat Robertson to garner funds for right-wing campaigns in Central America.)

Once reinstalled by the military, Ríos Montt began a "beans and rifles" policy that quickly became notorious. Food distribution, health care, and literacy campaigns among the Indian population coincided with massacres of whole villages and the resettlement of large populations of Indians in concentration camps, on the model of the "strategic hamlets" of Vietnam; all in accord with lessons learned by Guatemalan army officers at the infamous U.S. School of the Americas. Church workers who declared the aid programs to be a mask for an escalated campaign of genocide against the Indians were expelled from the country; but Ríos Montt's own contented reference to his "scorched-Communist" policy gave the accusations plausibility.

While televangelists like Pat Robertson and Jerry Falwell hustled for funds and support for the regime from their U.S. audiences,[4] Evangelical missionaries in Guatemala fronted for the government's "hearts and minds" campaign among the Ixil Indians. Despite testimonies of widespread torture and killing by the military *and* the guerrillas, some missionaries and their native Evangelical colleagues preferred to support the army's atrocity-scarred campaign rather than acquiesce in a feared "communist" takeover of the country.

In an interview with a North American visitor, one pastor from Salquil reported leading his congregation into government-held territory and internment at "Camp New Life," a refugee camp ringed with barbed wire and machine-gun nests, after government soldiers had burned their crops and destroyed their homes. The pastor said he had feared more of his people might die in guerrilla reprisals: Six members of his congregation had already been killed after they sabotaged booby traps laid by the guerrillas. "Here we were in a situation where the guerrillas would kill anyone who refused to do what they said," he declared, "and they've actually killed some of us."

But the army, too, had killed members of his church, he acknowledged. When government helicopters landed in the hamlet of Tu Chobuc, three families, twenty-nine persons in all, gathered to pray. After troops discovered an empty guerrilla storage pit nearby, they took the men, women, and children there and cut their throats.

The pastor nevertheless led his people into the embrace of the military. Part of the reason may have been quite pragmatic. With massive U.S. support, the army was vastly better armed; it was also demonstrably less discriminating in its brutality. Guatemala remains a textbook example of "low intensity conflict," the Pentagon's preferred form of population control through terrorism—"total war at the grassroots level," as one general described it. Military analyst Michael Klare defines it as "that amount of murder, mutilation, torture, rape and savagery that is sustainable without triggering widespread public disapproval" in the United States. Refined over the years since Vietnam, the doctrine was embraced by both the Reagan and Bush administrations.[5]

The concept is simple enough, as an interned Ixil explained: "If we obey, they don't kill us anymore."

The pastor, on the other hand, supported his decision to lead his congregants into the arms of the Guatemalan military by reference to the Bible. "We kept remembering that the Bible says that we should obey the President. . . . The Bible tells us that we shouldn't join ourselves to the guerrillas."[6]

One would search a Bible concordance in vain for the terms *President* or *guerrilla*. The pastor was evidently alluding to Rom. 13:1, a favorite verse among Ríos Montt's colleagues at The Word as well: "Let every person be subject to the governing authorities. For there is no authority except from God, and those that exist have been instituted by God." The apostle's words offered the pastor from Salquil a clarity more sublime than the villager's harsh explanation of the terrorist state, although from the perspective of the Guatemalan military the result was the same.

THE PAULINE LEGACY AS AN IDEOLOGICAL WEAPON OF DEATH

What have these accounts to do with Paul of Tarsus, a Jew of the ancient Roman world?

If these brief narratives read as exhibits in an indictment of Paul, our immediate response might be to try to minimize the connection, to exonerate Paul of deeds that were done in his name by others, centuries after his death.

The usefulness of the Pauline letters to systems of domination and oppression is nevertheless clear and palpable. This observation must be our starting point. It is not enough to protest that one or another remark in Paul's letters has been torn out of context to justify acts of horror. Such distortions are too widespread and consistent in the history of Christendom to allow such easy dismissal. These distortions also rest too easily on generally accepted perceptions of who Paul was and what he was about. I am concerned here neither to write a history of the popular interpretation of Paul nor to catalogue injustices in modern history. I want instead to describe what I see as the most important feature of the situation in which Paul is read today: the empressment of his voice to serve ungodly and inhumane forces, what the baptismal rite of my church calls the "evil powers that corrupt and destroy the creatures of God."[7]

However unnaturally, Paul has been made an agent of oppression in our age. Of course he was not the architect of the North American slave economy that so constrained the Reverend Le Jau's ministry. But the canonical Paul served the slave economy quite well. In fact it is hard to imagine institutional slavery thriving in so thoroughly Christian a society as the antebellum U.S. without the prop of apostolic legitimation that Ephesians and 1 Timothy provided.

The Reverend Le Jau was evidently quite aware that there was more to the Bible than those Pauline letters. He was alarmed, for instance, at "the Confusion our best Negroe Scholar was like to Create here among his fellow slaves on having put his own Construction upon some Words of the Holy Prophet's which he had read." More than a century later, another minister in the southern states would complain in a farmer's journal that "on almost every large plantation of Negroes there is one among them who holds a kind of magical sway over the minds and opinions of the rest; to him they look as their oracle, though most generally a *preacher* is, in ninety-nine cases out of a hundred, the most consummate villain and hypocrite on the premises. It is more than likely that he has seen miraculous visions, equal to those of John on the isle of Patmos; angels have talked with him, etc. The influence of such a Negro on a quarter is incalculable."[8]

That anxiety was well founded. Two decades earlier, the slave revolt that struck terror throughout rural Virginia had been fired by Nat Turner's apocalyptic visions of black and white spirits warring in the heavens.[9] In 1800 a slave named Gabriel had organized over a thousand Virginia slaves during gatherings "under pretext of attending preachment"; according to a deposition from a captured and condemned participant in the abortive revolt, debates about strategy had turned on the interpretation of Bible passages from the books of Exodus and Joshua.[10] The "Vesey conspiracy" that terrified white Charleston in 1822 centered on Denmark Vesey, an African veteran of slave rebellions in the West Indies, who inflamed black churches with fiery images of the Israelites' deadly assault on Jericho.[11]

Against this subversive reading of the Bible by slaves, the slaveholders' reliance on Paul was deliberate, calculated, and systematic. "It is rarely that any one can attend a house of religious worship without gaining some wholesome information. And the slave will generally learn, at such places, the reasons which sanction the master to exact of him his respective duties."[12] This divine "sanction" is, of course, derived from the Pauline letters. To the degree that these letters served a dependable and systematic function within the institutionalized brutality of American slavery, the canonical Paul was made complicit in the whipping of slaves, as surely as Saul of Tarsus held the coats of those who stoned Stephen to death at the gate of the Jerusalem Temple (Acts 7:58).

Similarly Paul did not conceive the terrorism against women in Puritan New England, any more than he invented male chauvinism or the patriarchal society. But the point remains that the canonical Paul has proved incalculably useful to patriarchy, sanctifying the intimate oppression of women (and children, and gays), far more useful, in fact, than any other section of the Bible. As feminist theologian Mary Daly remarks, "The most strikingly antifeminist passages are, of course, the Pauline texts."[13]

The oppressive legacy of the Pauline writings extends beyond the few passages that specifically address "the role of women." John Winthrop's haggling over prooftexts with Anne Hutchinson was, perhaps, mere pretext. His motives, and the vision of the Puritan theocracy, are surely to be sought in more elevated reflections, as in Winthrop's sermon, years earlier, to his fellow pilgrims on the deck of the *Arabella*. While enjoining mutual affection and consideration, Winthrop allowed that "in all times some must be rich, some poor; some high and eminent in power and dignity, others mean and in subjection." The assumption that the rich and powerful inevitably and properly dominate the poor and powerless was already the cornerstone of Aristotle's *Politics* and was a commonplace in discussions of civic and household government in classical antiquity.[14] For the Puritans, however, the far more relevant text was the apostle's injunction to be satisfied with one's calling (1 Cor. 7:17, 24) and the commands to subordination addressed to wives, slaves, and children in 1 Timothy and Ephesians.

It was in this form, spliced with Aristotle and metastasized, in the work of medieval European scholastic theologians, into a virulent code of divinely sanctioned domination, that the Pauline legacy was introduced to the "New World." When, in 1511, the Dominican Father Antonio de Montesinos decried the brutality of Spanish colonists on the island they renamed Hispaniola ("You are all in mortal sin because of the tyranny you practice among these innocent peoples!"), the colonists, good churchmen all, were as surprised by his "new and strange doctrine" as they were angry. They appealed to the island's governor, Christopher Columbus's son Don Diego, who had the priest summoned and demanded to know why he had preached things "in such disservice to the king and so harmful to the whole land."[15] Courageous and compassionate men like Father de Montesinos, or like Father Bartolomé de las Casas, who left us an account of the scene, confronted more than the wrath of Spanish conquistadores. As Chilean theologian Pablo Richard writes, "The genocide and the massacre which began in 1492 would not have been possible without an appropriate theology." Richard finds this theology articulated in a "Treatise on the Just Causes of the War against the Indians," published by Juan Ginés de Sepúlveda in 1545. Sepúlveda, a valuable witness because "he says clearly what everyone thinks and does," wrote that "it is just and natural that prudent, honest and humane men should rule over those who are not so . . . [and therefore] the Spaniards rule with perfect right over these barbarians of the New World and the adjacent islands who in prudence, intellect, virtue and humanity are as much inferior to the Spaniards as children to adults and women to men."

This logic of subordination generated a certain ambivalence in the Spaniard toward the "Indian," who was simultaneously the target of "evangelization" and of genocide. As Sepúlveda wrote, "The greatest philosophers declare that this war is just by law of nature" which seeks to bring "to submission by force of arms, if this is not possible by any other means, those who by their natural condition should obey others but refuse their authority."[16]

The subjection of Puritan women within the patriarchal household is only a particularly intimate form of the same sacred economy of subjugation.

The canonical Paul is no less indispensable to the Christian ideology of patriarchy in our own time. Much of the emphasis on biblical inerrancy in early Fundamentalism was designed, as historian Betty DeBerg has shown, to rejuvenate the troubled Victorian ideal of the family with its sharply divided sex roles in an earlier Christian backlash against women's emancipation.[17] The antifeminist backlash of the last decade incorporated the same Fundamentalist ideology, as documented by journalist Susan Faludi and demonstrated in the 1992 Republican presidential campaign's emphasis on "family values." Faludi observes that "in their sermons, the New Right ministers invoked one particular Biblical passage with such frequency that it even merited press attention: Ephesians 5:22–24—'The husband is the head of the wife, even as Christ is head of the church'—became an almost weekly mantra in many pulpits."[18] As Faludi notes, this appeal to the biblical Paul is an integral part of the social control of women. She cites an Evangelical minister's comment to a sociologist: "Wife beating is on the rise because men are no longer leaders in their homes. I tell the women they must go back home and be more submissive."

Variations on that anecdote have become too common to require documentation. In fact the Bible plays so pervasive a role in perpetuating "the legacy of the 'appropriate' victim" as to merit discussion in a treatment of violence against wives by sociologists, in which the Pauline writings are singled out as best summarizing the "so-called Christian attitude toward women, which surely reinforced their subjugation through force."[19] The sacred legitimation of victimage is well charted by now, particularly by feminist critics.[20] Pastors, therapists, and theologians have the Pauline letters particularly in mind when they suggest plastering a warning label across the Bible: "Caution: may be hazardous to women's health and survival."[21]

The hazards apply to gay men and lesbians as well. Political campaigns against civil rights for gays and lesbians regularly cite Paul, practically the only New Testament author to give homosexuality even momentary attention (Rom. 1:24–27; 1 Cor. 6:9–10, declaring that "homosexuals" shall not inherit the kingdom of God [RSV]). The same correlations that sociologists Dobash and Dobash have made between religious ideology and violence against wives could be extended to violence against homosexual men and women as well; the Pauline writings function as instruments of the "tyranny of the nuclear family" at the cost of violence to "the appropriate victims."

Nor should we underestimate the Pauline legacy's role in the impoverishment of nontraditional families. To provide ideological justification for gutting federal welfare programs like Aid to Families with Dependent Children (AFDC), the Reverend Jerry Falwell recites the Pauline dictum "If any one will not work, let him not eat" (2 Thess. 3:10) as one of ten "Judeo-Christian principles" at the foundation of American democracy.

Violence against women often occurs in quiet domestic isolation. But the murder of six million European Jews was a public effort, requiring tremendous coordination across many sectors of German society.[22] Since the mid-1970s, the question of Paul's contribution to the Christian anti-Semitism that led to Auschwitz and Treblinka has convulsed Pauline studies. Authors of articles and monographs on Paul's theology now routinely situate their work in the "post-Holocaust era."[23] Of course, Paul did not conceive Hitler's "final solution" to "the Jewish problem." But the words from 1 Thessalonians ("The Jews . . . killed both the Lord Jesus and the prophets. . . . God's wrath has come upon them at last!") stand at the source of a terrible stream of prejudice and hatred, a tradition given sharp and vindictive form in part through Martin Luther's gratuitous recommendation that "synagogues should be set on fire," Jewish homes "broken down or destroyed," Jews themselves dispossessed, "put under one roof, or in a stable, like Gypsies, in order that they may realize that they are not masters in our land," and set to harsh labor, "for all time."[24]

Not only did texts like 1 Thessalonians 2 facilitate the murderous anti-Semitism of Nazi Germany; Paul's voice in Rom. 13:1 ("Let every person be subject to the governing authorities; for there is no authority except from God") also served to stifle Christian opposition to Nazi policies, indeed to promote enthusiasm for Hitler in ecclesiastical councils. In his magisterial study of *The German Churches under Hitler*, Ernst Helmreich observes that "there were no protests by the church against the war when it started, nor were there any antiwar statements, pacifistic utterances, or support of conscientious objectors in the many church pronouncements during the war. There is no record of pastors refusing to serve when called in to the armed services." In fact, Helmreich observes, prayers on behalf of the Nazi government were routine almost everywhere in the churches; even the oath of personal loyalty to Hitler was finally objectionable to only a few ministers, notably the Swiss pastor Karl Barth.

Helmreich summarizes the dilemma churches faced:

What governmental actions are unlawful and what position an individual should take against such actions has long been controversial within the Christian church. Hard as these questions are for individuals, they are even more difficult for the church as an organized body, since it is bound by creedal statements, and the necessity of following established procedural methods. The churches, Protestant and Catholic, were haunted by the words of Paul in Romans 13:1–7 on the duty of obedience to those in authority.

Of course the chief responsibility for silence in the churches lies with the coercive mechanisms of the Nazi police state, as Helmreich acknowledges: "During the war years it was impossible to debate the issue as a theological problem; the lack of a church press, censorship, and the police took care of that." Only after the war did this become "an issue that was pounced upon in theological discussions," resulting in "a clear and unqualified affirmation of the right to oppose an unjust government, even at times of the right to kill a tyrant." But as Helmreich points out, if this became "the ethic of the postwar world—clarified and formulated as a result of the experiences of the recent past—it was not the one which prevailed in Hitlerian Germany."[25]

Nor has this ethic prevailed yet in South Africa, where the same passage from Paul has been quoted to defend apartheid in official declarations of the Dutch Reformed Church.[26] In the 1985 *Kairos Document,* opposition theologians in South Africa assailed the "State Theology" of the apartheid regime, opposing to it a prophetic theology that proclaims a "God who sides with the oppressed." The *Kairos* theologians declared that State Theology "is simply the theological justification of the status quo with its racism, capitalism and totalitarianism. It blesses injustice, canonizes the will of the powerful and reduces the poor to passivity, obedience and apathy. How does 'State Theology' do this? It does it by misusing theological concepts and biblical texts for its own political purposes. . . . The first would be the use of Romans 13:1–7 to give absolute and 'divine' authority to the State."[27]

The same passage of Scripture is as important a component of tyranny in Central America, where Evangelical pastors insist that "the Bible says that we must obey the President." The authors of *Kairos Central America* (1988) declared that the U.S.-sponsored "death project" in Latin America involves "a religious and theological war, a struggle between gods that are situated on both sides of the conflict. The God of the Poor, revealed by Jesus, has once more heard their cry and has made Himself present to lead the oppressed to liberation against the oppressors and against their gods." The God of the Poor stands opposed to "the God of Western Christian society," who "justified the conquest and lent itself for blessing successive empires, the very God whom so many Christians of today keep on invoking while they bless and support the imperial system itself."[28]

In the next year, third world theologians from Asia, South America, and South Africa issued *The Road to Damascus: Kairos and Conversion,* exposing and denouncing the idolatry of imperialist theology:

> Right-wing Christianity under whatever name is a way of believing that rejects or ignores parts of God's revelation and selects or distorts other parts in order to support the ideology of the national security state. We are convinced that this heretical choice is made for selfish political purposes, although not all the adherents of right-wing Christianity are necessarily aware of this. Consequently right-wing Christianity is the conscious or unconscious legitimation of idolatry.
>
> One of the characteristics of this new heresy is that it denies Christian freedom by insisting upon blind obedience to authority. The famous text from Romans 13 is misused to demand unquestioning and uncritical allegiance to the political authorities who exercise the politics of death and deception.[29]

The analyses in these three documents converge upon a single, massively oppressive pattern. When theology replicates the military and economic dimensions of the "New World Order," the canonical Paul's contribution to the ideology of Death is clear, and integral. As in that horrific scene in the Acts of the Apostles, the canonical Paul is still made to cooperate in the murders of Jesus' witnesses.

I emphasize that this conflict is not merely a matter of Christians disagreeing over the interpretation of Scripture in an essentially neutral environment. The *Kairos Central America* theologians observe that "the Empire itself supports, promotes, finances and adopts this theology as a deadly weapon against the poor . . . and especially against the God of the poor." The facts bear out their charges. Whatever the extent to which conservative Christians in the U.S. are aware of it, the American empire's propagation of imperialist theology is a multi-million dollar project.

The policy document prepared by Reagan's national security advisers in 1980 proposed that "U.S. foreign policy must begin to counter (not react against) liberation theology as it is utilized in Latin America by the 'liberation theology' clergy. The role of the church in Latin America is vital to the concept of political freedom. Unfortunately, Marxist-Leninist forces have utilized the church as a political weapon against private property and productive capitalism by infiltrating the religious community with ideas that are less Christian than Communist."[30] The doctrines of imperial theology elaborated in this policy document include the axiom that "war, not peace, is the norm of international affairs." In this global war of good (that is, the enhancement of U.S. corporate profits) against evil (that is, sinister attempts to redirect a society toward serving its people), the church's proper role is to defend "private property and productive capitalism" against the heresy that human need should determine the disposition of the earth's resources. According to the insidious political correctness of the document, the *real* violence in Central America is not the carnage wrought by U.S.-supplied helicopter gunships, bombs, and machine guns, or by machetes and electrodes applied with skills taught at the U.S. School of the Americas; it is rather the "violence" of ideas wielded by such dangerous men as the Jesuit priest Ignacio Ellacuría of El Salvador, who was murdered by the army's Atlacatl Battalion in 1989.

The imperialist theological project is also evident in the work of the neoconservative Institute for Religion and Democracy, which (since its founding a few months after Reagan's inauguration) has waged a propaganda and disinformation war against liberation theology and against purported "Communism" at the World Council of Churches;[31] in the Reagan Justice Department's extraordinary campaign of infiltration, intimidation, harassment, and prosecution against American church groups involved in the Central America movement;[32] and in the work of White House operatives like General John Singlaub and Lt. Col. Oliver North, who organized a network of sympathetic evangelists as fundraisers for "pro-democracy" terrorist armies in Central America and Africa.[33]

Here again we recognize immediately that Paul did not conceive of the "New World Order" or the national security state. On the other hand, once we observe that Rom. 13:1–7 played a central role in "mainline" church criticisms of liberation theology during the very years in which right-wing evangelists were stumping for money and support for "freedom fighters" in Nicaragua and Angola,[34] we begin to grasp the usefulness of Paul's legacy for systems of injustice and oppression. The canonical Paul is readily made into an instrument in the manufacture of consent, whether the propaganda task is to legitimize state-sponsored terrorism abroad, to inculcate public docility and suppress dissent at home, or to obscure the actual dynamics of global exploitation. If, as Karl Marx wrote, religion is the opiate of the people, the Pauline writings would seem to provide a more potent derivative, ready to be mainlined into the public bloodstream on demand.

Indeed, we may find this Pauline compound coursing through our veins already. For some of us, the figure whom I have just implicated in a torrent of violence is an intimate acquaintance.

My earliest awareness of the apostle Paul's distinct voice within the New Testament arose as I listened to my father's sermons in a small, white, Fundamentalist church in red-dust Gallup, New Mexico, in the early 1960s. Although the citizens of Gallup included only a handful of black families (none of whom attended our church), my father repeatedly drew the congregation's attention to Martin Luther King, Jr., and his campaign of nonviolent resistance in Mississippi and Alabama. Despite a sympathy with African Americans that left a lasting impression on me, my father found in Romans 13 the clear biblical mandate for the Negro to submit to civil authority, even if that meant quiet acquiescence in the face of segregation laws, contemptuous court injunctions, or police brutality. The Negro's proper hope, as my father read the Pauline letters, was to *wait* for just changes through the grindingly slow process of legislation.

I remember my father's appreciation for several very intelligent and industrious women who taught or supervised Sunday school classes; I also recall his unease around many of the belligerently conservative men who governed the congregations he served. I noted his evasiveness when invited by church elders to Christ-against-Communism rallies or, later, to meetings of the John Birch Society. And I understood, from an early age, the scriptural reason why these men, and not those women, governed our churches: in the Pastoral letters, the canonical Paul clearly stipulated that elders and deacons must be *married men* (1 Tim. 3:2, 12) and declared that "I permit no woman to teach or to have authority over men; she is to keep silent" (1 Tim. 2:12).

The canonical Paul's voice has been close, persistent, enduring. As my high school classmates debated Richard Nixon's impeachability, or the morality of the U.S. conduct of the Vietnam War after My Lai and Kent State, I heard Paul's voice. At college, classmates debated women's participation in religious activities on campus, and I heard Paul's voice. A shocking number of women friends confided that they had been sexually abused by fathers, stepfathers, or uncles, and then shamed into silence. Two men, one a close friend, committed suicide when their homosexuality was discovered by their churches. Yet another friend was ostracized as a homosexual by her church when she gave shelter to a woman whose husband had quoted Ephesians 5 to extort sexual favors in their bedroom. In all these episodes the canonical Paul was present, intricately involved in the network of prejudices and policies that coerced conformity and submission: a dependable spokesman for an Establishment that remained overwhelmingly conservative, oppressively straight and male, and impenitently prone to war.

In seminary I listened to emotional debates over the ordination of women in various Christian denominations. An Episcopal parish ruminated over sheltering Salvadoran refugees. More recently, students in my college classroom have agonized over leaving physically abusive husbands or boyfriends, or have struggled with memories of rape or incest. Throughout these conversations across the years, that single, clear voice—the voice of the canonical Paul—has continued to ring in my ears as the unbaptized voice of a sanctified status quo, of shameless patriarchy, of the Church Militant and Militarized.

I hasten to add that other, brighter tones have sounded within the blend that I have known from childhood as Paul's voice. Paul's voice rang out over the water in which my father baptized me at age nine: "We are buried with Christ by baptism into death, so that as Christ was raised from the dead by the glory of the Father, we too might walk in newness of life" (Rom. 6:4). Paul's solemn warning taught me to approach the Table of the Lord with reverence and regard for my brothers and sisters, "for any who eat or drink without discerning the body eat and drink judgment on themselves" (1 Cor. 11:29). Later, when My Lai and Kent State washed away my adolescent confidence that God's will coincided with what our president called "national security," it was Paul's voice that gave me another place to stand as a Christian: "Do not be conformed to this world but be transformed by the renewal of your mind, that you may prove what is the will of God" (Rom. 12:2).

But these are not the dominant tones when Paul's voice is heard in our public life. The apostle is perhaps never closer to the hearts and minds of the American people than when war must be promoted. A decade ago, my seminary class was galvanized by the assassination of Salvadoran Archbishop Oscar Romero and the rapes and murders of Dorothy Kazel, Ita Ford, Jean Donovan, and Maura Clark; not only because of the heinousness of these crimes—we were accustomed to remembering hundreds of murdered Salvadorans in our chapel prayers—but also by the contemptuous duplicity of our government's response. Jeanne Kirkpatrick, Reagan's ambassador to the U.N., declared the nuns partisans of the rebel front; Secretary of State Alexander Haig offered the press a fantasy of the women running a government roadblock, guns blazing. These official obscenities kindled an anger in me that I sought to communicate to other Christians. But in one church after another I encountered both a dizzying ignorance of the war in El Salvador and a sickening apathy toward learning more about it. Again and again I heard Christians respond that they were content to "leave politics to the politicians," since, after all, Saint Paul had commanded us to "be subject to the governing authorities."

A decade later, on Martin Luther King Day, 1991, George Bush flouted international law by ordering the bombing of Baghdad, the beginning of the most brutal war in our nation's history as measured either by deaths per day or by tons of explosives dropped. As in the invasion of Panama, the Pentagon imposed stringent restrictions on press coverage, and the White House generated a blizzard of disinformation. Despite the determined efforts of some American Christians to oppose the war, including clear, public denunciations from the official heads of the mainline Catholic, Orthodox, and Protestant denominations—including the presiding bishop of the Episcopal church, of which Bush is a member—the president exulted that "there is no peace movement" and that "we have licked the Vietnam syndrome." Even the possibility of informed dissent was forestalled. The Bush administration banned the broadcast of videotape showing the war's effects on Iraqi civilians. The Defense Department steadfastly refused to stoop to "body counts,'' repudiating the highly respected estimates by the government's own team of Harvard scholars (more than two hundred thousand killed by summer 1991).[35] A U.S. Census worker was fired for publishing an estimate of war casualties in Iraq. In the 1992 presidential campaign, the Bush administration tried to render their complicity in creating the Iraqi military machine, and in the fabricated Iraqi atrocities that goaded Congress into approving the war, political non-issues.

Since reasoned moral assessments of the war were often lacking in Christian churches, I was grateful for one Episcopal church's invitation to discuss the classical criteria of the "just-war tradition," and its applicability to this war, some two weeks after the bombing began. But in a chilling echo of ten years earlier, one of the first responses to my talk was an amiable shrug and the question, "But doesn't Paul tell us simply to obey our government?"

THE DYNAMICS OF PAUL'S ENSLAVEMENT

Why does a scrap of a letter from Roman antiquity hold such sway in our thinking about modern warfare? I doubt that it is because we Americans are so devoutly biblical a people. Numerous other Scripture passages that decisively condemn injustice, national arrogance, and militarism, or that portray the nonviolent glory of the reign of God, are much less well known in our public life together. I suspect the reason is rather the usefulness of this fragment of Scripture within a propaganda system that seeks to instill in us a benign acceptance of our government's brutal militarism.

Many Americans, I know, will be reluctant to allow that our "free press" functions as a propaganda system; how much more reluctant are U.S. churchgoers to conceive of our churches as cooperative participants in such a system. Yet how difficult it is for many of these same Americans to explain why they are not more disturbed by reports of systematic torture and murder campaigns in U.S. client states. Why is it so easy for us to judge the Christians of Germany who made their peace with Hitler while we utter hardly a whimper of protest about our own government's complicity in covering up the El Mozote massacre in El Salvador?[36] It would appear that, in circumstances in which more brutal methods of coercion and population control are simply unacceptable, the public submissiveness required for low-intensity wars to continue can be promoted through "a properly functioning system of indoctrination" (political analyst Noam Chomsky).[37] Anyone who has seen Christians shrug away questions about U.S. responsibility for atrocities in Central America (or, of course, elsewhere) can only marvel at how effectively this single scrap of Scripture, Rom. 13:1–7, diverts our attention and thus shields a massive war-making economy—the defense industries, the banking, the diversion of funds from domestic programs, the diplomatic subterfuge, all the mechanisms of what Jesuit priest Daniel Berrigan has called "the interlocking directorate of death"—from moral analysis and critique. Powerful political and economic interests are served, to murderous effect, whenever Romans 13 causes Christian populations to acquiesce in well-mannered and pious docility. Where the social machinery of war is concerned, the canonical Paul is simply good for business.

TOWARD THE LIBERATION OF PAUL

I have repeatedly referred to "the canonical Paul," and in the preceding pages I have intentionally used such phrases as "the biblical Paul" or "the Pauline legacy" in order to distinguish the voice that echoes in our ears today from the genuine voice of the apostle himself. Most of us can readily recognize the self-serving distortion of Paul's writings at work, for example, in nineteenth-century apologies for slaveholding. When the issue is closer to home, however—whether in contemporary attitudes toward homosexuals, or the feminist movement, or U.S. foreign policy, similar patterns of distortion serving to protect power and privilege may be more difficult to discern without the efforts of cultural critics (sociologists, nonmainstream journalists, or political activists, for example) to bring them to light. Such is the effectiveness of the propaganda system within which we live. But my point is that *these are patterns of distortion*: distortion of the suffering of other people, distortion of the effects of our own actions, and, as the preceding indictment suggests, distortion of Paul himself.

This book intends to reduce the distortion of Paul. I have written it in the conviction that the voice that rings so insistently in our ears today is not the apostle's own voice. That may seem a banal observation: Of course Paul is not responsible for many of the things said in his name today. But more is at stake here than correcting occasional and isolated examples of tendentious Bible-thumping. I contend that the distortion of Paul has become so pervasive, and has gone unchallenged for so long, that it is often impossible for us to hear Paul in any other way. But that means that Paul himself has been made a prisoner of the power of Death.

I speak of Paul's captivity in shockingly personal terms. Those who believe in the Christian doctrine of the communion of saints will accept this as more than a metaphorical conceit. Can we imagine Paul's reaction if he could hear his own words perverted toward violent ends, as we have so often heard them? I believe he might express his anguish in words like those he wrote in Romans 7:

Sin—so that it might be revealed as sin—worked death in me through what is good. . . . I am mere flesh, and now stand sold as a slave to Sin. I do not recognize what I have brought into being. For I am not accomplishing what I want, but rather the very thing I hate. . . . Now if what I am doing is not what I want, it is no longer I that do it, but Sin which has domesticated me. So I find this principle at work: while it is my will to accomplish the right, evil is close at hand. For my part, I delight in the law of God in my inmost being; but I see in my "members" another law, at war with the law of my mind, making me captive to the law of Sin which has moved in on my "members." Miserable man that I am! Who will deliver me from this body, which has come to belong to Death?

Paul is in chains today, a slave of Death. That is the premise of this book. In the following chapters, I turn to examine the dynamics of Paul's enslavement. How could so ardently faithful a man, a Pharisee devoted to "the justice of God," an apostle of Jesus Christ announcing God's triumph over the powers of this world, have come to be empressed into "alien service" (the phrase his contemporaries used for idolatry)? Why is Paul so easily accommodated to the dynamics of oppression and death?

This is not a book about the "New World Order," however, or about the antifeminist backlash of the religious right. It is a book about the conventions and assumptions that still hold sway when Christians read Paul, the habits of interpretation that effectively abandon Paul's letters to the ideological arsenal of the oppressor. It is time (to resort to another Pauline metaphor) to relieve the Powers of these weapons and turn them over to the service of God's justice (Rom. 6:13).

How has Paul fallen into the service of Death? I find three explanations surfacing in the recent study of Paul by biblical theologians and historians.

First, many of the passages from the Pauline writings that have played so notorious a role in history, that have served most readily to legitimize structures of injustice, occur in pseudonymous letters, that is, *in letters not written by Paul himself.* Other individuals wrote them, seeking to capitalize on the apostle's authority to advance their own policies and prejudices. Still other passages are interpolations by such individuals into the genuine letters of Paul. Since some of the perpetrators of this literary subterfuge aimed to deflect pagan suspicion away from Christians by endorsing the subordinationist values of conservative Roman society, a degree of accommodation to coercive violence was effectively built into the canonical Paul almost from the beginning.

A second explanation has to do with what in much current research remains the dominant picture of Paul's own "social conservatism," a picture I will have occasion to dispute in a later chapter. Scholars often contrast the robust radicalism of the early "Jesus movement" in Roman-occupied Palestine with the intimate "love-patriarchalism" that prevailed in the intimate Pauline house churches in the cities of the Hellenistic Diaspora. As a well-educated and ambitious male, a financially independent Roman citizen, and a Pharisee (so this argument goes), Paul moved in this urban environment with ease and managed the affairs of the nascent Christian communities with a keen sensitivity to Roman propriety. On this view, Paul's letters serve to protect privilege today partly because Paul's own origins and the interests of his congregations lay within Roman society's privileged strata. Despite the brilliance of his theological ideas and the fervency of his religious experience, he found no reason to allow these to challenge the conventions of privilege from which he and his network of upper-class householder-citizens so clearly benefited. Paul's paramount concern, according to this view, was for the quiet cohesion of his churches, not the disruption of social roles in pursuit of some ideal of "justice."[38]

Such generalizations, I will argue, have had the effect of isolating Paul from the more progressive and liberative impulses of his own day—and of ours.

A third line of explanation points us to the way the theological tradition of the last fifteen centuries has shaped our perceptions of Paul as a theological genius, propounding his own rather idiosyncratic doctrine of salvation in competition with other religions, especially Judaism. As we shall see in later chapters, the tremendous ferment in the study of Paul over the last twenty years stems from the recognition that the Christian tradition has *imposed* these concerns on Paul: They are not his own concerns—or at the very least, not his primary concerns. The frequency with which Paul's interpreters today speak of a "new perspective on Paul" or call for a "paradigm shift" in the interpretation of the apostle[39] opens the door for a thorough reexamination of Paul's apostolate in its historical and political context.

Paul has been pressed into the service of Death in our own time, but contemporary scholarship allows us to see that this is artificial, and that it has been made possible, in part, by the betrayal of Paul in the New Testament canon, in part by generalizations about Paul's own privileged position within Roman society, and in part by the way the theological tradition has mystified and depoliticized him. Each of these factors is examined in the chapters that follow.

PAUL IN THE SERVICE OF LIBERATION

As we have seen, Paul has been made an instrument in the legitimization of oppression. But he is only one of its victims. Our resistance to Paul's enslavement must be grounded in a broader and deeper horror and outrage at the dominion of violence and death that sweeps, unabated, through our history.

In her book *Victimization: Examining Christian Complicity*, Christine Gudorf explores "the ways that the Christian gospel is used to mask and thereby maintain ongoing victimization in our world." Gudorf cites Eph. 5:22 to illustrate the potential of Scripture "to set the conditions for, excuse, or even demand, the victimization of women." She asks her readers to imagine the effect of Rom. 13:1 or Titus 3:1 "on Salvadoran peasants jailed and tortured for participating in literacy drives, or agricultural cooperatives, or human-rights marches, or on the black Christians of the South who risked their lives in the civil rights campaign, or on German Christians who conspired against Hitler." They would, she suggests, hear these words as "divine betrayal"; and she asks "how many more would have joined them in their work for justice had they not been reminded of these passages and similar scriptural messages?"

Gudorf cites Rom. 1:26–27 as supporting "those who advocate adding to the social hate and discrimination against homosexuals by excluding them from the Christian community." She observes that therapists turning to Scripture for resources in helping victims of incest find unqualified commands to children to honor and obey their parents (in the New Testament, Eph. 6:1 and Col. 3:20), but in the absence even of scriptural recognition of incest as a form of victimization, she concludes that what Scripture does say "is not helpful and can actually support abuse."[40]

I note that although Gudorf speaks of the potential of Scripture in general to legitimize violence, most of her examples are taken from the Pauline letters. With many scholars, I would argue that much of the dangerous potential of which Gudorf speaks is due to the *misinterpretation* of Paul, the misreading of his letters, and the (often intentional) distortion of his voice. Indeed, correcting for that distortion is my purpose in the following chapters. But we must bear in mind from the start that Paul is not the chief victim when his words are perverted.

Gudorf points out that "the uncritical use of Scripture as revelatory and authoritative, even among many committed to the liberation of victims, is dishonest and contributes to maintaining victimization." That point is critical for what I intend in this book. It could be dangerously counterproductive to discover and reject "misreadings" of Paul, and to recover the "genuine voice of the apostle," if the result were simply to restore a rehabilitated Paul to a position of unquestioned authority to which men and women must submit themselves. The ultimate horizon of any effort to liberate Paul from his metaphorical chains must be the liberation of men and women who suffer very real oppression and violence in our own day.

But I intend even more. I am convinced, and mean to convince my reader, that Paul himself is far more an advocate of human liberation than the inherited theological tradition has led us to think. The liberative horizon of this book is, I believe, also the horizon of Paul's own apostolate. In his letter to the Romans, for example, Paul declares his confidence that "the sufferings of this present time are not worth comparing with the glory that is to be revealed to [or in] us." In contrast to our own tendency as American Christians to a buoyant triumphalism, which may owe more to centuries of global exploitation and materialism than to faith, Paul never waves aside the sufferings of this present time in order to meditate contentedly on the glory of the new age. Rather he dwells on the anguished groaning of a world "in travail": The very cries of the tortured are part of a global chorus of yearning for liberation. When we attune our hearts to those cries and join our voices to that chorus, Paul declares, the Spirit of God is given voice (Rom. 8:18–27).

The immediate goal of this book is to recover the voice of Paul, a voice stifled and obscured through long centuries of interpretation. But that project can only be liberating if it is put in the larger context of a hearkening to the Spirit that attends to the cries of victims. In this sense, "liberating Paul" must be seen as one small part of the much broader liberating work of the Spirit.

2

The Canonical Betrayal of the Apostle

I declared at the end of the preceding chapter that the oppressive face of the "canonical Paul" is largely the reflection of words Paul never wrote, which nevertheless appear under his name in the New Testament. Obviously, a preliminary step in interpreting Paul must be to sort out which writings are *pseudepigrapha*, that is, writings falsely attributed to him. The next step is even more urgent for our purposes here, however: to determine the effect of the pseudepigrapha on our perceptions of Paul, and to control for it. As we shall see, the centuries-long acceptance of inauthentic writings as genuine letters of Paul not only has resulted in a skewed picture of the apostle's thought in general; the inauthentic letters have even contaminated the way we read Paul's genuine letters.

FACING THE FACTS OF PSEUDEPIGRAPHY

Which purportedly Pauline writings are not, in fact, his? Although scholarly consensus is always somewhat elusive, even a cursory review of reference works written from the historical-critical perspective (for example, the *Anchor Bible Dictionary*) and of articles in journals like the *Journal of Biblical Literature* will reveal a wide agreement among many scholars on the following points.

(a) Paul did not write the Pastoral letters (1 and 2 Timothy and Titus), Ephesians, or Colossians (although the case with Colossians is more ambiguous, and consequently more controversial, than with the others).

(b) The verses pronouncing God's judgment upon "the Jews" who killed Jesus (1 Thess. 2:14–16) or commanding women to silence (1 Cor. 14:34–35) are interpolations into Paul's genuine letters, made after the apostle's death.

(c) A significant minority of scholars likewise contend that the commandment to submit to governments (Rom. 13:1–7) is also a late interpolation.

This is not the place to rehearse those arguments at length: I happily refer the interested reader to standard critical introductions to the New Testament,[1] and to literature cited in what follows, for the relevant arguments pro and con. The judgments that will guide my interpretation of Paul in the subsequent pages are as follows:

(a) With the majority of historical-critical interpreters, I do not consider 1 Timothy, Titus, or Ephesians to be from Paul himself. Beyond the conventional observations that these letters differ in style and vocabulary from Paul's other letters—observations often explained by defenders of authenticity as the result of Paul having dictated these letters to assistants—this judgment relies on the different social and historical situation presupposed, or advocated, in these letters.

The concentration on conventional Roman morality as the qualification for church office, the alignment of Christian morality to the customary gender and master-slave roles within the household, and the more favorable attitude toward civil government all mark 1 Timothy and Titus as products of the second or third Christian generation, closer in situation to the letters of Ignatius and Polycarp (early second century) than to Paul himself. Further, where these letters deviate from Paul's genuine letters (as when 1 Tim. 2:11–15 commands women to silence in the churches; compare 1 Cor. 11:5), they constitute a deliberate reversal of the apostle's own position.

Ephesians shows a similar distance from Paul himself when its author writes that the Law has been "abolished" (Eph. 2:15), a suggestion Paul explicitly rejects as blasphemous (Rom. 3:31)! The author of Ephesians also distills "the mystery" of Paul's proclamation as the already achieved unity of Gentile and Jew within a single new people, the church (Eph. 3:1–7), while for Paul himself the "mystery" he reveals involves the destiny of still distinct peoples in a consummation he still awaits in the future (Rom. 11:25–36).

My judgment also depends on the presence of pseudonymity as a literary device in these letters. In other words, statements that would work to make a letter particularly effective in the situation of the supposed author's extended (or permanent!) absence are a strong indication that the letter is inauthentic. "Paul's" remarkable prescience in 1 Tim. 3:14–15 is a good example of such a literary device: "I hope to come to you soon, but I am writing these instructions to you so that, *if I am delayed*, you may know how one ought to behave in the household of God." (There follow extensive instructions regarding church order, written as if "Timothy" had never heard these things from Paul previously.) Another good example is Eph. 3:1–7, which puts Paul's theology in a nutshell for an audience that knows him only by reputation.[2]

(b) I regard Colossians as inauthentic, though with somewhat less certainty than in the case of Ephesians, since the elements of the sort of literary device I have just described are less obvious in Colossians. (The letter's distinctive vocabulary and theological perspective are less conclusive for pseudepigraphy than differences of style.) Nevertheless, we may detect the pseudepigraphic device when the "Paul" who speaks here claims to strive for the Colossians, the Laodiceans, "and for all who have not seen my face" (2:1). Paul's relevance for a post-apostolic generation is thus potentially guaranteed.[3]

(c) The passage urging women to "keep silent in the churches" (1 Cor. 14:34–35), and the brazen announcement that "God's wrath" has overtaken "the Jews, who killed both the Lord Jesus and the prophets" (1 Thess. 2:14–16), are surely interpolations. The plain sense of the first passage flatly contradicts 1 Cor. 11:2–16, where Paul clearly expects women to pray and prophesy in public worship. Further, a comparison of early manuscripts shows the interference of copyists at just this point in the letter.[4] The second passage, as it now stands in 1 Thessalonians, is a remarkable contradiction of Paul's nuanced and agonized argument in Romans 9–11, and transparently expresses the views of (Gentile) Christians living after the Roman war against Judea, a decade after Paul's death. Moreover, the "punchline" in verse 16 is absent from a number of Old Latin and bilingual manuscripts (dating from the mid-fourth century). Here as well we see the interference of copyists at precisely the point in question.[5] The coincidence of "internal" evidence (contradictions with what Paul says elsewhere) and "external" evidence (disturbances in the manuscript tradition, indicating interference from copyists) allows us to declare with confidence that *Paul did not write these words*.

(d) The situation is more complicated with regard to the command to "be subject to the ruling authorities" who derive their position from God (Rom. 13:1–7). On one hand, we must take seriously the tensions between this single passage and other places where Paul announces that "the *schēma* of this world is passing away" (1 Cor. 7:31) or represents the "subordination" of all earthly powers to God as an end-time event for which he longs (1 Cor. 15:24–28), rather than as a present reality that is in essence good. As James Kallas remarks on Rom. 13:1–7, "Paul could not have ascribed such an exalted status to Rome without being not only hypocritical and servile but untrue to his whole theological position."[6] On the other hand, the absence of any manuscript evidence for the interference of copyists should prompt caution. With most historical-critical scholars, I believe we must find some satisfactory explanation for the very uncharacteristic remarks in Rom. 13:1–7 without dismissing the passage as an interpolation. Several recent attempts to explain the passage have focused on political realities in Rome or in Palestine; these urgent questions will occupy us in chapter 6.

(e) Finally, I observe a series of interventions by ancient copyists *and* misjudgments by modern translators that have obscured Paul's close and collegial relationships with women peers and have thus effectively effaced the leadership of women in the congregations Paul served. Phoebe, *diakonos* of the church in Cenchrae (Rom. 16:1), was as much a deacon as any other *diakonos* in early Christian literature; she has nevertheless become something else, a "deaconess" (Revised Standard Version) and has suffered demotion from Paul's patron (*prostatis*) to his "helper" (Revised Standard Version) or "good friend" (Revised English Bible). Co-workers for whom Paul has obvious respect, Apphia (Philem. 2) and above all Prisca, toward whom Paul feels obvious fondness, respect, and gratitude, for she and Aquila "risked their necks for me and were in Christ before me" (Rom. 16:3–4), have routinely been marginalized as wives of the "real" co-workers, their "husbands" (for Apphia is usually assumed to be Philemon's wife). Why else, commentators apparently assume, would these women have merited the apostle's mention?

Such erasure of women's contributions is more difficult, of course, with women who are partners with other women, like Tryphaena and Tryphosa (Rom. 16:12) and Euodia and Syntyche (Phil. 3:2); so their contributions must be "feminized" and thus marginalized (consult any commentary on the "women's squabble" between Euodia and Syntyche). In the extreme case, women themselves must be "disappeared" from the text: so Julia, declared "eminent among the apostles" in Rom. 16:7 in our earliest manuscript of Romans (p46, circa 200 C.E.), was promptly renamed Junias in later manuscripts and now remains one of Paul's "fellow countrymen" and one of the "men of note among the apostles" (Revised English Bible).[7]

The cumulative effect of all these observations regarding mistranslations, changes and insertions made in the manuscript tradition, and probable pseudepigraphy is to cast doubt not only on the specific passages and letters I have just discussed but more broadly on the collection of Paul's letters as they appear in our New Testaments. I am less interested in arguing specific cases of pseudepigraphy than in asking, What difference should these judgments make for the way we read Paul?

First, we must face the fact that there are pseudepigrapha within the New Testament collection of Paul's letters. In the light of the historical evidence, to imagine that these letters were somehow providentially protected from the tampering of copyists, or that the canon itself was divinely insulated from fraudulent writings, is nothing but pious fantasy. As New Testament scholar William O. Walker writes, the question the interpreter is compelled to ask about any of these cases is "no longer simply, 'Is this passage an interpolation?' Rather, it becomes, 'Is this passage one of the interpolations that almost certainly are contained within the Pauline corpus, and indeed, in this particular letter?' "[8]

To put the point in strong language, we must recognize, on principle, that the Paul who speaks to us in the New Testament as a whole is an artificial composite, resulting in part from a campaign of deliberate revision of the memory of Paul. Judgments as to whether that revisionism was a faithful "adaptation" of Paul's teaching to a new situation, as some apologists argue, or a sinister deceit may differ from case to case. But we must not minimize the fact that pseudepigrapha by nature reflect the "deliberate alteration of the received tradition" (New Testament scholar E. Elizabeth Johnson).[9]

Pseudepigrapha are forgeries, however devoutly motivated they may have been. We must not allow discussions of how differently the ancients understood "authorship"—as they ascribed a philosophical treatise to an esteemed mentor, for example, or wrote an apocalypse under the "inspiration" of an ancient hero of the faith—to obscure the import of the act of forging a letter under someone else's signature. As New Testament scholar Luke T. Johnson writes, observations about the frequency with which ancient authors wrote under pseudonyms "are without either general or specific pertinence" to the Pauline writings, for literary pseudonymity was practiced "as a transparent fiction," while the Pauline pseudepigrapha, on the other hand, "deliberately [use] signals—his autograph, the network of names—that make the enterprise much more like a deliberate forgery."[10]

For just this reason, I cannot accept the broad definition of "authenticity" that this same scholar applies to the Pauline writings. Basing his judgment on "the persuasiveness of their literary self-presentation," Luke Johnson goes on to declare that "the whole Pauline corpus is one that Paul 'authored' but did not necessarily write."[11] This seems to me a dubious wordplay that muddles more than it clarifies. Nor am I prepared to accept any of the other euphemisms for the Pauline pseudepigrapha that are current in textbooks and commentaries, including references to "post-pauline Paulinism" or "the Pauline school," or to "interpreters" or "disciples" or "heirs" or "followers of Paul" or "continuity in the Pauline tradition," without considerable qualification.

It is not enough to observe that the pseudo-Pauline letters appropriated much of Paul's own language and concepts. We must ask to what new use these materials were put. To the extent that the pseudepigraphist's "alteration of the received tradition" in fact contradicts the plain sense of Paul's genuine letters, we must be prepared to judge that the author of 1 Timothy, for example, was as much a betrayer of Paul as his "disciple," a saboteur of one form of Pauline community as much as a member of a Pauline "school."

We should not retreat from such conclusions simply because 1 Timothy appears in our New Testaments. Of course, I recognize the difficulty such historical judgments present for those concerned with the theological status the pseudo-Pauline letters enjoy within the canon.

As E. Elizabeth Johnson succinctly remarks, "If Paul did not write them, they do not cease to be the church's scripture."[12] But as Johnson herself notes, that fact *raises* theological questions; it does not answer them.

I respect the efforts of biblical theologians to honor the constraints of the canon even in the face of pseudepigraphy, in effect making the best of a bad situation, as J. Christiaan Beker does when he urges that "even in their failures the early interpreters of Paul provide the church today with important guidelines and warning signals." I note, however, that the lesson Beker would have us learn from the pseudo-Paulines is the necessity of adopting Paul's gospel "to new historical circumstances" so that it may "remain a living word for new times and seasons." That is, *what* the pseudo-Paulines attempted in reactualizing Paul's voice, *not how* they went about it, seems to be what Beker considers authoritative for us.[13]

I hesitate to give the pseudo-Paulines any more authority than this. Indeed, in order to evaluate their significance for us today, I would urge Christians to weigh the fact that these pseudepigrapha are in the canon against the probability that they were canonized under a *misconception* (for they certainly were canonized as letters of Paul, not as "adaptations" of Paul).

Seen from the historical point of view, the fact that 1 Timothy or Ephesians stands in our canon shows only that the pseudepigraphists were hugely successful in their attempt to rewrite Paul and to suppress other understandings of the apostle's legacy. *The pseudo-Pauline writings emerged from conflict between rival interpretations of Paul, a fact easily obscured since only one side of this conflict "won,"* having been assured a place in our New Testament. The notion that the Pastoral letters emerged in an organic development from the earliest churches through a simple and continual process of "institutionalization" remains a naked postulate, more often assumed than argued in current scholarship.[14] Rather, the Pastorals were written by some Christians to combat the views and practices of other Christians, conventionally dismissed as "heretics" by virtue of the historical triumph of the Pastorals, but no less "interpreters" and "heirs" and "disciples" of Paul.

As church historian Hans von Campenhausen wrote decades ago, the Pastorals

> portray a Paul who rejects all exaggerated asceticism, and directs his readers toward an officially organized Church life, bourgeois virtues, and respect for the ordinances of creation . . . in other words: they portray the sort of Paul who was needed in the fight against gnosis, and who was quite definitely not to be found in the genuine epistles. Only when combined with these inauthentic letters could the genuine legacy of the apostle be tolerated by the Church and made "canonical."[15]

Von Campenhausen's comments are very much to the point, provided we recognize that "Church" here refers to those elements within second-century Christianity that found "officially organized church life, bourgeois virtues, and respect for the ordinances of creation" more tolerable than the leadership of charismatic women, egalitarian community life, and resistance to Roman coercion.

Speaking so generally of "the Church" is an example of what church historian Dennis MacDonald sees as the failure of earlier scholarship "to account for the tremendous diversity of ways the early church remembered the apostle." As a consequence, MacDonald writes, "we have too often seen the apostle of freedom as the priest of social convention. The domestication of Paul in the Pastoral Epistles was not an inevitable, linear development of the Pauline mission, as is usually assumed." To the contrary: When we read the *Acts of Paul and Thekla*—a third-century apocryphal writing that incorporates much earlier Pauline traditions, as MacDonald has shown—"we recognize that not all Christians in the Pauline circle would have silenced women from teaching, trimmed the order of widows, exhorted slaves to continued servitude, and commanded obedience to Roman authority. We can, in short, no longer assume that the Pastoral Epistles were the rightful second-century heirs of the Pauline legacy."[16]

To elaborate on this point, we may observe that other second-century heirs of Paul included the passionate, ascetic women who found their experience of spiritual emancipation echoed in the *Acts of Paul and Thekla,* and the individuals who in their pursuit of truth gathered around the bold interpretations of Marcion, who regarded himself as the champion of the Pauline gospel. Thekla's spiritual daughters, however idiosyncratic their appreciation of Pauline theology, might have taught Paul's other heirs the equality in the Spirit of men and women. The companions of Marcion, despite the principled extremism of his approach and its vulnerability to anti-Semitism (a flaw equally endemic to his orthodox opponents),[17] might have bequeathed to the larger church the legacy of a Pauline gospel of nonviolence. The pseudo-Pauline writings not only risked betraying Paul, they were written to subvert other second-century Christian communities that had preserved elements of Paul's truth.[18]

REEXAMINING PAUL'S "SOCIAL CONSERVATISM"

Once we recognize the existence of pseudepigrapha within our collection of Paul's letters, we cannot be content simply to draw a line between "genuine" and "inauthentic" letters. More insidious than their capacity to skew our general perceptions of Paul at the level of the canon is the power the pseudo-Pauline writings continue to exert in contaminating the way we interpret even the genuine letters.

This contamination is particularly evident in two issues of critical importance for any attempt to assess Paul's social or political position:

Paul and slavery, and Paul and women. Unfortunately, it is just where the social and political consequences are greatest that scholarship has too often abdicated its responsibility, retreating to safer historical questions about ancient manuscripts and the making of the biblical canon.

Paul and Slavery (I): 1 Corinthians 7:21

There are two passages, and only two, in Paul's undisputed letters where he gives advice concerning Christian slaves: 1 Cor. 7:21 and the letter to a house church that includes the owner of the slave Onesimus (customarily named after the first addressee, Philemon). These two passages bear scrutiny here precisely because (once the pseudo-Paulines have been bracketed from discussion) they have been made to bear the enormous weight of scholarly generalizations about Paul's social ethic.

We may take as one example—there are many others—Leander E. Keck's statement in his widely used handbook on Paul, written for pastors and students: "Paul's ethic appears to be so thoroughly influenced by his expectation of the imminent parousia that it produces a 'conservative' stance, for he actually urges his readers not to change their roles in society (1 Cor. 7:17–24)."[19]

This assessment is stated so firmly, here and in so many other handbooks and dictionaries, and with so little qualification, that the average reader would have no idea how questionable its exegetical basis is—although many of the scholars who have disseminated this judgment are of course well aware of the lexical, grammatical, and contextual difficulties lying just beneath the surface. Just because this view is so widely accepted, it deserves sustained scrutiny. In fact, three critical objections undermine this generalization about Paul's "conservative ethic."

First, the generalization that Paul "urges his readers not to change their roles in society" hangs on 1 Cor. 7:21, where according to most Bible translations, commentaries, and interpreters, Paul tells the Christian slave, "Even if you have the opportunity to become free, make use of your slavery instead." We may suspect that something is amiss, however, as soon as we notice that other translations, commentaries, and interpreters *render the same Greek words with an opposite meaning:* "if you have the opportunity to become free, by all means take it!"

Neither of these translations is arbitrary (though we may well wonder, then, why one reading has so predominated in the Christian imagination!). Here, as so often in his letters, Paul speaks elliptically: his Greek phrase, *mallon chrēsai,* can reasonably be translated either "by all means take advantage" or "rather make good use." But "take advantage" of what? "Make good use" of what?

Some interpreters supply the direct object "slavery" (*douleia*)—"make use of your slavery instead"—on the assumption that what Paul says here aligns with the rule they see repeated in verses 17, 20, and 24: "let each person remain in the calling in which they were called" by God.[20] But other interpreters, with as much grammatical justification, supply "freedom" (*eleutheria*), reading this imperative as an urgent exception to that same rule.[21]

Since either translation is possible, the decision must be determined by how one reads the immediate context, 7:17–24. But here the second objection arises: Just what does the context mean? The rule Paul repeats seems clear enough, for example, in the Revised Standard Version: "let everyone lead the life which the Lord has assigned to him, and in which God has called him" (7:17); "everyone should remain in the state in which he was called" (7:20); "in whatever state each was called, there let him remain with God" (7:24).

But this apparent clarity is misleading. In fact the English phrases used here, "the life . . . assigned," "state," or in other translations "condition," "situation," "station in life," "role in society," are all questionable attempts to render the Greek word *klēsis,* which means literally "calling." Now, in English we can speak of a person's occupation as his or her "calling"; but (as K. L. Schmidt has shown in his word study in the *Theological Dictionary of the New Testament*) *klēsis* never carried that extended meaning in ancient Greek literature. Within the New Testament, in fact, and especially everywhere else in Paul's writings, the word *klēsis* and the cognate verb *kalein* (to call) were used to indicate the general Christian "calling" to belong to Christ, or (at Rom. 11:29) the analogous "calling" of Israel.[22] It would appear, then, that translating *klēsis* with "station in life" is "totally anachronistic," revealing "an inappropriate preunderstanding for the interpretation of this text" (New Testament scholar Allen Callahan).[23]

Further, the rules of syntax make translations like "station in life" impossible, for such translations force the occurrences of the single term *klēsis* in these verses to mean several different things at the same time. For example, in his extensive commentary on 1 Corinthians, Gordon Fee patiently explains that "by saving a person *in* that setting, Christ thereby 'assigned' it to him/her as his/her place of living out life in Christ."[24] This seems a reasonable enough interpretation of 7:17–24, until one recognizes that only one Greek word, *klēsis,* is represented by four different phrases here: (1) the act of "saving a person" (the lexically justified meaning of the word in early Christian literature); (2) the social "setting" in which one received that calling—a meaning without any attestation in this period; (3) the act of "assigning" a social location, similarly unattested; and finally, (4) the social role itself, the "place of living out life," also without lexical precedent. We will get some sense of how artificial this interpretation is if we substitute "calling" for each phrase that expresses *klēsis:* "by *calling* a person in that *calling*, Christ thereby made a *calling* of it to him/her as his/her *calling* in Christ."

This is awkward, dubious, and far more complicated than what Paul actually wrote. Far from being "the only solution that respects the context" (Gregory Dawes),[25] translating *klēsis* this way would seem to require a lexical and syntactical impossibility. But what is impossible with New Testament Greek seems remarkably easy for some modern-day theologians, who seem to have the advantage of knowing what Paul must have meant! In fact throughout early Christian literature, and particularly in Paul's letters, *klēsis* means one thing: the "calling" to belong to Christ. Thus Paul writes in the parallel verse 7:18, "Was anyone at the time of his call circumcised?" Surely no one would argue that the "calling" here was a matter of God calling a man *to be circumcised*. Why, then, should anyone suppose that in 7:21 Paul speaks of God calling a person *to be a slave?*

More to the point, why have so many interpreters lent their weight to just that interpretation of the verse? The third objection to the conventional interpretation is that interpreters have made decisions about the troublesome phrases *mallon chrēsai* and *klēsis* on the basis of what they took to be the general principle or rule that informs everything Paul says in 1 Corinthians 7. Indeed, as our quotation from the student's handbook shows, this rule is often taken to reveal the very heart of Paul's ethic: "He urges his readers not to change their roles in society."

How surprising, then, to observe that throughout 1 Corinthians 7 Paul repeatedly allows that under appropriate circumstances, *Christians may change their status* without "sinning" (7:28, 36) or transgressing God's "call to peace" (7:15). In fact, *the whole chapter is structured by a series of concessions, in each of which Paul allows, in the light of circumstance, an alternative to his personal preference for conduct or lifestyle.*

Paul endorses sexual relations in marriage, although his preferred ideal is celibacy (7:1–7); he allows unmarried and widowed persons to marry, although it is not his first choice (7:8–9); he allows a wife to remain separated from her husband, although it is not only Paul's preference, but the Lord's command(!), that Christians not divorce (7:10–11); he allows Christians to be divorced if their pagan spouses initiate the separation, although the Christian partners do not need to initiate divorce (7:12–16). Paul repeats that unmarried Christians do not sin if they marry, although he feels quite strongly that this is not the best action given the "impending distress" (7:25–31). He insists that he will not lay any restraint on the Corinthians, although he is very concerned to free them from anxiety (7:32–36). He allows that a man who feels he is disgracing his fiancée (or his daughter) may marry her (or allow her to marry), although the man who can resist marriage in confidence does better (7:36–38). And finally he rules that a widowed woman may remarry, "in the Lord," although he feels she will be happier if she remains single (7:39–40).

Each use of the word *although* represents a Greek adversative particle, either *de* (but: 7:2, 9, 11, 15, 28) or *alla* (but rather: 7:7). These particles give a common structure to all of Paul's concessions. In each case, Paul

(a) lays down a general rule that expresses his own preference, then
(b) introduces an exceptional case, marked with a phrase like "but if . . . " for which
(c) he allows that variance from his general rule is unobjectionable; he then
(d) justifies the concession he has just made ("for," "because," "on account of").

Just this pattern is repeated in 7:21–23, as the translation in the Revised Standard Version shows: "[a] Were you a slave when called? Never mind; [b] but if [*all' ei kai*] you can gain your freedom, [c] avail yourself of the opportunity, [d] for [*gar*] he who was called in the Lord as a slave is a freedman of the Lord." This pattern shows that throughout the chapter it is Paul's intention not to lay down a hard-and-fast rule to be followed by all Christians everywhere; to the contrary, he allows exceptions to what he himself would prefer. His point is that his own personal preferences regarding sexual expression are not the final authority for how his readers live their life. He would like to see everyone remain celibate, "in view of the present distress" (7:26), so that they would be "free from anxieties" (7:32); but he knows this is not God's way. God has given different gifts (*charismata*) to different individuals (7:7). To some, God gives the ability to live a celibate life without distraction; to others (obviously not to Paul), the single life itself is a distraction from which marriage may bring release. This is a matter of individual *charisma,* individual discernment, and individual responsibility to God.

Clearly one's "station in life" does not determine the outcome of the sort of discernment Paul envisions here. If there is a single "rule" to which Paul wants all his readers to be alike responsible, it would seem to be the "calling" specified in 7:15: "God has called us to peace." In response to that calling, Paul hopes his readers will not be preoccupied with their present social circumstances, but he certainly does not absolutize those circumstances themselves as "God's calling." *"Staying in one's position" is not the governing principle in 1 Corinthians 7,* or even in 7:21. To the contrary, it makes far better sense to read the verse as Paul's urgent wish not to be misunderstood as encouraging slaves to continue in their state longer than they have to!

Despite the appearance of this preferable translation in some very successful recent Bible versions, however, one will search in vain for any general presentation of "Paul's ethic" built around this translation of 1 Cor. 7:21. The exegetically more dubious translation still holds undisputed sway in the common perception of Paul's "social conservatism."

The conventional interpretation of 7:21 would appear to rest on a series of exegetical misjudgments. Those misjudgments are hardly accidental. In his word study for the *Theological Dictionary of the New Testament,* K. L. Schmidt traced the translation of *klēsis* in 1 Corinthians 7 with "state" or "station in life" to Martin Luther, who used the German *Beruf* (occupation) rather than *Berufung* (calling) to translate the Greek. As Schmidt observes, Luther was concerned to demonstrate "that not only the monk has a vocation, but every Christian in the world and in secular employment as well."[26] Luther was also impressed by the similarity between 1 Cor. 7:17–24 and other passages, including Col. 3:18–4:1, Eph. 5:22–6:9, and 1 Tim. 2:8–15, 6:1–2—all of which he assumed to be genuine Pauline letters. The terms he coined to indicate this similarity, *Haustafeln* and *Standestafeln,* refer to tables of reciprocal locations or roles within the Roman household and city: husbands and wives, parents and children, masters and slaves, governors and subjects. Although 1 Corinthians 7 does not include a *Haustafel*—nothing is said to masters, for example, or to parents and children—it does address comments to husbands and wives and refers once, in 7:21, to slaves. Those points of contact were apparently enough to allow Luther to read *klēsis* in 1 Corinthians 7 in terms of the sort of reciprocal social roles delineated in the *Haustafeln.*

For Luther, and throughout the subsequent exegetical tradition, it would seem, Paul's voice in 1 Corinthians has been filtered through the operative grid of what the pseudo-Pauline letters present as "Paul's views on slavery."

The pseudo-Pauline writings continue to contaminate the interpretation of 1 Cor. 7:17–24 today, as some of the most renowned scholars and theologians set about to explain Paul's supposed command to "remain in your station in life." Hans Conzelmann explains that the command to remain in slavery is consistent with Paul's belief that he is living in the end time, as a result of which "civil freedom is seen to be merely a civil affair. In the church it is of no value." (As if to reassure the troubled reader, Conzelmann adds in a footnote, "the slave often does not wish to be freed.")[27] Other scholars offer that "Paul felt that social institutions as institutions did not deserve first attention. He was interested in relationships" (Peter Richardson);[28] or that the "desire of Christian slaves to obtain their freedom" was "not as crucial for Paul" as his adamant opposition to circumcision (James E. Crouch);[29] or that Paul was concerned chiefly with the individual's attitude: "The rules and structures of society are outwardly respected, but inwardly rejected" (John Ziesler).[30]

At length, these explanations of 1 Cor. 7:21—or rather, of the more dubious translation of 1 Cor. 7:21—become the basis for even broader generalizations about the texture of Paul's thought and the relation between his "theology" and his "ethics." Thus E. P. Sanders summarizes Paul's position on Christian "behavior": "In view of the shortness of time people should not change. This applied to being married or single, slave or free, circumcised or uncircumcised (7:17–24). . . . *The net result was extremely conservative: do not change.*"[31] A similar view appears in J. P. Sampley's small book on Paul's ethics, again quite representative of current scholarship: "Grounding this *quite conservative, even quietistic, social posture* is Paul's expectation of the imminent Parousia. . . . In the very section where Paul told the Corinthians to remain in the situations where they received their calls, he laces the eschatological thread that is the basis for his *reluctance to shake up social structures:* 'the appointed time has grown very short. . . . The form of this world is passing away.' "[32]

Here we can see that Paul's supposed "reluctance to shake up social structures," derived from a flawed reading of one verse in 1 Corinthians, has become a matter of theological principle. Significantly, none of these interpreters is concerned to give an account of the underlying structure of concession that shapes 1 Corinthians 7. Nor does any of them bother to offer any explanation for the alternative reading of 1 Cor. 7:21, let alone to base broad generalizations about Paul's social posture on it.

Ironically, the influence of the pseudo-Pauline letters has become so pervasive today that the view of Paul's alleged social conservatism is widely accepted, whether or not Colossians and Ephesians are regarded as genuine. For some who consider Colossians and Ephesians, with their full-blown Haustafeln, to be genuine, 1 Corinthians 7 displays only the initial stage of Paul's fight against a radical "misinterpretation" of the gospel that advocated "shaking up social structures." Thus Peter Richardson writes that "when Paul deals with slavery in his later correspondence [that is, Colossians and Ephesians] he seems to have become even more conservative than he was earlier, probably because of *the developing danger of radicalism.*"[33]

But the pseudo-Paulines extend their influence even where they are recognized as inauthentic. Widely recognized studies by David Schroeder and James E. Crouch have made the "danger of radicalism" the preferred explanation for the conservative posture of the Colossian Haustafel.[34] Crouch goes even further, arguing that Paul faced that danger already in 1 Corinthians. He reads the exhortation in 1 Cor. 7:21 as evidence that slaves in the Corinthian congregation had succumbed to a "superficial understanding of Paul's gospel," by which Crouch means that they had taken Paul at his word: "there is neither slave nor free . . . in Christ Jesus" (Gal. 3:28). Eager to correct this "misunderstanding," Paul urged slaves to "remain in the condition of slavery." Crouch justifies this translation of 1 Cor. 7:21 by appeal to "the entire context" of chapter 7, to the "principle" in 7:17, 20, and 24, and to the parallel in 1 Tim. 6:2 ("rather [slaves] must serve all the more"), which (although Crouch considers 1 Timothy pseudonymous) he describes as a "real as well as formal" parallel. Of course, the terrible "threat" that so exercised the author of 1 Timothy was precisely that Christian slaves might misunderstand the communal language of "brotherhood" within the church and forget their place, showing disrespect for their masters by daring to approach them as equals (1 Tim. 6:1). Crouch locates this threat in Corinth as well—and beyond. He contends that 1 Cor. 7:20 "is the principle which [Paul] applies in every situation in which the social order is threatened by an outburst of religious enthusiasm."

For this Paul, a slave's concern for his or her legal and material circumstances is not only unnecessary, it is inappropriate: "In Christ the social distinction between slave and free loses its meaning. Consequently, the Christian slave is to abandon his concern for freedom and concentrate upon fulfilling his commitment to Christ in the social situation in which he became a Christian." For this Paul, Crouch declares, the "more destructive kind of slavery" is the slave's concern for his or her own plight; and surprising as it may seem, Paul's warning against becoming slaves to human beings (1 Cor. 7:23) "can only refer to the demands of Christian slaves for social freedom."[35]

The Paul whom Crouch has discovered in 1 Corinthians, defending "the social order" against "outbursts of religious enthusiasm," protecting slaves from the "more destructive slavery" of yearning for freedom, would be right at home in the world of the Pastoral letters. But this *is* the Paul of the Pastorals, now read back into the genuine letters! This Paul alerts us to the "danger of radicalism," the "excesses created by an overemphasis on the equality created by the Spirit," in Crouch's words.

Turning to other scholars, we learn that the "danger of radicalism" is not merely a matter of political point of view but is at heart a theological failing, the reflection of lack of faith in God: "Attempts to change one's [social] status tacitly make that status more important than it is for one whose relation to God is a matter of trust/faith. What matters is not socio-economic freedom but inner freedom in Christ" (Leander E. Keck). Paul's concern is "the liberating of the individual," which must not be confused with seeking to change "the facts," as for example "through the realization of a social program." That would be "a misunderstanding of grace" (Hans Conzelmann). Rather, "liberation" must be understood "eschatologically" (which apparently means without connection to "the facts"); therefore remaining in one's own particular status is "a logical consequence of genuine theology."[36] All that remains to complete this intricate web of "genuine theology" is to damn social egalitarianism as heretical. So Crouch offers that "the drive toward emancipation was but a logical result of the self-understanding which eventually came to be designated as 'gnostic.'"

As those familiar with the conventions of scholarly writing have learned to expect, however, the political consequences to be drawn from "genuine theology" do not bear examination, remaining in the serene realm of the self-evident. Thus the apostle of the status quo not only stands ensconced in the canon by virtue of the presence of the pseudepigrapha; he is discovered, through the tortuous process of conventional exegesis, to be the Paul of the genuine letters as well.

To be sure, a few scholars have refused to hail Paul's supposed accommodation to the social "facts" as a virtue. One alternative is to see Paul's social conservatism less as the logical expression of his end-time expectation than as a personal failure of nerve. Noting that in earliest Christianity, "social conservatism and apocalyptic enthusiasm . . . seem to coincide," J. Christiaan Beker protests that the logic of Paul's thought ought to suggest, to the contrary, that

> the church as the blueprint and beachhead of the kingdom of God would strain itself in all its activities to prepare the world for its coming destiny in the kingdom of God. The hermeneutical consequence of Paul's thought on this matter suggests an active vocation and mission to the created order and its institutions, that is, the execution of our "spiritual worship" in terms of "bodily and responsible life in the world" (Rom. 12:1–2).

But Paul disappoints these expectations:

> Apart from the possibly revolutionary extension into society of the "neither Jew nor Greek" clause, Paul's attitude toward women, slaves, wealth, poverty, and the state is characterized by a social conservatism that does not extend the "ecclesial revolution" into society at large. . . . The ethic does not struggle with the issue of the empirically possible versus the religiously necessary, and it does not wrestle with strategies for political and social action. Rather, we get the impression of something like a religious accommodation to the social sphere.[37]

Apparently similarly disappointed, Calvin J. Roetzel resolves to attend to what Paul says, not what he does: "It is the gospel which Paul preaches rather than his limited application and witness to it that is definitive for our time."[38]

But this sort of qualification remains the exception in Pauline studies. Given conventional assumptions, interpreters have usually limited themselves to *explaining* Paul's "social conservatism," which remains an unquestioned theological "fact" derived largely from Paul's supposed "attitude toward slavery" in 1 Cor. 7:21.

If, as I have argued, that single verse has been consistently misinterpreted in an exegetical tradition still shaped by the force-field of the pseudo-Pauline writings, then the architecture of theological explanation I have just reviewed rests on an insubstantial foundation.

This is a profoundly disturbing insight, for it exposes a network of tacit assumptions about Paul that have far-reaching social and political consequences for our day. That these assumptions remain tacit, as do the political consequences to be drawn from them, casts a shadow over modern Pauline scholarship. Amos Jones, Jr., who has made some of these same observations about the interpretation of 1 Corinthians 7 in his study of *Paul's Message of Freedom,* presses a similar indictment:

> It may not be fair to say that the history of failure to grasp Paul's understanding of slavery in light of Christian freedom on the part of the Christian church and its scholars is a racist proclivity (i.e., bent on keeping in subjection and even destroying a certain class or race of people), but it would be fair to say that there has not been a mad rush on the part of white theologians to the opinion that, for Paul, Jesus meant freedom for the slave in the church as well as in society. It has been because of this negatively skewed interpretation of Paul that the black church and black theologians have ignored the Apostle to the Gentiles and, in fact, have held him as an object of scorn.[39]

Paul and Slavery (II): Philemon

We can make a similar account of Paul's letter to the owner of the slave Onesimus ("Philemon" in our Bibles), a letter widely regarded as a fortuitous window into Paul's attitudes and practice regarding slavery. Yet even here a number of details concerning the concrete situation that prompted the letter are unspecified, leaving the way open for the historical imaginations of interpreters.[40]

It is even disputed whether the owner of Onesimus was named Philemon. It is just as plausible that Philemon and Apphia were named first as a team of evangelists, Paul's co-workers (*synergoi*), and that Archippus is addressed because *he* was the owner of Onesimus.[41] But other questions abound as well.

(1) How did Onesimus come to be with Paul? Paul's remark that Onesimus "was separated" from his master (*echōristhē,* v. 15) appears deliberately vague. Was he sent by his master, or did he run away? If the latter, has he come to be with Paul in prison by accident, or has he sought Paul out, hoping to secure asylum from the slave chasers, or at least to find an advocate who will intercede on his behalf with his master?

(2) Has the slave in fact "wronged" his master (*ēdikēsen,* v. 18)? If so, how? Has he stolen money or goods, beyond the obvious "theft" of himself?

(3) Paul has "converted" Onesimus, "becoming his father" in his imprisonment (the usual interpretation of v. 10). Should we therefore suspect that the slave's motives in accepting baptism have been tainted

by the anticipation that conversion would bring either freedom, or at least better treatment from his new "brother" in Christ?

(4) What is the exact character of Paul's request "concerning my child" Onesimus? As John Barclay writes, the "peculiar paradox" of this letter is that it "is skillfully designed to constrain [the addressee] to accept Paul's request, and yet, at the same time, it is extremely unclear what precisely Paul is requesting!" When Paul asks the master to receive the slave "no longer as a slave but as *more* than a slave, as a beloved brother" (v. 16), does he mean as a slave *and* as a brother? Is the master implicitly asked to manumit the slave, or to forgo his legal right that he punish the slave, or only to soften the punishment? Is the prospect that Onesimus "serve" Paul (as the Revised Standard Version translates *diakonē,* v. 13) backed up by a possible offer of money (v. 18), equivalent to a request to buy or to borrow the slave's duties indefinitely?

(5) Finally—and most important for our purposes—what strength does Paul's request have, and to what extent can we generalize from this appeal to Paul's views on slavery as such?

The answers one routinely meets in commentaries and journal articles often seem to have less to do with what can be ascertained as fact than with the healthy imaginations—and prejudices—of interpreters. The cumulative effect of these studies is to insulate Paul, and "the Pauline gospel," from any real engagement with the social or political reality of slavery and to conform the apostle to the worldview and ethos of the Pastoral epistles.

In independent studies, New Testament scholars Sara Winter and Clarice Martin have called to our attention a series of unsubstantiated assumptions that continue to predominate in scholarship on this letter:

(a) that Onesimus is a runaway slave (a "fact" never specified in the text);

(b) that Onesimus *stole* from his master (a "fact" that depends on reading the conditional clause in v. 18 as an indicative statement of reality);

(c) that the slave's unworthiness is thus clearly established ("Paul knew precisely the sort of person Onesimus had been and the dubious manner of life in which he had engaged," writes New Testament scholar John Nordling);

(d) consequently, Paul's intervention on Onesimus's behalf must be attributed to the apostle's "altogether astonishing" generosity, his "wonderfully gracious offer" attributed to "warm feelings" toward Onesimus (so A. Rupprecht).[42]

These assumptions received a classic formulation in the erudite Bishop Lightfoot's commentary on Philemon (revised edition 1879).

Lightfoot regarded this letter as "the only strictly private letter" in the Pauline corpus, touching "not once upon any question of public interest."[43] However unpleasant the reality of a slave's life in the Roman world, Onesimus's motives for running away were, in Lightfoot's view, unequivocally base: He represented "the least respectable type of the least respectable class in the social scale," a slave who lived up to the worst stereotypes in Roman culture. "He was a thief and a runaway. His offence did not differ in any way, so far as we know, from the vulgar type of slavish offences." The slave encountered Paul in Rome, an appropriate destination for a runaway slave, "the natural cesspool for these offscourings of humanity. . . . In the dregs of the city rabble [Onesimus] would find the society of congenial spirits." He came to Paul either by accident or from a guilty conscience and was converted by the persuasiveness of Paul's evangelization.

As a result of that miraculous conversion, the slave turned out to be positively likable! "The genial, affectionate, winning disposition, purified and elevated by a higher knowledge," Lightfoot wrote, would provide "a solace and a strength to the Apostle in his weary captivity." Paul's motive in the letter, Lightfoot assures us, was personal affection for this particular slave. Whatever the apostle's private thoughts about the institution of slavery (in Lightfoot's view, "the word 'emancipation' seems to be trembling on his lips") these thoughts never interfered with the clear call of duty. The "imperious demand" of Roman law bound Paul to return the slave; and Christian morality bound Onesimus to return, penitent and submissive, to "place himself entirely at the mercy of the master whom he had wronged" and to "make restitution." Roman law and Christian morality thus converged: Onesimus, "a thief and a runaway," had "no claim to forgiveness." Paul's intercession for the slave was thus completely gratuitous and benevolent, an expression of "the nobility of the Apostle's character."

Since Lightfoot considered Colossians, Ephesians, and the Pastoral letters to be genuine, he could arrange these alongside Philemon and 1 Corinthians 7 under the heading "the attitude of Christianity towards slavery in general." Whatever Paul's personal feelings about slavery, the gospel that he proclaimed publicly involved "the absolute equality of the freeman and the slave in the sight of God" as a spiritual, not a political, truth. Thus "the slave may cheerfully acquiesce in his lot, knowing that all earthly distinctions vanish in the light of this eternal truth"; the only "duties" that Paul perceived to flow from this eternal truth were the masters' benevolent treatment of their slaves and the slaves' submissive obedience to their masters (Col. 3:22-4:1, Eph. 6:5-9). Paul "has no word of reproach for the masters on the injustice of their position; he breathes no hint to the slaves of a social grievance needing redress."

Lightfoot, to be sure, was no apologist for slavery. He wrote passionately of the historical process through which the principle of Gal. 3:28 had brought the institution of slavery crashing to the ground. Although centuries of Christian slave societies could find in the Pauline writings a spiritual comfort, Lightfoot considered that given the "eternal truth" of the equality of all before God, the eventual abolition of slavery was "only a question of time." Lightfoot nevertheless contented himself with theological explanations why Paul and his contemporaries had not pressed against the social facts of slavery. This was so, not merely (as later interpreters would argue) because altering the structures of Roman society was beyond the power of the empire's subjects to conceive, but rather because "slavery was interwoven into the texture of society; to prohibit slavery was to tear society into shreds." That tearing a slave-owning society "into shreds" would naturally have been abhorrent to Paul will of course be self-evident to Lightfoot's reader, who will recognize that the "spirit of the Gospel" Paul preached, which "belongs to all time," was "not concerned with any political or social institutions; for political and social institutions belong to particular nations and particular phases of society"—unlike the apostle's transcendent gospel, which is readily embraced by slaves and their masters at the same time!

Some more recent authors have enlarged upon what Lightfoot saw as Paul's concern for Roman law and for social obligation to the slave-holder. Expressing doubt that either Paul or his associates would have given any aid to a fugitive slave, they point out that not only would harboring a fugitive jeopardize Paul's own chances for freedom (N. T. Wright), but also that "such behavior" would have violated "Paul's commands to dutiful obedience of the secular authority (cf. Rom. 13:1–7)" and would have risked alienating "a coworker, his household, and perhaps the other churches of the Lycus Valley" (B. M. Rapske).[44] Such risks, we are to understand, would naturally and properly have impressed the apostle more than the risks of beating, whipping, or even death that might have prompted a slave to run away and almost certainly awaited a fugitive slave's return.

If these judgments imply that Paul speaks from the perspective of the privileged in a slave society, J. Duncan M. Derrett argues that case explicitly. Insisting that Philemon 10, "I have become his father in chains" (en tois desmois), be read as Paul's stipulation that he has baptized Onesimus "in *his* [that is, Onesimus's] chains," that is, with no prospect of manumission, Derrett concludes that the letter "was directed in reality to pagan scrutineers of [Paul's] church." Paul was eager to avert any suspicion on the part of Roman magistrates that his conversion of Onesimus had secured the slave's emancipation. The letter effectively "absolves the church from [the] suspicion" that Paul "was developing . . . a sanctuary" for slaves. Noting that in later centuries the Christian church limited its scope "as a sanctuary for fugitives," discouraging flight "in cases where the State would suffer,"

Derrett declares the attitude behind that decision—that "slaves would be discriminated against so far as necessary to keep the goodwill of the State"—to be "in harmony with Paul's."

The letter's message to the civil authorities, Derrett claims, is that "the church is no sanctuary (*asylum*), it extends no civil rights to fugitives, and diminishes in no way the rights of the outraged parties"— the "outraged parties" here of course indicating the slaveholder, who will be relieved to find his legal right to beat his slave to death secure. The message to Christian slaves is that "salvation deprives them of all claim! The freedman-of-Christ image (1 Cor. 7:22) is not to be taken literally" (again, sighs of relief from the slaveholders' bench); the message to the church, that "the State had a divine task (Rom. 13:1–4). The church, doing no wrong (Galatians 5:23), would be protected by it. Hence its relations with the owners of vagabond slaves must favour the former rather than the latter."[45]

Derrett's reading of Philemon is extreme. It nevertheless exemplifies the common tendency to conform this letter to the interests of a slave society as they are represented by the pseudepigraphic Pastoral letters, and by the exegetically notorious passage Rom. 13:1–7.

Contrast the easy confidence with which scholars discuss Paul's meticulous consideration of slave owners' rights, and his deep concern to foster "obedience to the secular authority," with the profound bafflement with which scholars greet Paul's forceful references to the slaveowner's "duty" (*to anēkon*, v. 8) or to what he might "command" (v. 8), as if he could expect the slaveowner's "obedience" (*hypakoē*, v. 21). "Just what Paul intended . . . is unknown," John Nordling admits; but (he hastens to add) such language probably refers to "the forgiving attitude which Philemon, as a Christian, ought to assume toward repentant Onesimus."

The net effect of such characterizations is to individualize the letter— Paul writes on behalf of this slave, in these specific circumstances—and thereby to bleach the apostle of any social or political commitments beyond the immediate situation. Thus exegetical judgments originally made within the force-field of the pseudo-Pauline writings (Lightfoot) are perpetuated; thus the clear intent of the letter is reversed so that one finds extended discussions of the slave's "duty" to his master; thus the modern reader's sensibilities are eased by explanations couched in terms of what is good for the slave economy. The interests of the slaveholders are maintained as self-evidently of supreme value: *Their* "risks" are assumed to be Paul's most important considerations.

In dramatic contrast to these conventional assumptions, other recent studies of how the letter works to persuade have emphasized Paul's use of various rhetorical techniques to bring argumentative force to bear on the slaveowner:[46]

- The letter's opening lines constitute what ancient rhetorical handbooks called an *insinuatio,* in which a speaker approaches a topic expected to meet resistance through an indirect route (that is, Paul does not mention the circumstances of Onesimus's "separation").
- Paul appeals to the master's sense of honor, to emotions (referring to Onesimus as "my heart" and asking the master to "refresh my heart").
- In a "transparent rhetorical device" (John Barclay), Paul simultaneously affirms and renounces his apostolic authority (vv. 8–9).
- Paul addresses the letter to a community that includes the slave owner, who consequently "will feel himself answerable not only to the distant Paul but also to the Christians who come regularly to his house" (John Barclay). Further, the local church will recognize that they are "a part of a wider community, and that the problem posed by Onesimus's return is one shared by Philemon [i.e., the slave owner], the local church, and the extended church" (Norman Peterson). The contrast with Lightfoot's sweeping judgment that the letter touches "not once upon any question of public interest" could not be more striking.
- The very lack of specificity in Paul's request indicates the rhetorical force behind it. Paul can refer obliquely to the master's expected response as a "duty," or "what is required" (*to anēkon,* v. 8), because he expects the preferred response to be clear enough to the master. According to the rhetoric of the letter, then, the "free will" accorded the master is a matter of complying with or refusing Paul's request, but not of choosing among any number of equally satisfactory alternatives.

This last insight is the key contribution of recent studies of the letter's rhetoric. As Norman Peterson shows in his in-depth study of the letter, Paul's appeal to the slaveholder runs on two tracks. On one hand, he *requests* that a "brother" do "the right thing" (*agathon*), willingly and out of "love"; yet simultaneously he speaks of a "duty" that he could *command* as an apostle, by compulsion. These tracks converge in v. 18, where the slave owner's "freedom" (undergirded as it is by Roman law) and Paul's active intervention on behalf of the slave intersect.

How do these tracks relate to each other? We must observe, first, that although the letter specifies neither the circumstances of Onesimus's "separation" nor the anticipated circumstances of his return, Paul's reference to the slave's former "uselessness" (v. 11) and his "request" of something that he could properly "command" or "compel" (*kat' anankēn*, v. 14) show that he anticipates, and seeks to overcome, considerable resistance from the slaveholder. Most probably, then, Onesimus is absent without his master's permission.[47] Second, as Peterson shows, Paul invokes his apostolic authority in the letter, not in order to waive it and turn instead to a friendly request between equals, but in order to secure obedience while simultaneously maintaining a sense of egalitarianism within the church.

Paul deliberately crafts his language to accomplish a desired result. His rhetoric, Peterson writes, "is a part of the sociological reality because Paul employs it in his social relations, and because it is an element of *his* social relations it is not independent of his actual social role. His rhetoric is the form through which he exercises his role" as an apostle. Thus even when Paul appeals to "a brother's love," this appeal is transparently the appeal of an apostle who seeks the obedience of his own convert. Further, because Paul and the slaveholder relate to each other in terms of specific social roles ("brother," "apostle") within a Christian community, "the consequences of compliance or noncompliance" are understood in terms of judgment "by the Lord." That fact renders Paul's requests "nonnegotiable and gives them their status of commands."[48]

As far as respect for legal and societal conventions is concerned (the focus of much scholarly attention, as we have seen), Paul stands ready to reimburse the master for whatever "loss" he has suffered. But this offer is laced with irony, as the conditional clause shows: "*If* he has done you wrong" (v. 18). But of course Onesimus has "harmed" his master! Whether or not he has stolen money, he has unquestionably stolen something of value from his master, namely, himself, as a number of interpreters have recognized.[49] This loss must be in the foreground of Paul's offer. The only "if" in question is the master's response. Paul's offer is, in effect, a challenge: "*If* you insist on owning this man as a slave, I will pay you his slave price." But this possibility—Paul's only concession to the legal rights of the slave owner—is clearly not what the apostle expects.

Careful attention to Paul's rhetoric shows that he anticipates three possible responses, which we can rank from least to most satisfactory:

1. *If* the master considers his slave's absence a financial loss, Paul will repay that loss; but what follows immediately, "to say nothing of your owing me even your own self" (v. 19), clearly indicates that such a transaction is the least satisfactory response. (Of course, the slaveholder's obvious prerogative under Roman law—simply to punish his runaway slave and to ignore the sentimental pleadings of an itinerant missionary—never comes into consideration as a possibility in Paul's letter.)

2. Against the possibility that the master should insist on having the debt paid, Paul not so subtly implies that he could with as much right insist that the master repay *his* debt to Paul; and if the master "owes" *himself* to Paul, repaying such a debt could mean only self-enslavement. The master is in effect pressured to renounce the financial claim that is his legal right as owner of the slave.[50] Here Paul appeals to his authority and role as an apostle. But he clearly means to discourage this second option.

3. The clearly preferable alternative is that the master will act instead out of "love," as a "brother," responding to Paul's "appeal."

Once we recognize the terms of option 1—that the slave owner sell his legal claim over the services of his slave—we can see that options 2 and 3 require the master to renounce his legal claim over the value of the slave either on compulsion, in "obedience" to Paul's command, or willingly, out of "love."

Paul never specifies that the master should set his slave free, but recent studies suggest that this is almost certainly his intention. In his full-length study of Paul and slavery, S. Scott Bartchy writes that given the social-legal context of the ancient practice of manumission, "the question . . . was most likely *when,* not *if,* Philemon planned to set Onesimus free."[51] It may be that Paul was not more specific because he did not see the legal process of manumission as the only way of fulfilling the requirement (*to anēkon*) of which he spoke. But this requirement, this duty, is clearly the master's obligation—*the only obligation operative in the letter*—to renounce the fact of ownership, the commodification of another man's labor and person, that constitutes his legal relationship to his slave.

Other scholars have focused attention on Paul's appeal that the slaveholder receive Onesimus as "no longer a slave, but more than a slave" (v. 16). Does this phrase allow that Onesimus will remain legally his master's slave? John Barclay asks pointedly whether it is "possible for Philemon and Onesimus to be truly 'brothers' while remaining master and slave" and disputes the common view that Christian masters and slaves could live together "as brothers," "as if slavery did not exist." In everyday household routines and in church assemblies alike, Barclay suggests, the result would be chaos. That dilemma could not have arisen on the terms given in the pseudo-Pauline writings, of course, where Christian obligation and duty coincided perfectly with the reciprocal roles of slave and master. In Philemon, by contrast, these obligations remain in tension.

On the basis of a meticulous analysis of Paul's language of social roles, Norman Peterson concludes that the tension between the social role "brother" and the social roles "master" and "slave" are in fact incompatible. Since "it is logically and socially impossible to relate to one and the same person as both one's inferior and as one's equal," Peterson argues, the slave's

> being a brother to Philemon means that he cannot also *be* a slave to Philemon in any domain. In other words, *being* in Christ or *being* in the Lord is a state of social being that governs the relationships between believers even outside the spatial and temporal boundaries of the church. Being in Christ/the Lord, therefore, excludes all other forms of social being for those who are "in" him. And this state of being is the norm which determines the behavior, the form of social relations that is appropriate, indeed required (*to anēkon*), between believers.

It follows that if the master "acts as Paul demands, his action in the domain of the church will affect his institutional position in the domain of the world, at least with regard to his institutional relationship with Onesimus as his slave." In short, "Paul's line of argument strongly suggests that the only acceptable action would be for Philemon to free his slave."[52]

The Pauline Gospel and the Redemption of Slaves

Do these conclusions regarding "Philemon" allow us to make generalizations about "Paul's opposition to slavery"? I see no reason to hesitate on the grounds that Paul's response to this concrete situation was ambiguous; the arguments just presented show that it was not. On the other hand, we should bear in mind that "slavery" in the early empire was a matter of legal status, not necessarily of socioeconomic level; it could therefore embrace a wide diversity of situations and circumstances. "Slaves" in wealthy households or businesses could enjoy positions of power and not inconsiderable prestige; many urban "slaves" lived in better material circumstances than the vast majority of peasants outside the cities. In an analogy proposed by Dale B. Martin, a general call for the legal manumission of slaves within the Greco-Roman class structure would, in many cases, be like advocating the promotion of low- or mid-level managers within a capitalist bureaucracy; it hardly calls the institutional structure into question.[53]

On that basis we might doubt that Paul had a single, comprehensive rule on the legal status of slaves as such. It is nevertheless clear enough that in this particular case, Paul sought to persuade the Christian community that the norms of life "in Christ" required the renunciation of the slaveholder's legal prerogative over the slave. Indeed, Paul has put all of his apostolic authority at stake for the sake of this runaway slave.

Frustratingly, even when scholars recognize the validity of a more liberative reading of Philemon, the step forward tends to be washed away in the sea of conventional assumptions based on the "status quo" reading of 1 Cor. 7:21, and on the pseudo-Pauline writings behind that. John Barclay, for example, accepts Peterson's groundbreaking study of Philemon, but "qualifies" Peterson's findings by subordinating them to the principle he finds in 1 Cor. 7:17–24: Christians, slaves and masters alike, should "remain where they are." Barclay concludes that "there was nothing especially revolutionary in the fact that Paul treated slaves as human beings, urged their humane treatment and even called them 'brothers,' so long as he did not spell out any practical implications which could conflict with the continuing practice of slavery."[54] But this verdict, that there was "nothing especially revolutionary" about Paul, relies on a premise that Peterson, Bartchy, and others have already overturned. The response Paul called for *did* conflict with the continuing practice of the slave relationship between Onesimus and his master.

Similarly, Margaret MacDonald hails Peterson's "thorough study," but assures her reader nevertheless that nothing in Philemon hints of manumission. Rather, "Paul's comments show a certain respect for the structures of the master/slave relationship," revealing the same "love patriarchalism" she finds in 1 Cor. 7:17–24: "Social distinctions between members are maintained. Those in authority are to respect and care for the needs of subordinate groups in return for their obedience."[55]

These characterizations resound with a Pauline voice that has been trained into harmony with the pseudo-Pauline writings. Real advances in understanding Philemon fail to impede the glacial pressure of assumptions about Paul's "social conservatism." The pseudo-Paulines have effectively set the limits of exegetical possibility, obscuring two essential facts from the view of some scholars: *the complete absence in Philemon of any reference to the slave's "obedience" and a forceful appeal for the master's "obedience" instead.* If some scholars find it difficult to imagine that Paul might envision manumission as the appropriate response in this specific case, how much more difficult to conceive of manumission as a "duty" that Paul might expect all slave owners to recognize by virtue of their being Christians!

But is that so inconceivable? There is considerable evidence that some early Jewish and Christian communities renounced slaveholding (the Jewish sectarians Philo describes in his *On the Contemplative Life,* ca. 30–50 c.e., for example), or secured the manumission of slaves by purchasing them from their masters (observed in 1 Clement 55:2, ca. 96 c.e.; encouraged by Hermas in Similitudes 1:8, Mandates 8:10, ca. 140–155 c.e.) or by promoting manumission within the church (to the dismay of Ignatius, *To Polycarp* 4:3, ca. 107 c.e.). Despite this evidence, however, one routinely reads generalizations—incredibly—that early Christianity never questioned the institution of slavery. James E. Crouch has observed that "Greek and Roman religions [afforded] the slave a degree of recognition and protection," and even "offered him an opportunity to procure his own freedom as well." Yet this observation never suggests to Crouch that Paul could have shared a certain egalitarianism with this environment. To the contrary, Crouch muses that in such an environment, a Christian slave might have come to expect "that his relationship to his heavenly [Lord] should nullify all obligations" to his earthly master—mistakenly, of course![56]

According to the conventions of scholarship, evidence of egalitarian impulses in his environment can tell us nothing about Paul's own attitudes toward slavery. Instead, scholars more routinely dwell on the urgency with which some early second-century "heirs of Paul" sought to contain the practice of slave redemption (Ignatius writes to Polycarp that slaves must not "desire to be set free at the church's expense, lest they be found to be slaves to lust," 4:3), and to stanch the egalitarian expectations of Christian slaves ("they must not be disrespectful [to their masters] on the ground that they are brothers," 1 Tim. 6:2). These efforts—rather than the equally well attested efforts to redeem and emancipate slaves—are routinely generalized as the early Christian *acceptance* of slavery, to which Paul is then assimilated.

There are occasional exceptions to this pattern, startlingly enough. In his "Note on 1 Corinthians 7:21," Allen Callahan has detected behind this verse "the Corinthian practice of ecclesial manumission."[57] He observes that in 7:22 Paul wrote that someone called as a slave "is now a *freedperson* of the Lord": The Greek word is *apeleutheros*, "freedperson," not *eleutheros*, "a noun applied exclusively to free persons who were born that way." Callahan reasons that if Paul were simply speaking metaphorically, we might expect to read that the person called as a slave is now "free in the Lord." But the unexpected term "freedperson" suggests that Paul is not speaking metaphorically, and that he is referring instead to the real experience of slaves who have received manumission upon conversion (that is, at their "calling").[58] He concludes that "the Corinthian church would have been in the practice of obtaining the freedom of enslaved members by marshalling their collective funds to pay the price of said member's manumission."

Along a more inferential path, Elisabeth Schüssler Fiorenza argues that, given the background of oriental cultic and Jewish religious manumission, the baptismal formula that Paul recites in Gal. 3:28 ("there is neither slave nor free") would naturally have encouraged slaves to "expect freedom from their initiation into the Christian community." She finds support in Ignatius's protest in his letter to Polycarp, since that letter "presupposes that slaves who joined the Christian community expected their freedom to be bought by the church."[59]

One other highly suggestive line of questioning would ask after Onesimus's expectations as he made his way to Paul. Recent studies by

Peter Lampe, B. M. Rapske, and S. Scott Bartchy have narrowed the list of possible scenarios behind the letter, arguing that Onesimus was most probably absent without his master's consent, that he had found his way to Paul by intention, and that he would not have done so if his intention had been to run away (that is, to escape slavery). These scholars conclude that Onesimus sought Paul out as an intermediary, a "friend of the master" (*amicus domini*), who would facilitate his reconciliation with his master.

The premises of this argument, deriving from discussions in Roman law concerning the prosecutability of runaway slaves, finally conceive only two possibilities: either Onesimus was a runaway who accidentally ended up next to Paul in prison, or Onesimus sought Paul out as an intermediary in order to be reconciled with his master. There is, however, another possibility, so far unconsidered by interpreters: that Onesimus might have come to Paul reasonably expecting Paul to respond in just the way he did, that is, to intervene by urging the slave's manumission.

Why hasn't this possibility been discussed? Asking how Paul would have appeared "in the eyes of Onesimus," Brian Rapske argues at some length that from observing changes in the routine of the household in which he served, Onesimus would have perceived Paul as a powerful patron of his own master, "fully capable not only of bringing pressure to bear in his case but also of commanding Philemon and expecting Philemon's obedience." Rapske points to verses 8, 14, and 20 as evidence of such capability on Paul's part. Yet he ignores how those statements serve Paul's rhetorical strategy, and he never speculates about the impression Onesimus might have formed about Paul on the basis of his proclamation.[60]

I have already asserted that Paul's appeal depends on the master's ability to recognize the desired response (apparently manumission) as the "duty" (*anēkon*) that Paul may "command." Given the constraints of the situation in which Paul makes his appeal,[61] this expectation makes sense only if, at some previous stage in their relationship, Paul had discussed the obligations of Christian "brotherhood" in such a way that the master could now recognize Paul's request as a concrete application of those obligations. Otherwise Paul's cryptic allusions to "duty" would be so vague as to be unintelligible.

I conclude that a master's "duty" to slaves, even to the extent of manumitting them, was among the expectations that Paul would have communicated to householders during their formation as Christians. That is, the master's duty to the slave, potentially including manumission, was an integral part of the gospel Paul preached. This suggestion also allows us to account for Onesimus's very deliberate flight to Paul, for he knew this as well as his master did. In the eyes of Onesimus, Paul was a powerful patron, yes; but more specifically, Onesimus had reason to see in Paul a patron who could be expected to urge the release of slaves as an expression of Christian duty.

The convergence of these distinct lines of argument suggests that Paul's attitude toward slavery was dramatically different from the conventional reading. That difference is not due to any lexical or rhetorical ambiguity in Paul's language. It is due rather to the pseudo-Paulines' contamination of the way we have usually read 1 Corinthians and Philemon. When the horizons of possibility are dictated by 1 Timothy, or Ignatius's letter to Polycarp, Paul is effectively held prisoner to his "canonical" portrait as the apostle of the status quo.

Paul and Women: The Curious Persistence of 1 Corinthians 14:34–35

One other dramatic example of the way the pseudepigrapha have contaminated our reading of Paul appears in an unexpected source: recent studies of 1 Corinthians by feminist critics.

Critical scholars generally reject Colossians, Ephesians, 1 Timothy, and Titus as pseudonymous. With those letters go the most offensively patriarchal texts in the Pauline collection. Given the evidence in the remaining genuine letters that Paul held a number of women church leaders in high esteem as his peers in apostolic ministry, the way seems open to regarding Paul as far more sympathetic with the experience and leadership of women than the canonical picture of Paul has suggested.

Indeed, only one obstacle remains: the "command" in 1 Cor. 14:34–35, "let women keep silent," a passage that many scholars regard as an interpolation made by someone sharing the views of the author of 1 Timothy. This verse is consequently dismissed as irrelevant for the interpretation of Paul himself.

That judgment is not unanimous, however, even within critical scholarship. Two of the most attractive recent proposals for interpreting Paul have come from Antoinette Clark Wire and Elisabeth Schüssler Fiorenza, who have advocated a "feminist reconstruction of Christian origins" based in part on a careful analysis of the way Paul argues in his letters.[62] Studies by both scholars are seriously flawed, however, by their acceptance of 1 Cor. 14:34–35 as genuine.

In addition to accepting 1 Cor. 14:34–35 as authentic,[63] both Wire and Schüssler Fiorenza read chapters 11–14 as a unit intended to rein in women's leadership in the Corinthian congregation. In offering explanations of Paul's attempt to subordinate the independent charismatic women in Corinth, Wire appeals to Paul's participation in a class of privileged males who find their status eroding in Roman society. Schüssler Fiorenza, on the other hand, has in her earlier work followed more conventional scholarship, emphasizing Paul's "mission" motivation: Paul sought to conform his congregations to the norms of their social environment in order to ensure their survival. He "wanted to prevent the Christian community from being mistaken for one of the orgiastic, secret, oriental cults that undermined public order and decency."[64]

These arguments are inconsistent in a number of ways. First, in light of Paul's acknowledgment of women among his fellow workers and fellow apostles, both interpreters acknowledge that the claim in 1 Cor. 14:34–35, that silencing wives is authoritative practice "in all the churches," would have been "preposterous" (Schüssler Fiorenza). Here Paul "seems to misgauge the women prophets," and "underestimates the depth of his opposition in Corinth" (Wire).[65] These are telling admissions. Resorting to the premise that a speaker has seriously misgauged his audience is a precarious move in a rhetorical-critical argument: Wire herself points out that her project, a historical reconstruction through rhetorical criticism, depends on assuming that the speaker has not seriously misjudged the audience![66]

Second, as Schüssler Fiorenza points out, Paul's advice in 1 Corinthians 7 to remain free from the marriage bond "was a frontal assault on the intentions of the existing law and the general cultural ethos"[67] — hardly what one should expect from someone more concerned with the impressions of outsiders than with the freedom of women of Spirit! Recognizing the same dilemma, Wire is compelled to read 1 Corinthians 7 as Paul's tactical, and perhaps grudging, concession to those women.[68] But now Paul is pitted against himself, the emancipatory aspects of his letters (which both scholars recognize) being compromised by the stubbornly patriarchal sliver in 1 Cor. 14:34–35.

Further, suggesting that Paul was responding to conservative pressures from the environment hardly serves by itself to explain the tension between Paul and the Corinthian congregation. If the early Christian mission movement was "a conflict movement which stood in tension with the institutions of slavery and the patriarchal family" (Schüssler Fiorenza),[69] why should Paul alone feel the norms of a patriarchal environment as an overwhelming pressure?

These attempts at explanation, running as they do against what both scholars recognize as the generally liberative current of Paul's thought, reveal themselves at last to be contorted attempts to order the disarray that results when 1 Cor. 14:34–35 is accepted as authentic. But why grant this dubious passage such overriding control over the interpretation of 1 Corinthians? Schüssler Fiorenza declares, curiously enough, that "since these verses cannot be excluded on textual-critical grounds but are usually declared inauthentic on theological grounds, it is exegetically more sound to accept them as original."[70] To the contrary, scholars have usually declared these verses inauthentic on both external and internal grounds. Further, it is reasonable enough to declare a specific verse an interpolation on "internal" grounds, that is, even if there is no manuscript evidence that a text ever circulated without it (although such an argument must of course bear the burden of proof). In this particular case, however, there is textual "disturbance" in the manuscript tradition. Why shouldn't these verses be excluded "on textual-critical grounds"?

Wire devotes an excursus to discussing the text-critical question. She considers two possible explanations for the variation in manuscripts: (a) someone inserted a marginal gloss into the text of 1 Corinthians at two different places in two different manuscripts; or (b) these verses were inadvertently dropped from one manuscript, then subsequently restored in a different place in a later manuscript. Wire declares the second option the more probable, but she has established only the plausibility of the second explanation, not its preferability.[71] Rather than allowing the dramatic contradictions between 1 Cor. 14:34–35 and the rest of Paul's genuine letters to influence this judgment, Wire has effectively surrendered the interpretive control over 1 Corinthians to this only possibly authentic fragment.

The answer we give to the text-critical question is extremely important, of course, because it shapes the way we read Paul's argument throughout 1 Corinthians. If we determine that 1 Cor. 14:34–35 is an interpolation, then although there are clearly charismatic women in the Corinthian congregations, the attempt to read the whole letter as Paul's effort to circumscribe their activities must lose its force. If we assume instead that 1 Corinthians is directed against the sort of elite male householders that Wire very briefly and tantalizingly describes, then Paul's arguments about relinquishing privilege will sound very different.

We will return in chapter 6 to Paul's purposes in 1 Corinthians. This brief discussion may suffice to show the tremendous power the canonical "revision" of Paul continues to exercise, persuading us to accept a grotesque caricature of Paul's "social conservatism" as the truth despite the contrary evidence of his genuine letters.

There are other spiritual chains that bind Paul in captivity to the power of Death in our own day, however. To these we now turn.

3

The Mystification of the Apostle Paul

Men and women in our time continue to hear Paul's voice as the voice of oppression. Part of the reason, as I maintained in the previous chapter, is that Paul has been subverted by his interpreters within the canon itself—the authors of Ephesians and 1 Timothy, for example—and turned into an earnest apologist for the status quo.

But I also observed a system of explanations by which modern interpreters seek to justify the resulting picture of Paul's "social conservatism" as the natural consequence of his theology. He was indifferent to the plight of slaves in his churches, some scholars patiently explain, because of his expectation of Christ's imminent return and the dissolution of the present social order (1 Cor. 7:29–31). Anyone surprised by the apparent contradiction—why would the imminent collapse of "the present evil age" (Gal. 1:4) inspire a reluctance to shake up social structures and a commitment to protect the social order from "the developing danger of radicalism" among Christians?—will be reassured in solemn tones that this is a typical Pauline "paradox."

Alternatively, we are told by other scholars that Paul's profound grasp of "genuine theology" led him to value "inner freedom in Christ" instead of "socioeconomic freedom," which was after all "merely a civil matter," and consequently "of no value" in the church; and to oppose the egalitarian "misinterpretation" of the gospel among slaves, whose desire to be emancipated was "the more destructive kind of slavery." Or again, we are told that this was merely a matter of priorities for Paul: "social institutions as institutions did not deserve first attention," being "not as crucial" to Paul as the more urgent questions. These supremely urgent questions were (self-evidently, we are to understand) whether Gentiles must observe the Torah and on what terms they were to relate to Jews within the church.[1]

To the degree that these explanations depict Paul as more concerned with his own religious convictions regarding "salvation," "freedom from the Law," and so on, than with issues of justice within his own

55

congregations, they imply a value judgment at the heart of his thought: Concern for justice—setting people and nations in right relation to each other—is far less important than setting individuals in the right relation before God.

If that value judgment strikes a familiar chord for us today, we recognize these are not merely remote exegetical questions debated by a small band of academicians. I vividly recall a Presbyterian adult class arguing in 1982 whether Christians had the right to debate U.S. policy in El Salvador, and a gathering of Episcopalians in 1991 wondering whether it was appropriate for Christians to second-guess the conduct of the Persian Gulf War. In each conversation, it was self-evident to some of the people present that the business of Christians was to evangelize, to save souls, but not to "get involved in politics," which was best left to the politicians. Remarkably, early in both conversations, Paul was cited to sanction this tidy division of labor.

In his profound book on "discernment and resistance in a world of domination," Walter Wink describes his conversation with a Chilean Christian who argued that "Christians have no business trying to change structures, that we are simply called to change individuals, and that as a consequence of changed individuals, the structures will automatically change." Wink goes on to argue that the dilemma "personal or social" is a false one. Just as the powers of evil are not merely "demonic beings assaulting us from the sky" but are "the inner *and* outer manifestations of political, economic, religious, and cultural institutions," so our struggle against these powers must have deeply intimate *and* broadly political dimensions.[2]

But that is not the way we are used to reading Paul. More typically, citing Paul's letters serves to perpetuate the dilemma, "salvation *or* justice?" "spiritual *or* material liberation?" and thus to check efforts toward social and political engagement. In the shadow of Paul, even Christians deeply committed to working for social justice may be made to feel uneasy about their own spirituality, as if they have chosen the second-best path.

One effect is a tacit endorsement of the prevailing order, as prophetic impulses are deflected and blunted. But another, subtler effect is to render Paul himself less and less intelligible to people seeking to understand him. I have lost count of the times I have heard informed, sympathetic individuals express their bewilderment at the "enigma" of Paul. How could this Pharisee, zealous for the Torah, have given such slight attention to the concern at the heart of the Torah for justice for the poor and the alien (Lev. 19:9–16), the "weightier commandments of the Law" according to the rabbis of the Mishnah (Yebamoth 47a, b, ca. 200 C.E.)? How could this apocalyptist, breathing in the charged air of Israel's prophets, have missed their unwavering insistence that the Lord required nothing else than "to do justice, and love kindness, and to walk humbly with your God'' (Micah 6:8)? How could this Jew, a ''Hebrew born of Hebrews,'' have been so oblivious to the trials of his own people under Roman rule as to make the dreadful instrument of Roman terror into the symbol of a purely ''spiritual'' redemption?

My argument in this chapter is that these questions are misplaced. Instead of talking about the ''enigma'' of Paul, we should examine the enigma of his mystification by well-meaning interpreters, the process by which his thought has been misrepresented and distorted by the habits of theological interpretation up to the present day. The voice we hear today as Paul's is a highly synthetic voice, thoroughly filtered, modulated, and fine-tuned by centuries of Christian theologizing. *The Paul we hear has been thoroughly depoliticized*, the social and political dimensions of his work have been suppressed, and a narrow band of theological tones has been amplified, even to the point where a phrase like ''the politics of Paul'' may strike us immediately as nonsensical.

By describing this process as the ''mystification'' of Paul, I mean to suggest that certain global assumptions about the apostle have come to be endowed with an aura of the self-evident, despite widely recognized evidence to the contrary. To the extent that those assumptions have served to legitimate Christian identity over against other communities, the picture and voice of Paul that we receive are recognizably synthetic. Furthermore, whenever we observe interpreters working hard to reinforce those assumptions in the face of contrary evidence, we should be extremely suspicious that the picture of Paul we are being given is a distortion.

As we shall see, the ''mystification'' of Paul can take different forms. First, long-held assumptions about the apostle's social privilege too easily translate into pronouncements about what Paul ''must have thought'' about social realities in his churches. Second, the emerging church's efforts to distinguish itself from Judaism led Christians to make Paul over into a ''convert'' from his ancestral religion, thus divorcing him from his own Jewishness and eventually to regard him as the champion of a fundamentally un-Jewish, and even anti-Jewish, doctrine of redemption. Finally, intramural church debates over theological concepts like the nature of grace, or justification by faith, have put an inordinate weight on what Paul thought about heavenly realities rather than on what he did in this world, or why.

Let us examine each of these mystifications in turn.

THE ''GENTRIFICATION'' OF THE APOSTLE

Paul's solid usefulness to slaveholders, in the nineteenth century or in the second, depends upon hearing Paul as a champion of social inequalities as God-ordained. We have already seen that the Pastoral letters,

1 Timothy and Titus, manufactured a pro-slavery Paul in the interests of slaveholding Christians. But even scholars who reject the Pastoral letters as inauthentic frequently perceive Paul as speaking from a position of social privilege. As a consequence, current scholarship frequently attributes Paul's "social conservatism" to his own privileged position in Roman society.

Was Paul in fact a man of privilege? And did his social position determine his posture toward questions of social justice in his congregations?

The Question of Paul's Social Location

The author of Acts portrayed Paul as a man of considerable status. He came from Tarsus, "a citizen of no mean city," and had been born a Roman citizen, a fact that caused considerable discomfiture to the civil magistrates and military officers who detained him. He had a superlative Jewish education and was an impressive speaker. He clearly belonged in the city, rather than the countryside, and moved easily in the circles of Roman proconsuls, Epicurean and Stoic philosophers, and synagogue officers, at ease even when standing accused before governors and kings.[3] To the social historian E. A. Judge, the evidence of Acts suggests we place Paul in "the privileged group of Hellenistic families which had also been accorded Roman citizenship in return for services rendered." Paul possessed "an unusually well balanced set of social qualifications," shared with only "a very small minority of persons in the eastern Mediterranean," as demonstrated by his free movement "in the best circles in that society."[4]

On the other hand, some of Luke's details cannot be confirmed from Paul's own letters (his Roman citizenship, for example, or his birth in Tarsus, or his formal education with Gamaliel). New Testament scholars customarily recommend we exercise caution in using the information in Acts, taking into account Luke's interest in a particular image of Paul. As Wayne Meeks reminds us, "The author of Luke-Acts evidently was interested in portraying the Christian sect as one that obtained favor from well-placed, substantial citizens."[5] And Richard Cassidy writes that "largely because the narrative portrays Paul interacting so naturally with various Roman military and political officers, Luke's readers rather easily form the impression that Paul is equally at home with the other aspects of Roman rule: Rome's economic and social, as well as its political innovations." Cassidy proceeds to offset that impression by drawing attention to the regularity with which the Lukan Paul confronts Roman magistrates with "boldness" or gets thrown into jail.[6]

Nevertheless, the evidence of Paul's genuine letters as well gives an overall impression of "urbanity" (Gerd Lüdemann).[7] At the turn of the century, Adolf Deissmann's discovery that the language of Paul's letters had more in common with the everyday language of the newly discovered papyri than with the polished prose of classical literature led him to assign Paul, and indeed the early Christians in general, to the lower classes. Deissmann cited 1 Cor. 1:26–31 ("not many of you were wise . . . powerful . . . of noble birth") to support his view.[8] Today that view appears somewhat romantic to scholars who recognize the rhetorical skill in Paul's letters, indicating a good education, a measure of status.[9] Others point out that the statement in 1 Corinthians clearly indicates that some of the Corinthians were wise, powerful, and of noble birth.[10] E. A. Judge goes so far as to write that "if the Corinthians are at all typical, the Christians were dominated by a socially pretentious section of the population of the big cities."[11] Both assessments are probably true *in part,* since as Gerd Theissen has shown, the Corinthian congregation was probably stratified, including both a majority coming from the lower classes and "a few influential members" from the upper classes.[12]

How do we go about making judgments about social class in a society so distant from our own? Social historians insist that we cannot simply measure social class in terms of wealth alone, for example. Wayne Meeks points out that a person's status in Paul's world was a combination of several different, and often inconsistent, factors, including "power (defined as 'the capacity for achieving goals in social systems'), occupational prestige, income or wealth, education and knowledge, religious and ritual purity, family and ethnic-group position, and local-community status." Antoinette Clark Wire names two additional factors: whether the person was a slave and whether the person was a woman.[13] The more factors we take into account, of course, the more complex the task of measuring social status becomes.

Since status is something recognized and effective in social relationships, however, Richard Rohrbaugh proposes that "instead of looking at how much money a person has, and thereby classifying him in relation to his neighbors, we must look at a person's position in relation to others that enabled him to acquire the money in the first place. *Position is the key.*" He recommends we speak of status in terms of power and exploitation, classifying people "by whether they do or do not make use of (control?) the labor of others."[14] If we analyze the New Testament evidence in this way, we find that "nearly all of the early Christians we know anything about were in that powerless situation that left them subject to the machinations of others."

Indeed, few Christians were in a position to control their own status through the exercise of power. Rohrbaugh thus speaks of "the precariousness of wealth . . . without power in the Roman world. The fear of loss, of the downward mobility that was so common, was nearly universal. It was often expressed by Roman writers as the fear of fate."[15] Similarly, Wire observes that in a Roman city like Corinth, "survival required that people on every social level broker their possessions and connections to gain the patrons, peers, or dependents necessary in times of need. No one factor of citizenship, wealth, family, or office could tell the whole story of one's status in this complex world made increasingly volatile throughout the first century by arbitrary exercise of imperial power."[16]

Within that "complex," "precarious," "volatile" world, poised on the slopes of what classical historian Ramsay MacMullen has called a "very steep social pyramid,"[17] where should we situate Paul?

Some scholars have emphasized Paul's efforts to cultivate a network of fairly well-off householders as his patrons and suggest that this is the group with which Paul most naturally fit in. Stanley K. Stowers has argued that Paul's preaching usually took place in private homes, which were "a center of intellectual activity and the customary place for many types of speakers and teachers to do their work." Since lectures by itinerant philosophers were routinely "private affairs and audiences came by invitation," this setting in private homes implies a more privileged class of people: "it became a commonplace that the well-to-do liked to have philosophers seen hanging around their houses." Further, since "the patron or host could provide the speaker with an audience and a kind of social legitimation," it is "no accident that patrons, households and house churches are so prominent in the letters of Paul the missionary." Stowers notes that a fundamental concern in all Paul's letters is to maintain this network of householders: "The importance of private residences for his teaching activity was crucial. Paul needed a platform."[18]

On the other hand, the status enjoyed by these householders was relative. Wayne Meeks concludes his detailed examination of evidence in Paul's letters by describing the people who made up Paul's social platform as fitting "the picture of fairly well-off artisans and trades-people as the typical Christians"; they were nevertheless "small people, not destitute, but not commanding capital either."[19]

We cannot simply lump Paul together with the interests of the upper classes. To the contrary, Stowers himself observes that Paul insisted on his independence from the householders who acted as his hosts, making it his practice to support himself with manual labor.[20] More recent studies by Peter Marshall and Margaret M. Mitchell have focused their attention just here. Paul's refusal to accept support from upper-class Corinthians, with the obligations such acceptance would imply, is an important key to understanding the Corinthian crisis (a point to which we will have occasion to return in chapter 6).[21] Furthermore, Ronald Hock regards Paul's practice of manual labor itself as an important clue to his social location. After investigating the status of artisans like leatherworkers (Acts 18:3 makes Paul a maker of tents), Hock suggests we envision Paul typically in the workshop:

His trade occupied much of his time . . . from before daylight through most of the day. Consequently, his trade in large measure determined his daily experiences and his social status. His life was very much that of the workshop . . . of wearying toil; of being bent over a workbench like a slave and of working side by side with slaves; of thereby being perceived by others and by himself as slavish and humiliated; of suffering the artisans' lack of status and so being reviled and abused.[22]

Relying on Hock's conclusions, Anthony J. Saldarini contrasts Paul with "the Pharisees who appear in Josephus as retainers linked to the governing class in Jerusalem." As an artisan, Paul was "in principle" a member of "a subservient class who were limited by their ability to produce only a small amount of work by hand."[23]

We should not make too much of the humble conditions of artisan labor, however. As Bengt Holmberg and Dale B. Martin point out, Paul's defense of his manual labor, undertaken "so as to win the weak" (astheneis: 1 Cor. 9:22), indicates that he did not imagine that he *had* to work; manual labor was something he felt free to choose (unlike the slaves Hock would have us picture toiling next to Paul in the workshop). Further, Paul viewed working with his hands as humbling—a view that could not have originated in the working class.[24]

The overall impression of Paul's social origins remains, then, that "Paul himself came from the upper strata" (Gerd Theissen).[25] But if Paul *came from* the upper strata, did he remain "at home" there? To what extent, and in what ways, did his higher-status origins shape his perceptions and attitudes as an apostle?

The Problem of Explaining Paul's "Conservatism," Again

As we saw in chapter 2, scholars have long sought a theological explanation for what they perceive as Paul's "social conservatism." In his study of *The Social Teaching of the Christian Churches* (1912), Ernst Troeltsch attributed the apostle's "patriarchalism" to his fervently "Jewish" belief in God's sovereign and mysterious will, a belief that "cut the nerve of the absolute and abstract idea of equality." Troeltsch was the first to describe a Christian "patriarchalism" in which "inner religious equality [was] affirmed," as befits the doctrine of equal sinfulness before God, while "the willing acceptance of given [social] inequalities" quite properly reflected the belief in the inscrutable and omnipotent will of God. It was therefore perfectly understandable, Troeltsch declared, that Christianity should always be "very cautious towards any attempt to carry over this [purely religious] equality into the sphere of secular relationships and institutions."[26]

Albert Schweitzer perceived the same conservative social posture on Paul's part since he, like Troeltsch, accepted the pro-slavery interpreta-

tions of 1 Cor. 7:21 and Philemon as self-evident. He gave his explanation for this posture in the title of his 1929 work, *The Mysticism of Paul
the Apostle*. Marvelously undistracted by the sorts of exegetical and
argumentative considerations I reviewed in the previous chapter,
Schweitzer proceeded not only to elaborate what he called Paul's
"theory of the *status quo*" as a general principle but to characterize it as
"*a necessary inference* [from] the doctrine of the mystical being-
in-Christ." As he explained, "From the moment that a man is in-Christ
his whole being is completely conditioned by that fact. *His natural
existence and all the circumstances connected with it have become of
no importance.*"[27]

Troeltsch and Schweitzer have cast giant shadows across Pauline
interpretation to the present day, and their explanations of Paul's
"social conservatism" continue to enjoy wide currency. These explanations suffer from serious weaknesses, however. First of all, they fail to
account for the consistent pattern of concessions in 1 Corinthians 7,
which tends to undermine a "theory of the status quo" rather than to
reinforce it; nor do they recognize the argumentative force Paul brought
to bear on Onesimus's master. Furthermore, their generalizations about
the "necessary" connections between Paul's religious ideas and his
social attitudes leave no basis for explaining how impulses toward real
social egalitarianism arose, as they apparently did, among Paul's Christian contemporaries: Apparently these connections were not so self-
evident for everyone!

Finally, these explanations betray a rather one-sided preference for
the power of religious and philosophical ideas to determine social
attitudes, with little recognition of the power of social experience to
shape religious convictions in turn. More recent social-scientific approaches to Paul's letters seek a way to *correlate* social experience with
religious belief, without collapsing either into the other.[28]

Antoinette Clark Wire's discussion of the social dimension of Paul's
"call" experience in *The Corinthian Women Prophets* (1990) is a
particularly illuminating example. Wire makes an important contribution to our understanding of Paul's thought when she correlates his
experience of social status loss with his proclamation of the cross as "the
divine path of chosen loss."

"Before Paul is called to believe in Christ," Wire writes, "he is wise,
powerful, and a person with rank." He came from a fairly wealthy
family background and enjoyed a good education. "Paul is also favored
in the other three status indicators—Jew, free, and male. The significance of these factors is basic to what he is able to accomplish before he
is called. The lack of any would have been prohibitive. In wisdom,
power, rank, ethnic security, caste, and sex, Saul—to use Luke's name
for him at this stage—has status."[29]

But Wire observes that Paul has suffered a loss of status. "Paul's calling to preach Christ to the Gentiles [had] a direct impact on his social status, cutting off his promising career among the Pharisees without providing him the kind of wisdom that can be a solid power-base in the Greek world." Although he continues to enjoy status as "a Jew, free, and male," his privileges as a Jew "have been severely compromised, his rights as a free person have been limited by the Christian slave's freedom in Christ, and his position as a male is now being lived out in the same world with the Corinthian women prophets. *Paul unquestionably sees himself as having lost status.*"[30]

Instead of trying to identify Paul's social location as a pinpoint on a socioeconomic graph of Roman society, Wire describes his experience of change, of movement, across that graph—or perhaps we should say, down it. She sets Paul's experience within more widespread patterns of social dislocation and status loss, especially among other freeborn, educated Jewish males in the Roman Empire, pointing to other Hellenistic Jewish writings (the Wisdom of Solomon, 4 Maccabees, Philo's "Life of Moses") that emphasize accepting moral and legal restrictions on one's advancement "as a voluntary self-limitation." At the same time, she observes, the gentry of Greek cities who have watched "their independence disintegrate under Roman rule" turn to "seek dignity in Stoic self-denial."[31]

Most significant, however, is Wire's ability to relate Paul's experience of status loss to his theology of the cross. "There is a close parallel between Paul's view of his status loss and his view of what God is doing in Christ," she writes. God's choosing to be known through the foolishness of the crucifixion (1 Cor. 1:20), like the preexistent Christ's willingness to empty himself (Phil. 2:5–11), reveal to Paul "the voluntary downward plunge of the divine," the "divine path of chosen loss" in which Paul himself has now come to participate. *Paul interprets his own status loss as a sharing in the cross of Christ.* In contrast, the Corinthians' "exaltation of the crucified One" correlates to "their rising social status, which is seen as Christ's wisdom and power, giving them honor, group solidarity, and respect as women and/or slaves."[32]

We should expect this insight to prove enormously helpful in interpreting the conflict reflected in 1 Corinthians, and more generally in understanding Paul's attitudes toward social realities in his churches. Wire herself provides hints of what such a study might look like when she writes that Paul's experience of status loss mirrors that of some of the Christian men in Corinth.[33] Since, as she concedes, "the Corinthian women prophets are only one part of Paul's audience," it would be "particularly helpful" to examine "some group of men in the Corinthian church," for "a Christology such as Paul's may challenge *people like himself* profoundly."[34] Since she also allows (in an occasional remark) that there are older, established families of privilege within the Corinthian congregation, she raises the prospect of hearing Paul's proclamation of "the divine path of chosen loss" *as the elite of Corinth might have heard it.*

Wire does not pursue this line of inquiry, however. She has another agenda: to explore Paul's interaction with the "women prophets" of Corinth who are evident in 1 Cor. 11:2–5. Unfortunately, she has placed a pseudepigraphic passage, 1 Cor. 14:34–35, at the heart of her study, and thus *The Corinthian Women Prophets* becomes an example of what so often goes wrong in modern interpretation of Paul.

Taking the infamous command silencing women (14:34–35) as the fulcrum of the letter, Wire reads 1 Corinthians as Paul's determined attempt to undermine the newly attained authority and status of independent women "holy in body and spirit."[35] As for the *real* elite in Corinth, Wire suggests that Paul seeks to protect their status against the encroachments of the women prophets "by calling all believers to remain in the positions they had when called."[36] The reference, of course, is to the notoriously misread passage 1 Cor. 7:17–24.

Wire then compounds her reading of the letter with a sociological explanation for Paul's conservative posture. Paul has refused financial support from the upstart women prophets because their offer constitutes "a breach of their assigned status." At the same time, Wire asserts, he continues to accept hospitality and support *from his social equals* in Corinth, who share with him "the stoic self-denial respected in more established society," and who will share his theology of the cross as expressing "the self-discipline characteristic of his class." At this point she relies on Peter Marshall's study of the social protocols of patronage, *Enmity in Corinth* (1987). But she has reversed Marshall's conclusion, which was that "Paul has refused support from Corinthians of his own privileged class," in order to place the Corinthian women prophets at center stage in the dispute.[37]

The Corinthian Women Prophets is one example of a more widespread practice. Again and again, important and insightful attempts to explain Paul's theological or ethical perspective in terms of his experience of social realities have gone awry because of the intrusion of the Pauline pseudepigrapha.

Gerd Theissen's groundbreaking essays on 1 Corinthians, collected in *The Social Setting of Pauline Christianity* (1978), are another case in point. Theissen has demonstrated that social forces shaped the crisis that letter was written to address. He relates theological differences among Paul and various groups in Corinth to social stratification within the Corinthian congregation.

This is a very promising line of investigation. Unfortunately, as so often happens in Pauline studies, Theissen has allowed 1 Cor. 7:21 to function as the pivot on which Paul's letters are swung into line with the pseudo-Pauline writings. Theissen characterizes Paul's strategy as an example of "primitive Christian love-patriarchalism," which he finds "particularly in the deutero-Pauline and Pastoral Letters" (as one might expect), but which he insists is "already evident in Paul (namely, in 1 Cor. 7:21ff; 11:3–16)." We never learn what Theissen makes of the exegetical difficulties in 1 Cor. 7:21. Instead he speaks quite broadly about a love patriarchalism that "takes social differences for granted but ameliorates them through an obligation of respect and love, an obligation imposed upon those who are socially stronger. From the weaker are required subordination, fidelity, and esteem." No evidence is produced from 1 Corinthians that Paul requires the subordination of "weaker members" of the Corinthian congregation. To the contrary, the evidence Theissen brings to light shows that Paul *restricts* the freedoms of the higher-status Corinthians on questions of eating idol meat and practices at the Lord's Supper.[38] On what grounds, then, does Theissen summarize these findings as Paul "guaranteeing" the practice of the privileged?

Theissen implies that it is Paul's "love patriarchalism, with its moderate social conservatism," that determined the strategy of the orthodox church in its struggle against Montanism and Gnosis in the second century, and that shaped the establishment of Christianity as the religion of the Roman empire in the fourth.[39] But he never explains why these later developments should control our interpretation of Paul's letters. "Social integration" might be a very helpful category for describing the strategy of emerging "orthodoxy" in the Pastoral letters, or in the writings of second-century church fathers like Ignatius or Irenaeus. But on what grounds are those later developments read back into Paul's letters?

Unfortunately, that seems to be the inevitable effect when interpreters rely, as Theissen does, on categories of analysis that predetermine the results. Certain concepts from functionalist sociology, like "social integration," focus our attention on the relatively smooth, stable, and continuous growth and development of groups across time. Applying such categories to Paul's letters tends to assimilate Paul's situation to later developments in "the Pauline churches" (a phrase that seems always to refer to the churches of Ephesians or 1 Timothy, curiously enough, but *not* to the churches of Marcion or of the *Acts of Paul and Thekla*). Ironically, in a functionalist model, organic metaphors of "growth" and "development" predominate. Metaphors of conflict or struggle, which more accurately describe the circumstances in which the Pastorals were written, find no place.

Margaret MacDonald's study of "the Pauline churches" provides another recent example. MacDonald declares, plausibly enough, that "if the [Pauline] writings can be viewed as representative of different stages or generations of the [Pauline] movement's development, they may be compared in the hope of tracing the formation of a cultural system." But instead of showing why one ought to view the Pauline writings in this way, she simply assumes as her "working hypothesis" that the literary fact that 1 Timothy or Titus are written in Paul's name reflects a social fact, the continuity of Pauline churches "over three church generations."

This effectively surrenders the interpretation of Paul to his most conservative "disciples" in the second century. It is hardly surprising, on these premises, that MacDonald takes any evidence of "authority structures" in Paul's own letters as evidence of continuity with the patriarchy of the Pastorals, or that she blurs the household codes of Colossians and Ephesians together with the "love-patriarchal attitude that one finds in Paul's letters," in which "those in authority are to respect and care for the needs of subordinate groups in return for their obedience."[40] Where, exactly, is this call for the obedience of subordinate groups in the genuine letters? MacDonald provides no answer beyond a reference to "what is usually understood as the ethics of the Pauline communities" on the basis of 1 Corinthians 7 and Philemon. But it is precisely this "usual understanding" that needs to be reexamined![41]

We have already seen (in chapter 2) how the pseudo-Pauline writings continue to contaminate the interpretation of the genuine letters. To the extent that recent sociological studies have accepted the Pauline pseudepigrapha as raw material for generalizations about "social integration," "development," and "institutionalization" within "the Pauline churches," such contamination appears to be built in from the start. The origins of the pseudo-Pauline writings in what Dennis MacDonald has called the second-century battle for the apostle Paul are thus obscured. One side of that struggle—the conservative side—prevails by default. And the modern interpreter becomes an accomplice in the ancient campaign to rehabilitate Paul as an advocate of the prevailing order and its values.

PAUL'S DEJUDAIZATION

A second way in which Paul's voice has been distorted by the Christian theological tradition consists in the virtual obliteration of his Jewish identity and of the Jewish character of his thought.

The Classical Reading of Paul-against-Judaism

Establishing a "magna carta" for early Christian congregations of Jews and Gentiles, the author of Ephesians announced that Christ "has made us both one, and has broken down the dividing wall of hostility by abolishing in his flesh the law of commandments and ordinances" (2:14–15). Ephesians replaced Paul's vigilant concern for the integrity of Torah—his insistence that his gospel did *not* abolish the Law (Rom.

3:31) and that the Law remained "holy and just and good" (Rom. 7:12), and his exertions to preserve the rights of those who kept kosher within his congregations (Romans 14–15)—with a "universalism" based on the suspension of Torah observance. Ephesians did this so successfully, in fact, that subsequent Pauline interpreters have hailed Ephesians as "the quintessence of Paulinism."[42] The author of Ephesians thus subverted one of the apostle's most crucial concerns, "retracting" Paul's statements in Romans 9–11 (A. Lindemann) and "catholicizing" Paul into "an apostle who has lost his anchorage in Judaism" (J. Christiaan Beker).[43]

Since the time of Ephesians and the Acts of the Apostles, the "catholic Paul" has appeared as a *convert* from Judaism to Christianity, who turned back to critique his ancestral religion. This picture has provided the theological foundation that continues to undergird the ideology of Gentile Christianity's uniqueness and superiority. Ironically, the very passages in Paul's genuine letters where he combats just such arrogant presumption upon the grace of God among Gentile Christians have been dismissed as the unfortunate remnants of the apostle's ethnic prejudice (F. W. Beare, C. H. Dodd, Robert G. Hamerton-Kelly).[44]

It is above all Martin Luther's legacy that teaches us to interpret Paul as a theological opponent of Judaism. Luther appropriated Paul's contrast of "justification by works of Law" with "justification by faith" in his indictment of Roman Catholic legalism. He thus bequeathed to subsequent Protestant interpreters a code that deciphered "the Jew" in Paul's letters as a symbol for "the religious and ecclesiastical man" (Karl Barth), "the community of 'good' people which turns God's promises into their own privileges and God's commandments into the instruments of self-sanctification" (Ernst Käsemann).[45] Once the Reformation made Paul's discussion of justification by faith in Romans into "the center, not only of the Pauline message but of the whole Christian proclamation" (Käsemann), nothing could prevent the apostle's perceived critique of Judaism in that letter from being similarly placed at the heart of his theology. Consequently the letter to the Romans is now read as Paul's "exposition of salvation as he understands it," made "through a contrast with the Jews' understanding of [salvation] and their claim to possess it exclusively." In Romans, and throughout his theology, "Paul's opponent is not this or that section in a particular church, but the Jews and their understanding of salvation" (Günther Bornkamm).[46]

Given the tremendous importance of this way of reading Paul for Christian, and especially Protestant theology, one may be dismayed, but can hardly be surprised, that it persists despite countervailing insights and repeated protests from historians of religion. Already in 1848, F. C. Baur complained that even among interpreters who gave lip service to the historical critical approach to Paul, "the dogmatic view is not to yield one step to the historical, lest the position of an Epistle such as that to the Romans should be impaired, and the Lutheran forensic process of justification, which it is of such moment to maintain in its integrity, suffer from the shaking of its great buttress." Indeed, Baur himself never moved beyond the philosophically determined categories of Hegelian dialectic, explicating Paul's theology as "the universalism of Christianity, in which all nations should be embraced," in dialectical relation to "that great opposing force," "Jewish particularism."[47]

More than a century later, Walter Schmithals blamed Karl Barth for the dramatic lapse in historical studies of "the historical problem of Romans" following the First World War. It had been Barth, after all, who by literary fiat had declared that the historical study of Romans had been completed and had turned instead to a theological interpretation of Paul's struggle against "the Jew," whom Barth decoded as "ecclesiastical man."[48]

In 1963 Krister Stendahl sought to set Pauline interpretation on a more adequately historical footing. Stendahl characterized as an anachronism the "introspective conscience of the West" that had dominated Pauline interpretation (especially as the legacy of Augustine and Luther). Ernst Käsemann promptly assailed Stendahl's approach, not as bad history, but as a threat to the foundations of Protestant theology, indeed, as having "fateful significance for the whole of Christianity." Curiously, Käsemann upheld the priority of the church's theology over historical judgments about Paul's writings on the Reformation principle of "the pre-eminence of the scriptures over the church."[49]

The last century has seen serious efforts to set Paul's theology in its proper historical context, to be sure. But these have rarely penetrated the realm of theological necessity where Christianity's assumed superiority over Judaism has set the bounds of the discussion.

Rudolf Bultmann's landmark work on Paul is an important example. Bultmann outlined the "historical position of Paul" concisely and brilliantly: "Standing within the frame of Hellenistic Christianity he raised the theological motifs that were at work in the proclamation of the Hellenistic Church to the clarity of theological thinking" and "called to attention the problems latent in the Hellenistic proclamation."[50] Bultmann promptly disregarded this insight, however, as he proceeded to discover Paul's basic theological position "more or less completely set forth in Romans," and to articulate that position through constant contrasts "between Paul and Judaism." After all, it is the Jew—not, as Bultmann's earlier statement might have led one to believe, the gentile Christian in the Hellenistic church—"with whom Paul is debating in all these arguments."[51]

Thus Protestant theology has often proceeded with business as usual, undisturbed by the complexities of historical fact.[52] The tremendous gravitational pull of the Paul-against-Judaism paradigm seems irresistible.

The Inadequacy of the "New Perspective on Paul"

As those familiar with current Pauline studies know, Bultmann's synthesis no longer holds sway as it did earlier in this century. Decades ago, scholars of Judaism insisted that Paul's attack on "Jewish works-righteousness" represented a "fundamental misapprehension" (Hans Joachim Schoeps), or was "from the Jewish point of view inexplicable" (George Foot Moore). More recently those criticisms have been supported by E. P. Sanders's extensive analysis of second-Temple Jewish literature (fifth century B.C.E. to 70 C.E.) in his study of *Paul and Palestinian Judaism* (1977).[53] The wide acceptance Sanders's work has received owes much, no doubt, to changed sensibilities in Christian theology after the Shoah (or Holocaust). This acceptance is evident in references in academic journals and monographs to "a new era in Pauline studies," the "post-Sanders era," a "paradigm shift," or the need for "reinventing Paul."

The implications of Sanders's work are indeed far-reaching. If he (and Schoeps, Moore, and others before him) is right, then Paul's supposed "attack" on Judaism does not correspond to the ordinary Jewish self-understanding evident in the great majority of ancient writings. Rather, that "attack" must either be taken to represent Paul's serious *misunderstanding* of Judaism, or else it must be evacuated of any logical force. Sanders himself takes the latter course: he argues that Paul thought "backward," "from solution to plight." He "was not trying accurately to represent Judaism on its own terms," but "simply saw the old dispensation as worthless in comparison with the new." Sanders summarizes, "In short, *this is what Paul finds wrong in Judaism: it is not Christianity.*"[54] Rather similarly, Heikki Räisänen argues that Paul backed into his theology of the Law as the result of church controversies that had little to do with Judaism itself. "In the course of his work among Gentiles [Paul] had fully internalized the Gentile point of view and identified himself with it." When challenged by Peter in Antioch (Galatians 2) with the fundamentally Jewish demand "that God's revealed law had to be taken seriously *as a whole*," Paul was forced to fabricate a theological justification for his now thoroughly un-Jewish perspective.[55]

The dilemma thus posed for Christian theologians today is at once critical and inescapable. On the one hand, it no longer seems possible to explain Paul's conversion from Judaism in terms of the inadequacies of Judaism. There are, so to speak, no intelligible *Jewish* reasons for Paul to have left Judaism behind. As Thomas Deidun points out, the dilemma we now face is, can one accept that fact and thus "pay respects to the 'new perspective' without being in principle disposed to go along with a far less flattering picture of Paul than the one on offer under the 'old perspective'?" Must one choose between the "Lutheran Paul," the opponent of a "Jewish works-righteousness" that we now recognize as a scholarly fabrication, and the "idiosyncratic Paul," whose theology is determined by his own very eccentric views?[56]

On the other hand, if we follow other scholars who hold to a "sociological" explanation, we will attribute Paul's "attack" on Judaism to his commitments to the gentile Christian church. In this way we may avoid the inaccurate and prejudicial stereotypes of the older "Lutheran" interpretation. But casting Paul's theology as an effort to justify the status of gentile Christians still assumes a "background" of tremendous Jewish opposition to the Law-free gentile church. That unproven assumption will involve us in another set of tendentious and prejudicial stereotypes about Jewish "particularism" and "ethnocentrism."

Despite this liability, the "new perspective," emphasizing Paul's opposition to Jewish "ethnocentrism," is the most popular alternative in Pauline interpretation today.[57] It nevertheless involves serious difficulties:

(a) First of all, it is hardly a "new perspective on Paul." It simply casts Baur's old dialectic of "Pauline universalism" versus "Jewish particularism" in sociological terms. It does not improve on Baur either by providing a more adequate explanation for the range of Paul's statements about the Torah or by asking to what extent a harsh "ethnocentrism" was characteristic of Judaism in antiquity.

(b) Given Bultmann's insight that the inclusion of Gentiles was already taken for granted by the church before Paul, it seems unlikely that Paul's purpose in Romans (or anywhere else) would have been to defend the inclusion of Gentiles from a broad opposition within the church. In fact, that purpose is presumed far more often than it is argued.[58] In contrast, scholars increasingly recognize that the letter to the Romans addresses gentile Christians and has as one of its primary goals a critique of gentile Christian "boasting" over against Jews and Judaism.[59] If the Paul-against-Judaism paradigm persists in the face of this recognition, it is apparently because historical interpretation is being made to serve a theological agenda.

(c) Although Christian scholars often offer this interpretation in the context of post-Holocaust interfaith dialogue, it hardly improves upon the theological anti-Judaism detected in the Lutheran paradigm. The only theological principle to be celebrated in the "new perspective" is a "universalism" that effectively excludes Torah-observant Jews (who are, by definition, "exclusivistic").[60]

This is hardly an advance in understanding. As William S. Campbell writes, "The most serious legacy of Baur was the view that since Christianity is the absolute religion, then Judaism (and Gentilism) must be negatively related to it." The same observation applies to the "new perspective" of the last twenty years. Contrasting Christian "universalism" with Jewish "particularism" has often gone hand-in-hand with

Christian chauvinism: "An abolition of all differences in the body of Christ has in the past . . . again and again led to the Christian view that the Jew as Jew no longer has a right to existence!"[61] Lest this be read as a hysterical exaggeration, one need only witness New Testament scholar Robert G. Hamerton-Kelly's equanimity as he attributes to Paul the views that the Jews "must persist until the eschaton" as a "negative presence," and that Christ had "revealed the real nature of life based on the Mosaic interpretation of the Law and made it clearly unnecessary and undesirable for the gentiles, or any Jew, ever to adopt that way of life again."[62]

(d) Finally, this interpretation merely postpones the question of intelligibility "from the Jewish point of view." That is, it suggests that Paul joined a community that already included Jews and Gentiles *on the basis of the Torah's suspension*. On this reading Paul only became that community's very prolific, if unreflective mouthpiece. The objections raised to the "old perspective" on Paul still remain, though now they pertain to the theological innovators in the Hellenistic-Christian community before Paul.

A Third Way?

There are a few voices suggesting a third approach to Paul that takes seriously the question of intelligibility "from the Jewish point of view" raised by Schoeps, Moore, and Sanders. This approach honors Johannes Munck's observation that Paul's letters are written to *gentile Christians*.[63]

Lloyd Gaston raises two questions that are at the heart of this new approach to Paul. First, recognizing that "Paul's letters were written to congregations that were overwhelmingly made up of Gentiles," Gaston suggests we ask "what a first-century Jew would have thought of the law *as it relates to Gentiles*."[64] Second, he asks how Paul might appear if he were "interpreted within the context of early Judaism" and "in continuity with the midrashic traditions of Judaism," rather than held up against an artificial "Christian concept of Judaism" derived "from what Paul denies."[65]

This approach to Paul is not yet widely accepted. I suspect part of the reason is that Gaston's perspective leaves no room for the conventional assumptions, so important to the theological tradition, about Paul as a convert from Judaism and about his theology as fundamentally opposed to Jewish thought.

One result of the general failure to adopt this approach is that in most post-Sanders scholarship, *Paul remains unintelligible from the Jewish point of view*. By default, Paul is interpreted not within his own historical context but within the framework of gentile Christian apologetics and polemics from the early second century and later. Now that we have begun to recognize Christian complicity in the Holocaust and to investigate the New Testament's contribution to Christian anti-Judaism,[66] assuming the Paul-against-Judaism paradigm leaves Christian theologians with an unpleasant choice: to continue to endorse Paul's (fundamentally anti-Jewish) theology in defiance of Jewish sensibilities or to abandon Paul as a keen embarrassment.

Another result of assuming that Paul's supposed opposition to Judaism was central to his life and work is that other concerns are pushed out to the periphery. We are left with the peculiar picture of a first-century Jew far more concerned with his own idiosyncratic, thoroughly un-Jewish views of Law-free religious "universalism" than with the actual welfare of his own people or of the members of his congregations. Thus Peter Richardson explains Paul's relative unconcern for the question of slavery: "Paul felt that social institutions as institutions did not deserve first attention. . . . The reason he was so interested in the Jew/Greek question is that a failure to resolve it would result in two separate churches, an intolerable contradiction for Paul."[67] Christian slaveholding, we are to understand, was not an intolerable contradiction for Paul.

According to this conventional way of thinking, *the heart of Paul's thought is his theological opposition not to oppression but to the structures of the Jewish religion.*[68] The dejudaization of Paul obscures the actual relation between his own historical context and his theological reflection and praxis. In this light, Paul's dejudaization is one more dimension of his being depoliticized by the theological tradition.

THE THEOLOGICAL MARGINALIZATION OF PAUL'S POLITICS

I mentioned earlier two occasions, almost a decade apart, at which I heard Paul's exhortation to "be subject to the governing authorities" (Rom. 13:1–7) cited to forestall conversation about my nation's militarism. This is no coincidence, of course. As we saw in chapter 1, third-world theologians from three different continents alert us to Paul's usefulness to "imperial theology" in our day. The value judgment I described at the outset of this chapter—that Paul was less interested in justice than in setting individuals in right relation to God—functions in many churches as a sort of checkpoint at which impulses to social reform and political activism must "halt and be recognized" before proceeding.

This is a third way in which the Christian theological tradition has distorted Paul's voice. We are accustomed to reading Paul as the architect of a distinctly Christian doctrine of salvation, in effect attributing to Paul a "preferential option" for theology and doctrine over ethics and activism, for right belief (orthodoxy) over right action (orthopraxis). That preference has often reflected the institutional church's own interest in reinforcing its distinctiveness over against rival communities.

Given the importance Paul's writings have always enjoyed within the theological tradition, it may be easiest for us to recognize the distortion in that tradition if we notice where theologians have had to struggle the hardest to keep those writings in harness. The interpretation of Paul's letter to the Romans is a significant case in point.

The Babylonian Captivity of the Letter to the Romans

As we have seen, Paul's letter to the Romans continues to play a central role in our conventional image of Paul as a convert from Judaism and as a theological opponent of Judaism. That this is a mystification is evident, first of all, from the persistence of the view that Romans is (a) a comprehensive statement of Paul's theology in its essentials, (b) written at a time when Paul was least constrained by external circumstances, and (c) concerned with the problem of relating the Christian gospel as Paul proclaims it to Judaism, the Torah, and the people Israel. It is evident, too, from the strength with which that construal of Romans resists insights into the specific circumstances that occasioned the letter.

Recent scholarly literature on Romans shows that the eclipse of historical explanation of Romans, so strenuously protested by F. C. Baur a century and a half ago, continues today. J. B. Lightfoot's view that Paul wrote to the Romans "at leisure, under no pressure of circumstances, in the face of no direct antagonism," presenting his teaching "generalized and arranged so as to form a comprehensive and systematic treatise," still finds support among prominent exegetes (F. F. Bruce, C. E. B. Cranfield).[69] Thus the sixteenth-century Reformer Philip Melanchthon's characterization of the letter as a "compendium of Christian doctrine" survives even in the age of historical criticism.

Yet even those scholars reluctant to endorse Lightfoot's view have usually not found their way clear to viewing Romans, *like any of Paul's other letters,* as a letter thoroughly constrained by a specific historical situation. Rather, the horizons of "the Romans debate" have been broadened just enough to ask about the specific circumstances that occasioned the letter—which is nevertheless still read along the lines of a comprehensive and systematic treatise. Thus Romans is a defense of Paul's theology directed, beyond Rome, to Jewish adversaries in Jerusalem (Jacob Jervell); or a theological charter meant to constitute the Roman community as a Pauline church (Günter Klein); or a sample of Paul's rhetoric (Robin Scroggs) or of his teaching (Stanley K. Stowers), transmitted to win the Romans' support for his activities; or a "speech of exhortation" by which Paul hopes to win the Romans' recognition of the truth of his "version of the gospel" (David E. Aune).[70] Common to all these explanations is the view that the letter's contents are a comprehensive summary of Paul's gospel, essentially unconditioned by circumstance, which has been packaged and sent off to meet some circumstantial need. The body of the letter (Rom. 1:15–15:13, or more usually the "core" in chapters 1–8) is treated as a dogmatic cargo, rather like Paul's theological portfolio (some scholars make the comparison explicit). Questions of occasion or purpose are peripheral, applying only to the packaging of this cargo, and ultimately unnecessary for interpreting the letter's content.

The impression conveyed in these studies, an impression so pervasive in church history as to take on the appearance of the self-evident today, is that if other letters show Paul responding to concrete situations in light of his theology, Romans presents that theology itself, projected onto papyrus with only the slightest refraction by historical circumstances. The tremendous privilege Romans thus comes to enjoy can hardly be exaggerated. It is Romans that shapes academic presentations of "Paul's theology," for example, by scholars as diverse as Rudolf Bultmann and Juan Luis Segundo.

The wider implication of the privilege accorded to Romans is that the character of Paul's thought is essentially a system of theological beliefs, which may be "applied" in practical situations without these practical applications becoming in any way constitutive of Paul's thought. The system of beliefs, Paul's doctrine of salvation, is primary; its application in practical situations, secondary and derivative.

That view of Romans in particular, and of Paul's thought in general, is inherently unlikely. As Pauline scholar J. Christiaan Beker has insisted, the gospel Paul proclaimed was a matter of action, meaning not only that Paul always writes "in order to bring about something," but also that "the gospel itself has as its content the 'in order that' of God's coming triumph." This is as true for Romans as for any other letter Paul wrote.[71] Indeed, we should not be surprised to discover that Romans is an instrument of apostolic action once we notice that Paul declares at the outset that the gospel is "the power of God" (1:15), or that he introduces himself as someone "called by God" to accomplish a very specific work, namely, securing "the faithful obedience of all the Gentiles" (1:5). His commission includes the Christians of Rome (1:6). Thus his intention to come to the Romans, "to impart some spiritual gift to strengthen" them (1:11), to "reap some harvest" among them, exactly coincides with his commission to all Gentiles (1:13), and with his obligation to "Greek and barbarian, wise and unlettered alike" (1:15).

In this light, we should be surprised, even scandalized, at the regularity with which commentators tear Paul's statement in 1:16–17 ("I am not ashamed of the gospel, for it is the power of God") out of its context and isolate it as the "theme" of a theological essay, thus obliterating the signs of the letter's character as *praxis.* Such an exegetical contrivance is theologically useful, of course, in that it elevates the doctrine of justification by faith above the situational contingencies of the letter. But it is artificial, as is evident from what we have observed in the letter opening and from the letter's conclusion as well. There Paul uses language parallel to that in 1:1–15 to reiterate his intention in writing to the Roman Christians. Through this letter he fulfills his apostolic commission "to be the minister of Christ to the Gentiles," securing the "sanctification of the offering of the Gentiles" (15:14–16). Thus his apostolic work extends the work of Christ, "what Christ has wrought through me to win obedience from the Gentiles, by word and deed, by the power of signs and wonders, by the power of the Holy Spirit" (15:18–19).[72]

The letter's character as paraenesis, that is, as exhortation intended to move people to act in a certain way, is clear from Paul's solemn appeal to "present your whole beings as a living sacrifice, holy and acceptable to God, your spiritual worship'" (Rom. 12:2). Just here Victor Paul Furnish sees the key to the letter's structure: Romans is designed to move the reader from a description of the horrors of Gentile immorality (1:18–32) through the transformation of baptism (chapter 6) to the new possibility of holy lives offered to God (chapter 12).[73] The letter takes its structure from what Bultmann identified as the "once—but now" schema of early Christian preaching; the "theological" argument in chapters 1–11 is meant to energize the exhortation to action that follows in chapters 12–15.[74]

Other scholars have given attention to the argumentative movement sustained by rhetorical questions throughout the letter (Hendrikus Boers) and to the parallelism of rhetorical questions in Romans 3— usually misread as part of Paul's "attack on Judaism"—and in Romans 6, where the transformation effected in Christian baptism is clearly in view (William S. Campbell).[75]

These different lines of argument converge in a new understanding of Romans as thoroughly determined by a concrete historical situation and as directed to gentile Christians as its primary target. In contrast to the exegetically dubious interpretation of the letter as a pre-packaged introduction of "Paul's gospel" in opposition to Judaism, these more nuanced rhetorical studies confirm that *Romans is, like Paul's other letters, a tool designed and deployed as part of Paul's apostolic work.* It is time to decentralize Romans from its current role as a "comprehensive and systematic" presentation of theological ideas, and rediscover the letter as an instrument of action.

Paul's Deployment in the Struggle against Liberation Theology

I remember very little of the coursework in my first year in seminary. I remember with crystal clarity the hush in the cafeteria the morning we learned that Archbishop Oscar Romero had been assassinated in El Salvador.

We read widely in the theology of liberation, of course, and debated its virtues and shortcomings in our seminars. Many of us also came to recognize, even at a great distance, what the Archbishop's brothers and sisters in El Salvador knew intimately: that his life had incarnated the preferential option of the poor at the heart of that theology.

"Our Salvadoran world is no abstraction," Romero told an audience of European academics a month before his death. "It is a world made up mostly of men and women who are poor and oppressed." His church's resolve to experience the daily realities of devastating poverty and "to let ourselves be affected by them, far from separating us from our faith, has sent us back to the world of the poor as to our true home. It has moved us, as a first, basic step, to take the world of the poor on ourselves."[76]

It also moved Romero to speak out, forcefully and often, against the repression in his own nation and against the nation whose interests the repression served. As we now know, he was murdered for his trouble by men to whom the U.S. government gave unwavering support as the "best chance for democracy" in El Salvador. As we knew even then, the Reagan administration considered Romero and his fellow liberation theologians the greatest danger to U.S. interests in Latin America. In that first year in seminary I learned that the theology of liberation was more than an interesting subject for academic debate. It was a precious instrument in another people's struggle for their own survival.

In this struggle, too, Paul has played a part.

As we have seen, the *Kairos* theologians complained that "imperial theology" has empressed Paul into its service in order to provide "theological justification of the status quo with its racism, capitalism and totalitarianism." The most blatant form of this abuse of Paul is the regular use of Rom. 13:1–7 to encourage quiet submission to governments. But the same purposes are served whenever the apostle is brought in to undermine the initiatives of the theologians of liberation, and to remind Christians that social justice must always remain a secondary concern.

Given the profound legacy of Catholic social thought over the last century, one could hardly describe the official teaching of the Catholic church as "imperial theology." To the contrary, the Latin American Catholics who were radicalized by their work in the slums of Rio de Janeiro or Santiago heard in the declarations of the Second Vatican Council a profound vindication of their experience and of their impulses toward rethinking theology in terms of human liberation. Surely one would have expected the theology of liberation to find a warm welcome within the bosom of the Catholic church.

Curiously, throughout the late 1970s and 1980s official Catholic church teachings about liberation theology tended to read like warnings to the faithful. I notice that when the apostle Paul is cited in these instructions, it is usually in order to emphasize the difference "between salvation and human welfare, between salvation and human rights."

That language comes from the "Declaration on Human Development and Christian Salvation" (1977) issued by a commission of the Roman Catholic Congregation for the Doctrine of the Faith. According to the Declaration, "it is easy to be mistaken about what constitutes true denial of human freedom, true slavery"—especially, one suspects, in circumstances like those prevailing in much of the Third World, where hunger, diarrhea, and state-sponsored violence might distract one from doctrinal truths. On the basis of generalizations about Paul's doctrine of justification by faith, the commission asserts that "the Bible speaks of sin in the first instance in terms of an explicit, personal decision that stems from human freedom," not in terms of institutional injustice. Similarly the commission relies on Paul to distinguish "the primary liberation from death and perishability, from the power of sin and from the law," from a secondary, derivative liberation, the alleviation of material conditions for the poor.

As to the liberation theologians' call for the church at last to commit itself to a "preferential option for the poor," the Declaration assures us that "a strong kinship with the poor" has always been "among the principal functions of the church," the historical record in Latin America notwithstanding. The Declaration has in mind a broad definition of "the poor," of course: "those who are afflicted by any serious spiritual, psychological, or material wants." At the same time, we are warned not to expect the church to embrace a single political option. It will always be appropriate for Christians "to opt freely among different paths"; there will always be "controversy on social and political issues" among Christians. Therefore, while Christians may properly "try to effect change by, e.g., shaping human consciences, entering into discussion, initiating and supporting nonviolent action," the church must always remember that political action "does not have a kind of absolute value."

The Declaration specifically repudiates only one political stance, namely, the perspective in which "the differences that exist between social 'classes' are taken up into a systematic 'class struggle.'" The quotation marks alone should make it clear that "class" differences are a dubious basis for analysis, an unacceptable vestige of "Marxism and Leninism" irrelevant to the real world.[77]

Paul is just as useful for promoting obedience to the church hierarchy. When Pope John Paul II spoke to delegates at the Puebla assembly in 1979, he first warned against depictions of "Jesus as a political activist," "the subversive from Nazareth." Such pictures are "'rereadings' of the gospel that are the product of theoretical speculations rather than of authentic meditation on the word of God and a genuine evangelical commitment"; they are causes of "confusion" to the faithful.

The pope then cited the Paul of the Pastoral letters to argue that "carefully watching over purity of doctrine" is "the primary and irreplaceable duty of the pastor, of the teacher of faith." That duty includes exhorting "prompt, sincere respect for the sacred magisterium, a respect based on the clear realization that in submitting to it, the people of God is not accepting the word of human beings"—a danger that arises, apparently, in the "theoretical speculations" of the liberation theologians—"but the authentic word of God."[78]

The standard lines on which the liberation theologians would be censured over the next decade were already evident. According to the "Instruction on Certain Aspects of the 'Theology of Liberation' " issued by the Roman Catholic Congregation for the Doctrine of the Faith (1984), it is important to learn from Paul that liberation "is first and foremost liberation from the radical slavery of sin." In contrast, "some"—by clear implication, the theologians of liberation—"are tempted to emphasize, unilaterally, the liberation from servitude of an earthly and temporal kind. They do so in such a way that they seem to put liberation from sin in second place, and so fail to give it the primary importance it is due."[79]

One might well ask which liberation theologians have "put liberation from sin in second place." Indeed, the final document from the progressive bishops' conference in Puebla (1979) insisted on a conception of "liberation from all the forms of bondage, from personal and social sin, and from everything that tears apart the human individual and society."[80] It would seem to be the Congregation, not the theologians of liberation, that has subordinated one form of liberation, that which is merely "earthly and temporal," to the "first and foremost" liberation, that from sin.

The Congregation goes on to repeat earlier condemnations of "concepts of an ideological inspiration," meaning of course social analysis based on class differences, as "incompatible with Christian faith." But must one be the victim of "ideology" to recognize that the massive exploitation of third-world people has been systematically orchestrated in the first world? The question brings to mind the comment of Roman Catholic Archbishop Dom Helder Camara, an indefatigable champion of the poor of Brazil: "When I feed the poor, they call me a saint. When I ask *why* they are poor, they call me a Communist."

However ambiguous or implicit these ecclesiastical warnings, their intention was made clear enough in the 1980s by the regular silencing or censure of liberation theologians (one thinks of former Franciscan Leonardo Boff, former Dominican Matthew Fox, or former Salesian Jean-Bertrand Aristide); by the newsphoto image of Pope John Paul II shaking a scolding finger at the kneeling figure of Ernesto Cardenal, a Catholic priest serving as Minister of Culture in Sandinista Nicaragua; and by the Vatican's monstrous action, alone in the world, of giving diplomatic recognition to the murderous military regime that ousted Haitian president Jean-Bertrand Aristide's elected government by force.

These ecclesiastical statements cite Paul in order to subordinate "earthly" to "spiritual" concerns. That is only one of the ways in which Paul has been useful in marginalizing the theology of liberation. Just as fateful is the acceptance of this ranking by liberation theologians themselves as an accurate representation of Paul's thought. As David Bosch has written in the *Journal of Theology for South Africa*, "In the circles of liberation theology Paul has a rather bad press. He is often looked upon as the one who transformed Jesus' message about God providing justice for the poor and the oppressed into a general and universalistic religion about salvation for sinners in the hereafter."[81]

For example, Clodovis Boff and George V. Pixley declare that Paul's preference for speaking of the cosmic significance of the cross rather than the historical Jesus "meant that in his letters, and most likely in his ministry as well, he showed a certain blindness to poverty as a social fact. For him, *true* poverty was anthropological, inherent in the human condition." They continue, Paul "was so impressed by the inherent poverty of humanity compared to the greatness of divine favor that the problem of human differences between rich and poor was relegated to a secondary level in his thought. He did not offer any theological outline of the option for the poor, though he did touch on it in some cases of intra-church conflicts."[82] Similarly the Jesuit martyr Ignacio Ellacuría wrote that "the gospel of Paul pays little attention to the Jesus of the flesh, to the historical Jesus. It moves, rather too rapidly, to the Christ of faith." Paul had not known Jesus personally: The result is a christology "aloof from fact."[83]

In the U.S., the theology of liberation quickly came under fire not only from conservative circles, but also from liberals laying claim to the "Christian realism" of theologian Reinhold Niebuhr, who died in 1971.

Widely hailed as the century's most important "theologian of public life," Niebuhr has left a complex legacy.[84] Niebuhrians on the "left" emphasize Niebuhr's critique of capitalism and his eventual estrangement from the U.S. policy of "containment" in Vietnam, and consider liberation theology an appropriate extension of his thought.[85] Those on the right, on the other hand, emphasize Niebuhr's critique of totalitarianism (which they invariably identify with revolutionary governments in Latin America, not with the murderous U.S. client states that Ambassador Jeanne Kirkpatrick politely described as "authoritarian states"), and Niebuhr's constant insistence that American Christians in particular must assume their global responsibilities with proper seriousness. Robert McAfee Brown quite aptly characterizes the neoconservatives as "listening to Niebuhr with only one ear."[86] Nevertheless Niebuhr's doctrines have been enormously popular among U.S. policymakers.

Niebuhr's Christian realism relies on a fundamental contrast between the impossible moral ideal held out by Christianity, on the one hand, and the possible approximation of that ideal in the political arena on the other. In that arena, Niebuhr wrote, "forces which are morally dangerous must be used despite their peril"; indeed, "the realities of sin make coercion and resistance a requirement of justice."[87]

Too often since Niebuhr wrote those words, that contrast has served to insulate the doctrine of inevitable violence and to legitimate inequalities of power and wealth from critique by the Christian gospel. But the defect is visible already in Niebuhr's argument for U.S. military involvement in the Second World War, which he couched in terms of assuming "our duty" as Americans "to defend the free world." In the course of explaining (in 1940) "why the Christian church is not pacifist," Niebuhr contrasted the "absolute and uncompromising ethic of Jesus," which he declared an impossible ideal, not "immediately applicable to the task of securing justice in a sinful world," with the Pauline doctrine of "justification," which "measures the full seriousness of sin as a permanent factor in human history" and offers "the assurance of divine mercy for a persistent sinfulness which man never overcomes completely."[88]

The 1940 essay suggested that the Pauline doctrine of grace meant accepting one's regrettable duty to participate in violence for a "just cause." Reflecting later on the saturation bombing of the Ruhr valley by Allied forces, Niebuhr wrote that once one understood "the religious fact that Saint Paul understood so well," that "there is no escape from guilt in history," one would be more willing to "cause innocent people to suffer with the guilty"—with due regret, of course.[89]

If Niebuhr was "the theologian most responsible for bringing the majority of the Christian churches out of their isolationism and into a realization of the global responsibilities of the United States,"[90] Paul's doctrine of justification by faith evidently provided the theological lever with which Niebuhr moved the churches to embrace the war. To the extent that Niebuhr's Christian realism provided a theological rationale for U.S. military interventions in the decades after that war, he continued to attract interest in Washington. In those years, as Niebuhr served on several "cold war" policy boards, his "lesson about the moral ambiguity of the uses of power remained subordinated . . . to the lesson about the necessity of resort to power," historian Paul Merkley writes.[91] As the United States extended its political and military domination in Southeast Asia, Niebuhr initially complained—quite against the record of history—that Americans suffered from "a strong anti-imperialist tradition." That unfortunate defect saddled us with "a certain hesitancy in exercising the responsibilities of our imperial power" and caused us to fear—quite reasonably, as history would show—"that we may violate the cardinal principle of liberalism, the 'self determination of nations.' " Such hesitancy, Niebuhr insisted in 1962, "we cannot afford."[92]

However seductive the logic of Niebuhr's so-called Christian realism, there is nothing particularly Christian or even particularly realistic in ecclesiastical endorsements of military force. In an important essay responding to the call for military intervention in Bosnia, Lutheran pastor and theologian Jack Nelson-Pallmeyer insists that since "today's crises were born out of yesterday's policy failures, we should not allow those most responsible for present crises to tell us self-servingly that nonviolence doesn't work."[93]

Nelson-Pallmeyer reveals the same moral anguish over Bosnia that Niebuhr expressed in his essays in the 1940s, the anguish that arises when the commitment to nonviolence confronts the magnitude of human injustice and violence. "We cannot in the spirit of Jesus, for example, cite a principled commitment to nonviolence as a reason to do nothing about 'ethnic cleansing.' " Such pervasive violence "is a judgment against unjust systems and against the ineffectiveness of my nonviolent peacemaking that results in great violence to others." It is just this "ineffectiveness" in the face of evil that led Niebuhr to renounce Christian pacifism, and to espouse the more "realist" position of accepting violence, under certain circumstances, as the regrettable duty of the responsible Christian. But Nelson-Pallmeyer rejects the logic of Niebuhr's conclusion, refusing the easy logic of a "Christian realism" that authorizes in advance the "last resort" to violence. He calls us instead to explore effective strategies of nonviolent direct action even more vigorously.[94]

Whatever the merits of Niebuhr's justification of violence, it is his theology of "global responsibility" that explains his continuing influence in the highest echelons of government as an "apologist of power," the premier "theological interpreter of the U.S. imperial vocation," "the religious pointman for the interventionist movement" (Bill Kellerman; Noam Chomsky).[95] Bearing in mind how the United States has exercised its global "responsibilities" in Latin America in recent decades, with the vigorous approval of self-declared Niebuhrians like Michael Novak,[96] one may understand why third-world observers frequently see in Christian realism "a religious ideology that serves to justify U.S. power, or the power of establishments in other countries in league with the United States, and the 'national security doctrine.' "[97] Niebuhr's contrast of the "impossible" ethic of Jesus with the "Pauline doctrine of grace" mirrors the contrast two-thirds-world *Kairos* theologians draw between a "state theology" that "is simply the theological justification of the status quo with its racism, capitalism and totalitarianism" and "the God of the

Poor, revealed by Jesus.'' It is hard to avoid the impression that in this dark side of Niebuhr's doctrine, Paul has become an acolyte of imperial apologetics, the theologian of necessary (though regrettable) violence.

The mystery to be explained here is not Niebuhr's popularity in the corridors of power. It is that Niebuhr could so easily convince us that ''conscious choices of evil for the sake of good'' was the essence of ''the Pauline doctrine.'' After all, Paul himself was aware of those in his own day who interpreted him as saying, ''Let us do evil that good may come.'' ''Such slanderers,'' he wrote, ''are rightly condemned'' (Rom. 3:8).

Paul's empressment into the ranks of liberation theology's opponents is more than the result of modern power politics. By causing the letter to the Romans, and especially the doctrine of justification by faith, to bear the weight of the ''essence of Paul's theology,'' the Christian tradition has effectively lifted the letter's rhetoric from its context, marginalized other concerns in Paul's thought, and reduced the other, more clearly contextual letters to the status of contingent ''applications'' of Paul's theology. The result has often been to subordinate concern for human liberation to other, ''higher,'' more urgent duties, whether these are conceived of as ''spiritual'' rather than merely ''material'' welfare (as in the Vatican statements against liberation theology) or as more ''practical'' rather than merely ''idealistic'' concerns (as in so-called Christian realism).

Thus the interpretation of Paul continues to protect the empire from critique. No wonder, then, that men and women involved in activism for peace and justice continue to ask, with no little urgency, ''What do we do with Paul?''

TOWARD A NEW APPROACH

In the preceding pages I have sought to evoke the critical situation in which we now read Paul. The patterns of canonical distortion and theological mystification that have had such disastrous consequences in the past continue to influence the way we read Paul today. Our situation with regard to Paul is critical not only because longstanding conventions in scholarship are crumbling, but because the predicament in which many scholars now find themselves provides a window of opportunity in which other conventional assumptions about Paul can be questioned as well.

I have described a pattern of mystification of the apostle Paul in which his praxis is subordinated to his thought, and both are effectively redirected toward safeguarding the interests of privilege and power. Fortunately, it has been possible at each stage of that argument to rely upon insights current in Pauline scholarship today into the nature and tendency of the Pauline pseudepigrapha, into alternative visions of the Pauline legacy in the second and third centuries, and into the inadequacy of the twin paradigms of Paul as convert from Judaism and as opponent of Judaism. If it is routine for scholars now to speak of our standing in the middle of a "paradigm shift" in Pauline studies, that means that we recognize the inadequacy of the conventional understanding of Paul and acknowledge the need for a more adequate portrait of the historical Paul. These insights, coordinated in a single, coherent perspective, may help us to train our ears to recognize the distortions in the voice we routinely hear—not only in scholarship, but also in churches, in politics, in conversation—as Paul's.

How should we move toward such a new perspective? We can start by recognizing, with J. Christiaan Beker, that Paul was less a systematic theologian than an apostle, less concerned with getting people to accept his ideas than with moving them to act in conformity with his vision of God's coming triumph.[98] Peter Tomson makes a similar point in his study of Paul's treatment of Jewish law:

> Paul's epistles display a logic which seem homiletical and pastoral rather than systematic, and they read most naturally as *ad hoc* letters written to various communities in different situations. Obviously these situations involved not only theological issues, but all kinds of practical questions reflecting the vicissitudes of daily life. In view of Paul's Jewish background we may even suspect that his concern with such practical questions was at least as important as his theological expositions.[99]

In all of Paul's letters—including Romans—we see the apostle engaged in the constant interplay of praxis and reflection. The appropriate object for the study of Paul's theology, then, is not a set of theological propositions, an "essence" or "core" of ideas, but the direction in which he sought to move others in the course of his apostolic activity. The proper approach to Paul's letters begins with an understanding of his thought that resembles Gustavo Gutiérrez's definition of theology. In Paul's letters we see the apostle engaged in "critical reflection on praxis in the light of the word of God."[100]

If, with Beker, we recognize that "Paul seems more interested in persuasion, emotional appeal and moral exhortation in his letters than in the academic pursuit of coherence and consistency of thought,"[101] we should adopt a method appropriate to the study of persuasion: rhetorical criticism. There is no reason here to enter into the debate over the level of Paul's training in ancient rhetoric, since the so-called New Rhetoric emphasizes the dynamics of argumentation in *any* discourse intended to persuade.[102] This methodology has already proven its usefulness in biblical studies.[103]

More important, approaching Paul's writings through rhetorical criticism, emphasizing their character as persuasive discourse, can free Paul from "the straitjacket of each generation's self-understanding," which "takes Paul's letters out of the public domain where argument is in order and where Paul's strong arguments could have social impact" (Antoinette Clark Wire). Wire points out that "understanding Paul's letters as argument may be possible in the church only when there is a shift in its view of the Bible's authority." Such a shift would allow us to hear Paul's voice more genuinely, for in his letters "Paul claims a hearing on the basis of insistent arguments from God's calling, from revelation, from hard work, and from modeling Christ. The letters do not claim to be authoritative in their own right or this argument would be redundant. For Paul, such intrinsic authority belongs to God alone. Paul's letters' authority depends on free assent to Paul's arguments because they are convincing."[104]

A "Quest for the Historical Paul"

No account of Paul's apostolic work should win approval unless it observes the constraints of historical reasoning that are routine in the modern study of "the historical Jesus." In fact the foregoing description of a massive theological misrepresentation of Paul suggests that the situation in Pauline studies now bears comparison with Albert Schweitzer's striking summary of nineteenth-century scholarship on the life of Jesus, published in 1906. Schweitzer wrote,

> The study of the life of Jesus has had a curious history. It set out in quest of the historical Jesus, believing that when it had found Him it could bring Him straight into our time as a Teacher and Savior. It loosed the bands by which He had been riveted for centuries to the stony rocks of ecclesiastical doctrine, and rejoiced to see life and movement coming into the figure once more, and the historical Jesus advancing, as it seemed, to meet it. But He does not stay; He passes by our time and returns to His own. What surprised and dismayed the theology of the last forty years was that, despite all forced and arbitrary interpretations, it could not keep Him in our time, but had to let Him go. He returned to His own time, not owing to the application of any historical ingenuity, but by the same inevitable necessity by which the liberated pendulum returns to its original position.[105]

A similar state of affairs pertains to the interpretation of Paul. Studies attentive to the character of ancient Judaism have broken Paul loose from the "stony rocks of ecclesiastical doctrine," but again and again the figure of Paul that is thus freed to approach us has turned out to be a projection of our own values (as Christians and as Americans). It is precisely the scholarly-theological constructs of Paul as a convert from Judaism, a champion of religious "universalism," a representative of middle-class interests, and an apologist of power that holds Paul manacled to engines of prejudice, exploitation, violence, and war.

The analogy with the quest for the historical Jesus suggests that we might employ a parallel set of criteria in our attempt to restore Paul to his own time and place, and thus to come closer to hearing the voice of "the historical Paul" in our own time.

1. Just as New Testament scholars use the "criterion of dissimilarity" to distinguish the self-interests of the Christian communities that produced the Gospels from the probable characteristic sayings and actions of Jesus himself,[106] so a "criterion of dissimilarity" applied to Paul would control the tendencies in the Christian tradition toward self-legitimation against rival religious communities (the theological anti-Judaism of Ephesians, for example) and toward accommodation within oppressive societies (the patriarchal morality of the Pastorals, for example). This criterion might state that *unless clearly required by the genuine letters of Paul, interpretations that assimilate Paul's thought and praxis to the recognized purposes of the pseudo-Paulines would be considered doubtful.*

2. Just as a "criterion of historical intelligibility" serves to make sense of Jesus within the context of first-century Palestinian Judaism,[107] so a criterion of historical intelligibility would seek to interpret Paul as well by constant reference to a Jewish environment of thought. Applying such a criterion would involve assuming as a matter of principle that "Paul knew as much about Judaism" as do modern scholars of the Judaism of Paul's time (Lloyd Gaston),[108] and that difficulties in understanding Paul "from the Jewish point of view" may reside with the modern interpreter rather than with Paul. According to this criterion, *interpretations that require the prior assumption that Paul's thought was characteristically un-Jewish or opposed to Judaism should be considered doubtful.*[109]

3. A criterion of rhetorical intelligibility would respect the context of Paul's letters in his apostolate among Gentile-Christian congregations, employing rhetorical criticism to discover how Paul has written "to elicit or increase the adherence of the members of an audience to theses that are presented to their consent," seeking to modify their "convictions or dispositions through discourse" in order to achieve a "meeting of minds."[110] Such a criterion—particularly relevant to studies of the letter to the Romans—stipulates that *interpretations that assume that Paul is not writing to persuade the audience to which he actually writes* (i.e., an audience of Gentile Christians) *would be considered doubtful,* as would any interpretation that fails to respect "the contexts of his whole apostolic praxis" (Juan Luis Segundo).[111]

4. In light of the preceding observations about the tendency of the Christian tradition to depoliticize Paul, the criterion of dissimilarity itself would suggest taking up again the political key that liberation

theologian Juan Luis Segundo tried, then rejected, in his book on Paul.[112] Segundo considered the political key unusable because he shared some of the widespread assumptions about Paul's thought that I have criticized in the preceding pages. If those assumptions are wrong, as I have argued they are, then Segundo's rejection of the political key was premature. After all, sometimes a key fails to work at first, not because it is the wrong key, but because a lock has become stiff and unyielding through long disuse—surely an apt metaphor, given the history of Paul's appropriation by the church. In such circumstances, a good sharp knock or two often serves to rattle things loose enough for the same key to work. The first three chapters of this book have been intended, so to speak, to knock loose some assumptions about Paul that have come under considerable criticism in recent Pauline scholarship. It is time now to try the political key again.

Reading Paul in a Confessional Situation

The criteria I have proposed respond to Elisabeth Schüssler Fiorenza's call in her 1987 presidential address before the Society of Biblical Literature for an "ethics of historical reading" that would "give the text its due by asserting its original meanings over and against later dogmatic usurpation." But Schüssler Fiorenza also called for an "ethics of accountability that stands responsible not only for the choice of theoretical interpretive models but also for the ethical consequences of the biblical text and its meanings."[113] Such responsibility would require us to recognize, name, and publicly oppose the sorts of destructive appropriations of Paul's writings in our own situation that we have had occasion to observe in the preceding pages.

"Our own situation" in North America is a confessional situation (*status confessionis*), by which I mean a situation in which "our understanding of the Christian message is *so clear* that taking exception to it is no longer possible. Those who now dissent remove themselves from the company of believers" (Robert McAfee Brown).[114] Asking what a *Kairos Document* for the U.S. would look like, Brown presents the statement of the Community of St. Martin in Minneapolis, who discern a confessional situation in what Jack Nelson-Pallmeyer calls the U.S. war against the poor: (1) "Structural injustice within the world economy is responsible for massive death and destruction of the world's poor"; (2) "The United States is actively engaged in warfare against the poor"; (3) "Present global patterns of production and consumption become a war against future generations"; (4) "The arms race victimizes the poor."[115]

I find that statement of our situation as a confessional situation utterly compelling, as I do the community's call for civil and ecclesial resistance (what the Reverend Carter Heyward calls the key to "doing theology in a counterrevolutionary situation").[116] With particular significance for the project here, Nelson-Pallmeyer writes of "a relationship between our relative affluence and our willingness to accept imperial myths and to ignore or be indifferent to U.S. foreign and domestic policies that victimize the poor." But if, as I argued in chapter 1, our indifference is routinely cultivated within American churches by the invocation of Paul's name, then throwing off our indoctrination in indifference will require us to reinterpret Paul.

Paul's Preferential Option for the Poor and Oppressed

In the pages that follow, I am guided by two hunches about Paul, alongside the criteria I have just named. The first, and perhaps the most provocative, is that Paul would have recognized what liberation theologians call "the preferential option for the poor" as an authentic expression of Israel's faith and, consequently, of the gospel of Jesus Christ of which he had been made a minister.

If the so-called option for the poor was in fact integral to the message of Israel's prophets (and I cannot imagine any more integral aspect of their message), it is reasonable to imagine that Paul, or any Jew in the Second Temple period for that matter, might have been familiar with that message and might have been in sympathy with it. After all, according to Paul's own account in the letter to the Galatians, when he met with the apostles in Jerusalem, he declared that being continually mindful of "the poor" was "the very thing I have made it my business to do" (Gal. 2:10, New English Bible). Indeed, Acts 11:27–30 makes a campaign for famine relief in Judea the occasion for Paul's first "mission"!

To be sure, Paul was no more a social analyst than he was a systematic theologian. As Beker points out, we never see Paul "wrestle with strategies for political and social action."[117] It would be extremely anachronistic, however, to expect Paul to think in terms of the sort of economic or political analysis that liberation theologians practice today. As to what informs and impels that analysis in liberation theology, on the other hand—"a commitment to think for the sake of poor and oppressed people" and to consider the links between theology and praxis in terms of that commitment (Juan Luis Segundo)[118] —there are indications in Paul's writings that he was no stranger to such a commitment. Paul admonished the Christians of Rome not to "set your minds on high things, but associate with the humble" (Rom. 12:16).[119] And in what is arguably the first Christian articulation of the preferential option for the poor, Paul appealed to members of the church in Corinth to remember that even in their own calling as a congregation, "God chose what is foolish in the world to shame the wise, God chose what is weak in the world to shame the strong, God chose what is low and despised in the world, even things that are not, to bring to nothing things that are"

(1 Cor. 1:26–28, RSV). It is significant that in that same letter Paul criticizes the wealthier Corinthians for distorting the life of the community by celebrating their own material advantages as God-given (4:6–11) and showing contempt for the poor in their ritual life (11:21–22).

We will return in chapter 6 to examine Paul's apostolic praxis among his congregations in greater detail. I should make my hunch explicit here, however: *Any interpretation that excludes the possibility of Paul's awareness of the poor, and his reflection on the situation of the poor in the light of the gospel he proclaimed, ought to be considered doubtful.* I will in fact argue that Paul's apostolate embodies the commitment to the poor that we recognize today as a distinctive feature of liberation theology.

A second hunch derives from the principle of reading Paul's letters, not as autonomous, disembodied artifacts of Paul's theological thinking, but as instruments of his apostolic activity. If we are to endow our vision of Paul with flesh and blood, wouldn't it be appropriate to contemplate Paul's bodily presence as he writes of a slave's freedom while he himself wears chains of Roman iron (Philem. 1, 10) or as he protests that he is a genuine apostle by reciting the record of his arrests and beatings (2 Cor. 11:23–27)? If Paul could describe himself and his fellow apostles as "last of all, as though sentenced to death, . . . a spectacle to the world, . . . weak, . . . dishonored, . . . hungry and thirsty, . . . poorly clothed and beaten and homeless, . . . weary from the work of our own hands, . . . reviled, . . . persecuted, . . . slandered, . . . like the rubbish of the world" (1 Cor. 4:8–13), why should we surrender the prerogative of interpreting Paul today to the interests of the powerful and comfortable? Why not assume that Paul's vision will be clearest when seen from the standpoint of the oppressed today, and of those who work for liberation—and suffer arrest, imprisonment, and torture for their trouble?

Ultimately, asking how Paul's theology was embodied in him leads us to ask about his experience of violence. His emphasis on the character of Christ's death as crucifixion was unusual (Phil. 2:8); so was the violence of his initial response to Jesus' followers (Gal. 1:13–14). Given the enormity of suffering inflicted on Paul's own people by the Romans in the first century, shouldn't we expect to find that the political violence of Rome played some role in his thought?

In her profound essay on "The Private Life of War," Susan Griffin argues that from our very first days, our pleasure and our suffering are "inscribed" in our bodies; they "settle into flesh and bone." This embodied experience becomes our truth, which is either embraced in love or suppressed in "mystification . . . passed from one generation to the next."[120] Psychoanalyst Alice Miller similarly finds the "roots of violence" in the bodily traumas of childhood punishment.[121] Can it be that the violence in the very air around Saul of Tarsus left no significant impression on the man? Given his own deliberate emphasis on the crucifixion of Christ as the heart of his proclamation (1 Cor. 2:2), the heart of his shared apostolate (2 Cor. 4:10), and the heart of the eucharistic common life (1 Cor. 11:26), are we really to imagine that the cross was no more than a religious symbol for him, the naked truth of the violence revealed there a matter of indifference for his theology?

My second hunch is that *any interpretation of Paul's thought that fails to account for the political aspect of the cross should be considered inadequate.* I will argue that Paul recognized the depths of political terror in the violence of the crucifixion, and saw specifically this violence overcome in Christ's resurrection.

A Personal Angle of Vision

My own perspective on Paul is influenced now by my vocation as an Anglican lay Franciscan. As such, I write from within a community of women and men who seek to live out the gospel imperatives in the spirit of the "little poor man of Assisi." Francis (or at least his pious biographers) considered the dream that called him to chivalrous obedience to his Lord a mirror of Paul's vision on the road to Damascus; his response to that dream took the form of the apostle's exhortation, "Since we live by the Spirit, let us follow the Spirit's lead" (Gal. 5:25–26).[122] For Francis, obeying Christ meant embracing poverty, standing in the place of the poor of the world; for just here the union of the love of God and the suffering of the world—the mystery announced and celebrated in the Eucharist—could be actualized.

I think it is no accident that some of the most widely recognized Franciscans of our own time are best known for challenging their churches to stand in the place of the poor. I think, for example, of Archbishop Desmond Tutu (Anglican lay Franciscan) of South Africa, and Leonardo Boff (formerly a Friar Minor) of Brazil; or of Terry Rogers, a sister in the Anglican lay Franciscans, whose desire to incarnate the love of God has led her to stand with the poor in the Israeli-occupied West Bank.

Francis sought wholeheartedly to realize, in his own bodily life among the poor, the love of Christ for the world and the suffering of Christ with and for the world. *But this is a union first contemplated by the apostle Paul* (Rom. 5:1–5; 8:18–39).

This striving is signified in the mystery of the holy wounds which Saint Francis received on Mount Subasio. As a consequence of that event, the church honors Francis on his feast day by reading the apostle Paul's description of his own wounds, "the marks of Christ I bear on my own body" (Gal. 6:17). Paul's wounds, however, were inflicted not in mystical rapture, but in "extrajudicial" beatings that were the routine consequence of his apostolic activities.

My intuition, these hunches informed by the example of a "great cloud of witnesses'' in our own day, suggest that an apostle who could speak so movingly of the love of God for a world groaning for liberation must have been alert to the suffering of real men and women around him. I suspect that the continual remembrance of the poor for which Paul expressed such resolve was not incidental to his theology, and that the scars he bore on his body were the measure of his commitment to that vision.

The "new approach" I have described, and which I will pursue in the following pages, will provide new understandings of some much-discussed and much-debated topics in Pauline studies. Chapter 4 reexamines Paul's theology of the cross from a political perspective. Chapter 5 investigates the apocalyptic and political dimensions of Paul's "conversion" experience. Finally, Chapter 6 looks at aspects of Paul's apostolic praxis in the congregations of the Roman Diaspora.

II

FROM DEATH TO LIFE

"If the trumpet's call is indistinct, who will prepare for the struggle?"

—1 Corinthians 14:8

4

Paul and the Violence
of the Cross

"When I first came to you, brothers and sisters," Paul wrote to the Christians in the Roman colony of Corinth, "I resolved to know nothing among you except Jesus Christ, and him crucified."

It is impossible to exaggerate the importance of the cross of Jesus Christ to Paul.[1] Not only did his encounter with Jesus *as the crucified* generate the revolution in his conviction and action that we customarily call his "conversion," it energized his entire apostolic endeavor (of which his letters represent only a small part), through which he sought to order the lives of Christian congregations by pulling everything into the tremendous gravitational field of the cross. His proclamation in the cities of the Roman Empire consisted in the "public portrayal of Jesus Christ crucified" (Gal. 3:1).[2] The entrance rite of baptism was in his eyes nothing less than co-crucifixion with Christ (Rom. 6:1-5); the common sacred meal, the "Lord's supper," a solemn and public proclamation of the Lord's death (1 Cor. 11:26). The atmosphere of the congregation was to be charged with constant regard for the brother or sister "for whom Christ died" (Rom. 14:15; 1 Cor. 8:11).

As soon as we recognize the centrality of the cross of Christ for Paul, the common view that Paul was uninterested in political realities should leave us perplexed. The crucifixion of Jesus is, after all, one of the most unequivocally political events recorded in the New Testament. Behind the early theological interpretations of Jesus' crucifixion as a death "for us," and behind centuries of piety that have encrusted the crucifixion with often grotesque sentimentality, stands the "most nonreligious and horrendous feature of the gospel" (J. Christiaan Beker),[3] the brutal fact of the cross as an instrument of imperial terror. If in his theologizing Paul muted or suppressed the politically engineered horror of the cross, then we would have to conclude that Paul himself mystified the death of Jesus, accommodating his "word of the cross" to the interests of the very regime that had brought about that death.

93

THE POLITICAL SIGNIFICANCE OF CRUCIFIXION

Martin Hengel's study of crucifixion in the Roman world highlights its political significance.[4] As a means of capital punishment for heinous crimes, crucifixion was the "supreme Roman penalty," yet "almost always inflicted only on the lower class (*humiliores*); the upper class (*honestiores*) could reckon with more 'humane' punishment" (such as decapitation). Crucifixion was "the typical punishment for slaves," practiced "above all as a deterrent against trouble," the most spectacular example being the crucifixion of six thousand followers of the slave rebel Spartacus in 71 B.C.E. A special location was reserved on the Campus Esquilinus in Rome for the public crucifixion of slaves: Hengel compares it to Golgotha, outside Jerusalem.[5] The Roman lawyer Gaius Cassius explained this use of crucifixion as he pressed in court, in the face of mass protest by people from the lower classes, for the execution of four hundred slaves after their master, the prefect of Rome, was murdered by one of them: "You will never restrain that scum but by terror" (Tacitus, *Annals* 14:42–45).[6]

Only those Roman citizens who by acts of treason "had forfeited the protection of citizenship" might be crucified, but this happened only very rarely. Much more commonly, crucifixion served as "a means of waging war and securing peace, of wearing down rebellious cities under siege, of breaking the will of conquered peoples and of bringing mutinous troops or unruly provinces under control." First among these "unruly provinces," of course, was Judea, where the Romans crucified tens of thousands of Jews. The Roman general Varus put down a rebellion there in 4 B.C.E., crucifying two thousand suspected rebels at once (Josephus, *War* 2:5:1–3). The Roman procurator Felix, confronted by widespread resistance and sporadic guerrilla action in the 50s of the common era, won the hatred of his subjects by indiscriminate mass crucifixions, putting to death "a number of robbers [*lēstaí*] impossible to calculate" (*War* 2:13:2: Josephus uses the pejorative term preferred by Rome for its most ungrateful subjects). His successor, Florus, provoked full-scale rebellion first by plundering the Temple treasury, then by suppressing the ensuing (nonviolent) protest with mass crucifixions even of Jews who held equestrian rank as citizens of Rome (*War* 2:14:6–7). During the subsequent siege of Jerusalem, the Roman general Titus crucified as many as five hundred refugees from the city per day, until "there was not enough room for the crosses" outside the city walls (*War* 5:11:1–2).[7]

These specific instances of mass crucifixion reported by Josephus are exceptional only for scale. We should suppose that summary crucifixions in smaller numbers were as "routine" in Roman Judea as are "extrajudicial" killings by covert police death squads or "accidental" deaths in police custody in apartheid South Africa, or Israeli-occupied Palestine, or Los Angeles, or Chicago (to cite only recent examples where government officials have acknowledged police complicity in such deaths).[8] Because crucifixion was primarily *an instrument of public terrorism*, however, a more precise modern analogy might be the widespread atrocities documented in some Central American and Caribbean states.

In the Roman practice, "whipping, torture, the burning out of the eyes, and maiming often preceded the actual hanging."[9] Josephus reported that Titus's troops captured poorer Jews escaping from Jerusalem to seek food outside the walls, and tortured, scourged, and crucified them in the sight of the city's defenders. In one instance they hacked off the hands of torture victims and drove them back, mutilated, into the city to coerce its inhabitants into surrender (*War* 5:11:5).

In El Salvador during the 1980s, the mutilated bodies of "disappeared" labor leaders, opposition journalists, or lay catechists were dumped in city streets to be discovered by the populace, their tongues cut out, severed genitals stuffed into their mouths; decapitated and burned corpses were propped up in the doorways of offices; campesino families were beheaded, their bodies then propped up around a table, hands folded on the severed heads.[10] The United Nations Human Rights Commission has found defense department officials at the highest level responsible for atrocities like the 1983 massacre of a thousand men, women, and children in El Mozote, where the bodies of children have been exhumed from beneath the church building in which they were shot or burned to death.

From Guatemala, Nobel Peace Prize laureate Rigoberta Menchú Fum has described the public torture and murder of campesinos, including her younger brother, by the Guatemalan army in a campaign against "communists." The army drove the people of neighboring villages at gunpoint to the site of the killings, where they were surrounded by more than five hundred soldiers. During a two-hour harangue against the captured "Cubans, Nicaraguans, and communists," the commanding officer invited onlookers to inspect the tortures sustained by the victims: lacerations, needle punctuations, electrical burns, ears bitten off, tongues split, breasts and genitals mutilated, faces meticulously flayed. At length the wretched victims were doused in gasoline and burned alive before the eyes of their families.[11]

In Haiti, army and police personnel ringed the church of St. Jean Bosco, where Father Jean-Bertrand Aristide was celebrating the Eucharist, while armed men in the red armbands of the Tontons Macoutes burst in on the congregation, firing pistols and swinging machetes in a massacre that lasted the better part of an hour, killing seventeen people and wounding seventy-seven (but failing to murder their target, Aristide himself). After a pregnant woman, slashed in the abdomen, escaped, the murderers prowled through nearby hospitals, prodding beneath the gowns of women patients, to complete their bloody work. Later that evening, state television entertained one of the massacre's ringleaders, who boasted that wherever Father Aristide preached "there will be a pile of corpses."[12]

With such extreme brutality the "New World Order" is maintained today, the order of Pax Americana, actually only as "new" as the massacres at Wounded Knee in 1890 or Luzon in 1900.[13] From a comfortable distance, such obscene savagery repels and sickens us. Its intended effect on the immediate witnesses, however, is terror and, consequently, social control. *Such was the intent of Roman crucifixion as well.* It was no mere rhetorical flourish when Archbishop Oscar Romero spoke of the "crucifixion of the Salvadoran people," or when Father Aristide describes the congregation in St. Jean Bosco "clothed in robes of crimson and of purple, waiting to be scourged and mocked, and crucified."[14] The metaphor conveys a precise symmetry of terrorism. In each case, ancient and modern, the public display of inescapable pain and deep degradation is calculated to terrify and coerce submission (the terms preferred by empire being "pacification" or "stabilization"). Stylized public murders and the routine dumping of mutilated bodies in public areas are effective for population control to the extent they are publicly recognizable as the actions of a particular group or government. The techniques are part of a single strategy in terrorist states;[15] both the strategy and the techniques serve the interests of the empire, however, which invests in their proliferation (for example, at the U.S. Army's School of the Americas in Columbus, Georgia).[16]

As Hengel summarizes the point with regard to crucifixion, the chief reason for its use was "its allegedly supreme efficacy as a deterrent." The Romans practiced crucifixion above all on "groups whose development had to be suppressed by all possible means to safeguard law and order in the state."

The brutality of crucifixion was not exceptional in the order established by Rome. The so-called Pax Romana, the cessation of "hot" wars of expansion and competition among military rivals, was celebrated in rhetoric and ritual as a new golden age, the gift of the gods; but it was a "peace" won through military conquest, as Roman iconography clearly shows. The "altar of the peace of Augustus" was placed on the Hill of Mars, god of war. Coins struck under Augustus link the armed and armored First Citizen with Pax, goddess of peace, trampling on the weapons of subdued enemies, and Victoria, goddess of conquest, treading upon the globe itself.[17]

Most of our literary sources for this period, coming from the hands of the upper classes, who benefited from the "sheer rapacity" of an empire that "plundered the provinces on a vast scale" (G. E. M. de Ste. Croix),[18] speak of the arrangement in the most admiring terms, as have many modern historians. There are significant exceptions. New Testament scholar Richard Horsley seeks to place Jesus in his context within the "spiral of violence" by which he comprehends the reality of the Roman Empire. Horsley borrows that analytical concept from Brazilian Archbishop and theologian Dom Helder Camara, who describes the First World's institutionalized injustice in the Third World as "the basic violence." "This established violence," wrote Camara, "attracts violence No. 2, *revolt*," which provokes a third level of violence, official repression. Horsley notes that "the Romans, of course, had their self-legitimating ideology of 'defending their friends and allies' and of bringing 'civilization' and 'peace' to the rest of the world. But their imperial conquests were carried out by massive use of violence, with whole populations either slaughtered or enslaved (30,000 at one time from Taricheae in 52 B.C.E., *Antiquities* 4:120; *War* 1:180). Not surprisingly, the imperial regime was hardly legitimate in the eyes of the conquered."[19]

The last point bears emphasis. In his sharp-edged little volume on "the Pax Romana and the Peace of Jesus Christ," New Testament scholar Klaus Wengst allows us to hear other voices, describing the Roman "peace" from the perspective of its victims; first from Britain, in a speech put on the lips of a Briton by the Roman historian Tacitus:[20]

> Harriers of the world, now that earth fails their all devastating hands they probe even the sea; if their enemy has wealth, they have greed; if he is poor, they are ambitious; East and West have glutted them; alone of mankind they behold with the same passion of concupiscence waste alike and want. To plunder, butcher, steal, these things they misname empire; they make a desolation and call it peace. Children and kin are by the law of nature each man's dearest possessions: they are swept away from us by conscription to be slaves in other lands; our wives and sisters, even when they escape a soldier's lust, are debauched by self-styled friends and guests: our goods and chattels go for tribute; our lands and harvests in requisitions of grain; life and limb themselves are used up in levelling marsh and forest to the accompaniment of gibes and blows. Slaves born to slavery are sold once for all and are fed by their masters free of cost; but Britain pays a daily price for her own enslavement, and feeds the slavers.

And again, a Judean voice, the seer of 4 Ezra describing a vision in which a lion (the messiah) addresses the Roman eagle:

> Are you not the one that remains of the four beasts which I had made to reign in my world, so that the end of my times might come through them? You, the fourth that has come, have conquered all the beasts that have gone before: and you have held sway over the world with much terror, and over all the earth with grievous oppression; and for so long you have dwelt on the earth with deceit. And you have judged the earth, but not

with truth; for you have afflicted the meek and injured the peaceable: you have hated those who tell the truth, and have loved liars; you have destroyed the dwellings of those who brought forth fruit, and have laid low the walls of those who did you no harm. And your insolence has come up before the Most High, and your pride to the Mighty One. And the Most High has looked upon his times, and behold, they are ended, and his ages are completed! Therefore you will surely disappear, you eagle . . . so that the whole earth, freed from your violence, may be refreshed and relieved, and may hope for the judgment and mercy of him who made it.

The "peace" that Rome secured through terror was maintained through terror:[21] through slavery, fed by conquest and scrupulously maintained through constant intimidation, abuse, and violence;[22] through the ritualized terror of gladiatorial games, where the human refuse of empire—captives of war, condemned criminals, slaves bought for the arena—were killed in stylized rehearsals of conquest, their fate decided by the whim of the empire's representatives;[23] through the pomp of military processions, which often culminated in the execution of vanquished captives;[24] and on the ideological plane, through imperial cult and ceremonial, the rhetoric of the courts (where the torture of slaves was a routine procedure for gathering evidence), and an educational system that rehearsed the "naturalness" of Rome's global hegemony.[25] It was within this civilization of terror that crucifixion played its indispensable role.

Unless we keep in mind the cumulative psychic effect of this systematic violence upon subject peoples—the deterrent effect that makes social control possible—an analysis of the Roman imperium in terms of the "spiral of violence" may seem tendentious. E. P. Sanders objects to "political" readings of Jesus of Nazareth, for example, that "in Jesus' day, the Roman troop presence in Judea and Samaria was very thin, not much of an occupation, and there were no Roman troops at all in Galilee."[26]

However appropriate such calculations might be in the case of a neatly symmetrical war, they rather miss the point with regard to the function of an efficient military and a system of client states within an empire characterized by extreme imbalances of power. One might as well purport to measure U.S. domination of the Caribbean and Latin America solely on the basis of actual U.S. troop deployments (the invasions of Grenada and Panama, for example, or the more routine "show of force" in military exercises, presently at an all-time high in Guatemala), neglecting the pedagogical role such extreme actions have in enforcing the more normal (and even legal) channels of domination. James Douglass draws the instructive parallel between Rome's policy in Judea and current U.S. policy in El Salvador: "A willing client state relieves the imperial power of the direct responsibility of policing that region with its own troops. Thus freed, the central authority can deploy its military forces more flexibly over a much wider sphere of influence. Rome used client states such as Herod's brilliantly to help it maintain control over huge areas, yet with a minimum number of legions garrisoned permanently in the occupied territories."[27]

Marxist historian de Ste. Croix concurs. From the Roman perspective, massive applications of force could be held in reserve as a last resort. He cites the enslavement of 150,000 Epirots in 167 B.C.E. and the destruction of Corinth in 146 B.C.E., to which we should add the best documented case, the suppression of Judea in 66–73 C.E. But the fetters of empire were more normally secured through the cooptation of local aristocracies, which "had mainly given up any idea of resistance to Roman rule and in fact seem to have welcomed it for the most part, as an insurance against popular movements from below."[28] Other historical precedents are equally to the point: Columbus subjugated and destroyed several million Tainos with a few hundred Spanish soldiers. Noam Chomsky notes that "Cortés conquered Mexico with perhaps 500 Spaniards; Pizarro overthrew the Inca empire with less than 200; and the entire Portuguese empire was administered and defended by less than 10,000 Europeans."[29] In our own century, "when hundreds of Indians nonviolently submitted themselves to the blows of police in Bombay on June 21, 1930, the men who clubbed them to the ground hour after hour were not British, but several hundred of their fellow Indian countrymen, under the command of only six British sergeants."[30] The Nazi death camp at Treblinka, where 840,000 Jews were gassed to death, was operated by some thirty German officers and perhaps a hundred Ukrainians.[31] Equally illuminating are more recent examples involving ongoing terror campaigns that have killed tens of thousands of people, campaigns conducted by relatively small "elite" military units in Panama (the "Dignity" battalion) or El Salvador (the Atlacatl), termed "elite" precisely because of their efficiency in murder.

Acts of exemplary violence such as crucifixion make large-scale social control possible. As Douglass summarizes the point, "the cross was a key to the security system of the Roman Empire."

THE POLITICS OF JESUS' DEATH

Insight into the fundamentally political and terroristic nature of crucifixion leads to a political understanding of the crucifixion of Jesus. New Testament scholar Paula Fredriksen's compelling reconstruction of the events leading up to Jesus' death revolves around two fundamental insights: first, that the Romans crucified Jesus because they perceived him, and the crowds he stirred up in Jerusalem, as politically disruptive; second, that the Temple priests who handed Jesus over to Pilate were acting as "the middlemen between the populace and the Roman occupation government," concerned to forestall the sort of punitive violence against the Judean people of which recent history had shown Pilate to be capable.[32]

This reconstruction, immediately intelligible in terms of the structural violence of the Roman Empire and its client states, is not what we read off the surface of the Gospels. Rather the passion narratives provide a sophisticated coverup for the political nature of Jesus' death.[33] Fredriksen challenges the church to renounce "a simplistic reading of identity-confirming narratives, even if these are the ones offered by the gospels," and thus to honor its theological claims about Jesus of Nazareth. "Only by meeting this obligation with intellectual integrity can the church, with integrity, continue to witness" to the gospel.[34]

In fact, a number of theologians have recently sought the theological significance of Jesus' death precisely in its historical causation.

Salvadoran theologian Jon Sobrino argues for a new understanding of Christ that stays in fundamental contact with the commitments and actions that led Jesus to his death. The crucifixion of Jesus shows in the first place that "Jesus was actually executed as a *political rebel,* not as a blasphemer. His conception of God necessarily entailed his proclamation of God's coming kingdom, and this could not help but bring him into conflict with those in political power. If the kingdom of God entails human reconciliation, then Jesus could not help but unmask a situation that did not correspond with that vision." The cross thus manifests Jesus' "political love, a love that is situated in history and that has visible repercussions for human beings."[35]

Richard Horsley's important study of the spiral of violence in Roman-occupied Palestine culminates in a similar understanding of Jesus. A thorough exegetical examination of Jesus' words and actions leads Horsley to conclude that Jesus

> consistently criticized and resisted the oppressive established political-economic-religious order of his own society. Moreover, he aggressively intervened to mitigate or undo the effects of institutionalized violence, whether in particular acts of forgiveness and exorcism or in the general opening of the kingdom of God to the poor. Jesus opposed violence, but not from a distance. . . . He rather entered actively into the situation of violence, and even exacerbated the conflict.

As a direct consequence, "Jesus and his followers . . . were prepared to suffer violence themselves and to allow their friends to be tortured and killed for their insistence on the rule of God."[36]

Arriving at comparable conclusions on the basis of a "feminist reconstruction of Christian origins," Elisabeth Schüssler Fiorenza regards the Palestinian Jesus movement as a "renewal movement within Judaism" which understands the ministry and mission of Jesus as that of the prophet and child of Sophia [i.e., Wisdom] sent to announce that God is the God of the poor and heavy laden, of the outcasts and those who suffer injustice. As child of Sophia he stands in a long line and succession of prophets sent to gather the children of Israel to their gracious Sophia-God. Jesus' execution, like John's, results from his mission and commitment as prophet and emissary of the Sophia-God who holds open a future for the poor and outcast and offers God's gracious goodness to *all* children of Israel without exception.

Distinguishing this historical context from the theological interpretations of Jesus' death that would soon follow, she writes that the God of Jesus "does not need atonement or sacrifices"; Jesus' death is not willed by God, but results from his all-inclusive, prophetic action, just as all the messengers of divine Wisdom suffer violence.[37]

Walter Wink offers similar insights in the climactic volume of his trilogy, *Engaging the Powers.* The "irreducible fact about Jesus is that he was executed," Wink writes, because "not only did he and his followers repudiate the androcratic values of power and wealth, but the institutions and systems that authorized and supported these values . . . indeed, every conceivable prop of domination, division, and supremacy." For that reason "the Powers that executed Jesus did so under a necessity dictated by the Domination System itself" (by which Wink refers to "what happens when an entire network of Powers becomes integrated around idolatrous values"), since Jesus, living out "God's domination-free order," posed "the most intolerable threat ever placed against the spirituality, values, and arrangements of the Domination System."[38]

MIMETIC CONFLICT, VIOLENCE, AND CHRISTIAN ORIGINS

The convergence in these studies is remarkable. They represent an emerging willingness by theologians to take the most likely historical explanation of Jesus' death—namely, his being perceived as a political threat to the Roman order in Judea—as a starting point for theology. Yet even more remarkable is the authors' evident preference for this starting point, the result of historical criticism of the Gospels, rather than the story as the Gospels tell it. That preference reflects a growing recognition among biblical scholars and theologians that the Gospels have obscured the political nature of the conflict that led to Jesus' death, by shifting responsibility for that death from the Romans (who in fact crucified Jesus) onto the shoulders of the Jewish leaders in Jerusalem, or the Jewish population of Jerusalem, or at last, simply "the Jews."

Although holding the Jews responsible for Jesus' death is "scarcely credible as history" (Paula Fredriksen),[39] these narrative features did accomplish something important for the Christian communities that originated the Gospels at the end of the first century C.E., providing an explanation for the trauma of the Roman war against Judea. According to Fredriksen, "By laying the blame for Jesus' death on the leaders of Judaism . . . Mark argued that the Jewish rejection of the Gospel foretold and indeed led to God's definitive and historical rejection of the Jews: the destruction of their nation, their city, and their Temple, all come about in Mark's own day." Such a story thus served the needs of a Gentile Christian community living in the wake of the Roman war, for that war had given the community "a vital political reason to disassociate both itself and its messiah from a people in such bad odor."[40]

Fredriksen's judgment rests on the assumption, a commonplace in modern biblical criticism since the work of Rudolf Bultmann, that the Gospel narratives do not represent the history of Jesus in a simple, straightforward way. Rather they also represent the experiences and perceptions of Christian communities decades after Jesus' death, projected back onto the events that led up to that death in such a way as to justify those communities' distinctive self-understanding.[41] This implies that "to understand the reasons [for Jesus' death] given in the gospel accounts we must explore not the social crisis occasioned by the historical Jesus which led to his crucifixion, but the social formation of the Jesus movement as it led away from the crucifixion."[42]

The "scapegoating" of the Jews in the Gospel passion narratives, increasingly acknowledged by biblical scholars and lamented by Christian theologians in the wake of the Holocaust, represents the response of some late first-century Christian communities to the spiritual trauma of the Judean war. When the hope of an earlier generation of Jesus' followers that he "would be the one to redeem Israel" (see Luke 24:21) appeared to have been disproved by history, the Evangelists responded by rewriting that history. In their narratives, the faith-shattering violence of Rome against the people of the presumed Messiah became God's just punishment against the Messiah's enemies and betrayers, who were in some way no longer his people. The Gospels protected Jesus' messianic authority from refutation by historical fact by projecting that authority into heaven, and into the indefinite future: Matthew's Jesus assures his disciples that "all authority has been given to me in heaven and on earth" as he leaves the earth to dwell in heaven "until the end of the age" (Matt. 28:18–20); John's Jesus patiently explains to his disciples, who have asked how the Messiah can be revealed to them alone "and not to the world," that the Father and the Son will come to the believers "and make our home with them" (John 14:22–23). Even the destruction of the Messiah's city is conformed to the Messiah's will, for it fulfills the Messiah's prophetic words (Matt. 24:15–22, Mark 13:14–20, Luke 21:20–24), and is divine punishment for the murder of the Messiah (Matt. 21:33–22:14, 23:34–39; Mark 12:1–12; Luke 20:9–19), an event that was itself predetermined by divine necessity (Matt. 16:21–23, Mark 8:31–33, Luke 9:22).

This narrative scapegoating of the Jews is readily accounted for by René Girard's theory of mimetic (i.e., imitative) conflict and victimage. That theory has won increasing acceptance from biblical scholars, for it proposes to explain how sacred narratives (myths) arise from the dynamics of social formation.[43]

Within human groups, Girard contends, the tension that develops between our desire to be like one another (mimesis), and the conflict that consequently arises when we find ourselves in rivalry for the same desired objects, can lead to a crisis in which mutual aggression threatens to destroy our group. The group can survive this crisis by spontaneously deflecting aggression onto an appropriate victim, whose destruction at once releases the group's aggression and brings about a sudden unanimity, "the unanimity of the lynch mob." At this point, Girard argues, a massive misperception can take place: The group projects its own conflictual desires onto the victim, who is consequently seen to have "caused" the crisis, and it attributes to the victim's death the sudden "peace" within the group.

The potential for conflict remains, of course, since the victim's death has not removed the imitative desires within the group that led to the crisis in the first place. But that death has opened a new channel for the redirection of violence away from the group, a redirection that can now be reactualized through mock rehearsals of the original crisis (in religious ritual, particularly sacrifice) and through a system of prohibitions (culture) and rationalizations of the appropriateness of the founding violence (myth). On Girard's theory, then, the role of religion is simultaneously to rechannel conflict away from members of the group and onto culturally appropriate objects (or victims) and to conceal this very fact from the members of the group: "Human culture is predisposed to the permanent concealment of its origins in collective violence."[44]

A number of biblical scholars have recognized the Gospel passion narratives as examples of the victimage mechanism that Girard describes. For the Matthean community in the 80s or 90s, for example, mimetic conflict with Rome would have been at once inevitable, since the fact of Roman supremacy in Judea symbolized the very dominion over the earth that the Matthean community ascribed to its Messiah— naturally suggesting that the Messiah had not in fact come; and intolerable, since direct confrontation with Roman power would have appeared suicidal. The Matthean narrative deflected this conflict onto the available victims, the Jews of Jerusalem who had died in the war, and projected onto these victims the mimetic rivalry itself (the Jews had "chosen" the path of war already in their preference for the murderous rebel Barabbas), and the "peace" that resulted from their action. Note also the irony of the high priest's comment in John, "it is better for you to have one man die for the people than to have the whole nation destroyed" (11:50).[45]

(Surprisingly, Girard not only refuses to identify the Gospel passion narratives as persecution texts, insisting instead that only the Gospels' exposure of the scapegoating mechanism makes its discovery possible;[46] he goes so far as to dismiss investigation of these insights as "a waste of time," among "the most foolish undertakings of mankind," pursued by those who would "explain everything in the New Testament in the most ignoble light."[47] Most biblical scholars sympathetic with Girard's program have nevertheless qualified his work at this point, frankly acknowledging the "scapegoating" of the Jews in the Gospels.[48] Perhaps Girard's resistance to this insight exemplifies his own axiom that "the only scapegoats easy to detect as such are those of our enemies; the scapegoats of our friends are harder to see, and, if they happen to be ours as well, they are completely invisible *as scapegoats.*")[49]

Of course, the interpretation of Jesus' death as a death "for us," cast in the language of a sacrifice for sins, did not first appear after the Judean war. Paul declares that he "handed on" to the Corinthian congregation "what I also received: that Christ died for our sins in accordance with the scriptures" (1 Cor. 15:3). It is not surprising that the same theologians who offer "political" readings of Jesus' crucifixion also criticize the early "sacrificial" interpretation of Jesus' death as a failure of nerve that would have fateful consequences for the subsequent tradition.

Thus Sobrino writes that Jesus' death has been "toned down and stripped of its scandalous aspect" already in the Gospels, and in "the conceptual armory of Greek thought in which the mystery of God and Jesus was formulated right from the beginning." The result has been a tendency throughout Christian history to "emasculate" the cross, to render Christianity "just another religion with a sacrificial worship of its own," to "isolate the cross from the historical course that led Jesus to it by virtue of his conflicts with those who held political religious power," and thus to promote "a mystique of suffering rather than a mystique of following Jesus, whose historical career led to the historical cross."[50]

Wink, who finds Girard's reading of the Gospels as revelations of the scapegoat mechanism compelling, nevertheless recognizes that "the earliest Christians were not able to sustain the intensity of this revelation and dimmed it by confusing God's intention to reveal the scapegoating mechanism for what it was with the notion that God intended Jesus to die. This in turn led to their reinserting the new revelation into the scapegoat theology: Jesus was sent by God to be the *last* scapegoat and to reconcile us, once and for all, to God (the Epistle to the Hebrews)."[51] In this emerging theology of sacrifice, the Powers that put Jesus to death are effectively "let off the hook". "Rather than God triumphing over the powers through Jesus' nonviolent self-sacrifice on the cross, the Powers disappear from discussion, and God is involved in a transaction wholly within God's own self." Thus the "God of infinite mercy was metamorphosed by the church into the image of a wrathful God whose demand for blood atonement leads to God's requiring of his own Son a death on behalf of us all. The nonviolent God of Jesus comes to be depicted as a God of unequaled violence."

The cross could thus become the focal symbol for a sadomasochistic piety cultivated by the Domination System itself: a piety that inculcates submissiveness and resignation in the oppressed and teaches the oppressor the divine necessity of "good" violence; the piety of subjugation identified by liberation theologians as one of the foremost pastoral concerns of the church today.[52]

PAUL AND THE MYTHOLOGIZING OF THE CROSS

If the Christian theological tradition has obscured the scandalous depths of the "word of the cross," the previous chapter's discussion of the mystification of Paul might suggest that Paul himself taught subsequent generations that collective amnesia. It is a commonplace, after all, that Paul "does not cite [Jesus'] words or recall his teachings. Gone are the key terms employed by Jesus to designate himself, his mission, and the immediate objects of that mission: the Son of man, the kingdom of God, the poor" (Juan Luis Segundo).[53] Indeed, this seems to have been a matter of principle: Paul insisted on knowing Christ "no longer according to the flesh" (2 Cor. 5:16). The same holds true for Jesus' death: "curious though it sounds," Paul "does not seem to have any precise knowledge about the concrete circumstances of the crucifixion" (Ernst Käsemann).[54] These observations might suggest that Paul himself attempted, to borrow Jon Sobrino's words, to "isolate the cross from the historical course that led Jesus to it." On the basis of such a judgment, the "theology of empire" criticized by *Kairos* theologians might well (like the garments of those who stoned Stephen to death for his witness) be laid at Paul's feet.

Further, despite efforts to deny the sacrificial aspects of Paul's thought, motivated either by a Protestant polemic against Catholicism which "oversimplifies the problem to an inadmissible degree" (Ernst Käsemann) or by Girard's nonsacrificial interpretation of Christianity (Robert Hamerton-Kelly), it is still evident that Paul regularly uses sacrificial language to describe Jesus' death.[55] Indeed, as Walter Wink writes, "it is not Hebrews and the later writings that proved most influential in the reassertion of the sacrificial hermeneutic [of Jesus' death], but Paul himself."[56] If Paul played so decisive a role in promoting the sacrificial interpretation of Christ's death, then Paul should be held responsible for infecting subsequent Christian theology with the fatal logic of the divinely sanctioned necessity of bloodletting, of "good violence"—a disastrous legacy in the eyes of some contemporary theologians (Rita Nakashima Brock; Rosemary Radford Ruether; Christine Gudorf).[57]

Some Jewish interpreters have simultaneously emphasized Paul's initiative in developing this sacrificial interpretation and have denied any legitimate basis for it within ancient Judaism. There it was clearly understood that the forgiveness of sins was God's gracious initiative, not a commodity secured by blood sacrifices in the Temple.[58] This "peculiar," "inexplicable" aspect of Paul's theology (C. G. Montefiore, G. F. Moore) seems to go hand in hand with his "fundamental misapprehension," the result of the "characteristic distortion" of his Hellenistic outlook (Hans-Joachim Schoeps; Samuel Sandmel), or of his unstable personality, or both (Hyam Maccoby):[59] namely, his implication of the Torah itself in Jesus' death, as when he declares that "Christ redeemed us from the curse of the Law, having become a curse for us" (Gal. 3:13).

Paula Fredriksen finds that in his theology of the cross Paul appropriates the originally political vocabulary of liberation, but "denationalizes Christ," "praises a reality that is utterly spiritual," and thus "shrinks the significance of contemporary politics."[60] More avowedly sympathetic with the Jewish resistance against Rome, Jewish scholar Hyam Maccoby uses harsher language: "It was Paul who detached Jesus from his mission of liberation and turned him into an otherworldly figure whose mission had no relevance to politics or to the sufferings of his fellow Jews under the Romans."[61] Paul thus provided the theological alibi for the powers that killed Jesus, "letting them off the hook." If we add to this judgment G. E. M. de Ste. Croix's remark that Paul proceeded to write those same powers "a blank check" in Romans 13, with which they could consolidate their power in the subsequent centuries,[62] or George V. Pixley's comment that Paul offered Rome's subjects "a religious opium" that "enables a suffering people to endure, by offering private dreams to compensate for an intolerable public reality,"[63] we begin to understand why modern Jews who have come to accept Jesus as "one of our own" nevertheless see Paul as "the real villain of the piece."[64]

If some interpreters seek an explanation for Paul's sacrificial theology in the hellenized religious milieu that was supposedly his background, others suggest that Paul deliberately clothed the crucifixion in sacrificial imagery in order to minimize the troublesome political aspects of the messianic movement and to make his message more palatable to his audience—Gentiles living in Hellenistic cities, remote from dusty Judea and more accustomed to the sacrificial logic of the savior cults.[65]

The issue at hand is clearly an urgent one. Did Paul, who devoted himself to proclaiming the "word of the cross" in the cities of the Roman Empire, through that very proclamation betray the cause of the one crucified by Rome, his own oppressed people, and the other victims of imperial power?

In my judgment he did not. I will argue in the following pages that such conclusions represent a misunderstanding of Paul's theology of the cross, and that—in startling contrast to common perceptions of Paul— his interpretation of Jesus' death has an irreducibly political dimension.

First, however, we should note that this issue strikes at the heart of Christian interpretation of Paul's theology. What may appear from a liberation perspective as liabilities in Paul's thought have usually been considered virtues in the European and North American theological tradition, well into this century. First of all, for an important stream of theological scholarship, Paul's doctrine of the saving significance of the cross *is* the gospel,[66] whether that theology is construed around "christological soteriology" (Joseph Fitzmyer) or (more Protestantly) "justification by faith."[67] But as Dorothee Sölle has observed, putting the saving death of Jesus at the center of Christian theology often isolates the theology of "the biblical Christ" from the historical Jesus. "The renunciation of the historical Jesus and the substitution of kerygmatic formulae for his [at once religious and political] language serve to enhance the depoliticizing of the gospel. . . . In other words, the Christ who rules in the church and who has supplanted the [true] biblical Christ is the Christ of the rulers."[68]

Second, we must note that the conventional reading of Paul's theology as centered on the saving significance of Jesus' death is the focus of a profound crisis of intelligibility in contemporary Pauline studies. In that crisis, what is sometimes called the "kerygmatic" approach to Paul (*kērygma* is the Greek word for proclamation) appears to be inalterably opposed to a more thoroughly historical approach.[69] The classical Protestant scheme opposes Paul's doctrine of justification by faith to "the Jewish doctrine of redemption," and reads Romans as an essay on salvation in which Paul explains how in Christ's death God had accomplished "what the Law was unable to do" (Rom. 8:3), namely, to set human beings in a right relationship with God.[70] In contrast to the Epistle to the Hebrews, of course, the comparison here is not the superiority of Christ's atoning death "once for all" to the temporary and necessarily repeatable sacrifices of the Temple cult, but rather the superiority of justification by grace, which is God's free gift to the unjust (Rom. 5:6), to the scheme of justification by works, the impossibility located (on this interpretation) at the heart of Judaism. Romans is read as moving from the "plight" of the human being before God (1:18–3:20)— a plight in which Jew has no advantage over Gentile—to the "solution" that God offers in Christ's death (3:21–8:39).[71]

The difficulty of this reading, and at the same time its venerable usefulness for Christian dogmatics, is that it attributes to Paul the view that Jews cannot be forgiven of their sins (and thus "saved") apart from the atoning death of Jesus. What Jewish readers see as Paul's "peculiar" omission of Israel's covenant is explained by interpreters in the tradition of the Reformers as Paul's "deep," "radical" insight into the failure of "religious humanity" (of whom the Jew is, of course, exemplary) to benefit from that covenant.[72]

The current crisis in Pauline studies results from E. P. Sanders's willingness to take seriously the Jewish viewpoint, from which this construal of Paul's thought is unintelligible. The crisis also results from a failure to take the next step, toward a fundamental rethinking of Paul's theology. Despite his understanding of the Jewish viewpoint, Sanders persists in the conventional conception of salvation, of "getting in and staying in," as the center of Paul's thought. This is evident from his method (he proposes to compare Paul and Palestinian Judaism in terms of their doctrine of salvation),[73] his reliance on Romans (where Paul presents a "restatement" of "his gospel"),[74] and especially from the terms of his conclusion, posed as a reversal of Bultmann's construction, that "Paul thinks backwards," "from solution to plight."[75] That conclusion, a necessary conclusion on Sanders's premises, means that Paul's theology is completely lacking in persuasive force for any Jew who had not shared Paul's peculiar experience. This conclusion has prompted criticisms that Sanders has replaced "the Lutheran Paul" with "Paul the muddled and self-contradictory thinker" (J. Christiaan Beker), "the idiosyncratic Paul who in arbitrary and irrational manner turns his face against the glory and greatness of Judaism's covenant theology and abandons Judaism simply because it is not Christianity" (James D. G. Dunn).[76]

Third, we should note two other conclusions that plausibly follow from the view that Paul's supposed doctrine of salvation in Christ is "idiosyncratic" or "incoherent."[77] His theology of the cross can also be reduced to a symbol for the group cohesion of his Gentile Christian congregations. Thus some scholars speak of Paul's attempt retrospectively "to legitimate the social reality of sectarian gentile-Christian communities in which the law was not observed," "a theoretical rationale for separation" (Francis Watson, Heikki Räisänen).[78] In addition, Paul's own insistence that he enjoyed considerable rapport with the Jewish Christian community in Jerusalem may come under profound suspicion. Thus some scholars see Paul as deluded at best, "an unstable, authoritarian person" (Burton L. Mack);[79] at worst, a liar and a charlatan, "an adventurer of undistinguished background," who "deliberately misrepresented his own biography in order to increase the effectiveness of his missionary activities" (Hyam Maccoby).[80]

Clearly the integrity and coherence of Paul's theology and apostolate are at stake in this discussion.[81] The conclusions reached by some scholars today regarding the origins of Paul's theology of the cross would suggest that the "toxic legacy" reviewed in the first part of this book derives from Paul's own misguided or opportunistic tendentiousness.

A warning is appropriate here. We must not approach this topic hoping to find some way to shore up Paul's theology against the ravages of historical criticism. On the contrary, my hope is to press beyond the dogmatic conceptions that still prevail in much Pauline scholarship in order to gain a clearer picture of the historical Paul. My approach is guided by the criteria outlined in the preceding chapter, which raise the suspicion that recent debate is still constrained by a "Lutheran captivity" of Pauline theology. I am happy to find myself in good company in that suspicion. Other scholars have criticized our common habit of "foisting onto Paul questions that come from the Lutheran debate," the questions "of the Fathers, the mediaevals, the reformers, or post-enlightenment historical scholarship," rather than the questions of Paul's Jewish contemporaries (N. T. Wright).[82] These scholars have insisted that such an anachronistic approach effectively *"blocks our access to the original thought and the original intention of Paul"* (Krister Stendahl).[83]

In the following pages I explore several samples from Paul's letters in order to determine answers to three questions: (1) Did Paul deliberately obscure the political character of Jesus' crucifixion? (2) Did his sacrificial interpretation of Jesus' death mystify the historical character of that death by submerging it within a conception of divinely sanctioned violence? (3) Did Paul turn Jesus' death into a weapon in a polemic against Judaism?

DID PAUL OBSCURE THE POLITICAL CHARACTER
OF JESUS' DEATH?

Paul's letters show little interest in recounting the words or deeds of Jesus. Of course, since these letters are written to already established congregations, we should not assume that they reproduce either the content of Paul's initial proclamation, the "teaching" or "traditions" he has handed on, or the extent of his knowledge of the Jesus tradition (with which he may be more familiar than his few explicit citations would suggest).[84] We should nevertheless take seriously Paul's declaration that he sought to know "only Jesus and him crucified" among the Corinthians (1 Cor. 2:2).

In his letters Paul does not rehearse the historical course that led Jesus to the cross. But that does not mean that he was unaware of, or uninterested in, the historical causes of Jesus' death. Comparing Paul and the Gospels on this point can be misleading. After all, reconstructing the historical events that led to the cross is never a simple matter of reading the Gospel story. Since the Evangelists themselves partially obscured the political character of Jesus' death by shifting responsibility for that death onto the Jews, using "the political key" to interpret Jesus requires a corrosive criticism of the Gospel narratives as they stand. For his part, Paul may be less interested than the Evangelists in recounting the words and deeds of Jesus because he does not share their need, in the wake of the Judean war, to provide Jesus with a dramatically messianic past (a point on which I consider Paula Fredriksen's presentation decisive).[85] He is, rather, concerned constantly to stir up among his congregations a fervent expectancy of the Messiah's future (see Rom. 8:18–25, 1 Cor. 15:59–58, 1 Thess. 5:1–11).

In contrast to the Gospels, Paul is content to say no more about Jesus than that he was "obedient," and that this obedience was the cause of his death, which Paul specifies was by crucifixion (Phil. 2:6–8). Whether or not that is Paul's modification of a hymn he inherited from the Hellenistic church, a hymn that spoke of Jesus' death "for our sins" (as in 1 Cor. 15:3, where Paul explicitly cites a church tradition), the result is striking. The obedience of the one equal to God (2:6) consists not simply in becoming human, but in taking a particular place within humanity, as a slave (2:7); not simply in taking on mortality, but in being so humbled as to accept the most humiliating of deaths, the form of execution reserved for slaves under Roman rule, crucifixion (2:8).[86]

That very emphasis on the manner of Jesus' death, shameful and horrific, yes, but also unavoidably political in its connotations, stands in sharp tension with the view that Paul sought to obscure or mystify Jesus' death. The cross was for Paul the signature in history of the forces that killed Jesus, a signature as distinctive in the eyes of his hearers as the handprint in white paint over the victims of a Salvadoran death squad in our own time.

Nevertheless, as Charles Cousar correctly observes, "Paul appears totally uninterested in tracking down and identifying the villains responsible for Jesus' crucifixion, nor does he offer any historical reasons why they did it."[87] There are only two possible exceptions to this statement: 1 Thess. 2:15–16, where "the Jews" are blamed for killing "the Lord Jesus," a passage rightly regarded as an interpolation made by a Christian scribe in the wake of the Judean war (see chapter 2), and 1 Cor. 2:8, where Paul writes that "the rulers [*archontes*] of this age" crucified "the Lord of glory." Since this latter passage might be the only place in Paul's letters where he alludes to the human actors in Jesus' death, it clearly merits our attention.

Just what does Paul mean by the phrase "the rulers of this age"? Unfortunately, this is one of many places where the apostle's style is abrupt and elliptical. To make matters more complicated, he uses a term, *archōn,* that can have a range of meanings in classical and koine Greek. Although elsewhere in the New Testament *archontes* refers straightforwardly to human rulers,[88] the word could also refer to superhuman beings (e.g., the angelic "princes" behind the Persian and Greek empires in Dan. 10:13, 20).

It is evident from the immediate context, however, that Paul is not interested in examining political tensions in Judea or the vicissitudes of Pilate's career some two decades earlier. *The context of his interpretation of Jesus' crucifixion is the mythic symbolism of the Jewish apocalypses.* In the cross of Jesus, the Wisdom of God decreed "before the ages" (2:7) has confounded the rulers of this age who are being destroyed (*katargoumenōn*, 2:6). The terms used here are echoed in the prophecy at the end of 1 Corinthians: At the end, Christ will "deliver the kingdom to God the Father after destroying every rule and authority and power" (15:24). The parallelism, including both the verb "destroy" (*katargoumenōn*, 2:6; *katargēsē*, 15:24) and the related nouns "rulers" (*archontes*, 2:8), "rule" (*archē*), "authority" (*exousia*), "power" (*dynamis*, 15:24), suggests that "the rulers of this age" in 2:8 should be taken to include potentially "every rule and authority and power" that remains hostile to God (as Death is "the last enemy," 15:26). Further, the language echoes the apocalyptic vocabulary of the book of Daniel, where we are told that God disposes "rule" (*archē*), "sovereignty" (*basileia*), "power" (*ischys*), "honor" (*timē*), and "glory" (*doxa*) to the rulers of earth (2:37, Septuagint), until at the end God establishes a kingdom (*basileia*) that will "shatter and bring to an end" all the other kingdoms of the earth (2:44).

Earlier scholarship, heavily influenced by the "religio-historical school," tended to find 1 Corinthians saturated with gnostic motifs; the "rulers of this age" were set within a gnostic scheme of supernatural powers through which a "redeemer" would descend to bring salvation.[89] More recent scholarship has decisively criticized this interpretation, however, pointing out that the construct of a pre-Christian gnostic redeemer myth is a retrojection into the time of Paul of a pattern that first appears in gnostic literature a century or more later, a pattern often dependent on Paul's letters.[90] Recent studies of 1 Corinthians 2 tend to set Paul's language within the conceptual world of Jewish end-time speculations, seeing "the wisdom of God as an apocalyptic power" (E. Elizabeth Johnson).[91] Indeed, Judith Kovacs argues that this passage is one of the most important evidences of Paul's apocalypticism in his letters.[92]

"Apocalypticism" is, of course, another scholarly construct, and its precise definition in relation to the ancient sources continues to attract debate.[93] It is sufficient for our purposes to observe, with Judith Kovacs, the symmetrical language in 1 Corinthians 2 and 15. She sees here the characteristic apocalyptic tendency to "view reality on two levels: behind the events of human history lies the cosmic struggle of God with the forces of evil." The references to "the rulers of this age" or to "rules, authorities, powers" reveal that *Paul experiences the present time as under the dominion of evil rulers.* That Paul describes the rulers as "being destroyed" (*katargoumenōn*, 2:6) shows that Paul sees in the cross the beginning of the destruction of the evil powers—but only its beginning. When Paul refers at "the climax of the whole letter" to every rule and authority and power being destroyed and all things being subjected to the Messiah, it is clear that Paul looks forward to the completion of God's victory in the imminent future.[94]

Recognizing that Paul conceives Jesus' death as the decisive event in a cosmic struggle, what Kovacs calls "God's war of liberation," may disappoint our sense of history. After all, other writers in Paul's age could describe Pilate's savagery in Judea in journalistic detail. For Paul, however, Pilate's individuality seems to have dissolved within the apocalyptic category of "the rulers of this age."

But this hardly means that Paul has softened the political force of the crucifixion.[95] Two illuminating comparisons are at hand in the writings of Paul's near contemporaries, Philo of Alexandria and Flavius Josephus, both Jews. When in his *Embassy to Gaius* Philo described Pontius Pilate as "naturally inflexible, a blend of self-will and relentlessness," guilty of "briberies, insults, robberies, outrages and wanton injuries, executions without trial constantly repeated, ceaseless and supremely grievous cruelty" (301–2), he took care to point out that Pilate's brutality violated the intentions of Tiberius, who had instructed his procurators to "speak comfortably to the members of our nation in the different cities" and to regard Jews and their customs with respect (161). Philo reserved the greatest praise for Tiberius's predecessor, "who first received the title of Augustus for his virtue and good fortune, who disseminated peace everywhere over sea and land to the ends of the world" (310). The point of Philo's argument is that even the barbarities of a renegade officer like Pilate did not come near the horror Gaius proposed to inflict on the Jews when he ordered that his statue be erected within the Temple itself. Thus Philo can contrast the depradations of Pilate, which he attributes to grave personal defects, to the benevolent policies of the preceding Caesars. His rhetoric suggests that Philo is prepared, of necessity, to make peace with the Roman order, so long as the excesses of a Pilate or a Gaius are curtailed.

In recounting Pilate's massacre of Jews protesting his expropriation of Temple funds for a building project, Flavius Josephus restricts his moral judgments to noting that Pilate's soldiers "inflicted much harder blows than Pilate had ordered" (*Antiquities* 18:60–62). When he relates the crucifixion of Jesus, apparently because he is aware that "the tribe of the Christians" persists in his own day, he is satisfied to note that Pilate condemned Jesus "on the accusation of men of the highest standing among us" (18:63–64); no questions of justice disturb the account. Pilate's massacre of Samaritan villagers in Tirathana was answered by an embassy from the council of the Samaritans to Vitellius, governor of

Syria, accusing Pilate of slaughtering refugees, not suppressing rebels. Vitellius sent Pilate to Rome to answer the charges, but Tiberius died before he could hear the case; Josephus shows no interest in pursuing the matter further (18:85–89). Josephus's concern in this section of the *Antiquities* is to emphasize the unscrupulous violence of Jewish agitators, motivated by personal greed, who infected Judea with perversely revolutionary sentiments and thus invited disaster throughout the decades leading up to the war (*Antiquities* 18:6–10); he is not prepared to question Roman policy in Judea.[96]

Neither writer impugns the legitimacy of Roman order as such. Paul shows no such reserve, however. The crucifixion of Jesus is not for him an instance of official misconduct, a miscarriage of Roman justice. It is an apocalyptic event. It reveals "the rulers of this age," indeed "every rule and authority and power"—procurators, kings, emperors, as well as the supernatural "powers" who stand behind them—as intractably hostile to God and as doomed to be destroyed by the Messiah at "the end." Jesus' crucifixion, Robert G. Hamerton-Kelly writes, "is the crux of God's plan for unmasking and overthrowing the powers of this world."[97]

Paul's view of the cross of Jesus is certainly informed by the symbolism of Jewish apocalyptic mythology. But it would miss the point to set this symbolic background over against the "naked facts of history," as if these were available to the impartial observer. If there were a position of neutral objectivity from which the violence of the cross might have been regarded, neither Paul nor Philo nor Josephus was apparently able to find it. Rather, we should compare Paul's apocalyptic interpretation of the cross with other interpretations of violence in Judea that acknowledge, however subtly, the legitimacy of Roman rule implicit in the mythology of empire. We should marvel, not that Paul can speak of his "word of the cross" without specifically identifying Pilate, but that his indictment goes beyond Pilate to include all the powers of heaven and earth together that stand hostile to God.

Nevertheless, the reference to crucifixion prevents this symbolic interpretation of Jesus' death from losing its moorings in history and becoming a strictly otherworldly drama. The word of the cross, Robert G. Hamerton-Kelly writes, is "blunt and honest talk about the violence that religion and philosophy cover over with ritual myth, and rhetoric," disclosing "the lie in Horace's fatal couplet, *Dulce et decorum est, Pro patria mori* [It is sweet and seemly to die for one's country], in Caiaphas' heavy public burden, which he so nobly bears when he sends just one more young man to his death for the sake of the people (John 11:49–50). The word of the Cross cries, 'Fraud!' to all this death-obsessed humbuggery."[98]

Far from "denationalizing" the cross, Paul has, so to speak, internationalized it. He insists that the Roman colonists of Corinth, thousands of miles from the troubles in Judea, must mold their lives into a constant remembrance of one particular crucifixion in Judea, because through that crucifixion God has revealed the imminent end of the Powers and has begun to bring "the scheme of this world" to an end (1 Cor. 7:31).

PAUL AND "THE POWERS"

The political force of the "word of the cross" could hardly be announced more powerfully. If we are unaccustomed to perceiving this force, part of the reason may be that it has occasionally been blunted by scholarship. Interpreters have often slighted these passages from 1 Corinthians as "less central" to Paul's thought than the more "anthropological" or "existential" understanding of what Bultmann called "the powers of this age: Law, Sin, and Death," as these appear in Romans 5–8.[99]

Even when Paul's thought is construed as genuinely apocalyptic, however, interpretation may slight the global horizon of God's struggle against the Powers as we find it in 1 Corinthians 2 and 15. J. Christiaan Beker, an advocate of an "apocalyptic Paul," has distanced Paul from the mythology of the apocalypses and emphasized his "transformation" of Jewish apocalyptic. Beker observes, first, that Paul "does not engage in apocalyptic timetables, descriptions of the architecture of heaven, or accounts of demons and angels; nor does he take delight in the rewards of the blessed and the torture of the wicked." Second, he asserts that even when "traditional apocalyptic terminology" does appear (in Rom. 8:38–39, 1 Cor. 2:6–8, and 15:24–28), Paul uses these motifs only "sparingly" and interprets them "anthropologically." Thus "the major apocalyptic forces are, for him, those ontological powers that determine the human situation," that is, "the 'field' of death, sin, the law, and the flesh" that figure in Romans 6–7. Beker finds Paul's own apocalyptic interpretation of the cross more in the latter texts than the former, and consequently writes that "the death of Christ now marks the defeat of the apocalyptic power alliance."[100]

But Paul never declares that the existential powers of sin, death, or the Law have been defeated. He says rather that those who are "in Christ" are no longer to let sin rule as lord over them, not because sin has ceased to exist as a power, but because Christians have "died to sin" (Rom. 6:2, 6). Similarly, Christians are "free from the Law," not because the Law has ceased to be valid (to the contrary, as Paul insists in Rom. 3:31; 7:12, 22, 25!), but because Christians have "died with regard to the law" (Rom. 7:1, 4).[101] Further, Paul clearly affirms that the cosmic power of death remains unconquered (1 Cor. 15:26). If for Paul the field of cosmic powers opposed to God "operates as an interrelated whole . . . no power can be viewed in isolation from the others," the powers continue as active and insubordinate to God, although (with the exception of death) they no longer have any dominion over the Christian.

Moreover, even when Paul does use more "traditionally apocalyptic" language, he clearly insists that the Powers remain unconquered (1 Cor. 15:24). This insistence plays an important role in Paul's argument in 1 Corinthians.[102] It is not clear, therefore, why the apocalyptic conception so important in one letter (1 Corinthians) should be subordinated to the so-called anthropological categories of another (Romans). Indeed, it appears arbitrary to declare that the Powers as understood in 1 Corinthians have in fact been "reinterpreted" as the Powers of Romans, and on this basis to conclude—contrary to the intention of 1 Corinthians 15—that Paul understands the Powers to have been decisively defeated; how much more arbitrary to support this judgment with texts from the pseudo-Pauline Colossians and Ephesians![103]

It may be to the point here to observe that what Beker describes as "traditional apocalyptic elements" do in fact appear in Paul's letters, although they are not emphasized. The "word of the Lord" in 1 Thessalonians 4 is a rudimentary "apocalyptic timetable," complete with archangel's trumpet. The "architecture of heaven" can hardly have been unknown to someone who had been caught up to "the third heaven" (2 Cor. 12:2), who refrains from describing "visions and revelations" only because their content is unutterable (12:5);[104] nor does Paul expect his congregations to be unaware of the eternal liturgy of the angels in which they join in their congregational worship (1 Cor. 11:10; 13:1).[105] Finally, Paul is evidently comfortable with judgment according to works (Rom. 2:6–11) and divine recompense for the wicked (Rom. 2:5; 12:19–20).[106]

The net result of these observations is to situate Paul's thinking even more within the apocalyptic tradition. There is no good reason to marginalize the clearly apocalyptic viewpoint of 1 Corinthians 2 and 15 within Paul's thinking.[107] Indeed, Kovacs has demonstrated "the importance of the theme of God's battle with cosmic forces of evil for the letter [1 Corinthians] as a whole"; and her argument confirms and extends the apocalyptic interpretation of Paul offered by Beker and J. Louis Martyn.[108]

Our unfamiliarity with "God's war of liberation" as a Pauline theme may also result from the way Colossians and Ephesians have shaped our perception of Paul's theology of the Powers. Walter Wink's work on "the Powers," and particularly his awareness that the theology of the Powers in Colossians and Ephesians is vulnerable to distortion and abuse, points up this issue sharply.

No one has done more than Wink to demonstrate the relevance of the New Testament theology of the Powers to our political life together. In his trilogy, *Naming the Powers, Unmasking the Powers,* and *Engaging the Powers,* he has presented an engaging interpretation of "the language of power" in the New Testament. He perceives a single, coherent conception of the Powers throughout the New Testament writings, coming to fullest expression in Col. 1:16: "In [Christ] all things were created, in heaven and on earth, visible and invisible, whether thrones or dominions or principalities or authorities—all things were created through him and for him."[109] As Wink summarizes this conception, "These Powers are both heavenly and earthly, divine and human, spiritual and political, invisible and structural"; they "possess an outer, physical manifestation," identifiable with social structures and institutions, "and an inner spirituality, or corporate culture, or collective personality."[110] The New Testament declares that "the Powers are good; the Powers are fallen; the Powers must be redeemed."[111]

Yet Wink is aware that this theology of the Powers is vulnerable to misunderstanding and abuse. If we listen to what Colossians or Ephesians say about the Powers with earthly realities in view, our first impression may well be that the view we find there is simply unrealistic: "The Powers most certainly have not been defeated. They were as strong the day after the resurrection as ever before. . . . The fact is that the Powers are as powerful as ever, as no people should know better than we who have survived into the grim twilight of the twentieth century since the crucifixion."[112] This is a significant concession that puts the theology of Colossians and Ephesians into serious doubt.

Paradoxically, however, Wink also affirms that after the cross, "everything had changed. For now the Powers were forced to 'listen for the silent step of the dead man's invisible feet.' "[113] If the New Testament language of the Powers refers to "the inner and outer aspects of manifestations of power," then (Wink suggests) we should interpret the theology of Colossians and Ephesians as refering to freedom from the inner aspect, the psychological and cultural mechanisms of coercion (so ably cataloged by Gene Sharp in his study of *The Politics of Nonviolent Action*).[114] Wink offers as an illustration the assassination of Filipino activist and legislator Benigno Aquino:

> After Benigno Aquino had decided to renounce violence and commit himself to a nonviolent struggle against the Philippine dictator Ferdinand Marcos, he deliberately chose to return from exile to almost certain death. He was shot by the military before he had even descended from the plane. His death changed nothing. Marcos was more powerful than ever, having disposed of his only viable rival. Yet his death changed everything. Two and a half years later, Marcos was nonviolently removed from power. But for those with eyes to see, Marcos fell when Aquino toppled to the tarmac.[115]

In a comparable way, Wink argues, the cross exposes not only "humanity's complicity with the Powers, our willingness to trade away increments of freedom for installments of advantage," but the cross also exposes the Powers as unable to make Jesus become what they wanted him to be, or to stop being who he was. . . . Death is the Powers' final sanction. Jesus at his crucifixion neither fights the darkness nor flees under cover of it, but goes with it, goes into it. He enters the darkness, freely, voluntarily. The darkness is not dispelled or illuminated. It remains vast, untamed, void. But he somehow encompasses it. It becomes the darkness of God. It is now possible to enter any darkness and trust God to wrest from it meaning, coherence, resurrection. . . . Those who are freed from the fear of death are, as a consequence, able to break the spiral of violence. . . .

The cross is God's victory in another, unexpected way: in the act of exposing the Powers for what they are, Jesus nevertheless submitted to their authority as instituted by God. . . . He submitted to their power to execute him, but in so doing relativized, de-absolutized, de-idolized them, showing them to be themselves subordinate to the one who subordinated himself to them.

Thus Wink explains the theological claim of Ephesians that Christ has been enthroned "far above all government and authority, all power and dominion, and any title of sovereignty that commands allegiance, not only in this age but also in the age to come. God has put everything in subjection beneath his feet" (Eph. 1:20–22).[116]

Wink's vision of the power of nonviolence is compelling. It remains a paradoxical vision, however, if simultaneously "everything" and "nothing" can be seen to have changed by such a death; or else a transitory vision, if "those who have eyes to see" that everything has changed can in the next moment recognize that nothing has changed!

The paradox results because Colossians (and Ephesians, which Wink believes Paul did not write) have in effect collapsed the final triumph of God into the cross. Wink has demythologized the resulting fusion in terms of freedom from coercion, the freedom that we gain when we embrace nonviolent struggle and are prepared to die in that struggle.

Whether Wink's insight is in fact more profound than that of Colossians or Ephesians, where the "fallenness" of the Powers is (to say the least) an undeveloped theme, is a worthwhile question that cannot be explored here.[117] It is to the point, however, to ask whether a vision of the power of nonviolence, of the possibility of breaking out of the myth of redemptive violence, can be gained simply by looking upon the crucifixion of Jesus. The question arises because Wink is trying to make sense of the affirmation made in Colossians and Ephesians that the cross of Jesus marks the final triumph over the Powers. And the question is important for our purposes because Wink believes he is interpreting Paul.[118] He writes, "Paul asserts that it was not through the resurrection that the Powers were unmasked, but precisely through the cross," and cites Col. 2:13–15, which he accepts as Pauline: "Unmasking the Principalities and Powers, God publicly shamed them, exposing them in Christ's triumphal procession by means of the cross."[119]

This is the theology of Colossians. There are good reasons to doubt, however, that it is Paul's understanding of the cross, as if the "unmasking" and "exposure" of the Powers exhausted the meaning for Paul of God's triumph over the Powers. To affirm, as Colossians does, that the cross itself is God's triumph risks mystifying the violence of crucifixion into a distinctly otherworldly, spiritual "victory." Ephesians makes the point explicit: "Our struggle is not against human foes, but against cosmic powers, against the authorities and potentates of this dark age, against the superhuman forces of evil in the heavenly realms" (6:12, Revised English Bible).

To be sure, there is nothing otherworldly about Wink's writing on the Powers, but that shows his improvement on the theology of Colossians and Ephesians![120] In contrast, I contend that *the cross of Jesus,* like the murder of Aquino, *by itself shows only the power of violence.* It therefore serves the purposes of the crucifiers quite well. *The cross alone does not, cannot, reveal the defeat of the Powers:* "No meditation on the cross alone would have turned its curse into its saving efficacy!" (J. Christiaan Beker).[121]

If, in fact, Aquino's death "changed nothing," are "those with eyes to see" in reality suffering a mirage of light as they grope their way, with Jesus, into a darkness that remains "vast, untamed, void"? In the years after the "people power revolution" swept Benigno's widow, Corazon Aquino, to power, her government managed to weather numerous coup attempts only through ever more intimate alliances with the military, who continued their anticommunist bush war in the jungles and repression in the cities, resulting in a human rights record "as bad as, if not worse than, during the time of Marcos," according to a 1988 human rights mission. The Filipino legislature has been preoccupied with working out extensions of the U.S. lease on military facilities at Subic Bay. Whatever changed with Benigno Aquino's assassination, the one relationship that has determined Philippine history for the last century—a relationship based on the dynamics of violence exposed already in the massacres of 1900—remains intact. However inspiring Benigno's courage, and the courage of hundreds of men and women who laid down in front of tanks, may be to sympathetic observers, to planners in the U.S. government their freedom in the face of death is but another variable to be factored in to the operating costs of empire.

For those "with eyes to see," the assassination of Archbishop Oscar Romero fulfilled his prophetic declaration a few days earlier that "if they kill me, I shall rise again in the Salvadoran people." Jon Sobrino, who worked closely with Romero in the months before his death, has written movingly of the profound influence this one man has had after his death in his own country and in the world, justifying Dom Pedro Casaldáliga's remark that "the history of the church in Latin America is divided into two parts: before and after Archbishop Romero."[122] The "resurrection" of which Romero spoke, Sobrino suggests, began already with the funeral mass for the archbishop. But that funeral mass was also the occasion for yet more murders, as soldiers in plainclothes attacked the congregation with machine guns and grenades.

After the outrage of another decade of atrocities, the war against the poor became a political liability in Washington, and so peace accords were signed between the Cristiani government and the FMLN. The continuation of disappearances and death-squad activity is only one reason to doubt the triumph of Romero's spirit, however. In 1993 the Cristiani government, dominated by the political party founded by Romero's murderer, chose the thirteenth anniversary of his assassination to announce its defiance of the United Nations "Truth Commission" report that identified mass murderers at the highest levels of government. Cristiani signed into law a general amnesty for anyone named by the Commission's report; within weeks, officers convicted and imprisoned for the 1989 murders of six Jesuit academics and their housekeeper and her daughter were released from jail into waiting limousines; and Roberto D'Aubisson, identified by the Commission as the author of Romero's death, is still celebrated as the savior of his country. The U.S. Army's School of the Americas, responsible for training two thirds of the murderers identified by the Commission, continues its operations in Columbus, Georgia; Reagan administration officials like Thomas Enders celebrate the Salvadoran war as a qualified success in properly solemn tones; and Clinton's ambassador to the United Nations, Madeleine Albright, congratulates El Salvador for having become "a working democracy."

In the weeks after his landslide election as president of Haiti, Jean-Bertrand Aristide began sweeping reforms in the military and judicial system, thus sealing the fate of his government. While Aristide tried to mobilize the popular Lavalas movement to bring people-pressure against a Macoute-dominated bureaucracy, military officers were already engineering the coup that would drive him into exile in the United States. Journalist Mark Danner describes the events leading up to the coup as a contest of "naked power" pitting an angry but woefully defenseless populace against a ruthless military junta. The coup itself began with gunfire throughout the capital. Soldiers fired on Aristide's house, and officers shut down the radio stations, cutting off "Aristide's most potent weapon—his voice."

Now squads of soldiers made their way into the *bidonvilles,* shooting anyone they saw, firing into the scrapwood hovels. When the people came out into the garishly lit streets, the soldiers shot them down. It was a simple tactic, with a long and honored history in Haitian politics. (The army last used it to devastating effect in 1957, before Duvalier was elected, to decimate the ranks of the populist who had been his most important rival.) The people, confused, frightened, and disorganized—they had received no *mot d'ordre* from their leader—stumbled into the streets and died. Automatic weapons, ruthlessly employed, had given the lie to Aristide's "unarmed revolution."[123]

Where shall even "those with eyes to see" discern Christ's lordship over the powers in Manila or San Salvador or Port-au-Prince, or in Washington, D.C.? In the cross, or in the murders of Aquino and Romero, Wink writes that for those with eyes to see, "the massive forces arrayed in opposition to the truth are revealed to be puny over against the force of a free human being."[124] But the crucifiers, to the contrary, regard these deaths as incremental advances in their divinely ordained struggle for order against anarchy. Who will tell officials at the U.S. State Department that Romero's death "has changed everything"?

The very genius of the Pentagon's "low-intensity conflict" strategy is that the terrorist state is ready to absorb "the force of a free human being," in fact the force of thousands of free human beings, without any diminution of resolve and stands willing and prepared to murder still more. What can it mean to affirm that the cross "exposes the Powers for what they are," when in the very public terrorist murders of Romero and Aquino the Powers themselves announce that there is no limit to the violence the rulers are prepared to employ to secure their perceived interests? What can it mean to affirm with Ephesians that Christ is enthroned "above all government and authority," "in this age" as well as in the age to come, when from the perspective of the powers themselves nothing has in fact changed?

I do not dispute Wink's discussion of the power of nonviolence; in fact I find it compelling. But I believe Colossians and Ephesians have underestimated the magnitude of the Powers' imperviousness to non-violence. The consequence (as Wink also recognizes) is that the language of Christ's present lordship over the Powers *now* too readily yields the interpretation that the Powers somehow enjoy God's blessing now. Thus (to cite a particularly grotesque example) participants at a White House prayer breakfast soon after the bombing of Baghdad in 1991 were encouraged to envision Christ seated on a throne behind George Bush, Norman Schwarzkopf, and Colin Powell, the architects of the recent slaughter. In the light of such extreme distortions of the imagery in Ephesians, how is Wink's insistence that "the Powers have fallen" to be balanced against the affirmation of Ephesians that Christ is lord over the Powers *now?*

The problem Wink addresses is an inadequacy inherent in Colossians and Ephesians. Where the Powers are perceived primarily as spiritual and heavenly, or in terms of their "inner reality" alone, it would be easy enough to say that God "*has* rescued us from the power of darkness" (Col. 1:13), "*has* reconciled all things . . . in the cross" (1:20), "*has* disarmed the rulers and authorities'' (2:15). We might expect such affirmations from those who are *already* "risen with Christ" (3:1). Ephesians carries this language even further, so that those who are *already* "seated with Christ in the heavenly places" (2:6) know that Christ is *already* "seated far above all rule and authority and power and dominion," and that God "*has* put all things under his feet" (1:21–22). To the extent that these letters do not confront the outer aspect of the Powers as obstinately hostile to the rule of God ("our struggle is not against flesh and blood . . . but against spiritual forces of evil in the heavenly places"), their theology is inherently liable to an otherworldly spiritualization that distracts us from the web of this-worldly power relations, or else baptizes those power relations as already "obedient" to Christ. Is it necessary to point out that Paul has been accused of just such spiritualization of the powers (though not by Wink!), usually on the assumption that he authored Colossians and Ephesians?

This is not an abstract point of biblical interpretation. It strikes at the heart of our confessional situation. As Carter Heyward points out, the justice-making church in the United States cannot afford to envision itself "as a partner or leader in government efforts to build a just society—because our government is not attempting to do this. . . . The forces of social oppression are too deeply entrenched in our religious and civil traditions and their effects too devastating to support individ-ualistic, 'spiritual,' and 'inner-directed' approaches to our prophetic mission."[125]

In this regard, I suggest, the theology of Ephesians may be a liability to the liberation church. The pseudo-Pauline letters already began to modify Paul to serve the churches' agenda in the postapostolic period,[126] and to an extent to accommodate the word of the cross to the interests of empire. In the ears of the Roman dynasts of ancient Corinth, talk of Christ's having already defeated the powers would have seemed, to borrow G. E. M. de Ste. Croix's words, "a pleasantly harmless" myth; one can almost hear their collective sigh of relief at the Christian reassurance that "our struggle is not against human beings."[127]

This is not Paul's theology of the Powers as it appears in 1 Corin-thians. Wink acknowledges what appears to be "a case of genuine contradiction" between Colossians and 1 Corinthians, where Paul affirms that "Christ must reign *until* he has put all things under his feet" (1 Cor. 15:25). He minimizes this difference, however, as "not funda-mental but a matter of emphasis."[128] In contrast, I want to stress the following differences between Paul's theology of the Powers as it appears in 1 Corinthians and that of the pseudo-Paulines:

1. Paul himself is not concerned to speculate on the origins of "the powers." It is not important for him to affirm that they are "created" (a point made in Col. 1:16 and repeatedly emphasized by Wink). Paul was presumably familiar with the myths of God apportioning the nations to

the "sons of God," that is, the "angels of the nations" (Deut. 32:8-9) and of the "fallen angels."[129] But he says no more than that "death entered by one man" (1 Cor. 15:21; Rom. 5:12, 18), that "God subjected the creation to futility [*mataiotēs*]," and that creation is consequently in "bondage to corruption" or "decay [*phthora*]" (Rom. 8:20-21). He seems simply to assume, with the apocalyptists, a worldview in which spiritual forces stand behind political powers on earth.

2. Nor does Paul speak of the rehabilitation of the Powers; he speaks rather of their "destruction" (RSV) or "neutralization" (Wink), their *katargēsis* (1 Cor. 2:6; 15:24). The language echoes the apocalypses, where God will give dominion to the saints of the Most High (Dan. 7:22, 27) and will "shatter these other kingdoms and make an end of them" (2:44). Further, Paul locates this divine triumph "at the end," *not* in the cross of Christ (vs. Col. 2:15).

3. Paul does not hesitate to describe the Powers as continuing in hostility against God. Death is "the last enemy to be destroyed" (1 Cor. 15:26). Similarly, the apparent intention of the "angels, principalities, things present, things to come, powers" is to "separate us from the love of God which is in Christ Jesus" (Rom. 8:38).

4. In Paul's own letters, the work of "heavenly" Powers opposed to God ("angels, principalities") is clearly described as being carried out through very human instruments: "oppression, distress, persecution, starvation, destitution, peril, sword" (Rom. 8:35-39). As Wink correctly observes, Paul here lists "the sanctions of primarily human powers," things that "the evil will of human beings can concoct."[130] These earthly sanctions cannot separate us from the love of God, Paul says; "no machete, no fusillade of rocks, no bullets or rifles or Uzis, no tear gas or bombs, will ever dissuade us," writes Jean-Bertrand Aristide.[131]

It is hardly incidental that this rhetorically powerful passage in Romans 8 gives way immediately to Paul's appeal for his audience's sympathy with the people Israel (Romans 9-11),[132] an appeal motivated not only by recent imperial legislation harshly restricting Jewish rights in the city of Rome, but perhaps also by the savagery in Roman Palestine during these same years.[133]

5. Corresponding to the view that the Powers continue to wreak violence and misery on earth, Paul understands "living in the Spirit" not as a turning away from earthly misery toward the contemplation of "things heavenly" (compare Col. 3:2), but rather as an agonized groaning in sympathy with an oppressed creation. The Spirit draws Christians into the trauma of a cosmic childbirth, as those who live in the Spirit await not only their own corporeal emancipation from the thrall of the Powers, but the liberation of the whole of creation itself (Rom. 8:22-23). (It is no accident that Wink's superb discussion of prayer as resistance to the Powers repeatedly returns to Romans 8 and mentions the pseudo-Paulines not at all.)[134] This experience of the Spirit issues

directly, for Paul and, he hopes, for his readers, in "great sorrow and unceasing anguish" for his own people, Israel, as they await the liberation of the messianic age which is their birthright (Rom. 9:1–5). (Nothing is said here about the absorption of Israel into the "new people of God" through the nullification of Torah, as in Eph. 2:14–15.)[135]

6. In contrast to the statement in Colossians that God "disarmed the principalities and powers and made a public example of them, triumphing over them" in Christ (Col. 2:15), Paul uses the metaphor of the triumphal procession more sparingly, and only to refer to his own physical abuse at the hands of very real earthly authorities. After his "affliction" (*thlipsis*) in Asia, when "we were so utterly, unbearably crushed that we despaired of life itself" and "felt that we had received the sentence of death" (2 Cor. 2:8–9), he describes himself as being "led about" by Christ in a triumphal procession, giving off the "stench of death" to those who see only the victim of Roman punishment (2 Cor. 2:14–16; compare 4:7–12).[136]

I conclude that, in contrast to Colossians and Ephesians, which have been allowed to play so dominant a role in scholarship on "the Powers," Paul's apocalyptic language about the Powers resists transposing the significance of Jesus' death from the earthly to the heavenly plane. It is precisely Paul's own insistence that the Powers remain unconquered until "the end," when they meet their decisive defeat at God's hands, that resists any narrowly spiritual interpretation of the Powers. Paul interprets Jesus' death as *the beginning of God's final "war of liberation" against all the Powers that hold creation in thrall* through the instruments of earthly oppression. The death of Jesus unmasks the rulers of this age as intractably opposed to the wisdom of God, but *they are not yet overcome*.

Further, Paul speaks eloquently about his own freedom from the persistently lethal threats of the Powers: "We are afflicted in every way, but not crushed; perplexed, but not driven to despair; persecuted, but not forsaken; struck down, but not destroyed" (2 Cor. 4:8–9). This freedom marks his own identification with the crucifixion of Jesus: "We are always carrying about in the body the death of Jesus" (4:10). Paul is sustained in that freedom by a very traditionally apocalyptic hope in the resurrection of the dead, though to be sure this hope is confirmed for him by Jesus' resurrection.

Thus Wink's summary of Paul's theology needs modification. Yes, the cross robs the Powers of Death of their "final sanction," exposing the Powers "as unable to make Jesus become what they wanted him to be, or to stop being who he was." As Robert G. Hamerton-Kelly writes, "On the Cross these stupid powers displayed for all to see the one secret that they had to keep if they were to retain their power, the secret of founding violence."[137] But this is an insight possible for Paul only in light of the resurrection, for the crucifixion alone would only rehearse, not expose, the logic of founding violence. *It is the resurrection of Christ the crucified that reveals the imminent defeat of the Powers, pointing forward to the final triumph of God.* As J. Christiaan Beker declares, "the death and resurrection of Christ in their apocalyptic setting constitute the coherent core of Paul's thought."[138]

We will have occasion in a later chapter to explore the practical dimensions of the Corinthian controversy. It may suffice here to point out that the mythological language with which Paul discusses the death of Jesus serves clear rhetorical purposes in 1 Corinthians, effectively extending the significance of Jesus' death at the hands of "the rulers" so as to determine how citizens of a flourishing Roman colony, hundreds of miles distant from dusty Judea, ought to conduct themselves toward the "scheme of this age, which is passing away" (7:31), on the one hand, and toward the "have-nots" in their own community (11:22) and in Judea itself (16:1–4), on the other. Given the profound distaste for the subject of crucifixion that Hengel documents for the Roman upper class, Paul's insistence on talking about the cross of Jesus, his insistence that this event has begun the dissolution of the Roman order, and his insistence that wealthy and prestigious Corinthians within the Christian congregation must now relate to the poor in a new way because of that crucifixion can scarcely be described as "minimizing the political aspects" of the cross!

DID PAUL MYSTIFY JESUS' DEATH WITHIN THE LOGIC OF SACRIFICE?

In Rom. 3:21–26, Paul speaks of Jesus' death as an expiation "put forward" by God. As the New Revised Standard Version translates these verses,

> But now, apart from the law, the righteousness of God has been disclosed, and is attested by the law and the prophets, the righteousness of God through faith in Jesus Christ for all who believe. For there is no distinction, since all have sinned and fall short of the glory of God; they are now justified by his grace as a gift, through the redemption that is in Christ Jesus, whom God put forward as a sacrifice of atonement [or "place of atonement," margin] by his blood, effective through faith. He did this to show his righteousness, because in his divine forbearance he had passed over the sins previously committed; it was to prove at the present time that he himself is righteous and that he justifies the one who has faith in Jesus.

Here it would appear that Jesus' death is no longer understood as the consequence of his own struggle against social and political injustice in Roman-occupied Judea. Rather, the reason for Jesus' death is a necessity on God's part, for it is God who "put Jesus forward" to be killed. Jesus' blood provides expiation (*hilastērion . . . en tō autou haimati*) for "sins previously committed," which God had "overlooked." These sins consequently presented a challenge to God's righteousness that could only be satisfied through bloodshed; thus God offered Jesus as a sacrifice "to prove that he is righteous."

Some interpreters have found in these verses an understanding of Jesus' death in terms of the Day of Atonement ritual (thus the marginal note in the NRSV). That view relies on Paul's use of a Greek word, *hilastērion,* that refers in Leviticus to the lid of the ark of the covenant upon which the high priest was to sprinkle the blood of a slaughtered goat (Lev. 16:3–19). But other scholars have pointed out that the blood shed in the Yom Kippur ritual did not atone for sins; it served to purify the tabernacle (or, later, the Temple). It was the second goat, the "scapegoat," that carried the people's sins out of the camp (Lev. 16:20–22). In fact Paul says nothing to indicate a specific correspondence between Jesus' death and the Yom Kippur ritual; that connection is made not by Paul but by the letter to the Hebrews, which makes just that correspondence its central principle. Nor does Paul anywhere articulate the sacrificial logic that informs the letter to the Hebrews ("without the shedding of blood there is no forgiveness of sins," Heb. 9:22). Other scholars have found a more adequate explanation for Paul's use of the term *hilastērion* in the Hellenistic Jewish conception that the death of a martyr could atone for the people's sins (as in 4 Macc. 17:22).[139]

Although the origins and provenance of these sacrificial ideas continue to excite vigorous debate,[140] clearly *some* sacred logic of expiation through bloodshed is apparent in the juxtaposition of the *hilastērion* and Jesus' blood. The pressing question is, What role did such expiatory logic play in Paul's thinking?

The Christian theological tradition has relied heavily on the letter to the Romans as the place where Paul articulated a doctrine of salvation through the atoning death of Christ. Just this traditional interpretation raises the most serious questions about Paul's possible mystification of Jesus' death.

Christian interpreters have usually read Romans as a more or less systematic treatise on the Christian theology of salvation. On that assumption, they have read Rom. 3:21–26, quoted earlier, as the "thesis" at the heart of Paul's theology, where Paul describes the divine necessity of Jesus' death, as if God could not dispose of "sins previously committed" apart from an expiation in blood.[141] Further, they have read the preceding chapters of Romans (1:18–3:20) as Paul's description of the human plight, which provides the "theological presupposition" for the thesis in 3:21–26.[142] In particular, those chapters have been taken as Paul's argument that the need for such a salvation as God now offers in Christ's blood is universal, a conclusion supposedly reached in 3:9 ("we have already charged that all, both Jews and Greeks, are under the power of sin").[143] That argument has been taken to be directed in particular at the Jew, who falsely supposes salvation can be found outside of the blood of Christ.[144] Thus interpreters have held the declaration in 3:20, that "no human being will be justified in God's sight through works of law," to sum up a preceding assault on the Jewish understanding of salvation, the "demolition of Jewish privilege" (Käsemann).[145] Interpreters have also perceived the conclusion that follows in 3:27, that "boasting is excluded," as excluding "the fundamental attitude of the Jew, the essence of his sin" (Bultmann).[146]

The greater part of my earlier work, *The Rhetoric of Romans,* was devoted to demonstrating that these interpretations, and the soteriological approach to Romans they share, are inaccurate, misleading, and unnecessary. Further, I argued that much of the current "crisis in intelligibility" in Pauline studies arises from the Christian soteriological reading of Romans but (on the premise that this reading misconstrues Paul's thought) is not pertinent to Paul himself. It must suffice here to summarize some of the findings of that work.

1. Far from being an essay on salvation, when examined in light of Paul's persuasive strategy, Romans is a paraenetic letter like all of Paul's other letters. Paul wrote the letter to secure the obedience of the gentile Christians in Rome and thus to guarantee the "sanctity of the offering of the gentiles" (so the purpose clauses in 15:14–16). As Victor P. Furnish showed, Romans is structured around the contrast between existence before and after baptism, between the futile mind and bodily dishonor of 1:18–32 and the transformed mind and sanctified body of 12:1–2. That structure corresponds to what Bultmann identified as the "once—but now" schema of early Christian preaching and exhortation.[147]

2. At Romans 1:18 Paul does not begin an abstract description of human sinfulness; rather, he invokes the sinfulness of the gentile world in terms of the apocalyptic drama that provided the context for the Roman Christians' own baptism.[148]

3. The direct second-person address beginning at 2:1 ("you have no excuse, whoever you are, when you judge others!") is not restricted to Jews, or even aimed particularly at Jews, despite the views of commentators and the headings gratuitously introduced into various editions of the Bible. (The *New Jerusalem Bible,* for example, supplies the heading "The Jews are not exempt from the retribution of God" at 2:1.) Such an assumption is "anachronistic and completely unwarranted" (Stanley K. Stowers) and obliterates the normal function of the direct address, or apostrophe, which is to teach or admonish the audience.[149] Rather, this address, which forms a unit with 1:18–32,[150] establishes a principle of absolute and universal accountability before God, in deliberately general terms that will gain specificity as the argument proceeds.[151]

4. A second address, beginning in 2:17, explicitly addresses the Jew in the stylized rhetoric of the diatribe. "You, then, that teach others, will you not teach yourself? While you preach against stealing, do you steal? You that forbid adultery, do you commit adultery? You that abhor idols, do you rob temples? You that boast in the law, do you dishonor God by breaking the law?" (New Revised Standard Version). Despite the massive efforts of generations of biblical scholars, it is both unnecessary and unnatural to hear this conversation as an indictment of the Jew (Stowers declares such a construal "impossible").[152] Reconstructing a Jewish "doctrine of redemption" that would be "demolished" by these rhetorical questions remains a thoroughly artificial and unconvincing task, as Sanders has decisively shown in his *Paul and Palestinian Judaism*. Practically everything Paul says in this stylized conversation could have won assent, in principle, in a contemporary synagogue.[153] This is not Paul's unsuccessful or incoherent attempt at the "demolition of Jewish privilege" (against Sanders, Räisänen, et al.). To the contrary, the very assumption that Paul is trying to "demolish Jewish privilege" must be called into question.[154]

If, on the other hand, these chapters are read according to the conventions of diatribal style, we overhear the conversation more naturally as an exchange between Paul and a Jewish peer, "a student or partner in discussion" (Stowers), intended for the benefit of the gentile Christian audience.[155] In that conversation, the Jew cooperates with Paul, moving the conversation along by answering Paul's rhetorical questions, demonstrating that (as any Jew would have known) the covenant did not provide a shield against God's judgment or a basis for presuming on God's grace. That conversation reaches a climax in Rom. 3:1–9, where Paul asks, "What then have we discovered—Do we [Jews] hold up anything as a defense [against God's justice]?" And his Jewish partner responds, "Not at all! For we already know that all people, Jews and Greeks alike, are under a verdict of sin, just as Scripture says." This hardly undermines the covenant! To the contrary, as G. F. Moore declared, anyone "who so presumes on the remission of sins through the goodness of God does not know the meaning of repentance, and annuls [in oneself] the very potentiality of it."[156] This is the message of the rabbis, and it is a message on which Paul and his Jewish conversation partner agree. And it is a point on which they agree for the benefit of the gentile Christians in Rome who "overhear" the conversation.[157]

5. This brings us to a crucial point for our present investigation. The ultimate targets of Paul's diatribal conversation with his Jewish "partner" are the gentile Christians in Rome. Paul's point is that the same absolute accountability before God that the Jew has confessed (3:1–9) also applies to the Gentiles (the scriptural passages cited in 3:10–20 focus on the wickedness of Israel's gentile enemies, and more naturally serve to demonstrate gentile sinfulness), even Gentiles who are "in

Christ" (the repeated emphasis in 3:21-31, where the "expiation in Jesus' blood" is in view, is on the demonstration of divine righteousness). That the thrust of argumentation here is against Christian presumption on divine grace is also clear from the correspondence of rhetorical questions in 3:1-9 and 6:1-15 (where baptism is in view), as William S. Campbell has recognized. His insight both integrates the dialogue with the Jew into the rhetorical structure of a letter addressed to gentile Christians and determines the sense in which Romans 3 may be identified as "the key to the letter."[158]

Between Romans 3 and Romans 6 stands Romans 5, in one sense the pivot of the whole letter. Here Paul seeks to qualify a series of christological statements that could be misunderstood *by Christians* as a ground for "boasting" over against God. Thus if the significance of Christ's death were simply that it achieved the forgiveness of sins, and thereby provided the remedy for Adam's sin which had brought culpability into the world, then one might say that "just as through one man sin entered the world, so also through one man sin was forgiven." But Paul rejects that typology for the sake of another, apocalyptic typology, according to which Adam introduced not only culpability but, far more seriously, the thrall of Death: "Just as through one man sin entered the world, *and through sin death entered,* and so death came upon all humanity, since all have sinned" (5:12). His point is that the thrall of Death, given entry into the sphere of human existence through Adam's fault, is far more serious than the fault of Adam or of his descendants; how much greater is the power of Christ's death and resurrection, which has brought not only the forgiveness of sins but life out of death (5:15-17).[159]

Here we are at the heart of what Paul wants to say about Christ in Romans. The extended argument of 1:18-4:25 is that no human being may raise a claim against God's justice. In Romans 5 that argument is brought home to the gentile Christian audience. While Paul can speak of the expiatory significance of Jesus' death "for us sinners" (5:8), through which we are "justified by his blood" (5:9; 3:25), he evidently considers that truth by itself to be inadequate and potentially misleading. For he immediately adds, "*how much more [pollō mallon]* shall we be saved from the wrath of God" (5:9); "*how much more [pollō mallon]* shall we be saved by [Christ's] life" (5:10), just as he insisted in 3:25-26 that the expiation in Jesus' blood served to secure, rather than to imperil, God's justice. The atoning significance of Christ's death for Paul is less important than the apocalyptic significance of his obedience (5:18, 19), to be sure an obedience unto death (compare Phil. 2:5-8), and his risen life, for in Christ God brings life out of death. Thus the free gift does not correspond to the trespass, it is "*much more [pollō mallon]*" (5:15); if Adam's sin brought the reign of Death, "*much more [pollō mallon]*" will God's grace cause the righteous to reign in life (5:17).

This is why the atoning significance of Jesus' death disappears in Romans 6, supplanted by an apocalyptic scheme of fields of power. Here the significance of Jesus' death is that through baptism it causes Christians to die to the dominion of sin, just as Christ died to the dominion of sin (6:2, 6–7, 11–14). This new possibility is created not by the death of Christ alone, but by God's power to raise the crucified Jesus from the dead. That power enables the baptized to "walk in newness of life" (6:4), to "live to God in Christ Jesus" (6:11), to "yield yourselves to God as those who have been brought from death to life, and your members to God as instruments of righteousness" (6:13). Through baptism, the death *and resurrection* of Christ transfers men and women from the cosmic sphere of the power of sin and death to the sphere of God's justifying, sanctifying, and life-giving power.

In the light of these observations, we can see, first, that Paul's intention was not a frontal assault upon Judaism or Jewish beliefs (he in fact relies upon a fundamentally Jewish perspective in significant parts of his argument); and, second, that Paul was more concerned with the life-giving power unleashed by the death and resurrection of Jesus than with Christ's death as an atoning sacrifice. To be sure, he did not deny the expiatory significance of Jesus' death, but he, apparently for the first time in early Christianity, sensed how vulnerable that expiatory christology was to misapprehension and abuse.

As the rest of the letter shows, this was no theoretical exercise. The situation addressed in Romans resulted from shifts in the population of the Roman congregations, as Jews and Jewish Christians exiled from the city under Claudius returned, under Nero's rescript, to new and more difficult circumstances.[160] It is likely the returning exiles had suffered the confiscation of their property and now faced (in addition to the currently fashionable anti-Semitism of the Roman elite)[161] widespread homelessness, the difficulty of securing kosher food,[162] and restrictions on assembly. The gentile Christian population in Rome, perhaps the majority in the congregations Paul addressed, were tempted to share in the antijudaism of their neighbors. Paul warned against cloaking racist contempt for the weak (14:1–15:13) in theological finery, as if "God has rejected his people" (11:1), "Israel has stumbled so as to fall" (11:11), or "God has broken off branches from the tree of Israel" (11:17–21). Paul countered these slogans by reiterating the faithfulness and justice of the God of the covenant (11:1–2), who can restore Israel (and "cut off" the Gentiles!) by the same power that raised Christ from the dead (11:15, 18–24).

Romans addresses the threat of gentile Christian "boasting" against Israel. Although that threat is explicit only at 11:25–32, it is in fact the goal of Paul's argumentation from the outset as he develops the antithesis of obedience to God (1:5, 13) versus boasting against God (1:18–2:5). To judge from the way Paul argues against it, the gentile

Christian boast threatens to vaunt freedom from the Law (6:15) against the misfortune the Jews have endured because of their obedience to the Law (see 9:31–33). Thus the Law threatens to become the instrument by which God vanquishes the Jews. Paul urgently repudiates this view in chapters 9–11, but it will nevertheless become the explicit teaching of the church a few decades later (see the *Letter to Barnabas,* ca. 135 C.E.). Thus N. T. Wright declares, "In Rome, Paul foresees the danger of the (largely gentile) church so relishing its status as the true people of God that it will write off ethnic Jews entirely as being not only second-class citizens *within* the church, still maintaining their dietary laws when the need for them has passed, but also now beyond the reach of the gospel *outside* the church, heading for automatic damnation."[163]

René Girard has called our attention to the terrible dynamic of sacrificial thinking. At the climax of the crisis occasioned by rivalry, we deflect our mutual aggression against a vulnerable victim; through the logic of sacrifice, we subsequently hide from ourselves our own abiding tendencies to imitative rivalry and aggression and project these into the cosmos as the immutable sacred necessity of violence. The gentile Christian boast against which Paul struggles in Romans reflects just such rivalrous impulses. The gentile Christian population, eager to claim for itself the covenantal privileges of Israel and to distance itself from the liabilities of Torah observance, stands on the brink of scapegoating the Jews in their midst. The theological instruments for mystifying the Jews' victimization are already prepared: Their suffering results from their own accountability to Torah, and now their "unbelief" in the Messiah has won them God's punishment. Moreover, their lapse was "necessary" in order for God's grace to fall to the Gentiles, who are of course invulnerable from the Jews' plight since they are "not under Law, but under grace."

This vicious double standard reflects the logic of the scapegoating mechanism; Paul counters it by insisting on God's impartial justice for all (1:16–17; 3:21–31).[164] Within the mystifying scheme that Paul apparently anticipates, one may imagine how easily the Gentiles in Rome might have heard the gospel of God's grace toward them as a gospel of God's favoritism. While the Jews continued to suffer divine punishment for their sins, the "expiation in Jesus' blood" atoned for the sins of the Gentiles who are "in Christ." The theology of "expiation in Jesus' blood" (Rom. 3:24–26) could readily have functioned as the symbol of the Gentiles' new privileged standing before God, a privilege taken over from the Jews. Paul militates against a way of thinking about Christ's death that would sacralize one group's material advantages while viewing another group's misery as an act of God.[165] At length, through the language of apocalyptic revelation ("I disclose a mystery," 11:25), he reinterprets God's apparent preference for one people over another as God's unexpected way of including both ("so that God may have mercy upon all," 11:25–32). And he reorients the Gentiles' hope rather toward the justice and sheer sovereignty of the gracious God who raised Jesus from the dead (11:15). His target, not only in Romans 11 but throughout the letter, is gentile Christian arrogance.[166]

It would appear from this analysis that far from being the author of the "sacrificial hermeneutic" in earliest Christianity, Paul was its first critic. Romans simply does not support a reconstruction of Paul's theology as a doctrine of salvation moving from "plight" (sinfulness without remedy before God) to sacrificial "solution" (the necessity of death before God can atone for sins). Although Paul apparently could not conceive, as Girard does, the inherent inadequacy of all sacrificial thinking[167] —for he did not repudiate the expiatory theology he inherited—he nevertheless intuited, and sought to expose and correct, the latent susceptibility of that theology to human presumption and rivalry.

This way of reading Romans differs considerably from the conventional view that Paul intended only to contrast one way of "being saved," namely, by grace made available in Christ's redeeming death (3:24), to another way of "being saved," namely, by "being justified by works of law" (3:20), these two phrases recapitulating Christian and Jewish doctrines of salvation, respectively. We have yet to address passages in Galatians where Paul brings Christ and Torah into direct opposition and relates Jesus' death to his submission to Torah.

DID PAUL THINK THE TORAH KILLED JESUS?

We turn at last to the question of the Torah's involvement in Jesus' death. There are, of course, many full-length monographs on the subject of Paul and the Torah, and no consensus among them on almost any point of interpretation. I have no intention of adding to their number here. The specific question with which we are concerned arises from passages in Romans and Galatians where Paul relates the Christian's freedom from the Torah to Jesus' death, in which the Christian shares through baptism. Does Paul understand that the Torah killed Jesus?

In Rom. 7:4–7 the apostle declares, "You have died to the law through the body of Christ so that you may belong to another, to him who has been raised from the dead. . . . Now we are discharged from the law, having died to that which held us captive, so that we serve not under the old written code but in the new life of the Spirit."

Since for Paul baptism is a "dying with Christ" (Rom. 6:3, 5), the implications of these statements would seem to be that Jesus also died to the law and that Christians are united with Christ in that death. Yet, significantly, Paul never says this. He says rather that *"Christ died to sin, once for all"* (Rom. 6:10), and that now *"death no longer rules over him"* (6:9). By virtue of their union with Christ's death in baptism,

Christians are therefore to consider themselves dead to sin (6:2, 6, 7, 11, 12–23) and to look forward to the resurrection from the dead (6:5, 8).

The point of the difficult argument in Romans 7 is that Christians are free from the Law's condemnation, not because the law has ceased to be valid, but because the law's condemnation of sin no longer pertains to the Christian who (through baptism) has died to sin (7:4–6). The analogy of marriage law is therefore perfectly appropriate: The prohibition of adultery does not apply to a widow who remarries, not because that law has ceased to be valid, but because the situation in which it is enforceable ends with her husband's death (7:1–3). Paul apparently wants to defend the Torah's validity (it is "holy, just, and good," 7:12; he delights in it, 7:22) while conceding that Gentiles who are "in Christ" are not bound to keep it. The Torah's "just requirement" is fulfilled, anyway, through the Gentiles' life "in the Spirit" (8:1–4).[168] The argument here evidently does not move from "plight" with regard to Torah to "solution." Paul simply explains that the Christian's changed relationship to Torah should not be construed primarily as a fault in the Torah itself, but is the corollary of a more fundamental change in which the individual has been transferred through baptism from the sphere of sin's dominion to that of righteousness.

More troublesome are the statements Paul makes in Galatians. In 2:19–21 he declares, "Through the law I died to the law, that I might live to God. I have been crucified with Christ; it is no longer I who live, but Christ who lives in me; and the life I now live in the flesh I live by faith in the Son of God, who loved me and gave himself for me. I do not nullify the grace of God; for if justification were through the law, then Christ died to no purpose."

Once again the "dying with regard to the law" is a sharing in Christ's crucifixion. Here, however, Paul does not offer the qualifications presented in Romans. Rather he opposes the idea of righteousness or justification through law (*dia nomou dikaiosynē*) to the salvation accomplished in Christ's death. He goes on to pronounce a curse on "all who rely on works of the law" (*hosoi ex ergōn nomou eisin,* 3:10), a curse he finds in the law itself: "Cursed be every one who does not abide by all things written in the book of the law, and do them" (Deut. 27:26). Finally he declares (3:13) that "Christ redeemed us from the curse of the law, having become a curse for us, for it is written, 'Cursed be everyone who hangs on a tree'" (Deut. 21:23), and again that "God sent forth his Son, born of a woman, born under the law, to redeem those who were under the law" (4:4).

Christian interpreters have usually read this passage as articulating a doctrine of salvation, in terms of "plight" and "solution," that poses the plight to be that of the Jews (those who "rely on works of the law" for salvation).[169] According to this convention, the Jews are under a curse, either because no one can possibly keep all the commandments of the

Torah (that is, they are "cursed" by Deut. 27:26)[170] or because the attempt to keep the commandments is itself necessarily opposed to the attitude of "faith" (that is, they are "cursed" because they wrongly assume that one *can* be justified before God by the Law),[171] or both. Since, on these terms, deliverance from the plight of the Law is impossible through the Law itself, those living in Judaism are in a no-exit situation. They can be "redeemed from the curse of the law" only through an intervention from outside their relationship to the law. The "solution" requires that someone else stand in for them, bear the curse that properly falls upon them; and this Christ has done by dying a particular form of death accursed by the Torah, namely, crucifixion. In this understanding Christ's death is propitiatory: He bears God's curse, deflecting it from others, and thus delivers them.

This interpretation is no less troubling to some modern interpreters, Jewish and Christian alike, than the soteriological reading of Romans. Some of the same challenges we noted with regard to Romans arise with regard to Galatians as well.

First, Judaism never understood that right standing before God was possible only through perfect observance of all the commandments, all the time, so that failure to do so automatically cut one off from God's grace; rather, "the cure for non-obedience is repentance" and atonement.[172] Further, the opposition between law and faith in 3:11–12 seems arbitrary to Jews, for whom faith and the observance of the Law are not mutually irreconcilable but belong naturally together. In this regard, characterizing Judaism as seeking to be "justified before God by the law" is inaccurate. If this is indeed an argument moving from plight to solution, it would seem at once to exaggerate the plight of those living in Judaism and to ignore the solution ready at hand within the covenant, namely, repentance and atonement. This, declares Hans-Joachim Schoeps, is Paul's "fundamental misapprehension" of Judaism.

Further, the assumption that Paul is describing the plight of Judaism from which the propitiatory death of Christ provides the only solution subtly implies that the covenant relationship embodied in the giving of the Torah has been inherently flawed from the beginning.[173] That is, God appears to have established a covenant based not upon mercy (*ḥesed*) but upon wrath, and the only deliverance from the no-exit situation in which God has shut up the Jews is the provision of a substitute victim, a propitiatory sacrifice onto whom God's unremitting wrath may be rechanneled. *This is the logic of redemptive violence,* embodied in Anselm's Christian doctrine of salvation (*Cur Deus Homo*). Christian interpreters have projected that logic onto the covenant at Sinai and at the same time have denied to the participants in that covenant the propitiatory benefit of the sacred Victim's death.[174]

Once one pays attention to the rhetorical situation addressed by Galatians, however, the assumption that Paul is arguing in an abstract, generalized way about some universal plight is undermined. Paul addresses gentile Christians who are being encouraged to accept circumcision,[175] and it is his perception of their motives that has shaped his response.[176] These are Judaizers—neither Jews nor would-be proselytes but Gentiles interested in adopting aspects of the Torah.[177] This is apparent in Gal. 5:3, for the "solemn warning" that those who accept circumcision must keep the whole Law would hardly deter those who in fact intended to do just that.[178] Paul anticipates that they are interested in adopting selected observances, and (as a good Pharisee) he resists the notion that the Torah could be "used in an attempt at self-justification" outside the context of the covenant.[179]

In light of the rhetorical context of the letter, it becomes evident that Gal. 3:1–14 is a single argument regarding how the blessing promised to Abraham may flow to the Gentiles; it is unnecessary and inappropriate to read 3:10–14 as a theological critique of Judaism. The argument is neither that Judaism is flawed, designed to communicate only curse not blessing, nor that Jews characteristically misuse Torah and thus repeatedly and inevitably come under its curse. "Justification through the Law" is a hopeless prospect from which Paul wishes to deter gentile Christians; he says nothing to imply that it is the normal Jewish understanding of the covenant.

This does not mean, however, that the "curse of the Torah" is merely a theoretical possibility.[180] Nor does it mean that Paul's reference to Christ's dying to "redeem us from the curse of the law" is an ad hoc improvisation.[181]

N. T. Wright has shown that the key to understanding the narrative implicit in Paul's thought is his citation of Deuteronomy, "the great covenant document." The final chapters of Deuteronomy are "all about exile and restoration *understood* as covenant judgment and covenant renewal." For Deuteronomy, and consequently for Paul, the plight bound up with the Torah "is not a matter of counting up individual transgressions, or proving that each individual Israelite is in fact guilty of as in. It is a matter of the life of the nation as a whole." In order to understand the force of Paul's argument here, Wright argues, we must recognize

> that at least some Jews in this period understood the exile to be still continuing, since the return from Babylon had not brought that independence and prosperity which the prophets foretold. Roman occupation and lordship was simply the mode that Israel's continuing exile had now taken. . . . As long as Herod and Pilate were in control of Palestine, Israel was still under the curse of Deuteronomy 29. This was not a matter of private theological judgment or insight, not a matter about which one needed to conduct theological debate. . . . It was publicly observable fact.[182]

This *covenantal* understanding of Israel's plight (and, by extension, the plight of the Gentiles to whom the promises given to Abraham were ultimately to come) is not uniquely Pauline or even distinctly Christian. It is perfectly explicit, for example, in the book of Daniel, when the pious Jew Azariah speaks to God from the furnace into which the foreign oppressor has thrown him (Dan. 3:26–45, Septuagint). Azariah praises the Lord, "the God of our ancestors," whose promises "are always faithfully fulfilled" (3:26–27), who has made a covenant with Israel (3:34) and promised descendants as countless as the stars of heaven to Abraham (3:35–36), who is "gentle and very merciful" (3:42), who has nevertheless

> given a just sentence
> in all the disasters you have brought down on us
> and on Jerusalem, the holy city of our ancestors,
> since it is for our sins that you have treated us like
>   this,
> fairly and as we deserved.
> Yes, we have sinned and committed a crime by
>   deserting you,
> yes, we have sinned gravely;
> we have not listened to the precepts of your Law,
> we have not observed them,
> we have not done what we were told to do
> for our own good.
> Yes, all the disasters you have brought down on us,
> all that you have done to us,
> you have been fully justified in doing.
> You have delivered us into the power of our enemies,
> of a lawless people, the worst of the godless,
> of an unjust king, the worst in the whole world.
>   (Daniel 3:28–32, Jerusalem Bible)

Here we see the same juxtaposition of God's promises to Abraham with God's subjecting Israel to their enemies because they have disobeyed the covenant. Azariah is tormented not by his own transgressions—nothing in the book of Daniel suggests he is less than a paragon of virtue, piety, and resolve in his observance of the Torah—but by the fate of his people and their land:

> Lord, now we are the least of all the nations,
> now we are despised throughout the world, today,
>   because of our sins.
> We have at this time no leader, no prophet, no prince,

> no holocaust, no sacrifice, no oblation, no incense,
> no place where we can offer you the first fruits
> and win your favor.
>
> (3:37–38)

Azariah appeals for deliverance in terms of the covenant itself:

> Oh! Do not abandon us for ever,
> for the sake of your name;
> do not repudiate your covenant,
> do not withdraw your favor from us,
> for the sake of Abraham, your friend,
> of Isaac your servant,
> and of Israel your holy one.
>
> (3:34–35)

Similarly Daniel rises from his anguished contemplation of the prophecy of Jeremiah to plead with God:

> O Lord, God great and to be feared,
> you keep the covenant and have kindness
> for those who love you and keep your
>   commandments;
> we have sinned, we have done wrong, we have acted
>   wickedly,
> we have betrayed your commandments and your
>   ordinances
> and turned away from them. . . .
> Integrity, Lord, is yours;
> ours the look of shame we wear today,
> we, the people of Judah, the citizens of Jerusalem,
> the whole of Israel, near and far away,
> in every country to which you have dispersed us
> because of the treason we have committed against
>   you. . . .
> The whole of Israel has flouted your Law and turned
>   away,
> unwilling to listen to your voice;
> and the curse and imprecation
> written in the Law of Moses, the servant of God,
> have come pouring down on us—
> because we have sinned against him.
>
> (9:5, 7, 11)

Daniel, too, makes his plea on the basis of God's loyalty to the covenant. Further, and most significantly for our understanding of Galatians 3, he prays,

> We are not relying on our own good works
> but on your great mercy, to commend our humble
>   plea to you.
> Listen, Lord! Lord, forgive! Hear, Lord, and act!
> For your own sake, my God, do not delay,
> because they bear your name, this is your city,
> this is your people.
>
> (9:18–19)

The covenantal plight described by Wright could not be more obvious. The "curse" (*katara*) written in the Law of Moses subjects the people of Israel to foreign oppressors, because "the whole of Israel" has breached the covenant, however pious individuals like Azariah or Daniel might be. Nor is it their piety that motivates God to act, even as they remain unswervingly loyal to God in the midst of deadly persecution: "We are not relying on our own good works"—literally, our "righteousnesses" (*dikaiosynas*). It is rather the humble and penitent appeal to God's mercy and to the covenant that is meant to stir God to act on Israel's behalf.

The covenantal understanding of Israel's plight evident in Daniel (and in a wide variety of other Jewish writings from this period) should inform our understanding of the "curse of the law" in Galatians 3, and of how Jesus' death "redeems" from that curse. According to Wright, "the solution is found, very precisely, in the death of the Messiah":

Because the Messiah represents Israel, he is able to take on himself Israel's curse and exhaust it. Jesus dies as the King of the Jews, at the hands of the Romans whose oppression of Israel is the present, and climactic, form of the curse of exile itself. The crucifixion of the Messiah is, one might say, the *quintessence of* the curse of exile, and its climactic act.[183]

One result of Wright's interpretation is that the argument in Galatians 3 is not about the nature of Torah in itself, or about the characteristic failure of the Jews to keep the covenant.[184] Rather, it concerns what God has accomplished in the death of Christ. Paul's argument "actually *depends on the validity of the law's curse,* and on the propriety of Jesus, as Messiah, bearing it on Isael's behalf."[185] Therefore Paul's efforts to dissuade the Gentiles in Galatia from judaizing is not motivated by a belief that the Torah is no longer valid; nor is Paul saying, "Don't adopt the Torah because then you would be like Jews, that is, necessarily under a curse." The region where "the curse of the law" pertains is not

Judaism as such. To the contrary, those Gentiles who are contemplating circumcision and other Torah observances are, in Paul's eyes, about to take a giant step backward, away from the cross, back into the realm of the curse. He wants to prevent them from seeking their own way with the Torah, as if they could find a path to "righteousness" apart from the historical course of Israel's covenant, as God has brought this to its climax in the Messiah's death and resurrection. "Relying upon works of the law" is something the pious Jew, like Azariah and Daniel, would have known to renounce, but for the gentile Christian dilettantes in Galatia it remains a real danger.

THE CROSS AND THE JUSTICE OF GOD

As we have seen in this chapter, Paul's perspective on the death of Jesus is thoroughly and profoundly apocalyptic. Paul thus participates in a broad current in Second Temple Judaism through which Jews sought to "make sense of and to respond to concrete historial situations of oppression and even persecution." Apocalypticism empowered people to "remain steadfast in their traditions and to resist systematic attempts to suppress them" (Richard Horsley).[186]

In the cross, God has annulled the wisdom of this age and of the rulers of this age. Further, since the one whom the rulers crucified has been raised from the dead, the rulers have clearly marked themselves out as doomed to destruction (1 Cor. 2:6–8; 15:51–58). The immediate consequence is that the Christian is no longer obligated to the scheme of this world, which is passing away (1 Cor. 7:31), but is called to obey the God who has chosen the weak, those "without rank or standing in the world, mere nothings, to overthrow the existing order" (1:28, Revised English Version).

This apocalyptic theology centers on the vindication of God's ancient purposes for the covenant people, and through them for the liberation of all creation. The questions at the heart of Paul's theology do not center on how the conscience-stricken individual may be saved, or on how a movement that includes Gentiles as well as Jews may be legitimized. His questions are the questions of his fellow apocalyptists: How shall God's justice be realized in a world dominated by evil powers?[187] For Paul, as for his pious contemporaries, the justice of God stood or fell with God's covenant faithfulness,[188] for the "plight" Paul conceived was dramatically focused in Israel's oppression, a "real, indubitable fact of first-century life. As long as Herod or Pilate ruled over her, Israel was still under the curse of 'exile.'" In this sense "nothing less than the framework of covenant theology will do justice" to Paul's thought (N. T. Wright).[189]

Paul's doctrine of the cross is thus a doctrine of God's justice and

God's partiality toward the oppressed. In the crucifixion of the Messiah at the hands of the Roman oppressors, God has recapitulated the history of Israel's exile and brought it to a decisive climax; indeed, in a slave's death on a cross (Phil. 2:8) the enslavement of the whole creation is embodied (Rom. 8:20–22). Thus for Paul, no less than for the liberation theologians of our own century, the most important aspect of Jesus' humanity is "the *partisan* quality of this humanity," revealed for Paul precisely in the Messiah's embodying the fate of a crucified people. In this sense liberation theology and Pauline theology share a common goal, "to safeguard the identity of the one who was raised as the one who had been crucified." Where liberation theology has, to this point, emphasized "the presentation of Jesus' history," Paul focused more narrowly upon the presentation of the cross of Christ; but both presentations are "polemical" and "directed against those who would seek to undermine, theoretically or practically, the truth of Jesus' humanity" (Jon Sobrino).[190]

Paul accepts the expiatory theology of the Christian movement into which he was baptized (Rom. 3:21–31), but reconfigures this in the light of his own conviction that God's justice must triumph over all human boasting, even that of the gentile church. The thrust of Paul's letter to the Romans goes against the inclination of gentile Christianity to dissipate this apocalyptic vision, to absorb the cross of Jesus within a cult of blood that saves the initiate while abandoning the people of the ancient covenant to the vicissitudes of Roman power. The rhetoric of Galatians resists the urge to lapse into the security of religious observances borrowed from Judaism without joining with the "children of promise" in "waiting for the hope of God's justice" (Gal. 5:5).

Paul has not obscured the nature of the cross as historical and political oppression; rather he has focused it through the lens of Jewish apocalypticism. Only a gentile church unaccustomed to that perspective, and more familiar with the sacrificial logic of the blood cults, could have transformed Paul's message into a cult of atonement in Christ's blood (the letter to the Hebrews) and a charter of Israel's disfranchisement (the *Letter of Barnabas*). Paul's own letters show that he recognized these tendencies within the gentile church of his own day, and opposed them.

5

The Apocalypse
of the Crucified Messiah

The last chapter took up aspects of Paul's theology of the cross; now we must address the origins of that theology. How did Paul come to look upon the crucifixion of Jesus as an event of world-transforming significance?

Some interpreters have insisted that we find "the origin of Paul's gospel" in his conversion experience on the Damascus road (Seyoon Kim).[1] Others have protested that it is anachronistic to speak of Paul's "conversion," as if he "changed his religion." We should rather speak of his call, in the manner of Israel's prophets: of his commission, that is, as apostle to the Gentiles (Krister Stendahl).[2] Accepting this qualification, we must nevertheless account for a radical reversal in Paul's conduct, and a very public reversal at that. The churches in Judea knew that "he who once persecuted us is now preaching the faith he once tried to destroy" (Gal. 1:23).

The public character of this reversal is evident in Paul's apostolate among the Gentiles. Paul later connects the revelation he received with his apostolic commission: God "was pleased to reveal [*apokalypsai*] his Son to me, in order that I might preach him among the Gentiles" (Gal. 1:15–16). But what sense are we to make of this connection? How are this "apocalypse" of God's Son, the reversal in Paul's conduct, and his apostolic commission related?

J. Christiaan Beker rightly insists that Paul's conversion experience "is not the theme of his theology." Paul "hardly fosters psychological speculation, for the thrust of his gospel runs the opposite way—away from introspective self-concern and mystic self-analysis to an objective, almost sober, assessment of his apostolic task. . . . The conversion experience and the accompanying mystical phenomena are simply absorbed by the content of the gospel and its universal claim," taken up into a great vision of "God's redemptive purpose for his whole creation."[3]

How, precisely, do the personal depths of Paul's "conversion experience and the accompanying mystical phenomena" relate to Paul's "sober assessment of his apostolic task"?[4]

The answer is to be found in the mystical traditions of Jewish apocalypticism, which in Beker's words provided "the indispensable filter, context and grammar by which [Paul] appropriated and interpreted the Christ event."[5] This does not mean that Paul's visionary experience was somehow prior to and separable from the symbolic world of apocalypticism, however.[6] What Beker calls "the accompanying mystical phenomena" had an inherent apocalyptic structure.

APOCALYPTIC MYSTICISM AND PAUL'S "CONVERSION"

In a discussion of "Paul's ecstasy," historian of early Judaism Alan F. Segal argues that if Paul was an apocalyptist, "as such, he was also a mystic."[7] Studies into the origins of the Jewish mystical tradition, previously known to us primarily from the rabbinic literature and the more obscure Hekhalot texts, have shown that this tradition was part of the milieu of ancient Jewish apocalypticism. At the same time, recent studies of apocalypticism, particularly Christopher Rowland's groundbreaking work *The Open Heaven,* have emphasized the importance of visionary and mystical experience for understanding the social reality behind the apocalypses. These distinct lines of investigation converge in the insight that "mysticism in first-century Judea was apocalyptic, revealing not meditative truths of the universe but the disturbing news that God was about to bring judgment." The heavenly journeys in these early apocalypses "usually begin after a crisis of human confidence about God's intention to bring justice to the world, and they result in the discovery that the universe is indeed following God's moral plan."[8]

Segal finds evidence in Paul's letters that he participated in this apocalyptic-mystical tradition and concludes that Paul is "the only early Jewish mystic and apocalypticist whose personal, confessional writing has come down to us." As such, he is "an important witness to the kind of experience that apocalyptic Jews were reporting and an important predecessor to merkabah mysticism."[9]

Segal points to 2 Cor. 12:1–10, where Paul describes a heavenly journey:

It is necessary to boast; nothing is to be gained by it, but I will go on to visions and revelations of the Lord. I know a person in Christ who fourteen years ago was caught up to the third heaven—whether in the body or out of the body, I do not know; God knows. And I know that such a person—whether in the body or out of the body I do not know; God knows—was caught up into Paradise and heard things that are not to be told, that no mortal is permitted to repeat. On behalf of such a one I will boast, but on my own behalf I will not boast, except of my weaknesses. But if I wish to boast, I will not be a fool, for I will be speaking the truth. But I refrain from it, so that no one may think better of me than what is seen in me or heard from me, even considering the exceptional character of the revelations. Therefore, to keep me from being too elated, a thorn was given me in the flesh, a messenger of Satan to torment me, to keep me from being too elated. Three times I appealed to the Lord about this, that it would leave me, but he said to me, "my grace is sufficient for you, for power is made perfect in weakness."

Here "Paul reveals modestly that he has had several ecstatic meetings with Christ over the previous fourteen years." That claim would not have raised eyebrows among first-century Jews, Segal argues, "since this experience parallels ecstatic ascents to the divine throne in other apocalyptic and merkabah mystical traditions" in early Judaism. He concludes that Paul "may have learned about ecstatic experiences as a Pharisee or merely known about them generally from his Jewish background."[10]

What is distinctive in Paul's experience is, of course, his insistence that the one he has seen in heaven is Jesus Christ: "God revealed his Son to me" (Gal. 1:15–16); "I have seen Jesus our Lord" (1 Cor. 9:1). Segal argues convincingly that even if the "revelation" reported in Galatians 1 was not the same event Paul describes in 2 Corinthians 12, the two experiences were similar, and that in fact Paul had a number of ecstatic experiences in his life.[11]

The context of early Jewish mystical experience is "critical to understanding Paul's experience of conversion," Segal writes, for Paul's "conversion experience and his mystical ascension form the basis of his theology."[12] Paul learned "from his personal, visionary experience that Christ was crucified and rose." Although as a Jew Paul knew "in ways that the later church cannot appreciate how difficult it was for a Jew to accept a crucified messiah," he maintained "that the difficulty is overcome by a conversion experience of the risen Christ, which proves that Christ is still alive."[13]

This insight into the apocalyptic content of Paul's vision is the key to understanding the force of his "conversion."

Unfortunately, Segal is unable to exploit this insight since he cannot explain "why a Pharisee would have a vision of Christ." He concludes instead that "Paul himself cannot be a good witness" to the meaning of what he saw. "In his writing, many years after the vision, he has completely subsumed the content of the vision into an acceptable Christian theophany." Segal thus gives up on explaining the Jewish character of Paul's vision and interprets Paul's subsequent reports as instances of the perfect hindsight of a convert. "The meaning of his experiences was mediated by the Gentile Christian community in which he lived"; it was "the influence of the Gentile community" that later told Paul what he thought he had seen.[14]

One might well ask why someone whose commitment to the Torah led him to "persecute the church to an extreme degree" (Gal. 1:13–14) would, to use Segal's banal phrase, suddenly "decide to change commitments from one religious community to another." But Segal suggests such questions are futile. "There is something deeply mysterious about Paul's conversion experience, something that will never be available to scientific analysis." We need not press beyond a fundamentally irrational understanding of Paul's conversion since "conversions do not follow the pattern of philosophical questioning."[15]

To the contrary, the sudden reversal that Paul's vision worked in his life makes good sense in terms of the very apocalyptic-mystical tradition that Segal has described. Segal himself observes that "no pre-Christian view of the messiah conceived of the possibility of his demise at the hands of the Romans," and that "the Jews believed in a messiah who would defeat their national enemies and usher in a period of tranquility. Such a concept virtually eliminated the possibility of a crucified messiah for Paul when he was a Pharisee." Now, however, Paul "knows from his mystical experience that there is a divine, crucified messiah."[16]

We must ask, then, what such a discovery would have meant to the apocalyptically-minded Pharisee who opposed and persecuted the churches of the crucified messiah.

SAUL THE PHARISEE'S MOTIVES
IN PERSECUTING THE CHURCH

Scholars have tended to explain Paul's preconversion persecution of the Judean churches without reference to his apocalyptic beliefs or experiences. This is odd, since Paul himself declares that it was the revelation he received that brought about the reversal in his conduct as a persecutor (Gal. 1:13–16):

> For you have heard of my former life in Judaism, how I persecuted the church of God violently and tried to destroy it; and I advanced in Judaism beyond many of my own age among my people, so extremely zealous was I for the traditions of my fathers. But when the One who had set me apart before I was born, and had called me through his grace, was pleased to reveal his Son to me, in order that I might preach him among the Gentiles, I did not confer with flesh and blood.

The fact that Paul speaks here of his "former conduct in Judaism" and of his "zeal for the traditions of his fathers" has led most interpreters to attribute his persecuting activity to the willingness of the early Christians to violate the Torah. Paula Fredriksen describes "an almost universal consensus" among interpreters that Paul persecuted Jewish Christians "because they challenged religious principles fundamental to Judaism. Whether because they preached a crucified messiah or because they received Gentiles without requiring circumcision, these Christians violated Torah in the name of salvation in Christ."[17]

Fredriksen proceeds to show, however, that all these explanations, however common and however theologically useful for the Christian church, are historically unsupportable.

One set of explanations relies on the premise that Paul persecuted early churches because they had abandoned observance of the Torah. But there is no evidence that Jesus' original disciples failed to keep the Law. And Paul never appeals to the fact that the Messiah has come as a reason for considering the Law invalid.[18]

Some scholars have found in Luke's reference to Stephen and the "Hellenists" in Jerusalem (Acts 6:1) evidence of a group of Jewish Christians from the Diaspora whose liberal theology already involved relaxing the Torah. It was this group's supposed laxity, on this view, that so incensed Saul the Pharisee.[19] But nothing in Acts suggests the Hellenists had a distinctive theology. To the contrary, Luke insists that the accusations that Stephen spoke words against the Temple and the Law are false (Acts 6:9–14) and reports that the Hellenists and "the Hebrews," including the apostles, cooperated fully. It is also hard to find any accepted precedent in Diaspora Judaism for the innovation supposedly taken by Hellenistic Jews in Jerusalem.[20]

Neither can the supposed innovation of the earliest churches be attributed to Jesus' teaching against the Law. The fact that in subsequent disputes neither Paul nor any of the Jerusalem apostles relies on a word of Jesus indicates that "*if Jesus during his ministry had abrogated the Torah, apparently neither his own disciples nor Paul himself knew.*"[21]

An explanation of a different sort, especially popular in recent years, holds that Saul the Pharisee understood Jesus to be cursed by the Torah by virtue of his crucifixion. After all, in Gal. 3:13 Paul the apostle quotes Deut. 21:23, "cursed of God is everyone hanged from a tree," as applying to Jesus' death. On this theory, the Pharisee Saul would have looked upon any crucified Jew as standing under the curse of the Torah; to hail such a man as the Messiah would have appeared in his eyes as rebellion against the verdict of the Torah itself. His conversion would consequently have meant recognizing that the one cursed by Torah was in fact the Messiah and concluding therefore that God had brought Torah to an end.[22]

The difficulties with this explanation are, first, that in fact the Torah had not condemned Jesus, nor does Paul ever suggest Jesus died because he had violated the Torah.[23] Second, this explanation imputes to Paul a line of reasoning that would have been exceptional, to say the least, among first-century Jews who did not ordinarily look upon their crucified countrymen as cursed by God (so far as we can tell from literary and archaeological evidence).[24] To the contrary, excavations of a family tomb just northeast of Jerusalem revealed the bones of a young Jew named Yehohanan, crucified by the Romans (his heelbones were still fixed to the Roman nail; his family had had to cut off his legs to bury him), next to the bones of Simon, named "the builder of the Temple" in the funerary inscription.[25] No presumed "curse of the Law" had prevented a pious Jewish family from burying the poor young man in the family tomb. Nor should we consider such a scruple plausible, in Fredriksen's eyes:

> Romans indeed saw in Christ *hominem noxium et crucem eius,* "a criminal and his cross." But why would a Jew? . . . Why would a nation that had seen generations of its own so executed agree with the hated imperial force responsible that such a death was a scandal? Why, in brief, would Jews reject a Jew for a Roman reason?[26]

Finally, we must recognize that Paul's argument in Gal. 3:13 is designed specifically to meet the situation in Galatia.[27] It should not be read back as Paul's preconversion understanding of the cross. In its present context it in fact assumes the continuing validity of the Torah whose curse Jesus bore.[28]

Yet another attempt to explain Paul's motives in persecuting Christians suggests that he was incensed by the early church's practice of including Gentiles. Perhaps Saul the Pharisee found the notion of Gentiles and Jews worshiping together intolerably offensive. But why would this be so? As Fredriksen observes,

> Diaspora synagogues routinely permitted interested Gentiles to attend services and hear the scriptures without making any "legal," that is, halakic, demands on them. The curious and occasional outside observer concerned simply to acquaint himself with a powerful God; the crowds who participated with Alexandrian Jews in the annual celebration of the Torah's translation into Greek; God-fearers who moved freely between the pagan and Jewish worlds; committed men and women studying for full conversion—all these Gentiles could and did enter the synagogue community as they would, just as those journeying to Jerusalem could and did offer sacrifices at the Temple. Under normal circumstances, the boundary between the synagogue as a religious community and the larger outside world was a fluid one.[29]

Thus "once in the Diaspora, the Gospel spread so quickly to Gentiles because Gentiles were present in the Diaspora synagogues to hear it." But this means that including Gentiles in ritual assemblies could not have been the issue between Paul and the communities he persecuted.

"Gentiles in Paul's own synagogue could attend services without receiving circumcision: why should Paul and his community then persecute a subgroup in their midsts that followed just this practice?"[30]

Perhaps the issue that provoked the Pharisee Saul was more narrowly legal: The church involved Jews eating at table with Gentiles. This explanation reads the conflict over the common table in the Antioch church (Galatians 2) back into the Pharisee Saul's opposition to the Judean churches. Even if we were to suppose that these two conflicts concerned the same halakic issue (which is certainly not obvious), why would a Pharisee have found the common meals of Jewish and Gentile Christians so offensive as to merit punishment? Such common meals would not necessarily have involved the violation of kosher laws. As Fredriksen points out, Jews ate with Gentiles regularly enough that the Mishnah would later give detailed instruction on the procedure to be followed on such occasions. In his study of the halakic issues involved at Antioch, Peter Tomson observes that "Jews did not refrain from table fellowship with Gentiles either in Gentile homes or their own, and were even proud of their hospitality." Tomson concludes that "we can quite well imagine a Jew like Peter dining at Antioch with his Gentile brothers and sisters. We may add Paul and Barnabas, and in fact the majority of Antioch Jewish Christians, realizing that this was apparently the prevailing view in Tannaic Judaism."[31] Neither would common meals have violated Jewish concern for maintaining purity rules in Diaspora congregations, for the Jewish presumption would have been that ritual purity was impossible in Gentile lands anyway.[32]

Moreover, assuming that the table fellowship practiced in the Antioch church would have constituted a violation of Torah renders the apostolic agreement between Paul and the Jerusalem apostles (Acts 15) nonsensical, for it implies that in the dispute with Peter over the common table, Paul would have violated the kosher laws and encouraged other Jews to do so in the presence of the apostolic delegation from Jerusalem. This is scarcely credible, for Paul would thus "have made the agreement null and void and his own apostolate impossible" (Peter Tomson).[33] Further, the energy Paul and the Jerusalem apostles later expended in the "apostolic conference" would be inexplicable if the churches had in fact abandoned the observance of kosher laws from the beginning.

We see, then, that the ancient sources, Christian and Jewish alike, fail to support the suggestion that Paul opposed the churches because of their violation of halakah. Indeed, we should abandon our conventional picture of Saul the Pharisee traveling from one Jewish community to another as a sort of halakic policeman, flogging Jews whenever they ate nonkosher food or sat down to eat with Gentiles.[34]

But why *did* Paul the Pharisee persecute the churches? Was it, Fredriksen asks, "because these apostles maintained that Gentiles, too, had a place in the world to come? But so did Isaiah, Micah, Zechariah, and Tobit; so did the Alenu [in the daily synagogue prayer service]; so, drawing on this tradition, did Philo and, later, the rabbis; and in this period, accordingly, so probably did the Pharisees."[35]

This is an important observation, and it leads Fredriksen to an insight that "has been universally missed": The early Jewish-Christian movement included Gentiles on eschatological, not halakic grounds. Jews

> looked forward to the nations' spiritual, and hence moral, "conversion": Gentiles at the End *turn from* idolatry (and the sins associated with it) and *turn to* the living God. But *moral conversion is not halakic conversion;* and non-idolatrous Gentiles are Gentiles none the less. When God establishes his Kingdom, then, these two groups will together constitute "his people": Israel, redeemed from exile, and the Gentiles, redeemed from idolatry. Gentiles are saved as Gentiles: they do not, eschatologically, become Jews.[36]

Thus "standard Jewish practice and a strong and articulated apocalyptic tradition," not some principled opposition to the Torah, informed the apostolic church's inclusion of Gentiles. "They saw in their response, as with their leader's resurrection, yet one more sign that the Kingdom approached—indeed, its results were already manifest." Consequently, "if Paul protested this opinion, then he and the leaders of the Damascus synagogue, not the members of its ekklesia, violated 'the traditions of [the] fathers.' "[37]

In summary, Fredriksen shows that several conventional explanations for Paul's persecution of the early churches are untenable. It follows that we should not equate the "zeal for the ancestral traditions" that impelled him to attack the messianic movement with "zeal" as "a fundamental religious attitude" endemic to "the whole of Palestinian Judaism," or as "an integral part of Pharisaical piety" that sought to enforce "a detailed keeping of the law" (against Martin Hengel). Unless we presume that the early followers of Jesus characteristically violated the Torah, all that Hengel and others have written concerning "zeal for the Law and the sanctuary [i.e., the Temple] in Palestinian Judaism and among the Zealots" is irrelevant to the question of Paul's persecuting activity.[38]

After refuting all these possible explanations for Paul's persecution of the churches, Fredriksen offers a convincing alternative. She asks us to imagine how the earliest evangelists would have been received in the synagogue at Damascus:

> Sometime shortly after the year 30 came apostles enthusiastically proclaiming the imminent subjection of the present order through the (returning) Messiah to the coming Kingdom of God. . . . Normally present on

such occasions would be Gentiles voluntarily attached to the synagogue. Their reception of this message and consequent abandonment of idols would only serve to confirm the apostles' conviction that the End was at hand. . . .

How would the larger community respond? The belief in a Messiah known to have died must have struck many prima facie as odd or incredible; a Messiah without a Messianic age, irrelevant. But the enthusiastic proclamation of a Messiah executed very recently by Rome as a political troublemaker—a *crucified* Messiah—combined with a vision of the approaching End *preached also to Gentiles*—this was dangerous. News of an impending Messianic kingdom, originating from Palestine, might trickle out via the ekklesia's Gentiles to the larger urban population. It was this (by far) larger, unaffiliated group that posed a real and serious threat. Armed with such a report, they might readily seek to alienate the local Roman colonial government, upon which Jewish urban populations often depended for support and protection against hostile Gentile neighbors. The open dissemination of a Messianic message, in other words, put the entire Jewish community at risk.[39]

Paul, then, sought to suppress the messianic movement in Damascus because their preaching posed a threat to the precarious position of the Jewish community within a gentile population. His "zeal for the ancestral traditions" was oriented not around some peculiar perspective on law observance, but around political considerations with which any Jew under Roman rule would have been intimately familiar.

Fredriksen admits her reconstruction is speculative. I find it nevertheless compelling for several reasons. It interprets Paul's activity as a Pharisee within the context of first-century Judaism rather than projecting onto him the issues of later intramural Christian conflicts. It posits the same motive behind Paul's persecuting activity that scholars increasingly recognize behind the betrayal of Jesus by agents of the Temple—namely, to suppress the sort of social unrest that might provoke Roman punishment.[40] Finally, it thus aligns Paul's concerns with one of the most urgent concerns of Jews living under Roman rule, namely, survival.

Fredriksen calls our attention to the immediate political context that she believes informed Paul's motives:

We should pause to consider seriously the casualty figures of Jewish urban populations at the outbreak of the first revolt [in 66 c.e.]: 20,000 in Caesarea; 2,000—the entire community—in Ptolemais; in Paul's home community, Damascus, variously 10,000 or 18,000 Jews slain. Alexandria's convulsions in 38–41, Antioch's in 40, and again in 66 and 70, stand as striking attestation of the Jewish community's vulnerability to the violent hostility of local populations if Rome's attention were alienated or withdrawn. And the pagan urban casualties at the outbreak of the War in 66, and in later rebellions in the Diaspora, underscore the reasonableness of Gentile anxieties should they hear of news originating from Palestine, disseminated through the local synagogue, of a coming Messiah.[41]

This historical reconstruction is pivotal for our discussion of Paul's conversion. After all, we are interested in the motives of Paul's persecuting activity, not for their own sake, but for their possible value in explaining what the "revelation of Jesus Christ" would have meant to him. If, as Fredriksen argues, his reasons for persecuting the churches arose from "the politically precarious situation of urban Jewish communities in the Western Diaspora,"[42] then we should expect that Paul's conversion, too, had a political dimension.

That means that *we are in touch here with the political key to interpreting Paul's theology*.

As we saw in chapter 3, Juan Luis Segundo abandoned the attempt to interpret Paul using "the political key" on the dubious assumption that Paul acquiesced in the harsh realities of Roman slavery. But if Paul's motives as a persecutor were both political and apocalyptic, we should expect his reversal in course to have had a deeply political and apocalyptic logic as well. Unfortunately, Fredriksen stops short at this point, convinced that once Paul had become an apostle of Jesus Christ, his thought and work became fundamentally apolitical.[43] To the contrary: Exploring the political and apocalyptic dimensions of Paul's persecuting activity will help us understand the fundamentally Jewish character of his conversion.

APOCALYPTICISM AND RESISTANCE
IN ROMAN-OCCUPIED JUDEA

Paul declares that he persecuted the churches out of "zeal for the traditions of my ancestors" (Gal. 1:14; see Phil. 3:6). Yet as we have seen, this "zeal" was not a concern to enforce halakic conformity on the early churches. In fact Paul's motives were shaped by apocalyptic traditions as these were operative in the political climate of Roman-occupied Judea. A review of those traditions will help us establish the context in which we can make better sense of Paul's conversion.

New Testament scholar Richard A. Horsley observes that "apocalypticism was the distinctive form taken by imagination in late second Temple Jewish society." As such, it could serve as the medium through which Jews held fast to their faith under foreign oppression. "The apocalyptic imagination thus had a strengthening effect on the people's ability to endure, and even a motivating effect toward resistance or revolt."[44] On the other hand, within the common symbolic world of apocalypticism, different Jews might interpret their circumstances, and respond to them, in very different ways.[45] If some were motivated to resist their oppressors, others might on equally "apocalyptic" grounds have preferred endurance rather than resistance. As Jewish historian Martin Goodman writes,

> Belief in future messianic upheaval sometimes encouraged not unrest but acceptance of the political and social situation. [On this view] there was nothing to be done to hasten the messiah apart from righteousness in influencing the divine timetable. Political intervention, violent or otherwise, was meanwhile irrelevant or even wicked in its presumption to pre-empt God. . . . The impulse to throw off the shackles of Rome cannot have been an inevitable reaction to universally accepted religious tenets because many, probably most, Jews before A.D. 6 espoused with a good conscience the more peaceful, passive reactions just described.[46]

To understand the relation between "apocalyptic orientation and historical action"[47] under the circumstances of occupation, we should take to heart Goodman's advice, speaking of opposition to Rome "when it appears to have provoked action rather than just words."[48]

To understand the role of apocalyptic hopes in the political turmoil of first-century Judea, we must back up to 6 C.E., when a Roman senator, Sulpicius Quirinius, was dispatched to Syria by Augustus to remove Herod Archelaus from power. Quirinius imposed direct Roman rule over Judea—the first time since the Jews' return from exile that the land had been directly subject to foreign rule—and initiated an accounting of Judean wealth in preparation for Roman taxation (Josephus, *Antiquities* 18:1–6). This census, which Luke takes as an anchor for his story of Jesus' birth (Luke 2:1), was at once an affront to Judean sovereignty and, from the Jewish perspective, a usurpation of divine prerogatives (see 2 Sam. 24:10). As Horsley suggests, it would also have provoked memories of a previous exaction during the Roman civil war (ca. 44 B.C.E.):

> When the Jews were slow in rendering up a special levy of taxes to Cassius, he had subjected and enslaved the population of the four leading district towns of Gophna, Emmaus, Lydda, and Thamna. . . . Suddenly the whole society was about to be subjected permanently to direct Roman rule and taxation. As Josephus indicates, "The Jews were shocked to hear of the registration of their property."[49]

Indeed, the census provoked an immediate and fateful response. A teacher of the Torah from Galilee, Judas of Gamala, and a Pharisee named Saddok appealed to the people to refuse the census, declaring it tantamount to slavery (*Antiquities* 18:4) and "upbraiding them as cowards for consenting to pay tribute to the Romans and tolerating mortal masters, after having God for their lord" (*War* 2:118).

Josephus found in the ideas of Judas and Saddok, which he dubbed a "Fourth Philosophy" among the Jews, the germ of the war that would destroy Judea six decades later. He decried Judas's "philosophy" as an infection of the Jewish body politic, "the seed from which sprang strife between factions and the slaughter of fellow citizens." From the catastrophe of the revolt Josephus drew a moral: "an innovation and reform in ancestral traditions weighs heavily in the scale in leading to the destruction of the congregation of the people" (*Antiquities* 18:9).

Since we want to know how apocalyptic beliefs and political ferment were related in this volatile period, we should ask whether Josephus has in fact provided our answer. Was what he called the Fourth Philosophy really "the seed" from which all the horrors of the Roman war against Judea grew?

The Fourth Philosophy

In his massive study *The Zealots,* Martin Hengel declares that Judas's "innovation," a "break with what had hitherto been the Jewish tradition," probably "had a deeper effect than any other doctrine had ever had on Palestinian Judaism during the first century A.D."[50] But what, specifically, was this radical new teaching? And what were the "ancestral traditions" (*ta patria*) from which the founders of the Fourth Philosophy had, in Josephus's view, so grievously departed?

Hengel rightly insists the Fourth Philosophy was not merely a nationalist freedom movement, as it is often misrepresented in modern studies. To the contrary, "there was for Judas and his followers no independent sphere of life which was removed from faith. . . . On the contrary, all spheres of life—everyday existence, the law, religion and so on—were regulated by God's will—that is, the law—and the political sphere could not be excluded from this." The guiding motives of the Fourth Philosophy were eschatological, combining a fervent devotion to the sole lordship of God with the conviction that God would act soon to vindicate the resistance within Israel and achieve the freedom for which they struggled. So much is clear enough from Hengel's discussion of the sources.[51]

It is far less evident, however, that Judas's Fourth Philosophy was a program of armed insurrection, as Hengel contends. To be sure, Judas appealed for resistance to the census by arguing that "the deity would only readily contribute to the success of this plan on condition that one actively cooperated in it oneself or rather, that those who had, in their convictions, become followers of a great cause did not avoid the trouble that would be involved" (*Antiquities* 18:5 [trans. Hengel]).[52] But this hardly requires, as Hengel asserts, that such "active cooperation" meant an effort "to bring about the redemption of Israel by force," establishing the rule of God "by violent means."[53]

Hengel writes that according to the Fourth Philosophy,

the coming of God's reign depended on human "revolutionary activity."
. . . This cooperation between God and the "true Israel" took place in the
form of a "holy war," which had to be conducted by means of guerrilla
warfare, a situation like the beginnings of the Maccabean rebellion. . . .
The ultimate goal was to stir up a general popular rebellion against Rome,
which was seen as the prerequisite for God's intervention.[54]

The "guerrilla warfare" Hengel describes was a very real phenomenon *in later decades.* Following Josephus, Hengel attributes the violent
extremism of the sicarii ("dagger-men") and of the Zealots in the
revolutionary period *to Judas and the Fourth Philosophy already in 6
C.E.*: "Going contrary to reason and against the real interest of the
people and taking no account of the existing power structures, the
members of Judas's party tried by violent means to establish the order
that was in accordance with their conception of the law, in other words,
the sole rule of God." It is "understandable," Hengel declares, "that
Josephus should have emphasized, among his many criticisms of the
Zealots, their absolute refusal to consider the real interests of the
people."[55]

But these criticisms properly apply to the Zealots who first appear as
a party decades later, in the years immediately preceding the revolt
against Rome.[56] What do they have to do with Judas's resistance to the
census in 6 C.E.? Josephus attributes all the violence of the sixty years
preceding the war to the poisonous ideas Judas introduced, but significantly he never accuses Judas himself of the rapacity or brutality so
common during the revolt.

In fact Hengel's portrayal of guerrilla activity in Judas's day is
unsupportable. Significantly, Josephus says nothing about Judas the
Galilean, the founder of the Fourth Philosophy, to suggest that he either
taught or engaged in armed revolt.[57] Hengel has made Judas the Galilean
into an insurrectionist by identifying him with another Judas, "the son
of Hezekiah," who according to Josephus seized weapons from a royal
armory in Sepphoris, armed his followers, and proceeded to "make the
whole of Judea one scene of guerrilla warfare" (*War* 2:4:1 [76]; *Antiquities* 17:10:5).[58] But that identification is faulty.[59] There is no evidence
for a continuous revolutionary "sect" between the census of Quirinius
and the upheavals of the 50s and 60s. To the contrary, Luke has Rabbi
Gamaliel I declare before the Sanhedrin that Judas "perished, and all
who followed him were scattered" (Acts 5:37).[60]

Josephus associated Judas of Galilee with the violence of the revolt,
but he contradicted this picture himself, admitting that Judas's ideas
never won a large popular following.[61] The connection is in fact part of
Josephus's political agenda. By attributing to Judas the beginning of a
new and alien sect, Josephus hoped to dissociate revolutionary teachings
from what he wanted to represent as the traditions and beliefs of most

Jews.[62] Horsley suggests instead that Judas and his "philosophy" were "a relatively small association of teachers and others who had come together in response to the sudden imposition of direct Roman rule and the concomitant tax-registration."[63] Nothing Josephus attributes to the poisonous legacy of Judas's teaching "is recognizable as an *action* of the Fourth Philosophy. At no point in this digression (*Antiquities* 18:6–9) is Josephus describing the supposedly violent actions of Judas, Saddok, and their followers. The point of his harangue is that their *philosophy* had contributed to subsequent troubles, chiefly because of its effect on the young."

What was that philosophy? To the extent Josephus allows us to reconstruct it,[64] it comprised an appeal for noncooperation with the census (*apostasis*, literally "withdrawing" from it: for the connotation of "revolution" we should expect the Greek word *antistasis*), an appeal supported by an array of arguments:

(1) Submission is cowardice. The denunciation of Jews who tolerated Roman rule is practically Judas's signature in every reference Josephus makes to him.[65]

(2) The census constituted slavery, while Judas encouraged an "unconquerable love of freedom" among his compatriots.

(3) Submitting to the Romans was absolutely incompatible with confessing God alone as lord and master (*hēgemōn, despotēs*).

(4) Although immediate success was hardly assured, any who resisted the census would be "laying the foundation for future happiness."

(5) Even if they failed, their efforts would nevertheless win them "honor and renown."

(6) God would cooperate with their efforts insofar as they were courageous and "did not shrink from the bloodshed [*phonos*] that might be necessary."

That this last was a call to steadfastness in the face of Roman violence rather than a call to commit violence in a revolutionary cause is evident from Josephus's description of the courage of the sect's adherents (*Antiquities* 18:23–25):

> Their love of freedom is, however, insurmountable and they recognize only God as ruler and Lord. They endured quite unusual forms of death and disregarded the death penalty in the case of their relatives and friends, if only they needed to call no man Lord. Since their stubbornness is universally known and evident, I shall refrain from reporting it in greater detail. I do not need to fear that what has been said by me about this may not be believed. On the contrary, I have rather to be concerned that the words of this account may be too weak to describe their disregard of the excess of suffering that they have accepted.

Despite the Hellenistic terminology, scholars usually recognize common Jewish beliefs, particularly Jewish eschatological beliefs, behind various elements in Josephus's description. The confession of God as Lord and the belief that God was involved in human affairs were common themes in biblical and contemporary Jewish literature.[66] Further, as Horsley observes, the "freedom" (*eleutheria*) and "happiness" (*eudaimon*) of which Josephus speaks expressed the common Jewish hope "for liberation from Roman rule that would bring a renewed society of peace and justice," as the prophets had announced; the "honor and glory" promised for the vanquished "would likely have been a resurrection" like that held out for the righteous in Dan. 12:1–3.[67]

Horsley is right to suggest that the Fourth Philosophy was distinctive less for a radical break with Jewish concepts than for the "insistence on the concrete practice or realization" of their beliefs, specifically, non-cooperation with Rome in the matter of the tax assessment.[68] On the other hand, we must not minimize what was distinctive about their "philosophy" as well. Judas's resolute call for defiance in the face of torture anticipates by twenty centuries the program of nonviolent resistance outlined by Mohandas K. Gandhi, Martin Luther King, Jr., and others, which requires that participants "must cast off fear . . . of the sufferings which may follow" (Gene Sharp).[69]

An Apocalyptic Rationale for Resistance: 4 Maccabees

Although Josephus tells us no more about the content of the Fourth Philosophy, we find the same constellation of arguments in a surprising source. The rationale for resistance that Josephus attributes to Judas is strikingly paralleled (though without specific reference to the census under Quirinius), and (most significantly) elaborated *as a philosophy,* in the account of Jewish martyrs under Antiochus IV (Epiphanes) in 4 Maccabees, usually dated to the mid-first century B.C.E.[70] Note particularly the following correspondences with the Fourth Philosophy:

(1) In 4 Maccabees, the martyrs reject submission to the king's decrees as "cowardice" (6:12–23; 10:14; 13:10).

(2) The martyrs are repeatedly described as "free" from the king's coercion. Thus the elder Eleazar defies the king, "You may tyrannize the ungodly, but you shall not dominate my religious principles either by word or deed" (5:38). Reason, therefore, is "more royal than kings and freer than the free" (14:2).

(3) Although "self-control" (*egkrateia*) is a common Stoic topic, the author is confident that the sovereignty of reason over the emotions is nowhere more evident than among the Jews, those whose appetites are restrained by the Torah (1:33–2:14). Furthermore, the author can use political language to describe the sovereignty of reason as "governor" over the emotions (*hēgemōn,* 1:30); God "enthroned the mind among the senses as a sacred governor [*hēgemōn*] over them all," entrusting to

this governor the holy Law so that "one who lives subject to this will rule a kingdom that is temperate, just, good, and courageous" (2:22–23). Devout reason, then, is "lord" (*despotēs*), providing "the power to govern" (6:31–33), to "nullify tyranny" (8:15), to "conquer the besiegers" (7:4). It follows that the Jews cannot obey the dictates of the king because they are already "governed" by the Torah of God alone (5:15); they are thus "unconquerable" (9:18; 11:27).

(4) According to Josephus, Judas preached that noncooperation with the census—whatever its immediate results—would "lay the foundation for future happiness." The author of 4 Maccabees declares that the martyrs furthered the cause of freedom, becoming "the cause of the downfall of tyranny over their nation. By their endurance they conquered the tyrant, and thus their native land was purified through them" (1:11; compare 6:28–29; 12:17). "Because of them our enemies did not rule over our nation, the tyrant was punished, and the homeland was purified—they having become, as it were, a ransom for the sin of our nation" (17:20–22).

(5) The martyrs repeatedly find courage in the assurance of their own resurrection and welcome by the righteous who have died (5:37; 7:19; 9:8, 31; 13:17) and confront the king with the prospect of his own condemnation after death (9:9, 32; 10:11, 21; 11:3; 12:12–14).

(6) The martyrs of 4 Maccabees are exemplary for the author's philosophical discourse precisely because of their courage in the face of coercive violence (1:8–9). They prove, by defying the threat of death and the tortures of their oppressors, that "reason is sovereign over the emotions," particularly those that "stand in the way of courage: anger, fear, and pain" (1:4). Josephus's grudging admiration for the courage shown by adherents of the Fourth Philosophy in the face of the most excruciating tortures corresponds to the detailed narratives of the martyrs' tortures in 4 Maccabees. Furthermore, to Antiochus's great consternation, not only do the Jews defy his orders on the threat of death, they do not submit even to the terror of watching their children or brothers die (4:24–26; chaps. 12–17). Indeed, the mother of the martyred youths is the supreme proof of the author's theme. Recall that Josephus stood amazed by the indifference of the Fourth Philosophy to the suffering of their loved ones.

It would appear, then, that 4 Maccabees presents as the supreme "philosophy" (1:1) a series of arguments similar to those Josephus attributed to Judas, the founder of the Fourth Philosophy, and illustrates them by the example of the Maccabean martyrs. The resemblances are striking, whether or not 4 Maccabees was written by an adherent of the Fourth Philosophy. (That the connection between the two has not been made before, so far as I am aware, may be due to the inclination of scholars to research the historical background of ideas rather than their political function.)

It is therefore all the more significant that nothing in 4 Maccabees gives even a hint of advocating armed revolt. Rather, the author presents *a rationale for nonviolent resistance to foreign aggression.* It is endurance, not force of arms, that defeats and paralyzes the king's tyranny, rendering his violence powerless (9:30; 11:24–26; 16:14; 17:2).

The Book of Biblical Antiquities and the Psalms of Solomon

There were other Jews, too, in this same period who advocated resistance to Rome without calling for armed insurrection. The anonymous author of the "Book of Biblical Antiquities" (*Liber antiquitatum biblicarum*), writing between the time of Jesus and the war,[71] presents an extensively reworked history of Israel from the time of Adam to the death of King Saul. The author highlights the period of the judges, feeling it most analogous to his own lifetime, in order to put forward the idea that "the time has not yet come for the ascendancy of a king of the house of David" (D. Mendels).[72] The expanded portraits of various judges are offered as idealized pictures of "good" and "bad leaders" for oppressed Israel in the time of the author.[73]

As Saul M. Olyan observes in a study of the author's ideology and background, "the theme of resistance to oppressors is characteristic of the whole" of the work. A series of episodes in the story show the author's "advocacy of various types of resistance to enemy oppression and his belief that God helps those who act and resist. . . . The defiant individual or group within Israel resisting the oppressor and having faith in God will find success; God will act with the resisters on Israel's behalf against the enemy."[74]

But the document is not a call to arms. The "resistance" practiced by Israel's leaders in the absence of a warrior messiah[75] is often of a more modest, nevertheless creative nature. Thus Abram simply refused to run and hide from his Mesopotamian neighbors who wished to coerce him, on pain of death, to worship idols (6:11); he was miraculously delivered from the fiery furnace into which they had thrown him (6:16–18). Amram's resistance consisted in having children, despite the desperate advice of Hebrew neighbors that "it is better to die without sons until we see what God may do." He thus became the father of Moses, the deliverer (9:1–16). Even when resistance takes the form of military action against an enemy, as in Kenaz's slaughter of the Amorites, the characters expressly insist that it is God who has secured the victory, *not* human combatants.[76] Furthermore, it is repeatedly observed that Israel's numbers are woefully inadequate to mount an effective military resistance against its enemies, and that Israel is therefore forced to rely upon the gracious intervention of God alone. Mendels finds a "motto" in

27:14, "Now we know that the Lord has decided to save his people: he does not need a great number, but only holiness."

The clearest statement of the author's position comes in 10:3, when "the Israelites debate their options at the Sea of Reeds" with Pharaoh's army bearing down upon them:

> Then in considering the fearful situation of the moment, the sons of Israel were split in their opinions according to three strategies. For the tribe of Reuben and the tribe of Issachar and the tribe of Zebulun and the tribe of Simeon said, "Come, let us cast ourselves into the sea. For it is better for us to die in the water than to be killed by our enemies." But the tribe of Gad and the tribe of Asher and the tribe of Dan and that of Naphtali said, "No, but let us go back with them; and if they are willing to spare our lives, we will serve them." But the tribe of Levi and the tribe of Judah and that of Joseph and the tribe of Benjamin said, "Not so, but let us take up our weapons and fight with them, and God will be with us."

As Olyan suggests, the three strategies considered here were options seriously considered by Jews in the years immediately leading up to and during the war with Rome.[77] It is not correct, however, that Levi, Judah, Benjamin, and Joseph "have the last word" when they "insist on fighting the enemy."[78] It is God who "has the last word," pointedly acting to deliver Israel before the tribes can mount any resistance on their own. Thus "through this episode our author expresses his practical message for the present time: do not fight the oppressor: God will, provided you believe in him" (D. Mendels).[79]

Meanwhile the suffering of the righteous can be understood, as in 4 Maccabees, as a sacrifice to God on behalf of the people (so Isaac's prayer in 32:3).

A similar response to Roman rule is evident in the Psalms of Solomon (dated from the mid-first century B.C.E. to the mid-first century C.E.).[80] Here Roman overlordship, beginning with Pompey's invasion and depradations against the community of the righteous, is acknowledged as God's punishment of Israel, and Jerusalem in particular, for the nation's sins. The tyranny of Rome is only temporary, however. As surely as God had brought the yoke of foreign oppressors upon Israel, so surely would God suddenly redeem Israel by subjecting the nations to Israel's messiah, "at the right time." This would be a miraculous deliverance, not the result of military preparation: The messiah "will not rely on horse and rider and bow, nor will he collect gold and silver for war. Nor will he build up hope in a multitude for a day of war" (17:33). Significantly, however, while the Psalms of Solomon apparently reject the option of armed insurrection against Rome, the theme of defiance or resistance to the oppressor so evident in 4 Maccabees or the *Liber antiquitatum biblicarum* is missing, or at best muted here.

The evidence from Josephus concerning the Fourth Philosophy, and from 4 Maccabees, the *Liber antiquitatum biblicarum,* and the Psalms of Solomon casts doubt on the widespread portrayal of Palestinian Jewish society as a hotbed of revolutionary violence. To the contrary, Horsley writes, "The people resisted their unacceptable situation with considerable patience and discipline. . . . For seventy years, from 4 B.C.E. to 66 C.E., the Jewish people, with the exception of the Sicarii, engaged in a series of nonviolent protests of different sorts, despite the often-violent response by the Romans."[81]

Josephus recounts some of the most spectacular incidents. When Pontius Pilate inaugurated his command in Judea by ordering his garrison to enter Jerusalem, under cover of night, carrying their sacred insignia, the Jews staged a massive sit-in at his headquarters in Caesarea for five days and nights. At last Pilate met the crowd in a stadium, where they were surrounded by soldiers with drawn swords; Pilate ordered them to disperse on pain of death. Hundreds of Jews dropped to their knees and bared their necks, offering to die rather than permit the desecration of their city. Pilate relented (*Antiquities* 18:55–59).

He was prepared for the next incident, however. When tens of thousands of Jews gathered to protest his expropriation of funds from the Temple treasury to build an aqueduct, he sent a large force of soldiers in plainclothes into the crowd. At his signal, they pulled clubs from beneath their clothing and massacred protesters and onlookers alike (*Antiquities* 18:60–62).

The people persisted in their strategy of resistance, however, until a series of embassies of protest secured Pilate's recall to Rome in 36 C.E. (*Antiquities* 18:89). When a few years later Caligula ordered his subordinate in Syria, Publius Petronius, to erect his statue within the Temple of Jerusalem, "the multitude of the Jews covered all Phoenicia like a cloud." The force of this nonviolent protest moved Petronius to swear by his own life to refuse his emperor's order (*War* 2:10; Philo, *Embassy to Gaius,* 32). Fortunately for the governor, Caligula died before his resolve could be tested.

These incidents show not only the Jews' resolve to resist Rome, but also their initial determination to use nonviolent strategies.[82] Horsley has studied other popular movements that gathered around prophet or king figures in defiance of Rome.[83] He concludes that while these movements may have been "revolutionary" in the sense of anticipating and working toward fundamental social change,

> There is no real evidence in our texts that any of these movements was in any way violent, let alone armed, as has sometimes been suggested. But they were apparently understood as a threat to the dominant order. Modern interpreters might dismiss their anticipation of divine action as mere apocalyptic fantasy. To Josephus and others of the ancient Jewish

ruling group, however, these movements appeared as a genuine threat. Indeed, the ruling group's brutal suppression of these movements by overwhelming military force indicates just how anxious they were about the "revolutionary changes" that these prophets and their followers apparently anticipated. At the very least, of course, if the participants in such movements abandoned their fields in anticipation of divine deliverance, the prophets and their followers posed a genuine threat to their continuing productive base that the ruling groups depended upon in their peasantry.[84]

David Rhoads concurs. The fact that "the prewar prophetic movements" were nonviolent "does not mean, however, that they were not a significant part of anti-Roman resistance":

> Their eschatological behavior had as its object the destruction of the present order and its replacement by a divinely ordained one. The apocalyptic promises of God's saving action may have provided an alternative to violent revolution for some who despaired of the efficacy of human revolutionary efforts against the Romans. . . . These movements certainly had the effect of stirring up the people (*War* 2:258). And although most may not have been violent movements, they fed the atmosphere in which revolutionary activity took place. The fact that the Romans dealt with them by prompt military suppression indicates that they viewed them as anti-Roman and a threat to the established order.[85]

Our examination of Jewish texts dated to these same years, and the incidents reported by Josephus and Philo, show that for many Jews, nonviolent resistance was a principled response to Roman oppression. For some of these Jews, at least, it was also a response informed by the confidence that God could and would act, decisively and soon, to end Roman hegemony and inaugurate a new social reality, "direct rule" by God or God's messiah.

Apocalypticism and "Political Realism" among the Pharisees

There are hints in the writings just reviewed that for other Jews, the more prudent path was to "live in peace by obeying the [foreign] king" (4 Macc. 8:26), intending that if the oppressors "are willing to spare our lives, we will serve them" (*Liber antiquitatum biblicarum* 10:3).

The authors of those works flatly rejected such compromise, but without appealing to the course of armed revolt. Similarly although Judas of Gamala was no guerrilla, he clearly advocated resistance to Rome, teaching and organizing mass noncooperation, a virtual intifada against the empire, based on the conviction that submission to Roman rule was incompatible with God's kingship. The dangerous "innovation" Josephus detected in the Fourth Philosophy, the divergence from

"ancestral tradition" that in his view contaminated subsequent generations and led directly to the catastrophe of 66–70, was more than a
desire to resist Rome (for Josephus considered desire for freedom noble).
It was rather the refusal on principle to accommodate religious belief to
the political realities of the day, the denial that God might rule Israel
through foreign nations. As Hengel writes, in the Fourth Philosophy *the
rejection of imperial rule "was given a clear 'theological' foundation"*:

> Judas' thesis marked a break with a tradition of foreign rule which had
> lasted for centuries and which the Jews had endured relatively willingly
> until the rule of Antiochus Epiphanes. Even later, under the Maccabees,
> subjection to foreign rulers had not been rejected so fundamentally as it
> was by Judas. Confessing the "sole rule of God" meant not only a life and
> death struggle with Rome, but also a break with what had hitherto been
> the Jewish tradition.[86]

*The "ancestral tradition" from which the Fourth Philosophy di-
verged was the plain teaching of Scripture.* For the prophets expressly
declared that Israel's subjection to foreign empires was God's punishment for the nation's sins. The corollary was that the invading armies,
one after another, enjoyed their successive periods of military and
political supremacy by the will of God (see 2 Kings 24:2–4). It followed
that the people's submission to the foreign power was submission to
God, so that rebellion against the foreign power was rebellion against
God. So Jeremiah relayed the Lord's message to the kingdoms surrounding Judah in the sixth century B.C.E. (Jer. 27:4–8, 11):

> "It is I who by my great power and my outstretched arm have made the
> earth, with the people and animals that are on the earth, and I give it to
> whomever I please. Now I have given all these lands into the hand of King
> Nebuchadnezzar of Babylon, my servant, and I have given him even the
> wild animals of the field to serve him. All the nations shall serve him and
> his son and his grandson, until the time of his own land comes; then many
> nations and great kings shall make him their slave.
>
>   "But if any nation or kingdom will not serve this king, Nebuchadnezzar
> of Babylon, and put its neck under the yoke of the king of Babylon, then
> I will punish that nation with the sword, with famine, and with pesti-
> lence," says the Lord, "until I have completed its destruction by his
> hand. . . . But any nation that will bring its neck under the yoke of the king
> of Babylon and serve him, I will leave on its own land," says the Lord, "to
> till it and live there."

This doctrine explained the savagery of the Seleucid king to the author
of the book of Daniel, the brutality of Pompey to the author of the

Psalms of Solomon, and the catastrophe of 70 C.E. to the author of 4 Ezra.

And this doctrine apparently taught the Pharisees to understand the facts of direct Roman rule in Judea. Josephus declares that the Fourth Philosophy "agrees in all other respects with the opinions of the Pharisees," with the significant exception that "they have a passion for liberty that is almost unconquerable, since they are convinced that God alone is their leader and master. They think little of submitting to death in unusual forms and permitting vengeance to fall on kinsmen and friends if only they may avoid calling any man master" (*Antiquities* 18:23).

The implication is that the Pharisees and the Fourth Philosophy shared an eschatological worldview, but that the Pharisees affirmed the biblical teaching that God's sovereignty could be exercised through foreign rulers. Just this Judas repudiated. We should exercise caution here, of course. Josephus's portrayal of the Pharisees serves his ulterior purposes. Although he indicates there were Pharisees among the revolutionaries, he often presents the Pharisees in his *Antiquities* as the most influential group among the Jews, perhaps in order to advance the cause of Judean Pharisees with the Roman government of his own day.[87] His portrayal of the three "native" Jewish philosophies (the Sadducees, the Pharisees, and the Essenes) describes an acceptable range of Jewish opinion within which the dilemma of the love for freedom versus the recognition of divinely decreed "fate" could lead to different positions; only the Fourth Philosophy is alien because it refuses to acknowledge that the "destiny" of Israel might lie in subjection to Rome. Josephus's representation of Pharisaic "doctrine" nevertheless appears plausible, although he clothes it in concepts more intelligible to Hellenistic readers.

It appears that Pharisaic teaching has an essentially political component. Indeed, the "political realism" of the Pharisees is becoming a commonplace in historical studies today: Martin Hengel, for example, contrasts the "fanatical" Fourth Philosophy with "the ideas of the more moderate Pharisees," who "were much more 'national' in the 'real political' sense."[88]

The "realism" of the Pharisees is sometimes read as their lack of interest in political matters. Oxford historian Cecil Roth has written, for example, that "the entire Pharisee theory and background . . . was non-political. They were interested in personal conduct more than in the government of the state." According to Roth, "the Pharisaic tradition" was "on the side of law and order and the maintenance of the *status quo*"; the "accepted Pharisee policy" was "to submit to alien rule with a good grace so long as Jewish religious institutions remain undisturbed."[89] Sayings recorded in the Mishnah (*Avot* 3:3, 5, ca. 200 C.E.) teach, in Roth's view, that "if a man devoted himself wholeheartedly to the study of the Holy Law the problem of the recognition or non-recognition of an earthly sovereign lost its practical significance. This was perhaps the accepted Pharisaic answer to the Zealot creed."[90] Similarly, the revisers of Schürer's *History of the Jewish People in the Age of Jesus Christ* declare that the Pharisees "were not a political party at all, or not essentially so. Their aims were not political but religious: the rigorous fulfillment of the Torah. Insofar as these were not obstructed, they could be content with any government. . . . To politics as such they were always relatively indifferent."[91]

These generalizations depend, in part, on Jacob Neusner's argument that by the first century C.E. the Pharisees were no longer involved as a party in political affairs. A critical reading of Talmudic traditions about the rabbis before 70 C.E. shows, according to Neusner, that the Pharisees were predominantly concerned with matters relating to table fellowship in private homes; their arena of interest had shifted from the Sanhedrin to the sanctification of the household.[92]

There are reasons to dispute this interpretation of the Pharisees as apolitical, however. Israeli historian Gedalyahu Alon admits that we should not expect "unity of *outlook and action* among the Pharisees as a whole" relative to political questions; he contends, nevertheless, that the Pharisees were in general "realistic nationalists." The assumption that they were a purely religious movement is disproved, he argues, by the evidence that "the *halakah* of the Pharisees is directed to the *welfare and improvement of society.*" He rejects Neusner's argument that the Pharisees were by the first century no longer involved *as a party* in the political life of the nation, emphasizing instead "the instructive fact, not stressed by scholars, that throughout the period from the time of the Hasmoneans to the destruction of the Temple, the Pharisees sat together with the Sadducees in the Sanhedrin, and even jointly formed a government at the beginning of the war against the Romans."[93]

Anthony Saldarini similarly disputes Neusner's view that the Pharisees were no longer a political party in the Roman period. To the contrary, he observes, both Josephus and the rabbinic traditions "agree that the Pharisees were a political, religious group which sought power and influence in Palestinian Judaism" . . . "The admittedly sparse and indirect first century evidence and the sociological probabilities both suggest that the Pharisees still desired influence and power but attained less of it in the first century than in Hasmonean and even Herodian times."[94] Their political influence had diminished, not because they had decided to pursue a program of private holiness, but because they had been violently suppressed by the Hasmonean Alexander Janneus (who on one occasion crucified more than eight hundred opponents and expelled eight thousand others from Judea) and then frozen out of their traditional channels of political influence when the Romans created an artificial Judean aristocracy in the time of Herod.[95]

The Pharisees consequently found themselves in a precarious position. As Horsley writes,

> The combination of a number of the features of this new arrangement in the imperial situation of the Temple-state as a client kingship would have left the Pharisees and other scribe-scholars in an acute dilemma. In order to continue to have any role in society, they had to acquiesce in the new arrangement. They were surely realistic enough to understand actual power relations . . . yet their actual power and influence were drastically diminished—by an illegitimate client king! Hence . . . many of them would have been sitting uneasy in an ambiguous situation, eager to find an opportunity to change it.[96]

The ambiguity of the Pharisees' position was reflected in a range of opinions regarding the acceptability of Roman rule. In the desperate years of the revolt itself, Alon observes, the Pharisaic camp embraced "a movement of zealots on the one hand, and, on the other, a policy of despair that sought to withdraw from the idea of a Jewish state and to cleave to the recognition of the advantage and necessity of Roman rule in Judea.[97] Nevertheless "the main path followed by the majority of the Pharisees remained unchanged" . . . "They were opposed to Roman rule and longed for political freedom and democratic government, while acknowledging that a realistic appraisal of the circumstances must decide the choice of the opportune moment for action and determine the scope of its purpose."[98]

In fact the apparently opposite extremes within the Pharisaic camp were consistent with the ideological premises of this "main path." That is, *the Pharisees' "political realism" corresponded to a biblical, more specifically a prophetic-apocalyptic rationale:* the teaching that historical events on earth—the rise and fall of kingdoms and empires—reflected the outworking of a heavenly timetable.

According to Josephus, the Pharisees "attribute all that happens to destiny and to God; and they hold that the working of justice or its opposite lies for the most part with mortals, but in every event destiny assists" (*War* 2:162–163). "Contending that all events are brought about through destiny, but not meaning to deny human initiative in contriving them, they declare that through God a combination occurs, so that what humans have contrived with virtue or wickedness has a place in the very council chamber of destiny" (*Antiquities* 18:3).

The term Josephus uses here, "destiny" (*heimarmenē*), was a common Hellenistic term. The substance of the idea, however, is authentically Jewish: It reflects apocalyptic belief as clearly as does the doctrine of reward or punishment in the afterlife that immediately follows in each passage. Any biblically literate Greek-speaking Jew would have recognized the "council chamber of destiny" (*boulestērion tēs heimarmenēs*) as nothing other than the throne room of God where the prophets and apocalyptic visionaries of Israel were permitted to learn the mysteries of what is to come (1 Kings 22:19–23; Isa. 6:1–13; Ezek. 1:1–2:7; Dan. 7:9–10, 24–27). The *heimarmenē* of which Josephus speaks is the apocalyptic doctrine that God, the supreme ruler of the universe, has given sovereign power over the earth to successive empires, according to a foreordained timetable.[99]

This "religious conception of the origin of sovereignty" (Gabriele Boccaccini) became "the mystery" to be revealed in heavenly visions in the book of Daniel.[100] In the seer's prayer, it is the God of heaven "to whom belong wisdom and power; who changes seasons and times; who deposes kings and seats kings; who gives wisdom to the wise and knowledge to the discerning" (2:20–21). This is the interpretation of dreams revealed to kings: "To you [i.e., Nebuchadnezzar] the Lord of heaven has given the rule and the kingdom and the power and the honor and the glory" (2:36 Septuagint).

The apocalypses are often interpreted as "consolation literature," and to be sure the oppressed may find some consolation in knowing that the foreign regime will not last forever. The "eternal kingdom" to be established at the end of history (2:44) will be a kingdom of "the saints of the Most High" (7:13–14, 18). But the book of Daniel draws attention, not to the blissful details of that future kingdom, but to the mystery of God's sovereignty over the oppressor now: "The Most High has authority over all that is in the heaven and upon the earth; he gives the kingdom to whom he wills and may appoint over it even the lowliest of mortals" (4:17). The lesson is repeated before various kings (4:25, 34–35; 5:18–21; 6:25–28) but is really directed to "the many" in Israel who are invited to receive the teaching of "the wise" (12:3, 10). For this audience, suffering the ravages of the foreign king, "what remains to be understood is not so much why God in freedom will grant sovereignty to a Gentile king, but why God will permit a power subject to God to 'afflict' God's people and even show itself rebellious to God without immediately being punished."[101]

The apocalyptist's answer is a doctrine of divinely preordained times. To the psalmist's agonized question, "How long, O Lord," the apocalyptist responds with a calculation: "For just this long." Indeed, as J. Louis Martyn notes, "the matter of discerning the time lies at the very heart of apocalyptic."[102] The "seventy years" of Jerusalem's devastation (Jer. 25:11–12) are, the angel Gabriel reveals to Daniel, rather "seventy weeks of years." After that interval "rebellion will be stopped, sin brought to an end, iniquity expiated, everlasting right ushered in, vision and prophecy ratified, and the Most Holy Place anointed" (Dan.

9:24). Until that time, however, "it is necessary to wait," and pray for God's mercy (Dan. 9:18–19). Similarly the Jesus of the Gospel of Luke reveals that Jerusalem must suffer devastation and "be trampled on by the Gentiles until the times of the Gentiles are fulfilled" (Luke 21:24); in the meantime, one watches and prays (Luke 21:19, 34–36). The seer of 4 Ezra is assured that the divine schedule can no more be arrested than a woman's labor contractions can be postponed—but neither can the schedule be accelerated (4:33–43); "the creation cannot make more haste than the Creator" (5:44).

This apocalyptic doctrine of times functions to promote a piety of endurance, possibly of submission, for those suffering oppression. Both Daniel 11 and the apocalyptic prophecies in the Synoptic Gospels provide a "list of disappointed eschatological hopes," as the violent try to bring in the reign of God. God's people, however, must "stand firm," "remain," "endure to the end" (Dan. 11:32; 4 Ezra 6:25; Mark 13:13). As Jürgen H. C. Lebram points out in a study of "the piety of the apocalyptists," the book of Daniel promotes in its readers

> an aversion towards eschatological groups which allow themselves to be provoked into revolutionary action in the hope of a swift fulfillment of prophetic utterances . . . [and] a refusal to participate in revolutionary riots, together with the passive endurance of the tribulations produced by the time of profanity. These are expressions of a behavior which submits itself to the social, as well as to the historical, events, and does not propose to interrupt them by force. . . . On the whole the pious man is required to live in accordance with the cosmic order . . . [which requires] passive endurance of evil in the world. . . . The most dangerous sin is obviously pride which does not know its own limits.[103]

In Josephus's writings, the apocalyptic doctrine of God's sovereignty over human affairs points unambiguously to the necessity of submission to Rome. Josephus knew that the revolutionaries were inspired by eschatological visions[104] and that Jerusalem was visited by portents and signs that he clearly regarded as real (*War* 6:288–315). Indeed, he speaks as a prophet himself, as an interpreter of heavenly mysteries, as he explains the triumph of Rome to his readers. He insists that although the masses had "disregarded the plain warnings of God," that is, that the Zealots' path led to destruction, the "wise" could recognize in these signs "the manifest care of God for mortals" (*War* 6:310; Philo finds the same lesson in history, *Embassy* 3). The revolt itself was caused by the Jews' fatal misreading of prophecy (6:312–313):

> What more than all else incited [the people] to the war was an ambiguous oracle, likewise found in their sacred scriptures, to the effect that at that time one from their country would become ruler of the world. This they understood to mean someone of their own race, and many of their wise

men went astray in their interpretation of it. The oracle, however, in reality signified the sovereignty of Vespasian, who was proclaimed Emperor on Jewish soil.

This purported interpretation of prophecy is of course a case of perfect hindsight on Josephus's part. Further, his role in Rome's postwar propaganda campaign to pacify the Diaspora could not be more evident than in this passage. In Morton Smith's words, we see in the *War* Josephus's effort "to demonstrate that the rebels had brought their ruin upon themselves by their own wickedness, that the Romans were not hostile to Judaism, but had acted in Palestine regretfully, as agents of divine vengeance, and that therefore submission to Roman rule was justified by religion as well as common sense."[105]

Such a lesson clearly served Rome's interests. But that does not diminish the power of the apocalyptic tradition to explain the outcome of the war to the personal satisfaction of possible Jewish readers. Indeed, the value of the work as propaganda would require that Josephus's use of the apocalyptic tradition be persuasive for at least some segment of Diaspora Judaism—and of Josephus himself.

We observe the role apocalyptic belief could play for individual Jews in a passage from the *War,* in which Josephus narrates his own capture by the Romans after the siege of Jotapata, which had been under his command. Having snuck out of the city ("by some divine providence") and hidden in a cave with other well-supplied refugees from the city's aristocracy, Josephus was discovered. The Roman general sent a Jewish comrade to coax Josephus out of the cave; meanwhile soldiers prepared to smoke out the cave, or to storm it, if that attempt at persuasion failed. At this point, Josephus narrates, he recalled

> those dreams by night in which God had predicted what was to come upon the Jews, and the future of the Roman rulers as well. An interpreter of dreams, capable of discovering the meaning of ambiguous divine oracles, a priest and the son of priests, I knew the prophecies in the sacred books. Just then I was inspired to understand their meaning; and recalling the dreadful images of my own recent dreams, I prayed silently to God: "Since it pleases you, who created the Jewish nation, to destroy your own work; since fortune has passed over to the Romans, and since you have chosen me to declare what is to come, I gladly surrender to the Romans, choosing life. But I take you as my witness that I go forth not as a traitor, but as your servant." (*War* 3:336–408)

Once presented before Vespasian, Josephus announces the "prophecy" that the Roman general will become a king.

Steve Mason believes the biblical prophecy foremost in Josephus's mind as he wrestled with his conscience in the cave outside Jotapata was the prophecy of four kingdoms in Daniel 2, which Josephus elsewhere cites as pointing to the final supremacy of Rome.[106]

Josephus's narrative is horribly self-serving, of course, not least when he explains how he tricked his fellow refugees into a suicide pact that ("by divine providence") left him and a companion the only survivors. But we should not doubt the power of the apocalypse to explain—that is, to mystify into an acceptably pious form—the brutal facts of empire.

No less honorable a sage than Yohanan ben Zakkai, who obtained Rome's permission to found the rabbinic academy at Yavneh, shared Josephus's perception of portents within the besieged city of Jerusalem and reached a similar conclusion regarding the will of God. Spirited out of the doomed city in a coffin and presented (as was Josephus before him) before the Roman general Vespasian, Yohanan also hailed him as a king, explaining, "This has been handed down to us, that the Temple will not be surrendered to a commoner, but to a king; as it is said [Isa. 10:34], 'And he shall cut down the thickets of the forest with iron, and Lebanon shall fall by a mighty one.' "[107]

Whether or not Yohanan's opposition to the war or his accommodation to Rome "continued the earlier policies of Pharisaism" (Jacob Neusner), his reasoning is informed by at least one accepted path within Pharisaism.[108] As offensive as Josephus's personal conduct may be, he nonetheless can appeal to the same apocalyptic tradition. It is inaccurate, therefore, to describe the Pharisees unequivocally as "the party of resistance against Rome" (Hyam Maccoby).[109] Whatever the proportions of the revolutionary and accommodationist factions within Pharisaism, we should expect that both groups could have taken their bearings not only from a "realistic" appraisal of their political situation vis-à-vis Rome, but from the apocalyptic knowledge that, however temporarily, for now "all things have been subjected to the Romans" by God (*War* 2:361).

Given the biblical pedigree for such a view, we should be less surprised to find Pharisees who believed this way than to find Jews who did not. From this perspective, the outright denial by the Fourth Philosophy that God could rule Israel "through" a foreign regime was both politically radical and a challenge to "ancestral tradition."[110]

SACRED VIOLENCE AND PAUL'S CONVERSION

Josephus is perhaps the best evidence that the apocalyptic doctrine of world sovereignty replicates the logic of sacred violence described by René Girard (see chapter 4). In the speech Josephus reports having made to the Jews on the ramparts of Jerusalem from the battle lines of his Roman captors, the brutal coercion of a military siege in which refugees were crucified to intimidate the city has been mystified into a law of divine necessity. Even beasts, Josephus protested, recognized as "supreme law" the rule of naked force: "Yield to the stronger." "Rule belongs to those with the more powerful weapons" (*War* 5:368).

But he was not speaking to beasts, and so a more refined argument had to be offered: "To scorn meaner masters might, indeed, be legitimate, but not those to whom the universe was subject. For what was there that had escaped the Romans, save maybe some spot useless through heat or cold? Fortune, indeed, had from all quarters passed over to them, and God who went the round of the nations, bringing to each in turn the rod of empire, now rested over Italy" (*War* 5:366–367). The rebels were therefore "warring not against the Romans only, but also against God" (5:378). Of course, it was the Romans who would benefit if the theological argument was persuasive.

To identify the sovereignty of God with the superior power to kill was hardly the discovery of the apocalyptists. It was a far more ancient proclivity of our species, and a more enduring one, familiar enough to our ears today ("By the grace of God we won the Cold War"—George Bush). But the apocalypses were the media through which the doctrine of sacred violence infected first-century Judea. "The Most High God gave Nebuchadnezzar your father kingship and greatness and glory and majesty," the prophet Daniel declared to Belshazzar: "he killed whom he wished, and kept alive whom he wished; he raised up whom he wished and put down whom he wished" (Dan. 5:18–19). No less had God authorized the savagery of Antiochus Epiphanes against Jerusalem in the author's day; no less did Pompey's subjugation of the city in the time of the Psalms of Solomon reflect God's punishment; no less did the city's destruction at the hands of Vespasian and Titus manifest God's judgment on an unruly or even wicked people, in the eyes of Jews as diverse as Josephus, Yohanan ben Zakkai, the Evangelist Matthew, and the author of 4 Ezra.[111]

The belief that God has given absolute power into the hands of the conqueror is particularly appealing to the survivors, who must explain to themselves why others have suffered and died around them. The psychological dimension of this apocalyptic doctrine is especially evident in 4 Ezra, where the seer must be taught to share God's own indifference to the fate of those who died in the catastrophe of 70 C.E.: "I will rejoice over the few who shall be saved, because it is they who have made my glory to prevail now, and through them my name has now been honored. And I will not grieve over the multitude of those who perish; for it is they who are now like a mist, and are similar to a flame and smoke—they are set on fire and burn hotly, and are extinguished" (7:60–61).

The seer protests: God's justice is too harsh! But he is rebuked: "The Most High made this world for the sake of the many, but the world to come for the sake of few. . . . Therefore do not ask any more questions about the multitude of those who perish"—they have deserved their fate (8:1, 46–62).

The apocalyptic doctrine even allows one to identify with the aggressor: Josephus may really have convinced himself that Titus felt profound sympathy for the five hundred or so refugees he crucified daily outside the walls of Jerusalem (*War* 5:450).

For the apocalyptists, the balance of forces arrayed against each other on earth reflected decisions made in heaven and revealed as "mysteries" to the elect. For "realistic" Jews, among them many (though by no means all) of the Pharisees, the apocalypses supplied the rationale for "constructive engagement" with Rome. As we have seen, the Fourth Philosophy broke with "ancestral tradition" by denying this logic outright. The violence of Rome was not the wrath of God; it was only the violence of Rome and, as such, a direct affront to God's sovereignty. The righteous had no choice but to honor God by defying the instruments of torture and death.

We do not know what Paul thought of the Fourth Philosophy, although since he was present in Judea during the intifada against Pilate, he cannot have been unaware of its rationale. We must suppose that as a Jew, as an apocalyptist, and as a Pharisee, he assumed that God's triumph over the Romans was inevitable, however indeterminate that day might be. Paul must have heard, and even joined in debates over, matters of strategy and timing, of resistance and accommodation.

We do know what Paul thought of the group that proclaimed the crucified Jesus as the Messiah of Israel. Once we recognize the historical context of his persecuting activity, we can understand his "conversion" as well. If a Pharisee like Saul of Tarsus had looked upon Roman power with the eyes of the apocalyptists, he might well have concluded that God had given the sovereignty of the earth to Rome, "for a time." For that time, he might have concluded, resistance to Rome—however much he sympathized with its motives—was not only futile but impious. After all, "the tradition of the fathers," as Josephus refers to the biblical legacy, taught that the duty of the righteous was to wait in holiness and to pray for God's deliverance.

We do not have to assume that Saul the Pharisee looked on Jesus' crucifixion as the death of a condemned criminal. Josephus apparently did not (*Antiquities* 18:63–64);[112] nor is it apparent that he thought all the refugees crucified by Titus deserved their fate. It is conceivable (though there is no way to know one way or the other) that, as a Pharisee, he might even have regarded Jesus' death as the regrettable execution of an innocent man (as did Gamaliel and Nicodemus according to the Gospels and Acts). If, as some scholars suggest, he was familiar with ideas expressed in 4 Maccabees or the *Liber antiquitatum biblicarum,* he might even have attributed atoning significance to that death as the death of one of Israel's martyrs, contributing in some incremental way to the eventual redemption of the people from their Roman overlords.[113]

None of this, of course, would have required him to accept the outrageous claims of the messianists. Paul heard in the proclamation of the crucified messiah an apocalyptic announcement *and thus a direct challenge to Rome.* If one crucified by Rome had been vindicated by God—vindicated *by being raised from the dead already*—then the "time given to Rome" was at an end, the time of "the kingdom of the saints of the Most High" was at hand. The proclamation of the crucified was a declaration that the changing of the ages was at hand.

The logic of that message would have been immediately clear. But Paul disagreed with its content, for reasons apparent enough to anyone with eyes to see: Pilate's vicious policies continued undisturbed, the number of his victims increasing daily. "Righteousness was not flowing down like waters; men continued to beat plowshares into swords; the dead had not been raised; the Land was still captive" (Paula Fredriksen).[114] It was obvious that the time given by heaven to Rome continued.

So the messianists were not only wrong about what time it was; they were dangerously wrong. By prematurely proclaiming the change of the ages, especially if they did so with the defiant courage (*parrhēsia*) that Luke attributes to them in Acts, they threatened to provoke further violence from the Romans, thus aggravating Israel's misery in this, the period of the messianic throes. For the sake of all who would suffer in the inevitable Roman reaction, for the sake indeed of all Israel, the messianists must be silenced.

We need not picture Paul the persecutor as a vindictive, cruel man. He may have been simply a "realist" striving to take his moral responsibility seriously, convinced, to use Reinhold Niebuhr's words, that "the realities of sin make coercion and resistance a requirement of justice." The persecution of the messianists was "terrible, however necessary"; no doubt Paul took "no satisfaction in the human misery" he caused. We may imagine him acting in profound awareness of the "religious fact" that Niebuhr would later articulate in his name, that "there is no escape from guilt in history," and thus he may have been willing to "cause innocent people to suffer with the guilty," of course with due regret, "without rancor or self-righteousness."[115]

We must be clear: I am not suggesting that all, or even most, Pharisees would have shared Paul's antagonism to the messianic movement as a matter of principle. Some Pharisees were quite sympathetic to revolutionary or anti-Roman impulses among the people. The apostle himself declares, albeit retrospectively, that he "surpassed my peers among my people, so extremely zealous was I for the ancestral traditions" (Gal. 1:14). Nevertheless, his persecution of the early church was intelligible on the basis of apocalyptic belief about the sovereignty of Rome, the sort of belief Josephus attributes to the Pharisees in general.

On the other hand, it would be illegitimate to distance Paul's violence from the normative Jewish tradition by attributing it to his own psychological idiosyncracies. However excruciatingly personal his motives, they were not private. All of Judea felt the terrible ambivalence toward Roman rule that found expression for some in apocalyptic belief; only the intensity and direction of Paul's response was extraordinary.

My suggestion allows us to understand one Pharisee's persecution of the churches without having to assume some legal offense on their part or some idiosyncratic perspective on Jesus' crucifixion on his part. Further, this suggestion explains how an apocalyptic perspective informed Paul's motives as a persecutor. Indeed, if Alan Segal is correct in supposing that before his conversion Paul already experienced mystical visions of heaven, he might have interpreted such experiences as powerful, direct confirmations that God continued to reign as sovereign in heaven, at the same time that Rome enjoyed political sovereignty on earth. In this way his mystical experience might even have reinforced his motives for persecuting the messianists, although at the cost of increasing ambivalence toward Rome. It would be appropriate to speak here of increasing "cognitive dissonance," provided we remember that this tension in Paul would have mirrored the tension felt by many Jews living under Roman occupation, a tension projected by the apocalypses themselves.[116]

We can also understand why this Pharisee's visionary experience generated the reversal in conduct we are accustomed to calling his "conversion." Predisposed by the apocalyptic-mystical tradition to accept and to experience visions of the heavenly court from which Rome had been granted its power, Paul would also have been taught by the apocalypses that the righteous martyred by Rome would "at the last day" be raised from the dead (compare John 11:24). We have only to suppose that this Pharisee experienced a vision of the martyr Jesus in heaven, a vision for which the Jewish apocalypses themselves provided the conceptual preparation. He might, even then, have continued his persecution of those who endangered their brothers and sisters by agitating in Jesus' name, but only until the point when such visions made clear to him an apocalyptic fact: that God had raised Jesus from the dead. He was already intimately familiar with that claim and may have realized that nothing in the apocalyptic tradition made the claim impossible.

The consequences of such a vision for an apocalyptic mystic like Paul would have followed an apocalyptic logic. That is, the vision would have confirmed to him that what the apocalypses promised God would do someday, God had in fact begun to do now. His rationale for persecution would have begun to disintegrate immediately. The link between apocalyptic belief and sacred violence that Judas of Galilee had earlier broken through ardent courage had been broken for this Pharisee through a mystical vision. Both men thought as apocalyptic Jews, however.

Setting Paul's "conversion" against this background immediately reveals that the cross of Jesus indeed "showed Paul that he had been the servant of sacred violence" (Robert G. Hamerton-Kelly); "the revelation of the significance of the Cross uncovered the sacred violence in the institutions of this world," specifically the religio-political institutions Paul had served as a persecutor.[117] But against Hamerton-Kelly, it must be insisted that this was not a "violence" inherent within Judaism as a religion, or within the Torah as such (as Hamerton-Kelly himself occasionally recognizes).[118] The violence Paul came to see in the cross was not primarily a "crime of ethnic violence"; it was *not* the supposed "violence" of "excluding Gentiles" from table fellowship or sabbath observance; nor was it the supposed "Jewish point of view" that had killed Jesus as "a transgressor of the Law."[119] Rather, *in the cross Paul saw his own willingness to "sacrifice" Jesus, and a certain number of other Jews who insisted on provocative action in his name, to the violence of Rome, in order that the whole nation be "saved" from that violence.* This was the violence of a scapegoating theology, practiced by some in Judea (not all!), that tolerated iron nails and swords and whips, though "only for a time": a theology "which deals with violence by means of violence, purchasing order by means of victims" (Robert Hamerton-Kelly)[120] depending upon a calculus of acceptable, even necessary deaths.[121]

The crucifixion of Jesus alone did not reveal this to Paul. To the contrary, he was ready enough to persecute those who proclaimed the crucified as Messiah, because he believed that in the dark interval in which God still drew back from intervening in affairs on earth,[122] the terrible logic of violence had to prevail. Trapped within the realm of Death, he obeyed its law of bloody exchange, accepting this as the very Law of God. Had he known the later Christian Lenten practice of walking the Stations of the Cross, he might have felt at home in the final Station's depiction of righteous men and women laying Jesus' cold and bloodied body within the tomb, obeying God by honoring the dead even within the confines of Death's own empire.

But if God had raised Jesus from the dead, then a wholly different logic, the Law of Life, had invaded the realm of Death with an unconquerable power. A different "realism" now overtook Paul's thought. His subsequent letters clearly show that he understood Jesus' resurrection, not as an isolated event, but as the "first fruits of those who have died" (1 Cor. 15:20). Therefore he also knew "what time it is," the time to "wake from sleep" (Rom. 13:11); that "the appointed time has grown short," that "the present scheme of this world is passing away" (1 Cor. 7:29, 31). From here Paul was not far from the belief of the messianists themselves, that the crucifixion and resurrection of the righteous man Jesus was the fate of God's Messiah; and therefore that God had chosen to recapitulate Israel's exile and oppression in the torn flesh of its Messiah, and thus to bring Israel to its climactic redemption.[123]

If God had raised to life a body pierced by Roman iron—a victim executed as an enemy of Roman peace, and thus submitting to his people's tormented history—then the calculus of sacred violence that had made such an execution appear a terrible necessity, the calculus that had motivated Paul's persecution of the church, was destroyed forever. So Paul would later sing:

> "Death is swallowed up in victory."
> Death, where is your victory?
> Death, where is your sting?
> (1 Cor. 15:54–55)

In Paul's understanding, the dread balance of terror upon which every empire is founded had been broken. For Judas of Galilee, courageous faith in God alone had neutralized the fear of death. But for Paul, perhaps more of a "realist" than Judas, the same revolution in his thinking could have arisen only from the dramatic manifestation in tortured human flesh of God's power to raise the dead.

At just the point where we expect Paul's vision to have had the most life-changing significance, Paul's letters prove most reticent. As Beker observes, "Paul's conversion experience is not the theme of his theology." In the polemical context of Galatians, he recounts only that over the next three years after the "revelation" of Christ he "went away into Arabia, then returned to Damascus" (1:17); and except for a visit to Jerusalem, he tells us nothing about the following fourteen years except that he was "proclaiming the faith" in "the regions of Syria and Cilicia" (1:21–24)! It is clear enough nevertheless that (a) Paul stopped persecuting the churches and that (b) he joined himself to these congregations instead. He must have embraced their proclamation that Israel's destiny was signaled in the destiny of Jesus the Messiah.

The force of his conversion is evident in Paul's willingness now to "live under a constant threat, facing death daily" (1 Cor. 15:30–31). During these years, Acts portrays Paul suffering the same sort of persecution he had once inflicted (13:45, 50–51; 14:1–7, 19–20), a portrayal compatible with Paul's own testimony (1 Cor. 4:9–13; 2 Cor. 11:23–33). In the same way, the power of death was broken for all in whom "the Spirit of the one who raised Jesus from the dead lives" (Rom. 8:11), for the Spirit you received is not the spirit of slavery [*douleia*], bringing fear into your lives again; it is the spirit of adoption. . . . I regard our sufferings of this present age not worth comparing with the glory about to be revealed to us. . . . What then are we to say about these things? If God is for us, who opposes us? . . . Who accuses God's elect? It is God who vindicates us. Who condemns us? It is Christ Jesus who died, yes who was raised; who is at the right hand of God, interceding for us. Who separates us from the love of Christ? Can affliction, distress, persecution, famine, nakedness, threat, the sword? As it is written [in the cry of Israel's pious martyrs in the Psalms]: "For your sake we are being killed all day long; we are accounted as sheep to be slaughtered." No: in all these things we are more than conquerors through the one who loved us. For I am convinced that neither death, nor life, nor angels, nor rulers, nor things present, nor things to come, nor powers, nor height, nor depth, nor anything else in all creation, will be able to separate us from the love of God in Christ Jesus our Lord. (Rom. 8:15, 18, 31–39)

For Judas of Galilee, such arguments had informed a rationale for an intifada against Rome. For Paul, writing five decades later, these arguments were meant to encourage resistance within Rome itself to the empire's contempt of Israel, a contempt that already threatened to infect the congregations of gentile Christians as well. Against all apparent evidence in Judea, where the weight of Roman cruelty had crushed the voices of moderation among the people, and in the capital itself, where the Jewish refugees returning after Claudius's expulsion were conspicuous for their vulnerability (*astheneia*, the "weakness" of Romans 14–15), Paul insisted on the basis of an apocalyptic "mystery" that God would remember the ancient covenantal promises and redeem Israel (Rom. 11:25–26).

But Paul now knew that God would not act through the calculus of strength over weakness, the balance of power between armies and nations. God would act through the sheer life-giving power that had raised Jesus from the dead (11:15). Paul defied the logic that set peoples in a fatal competition with each other. Not even the threat of death could tear the Gentile away from the love of "the God who raised Jesus from the dead" (Romans 8); not even the threatening collapse of Judea could prevent the salvation of Israel by the same God (Romans 9–11). The logic of sacred violence had been vanquished by a more powerful Law, the "Law of Life" given by God the Giver of Life. For Paul, "salvation always means resurrection from the dead. . . . Paul basically defines God, on the model of a Jewish prayer, as the God who raises the dead and never does anything alien to that" (Ernst Käsemann).[124]

We see, then, that the resurrection of Jesus confirmed God's integrity to the covenant with Israel. Far from representing a lapse into Jewish "chauvinism," Paul's "inability to cut the links clearly between the old and the new religion," a "case of nostalgia overwhelming his judgment"

(Robert G. Hamerton-Kelly),[125] Paul's ringing affirmation of Israel's future is an inclusive vision that shatters the incipient scapegoating theology and practice of the gentile church. False "boasting" on the part of gentile Christianity (Romans 11), and the abuse of Jewish sensibilities at the common table, which constitutes the "scapegoating" of the Jews (Rom. 14:1–15:14),[126] must be overcome so that the Gentiles can fulfill their function in God's purpose, which is nothing less than the salvation of Israel.

THE APOCALYPTIC CONTOURS OF PAUL'S APOSTOLATE

In the early 30s, Paul ceased to persecute the messianists in Roman-occupied Judea and Roman Syria. From then on, he embraced their vision of the future held open by the Messiah's resurrection. In so doing, he did not turn his back on his people's hopes; rather, he discovered another route, God's route as he came to believe, to the fulfillment of those hopes. *From beginning to end, Paul's apostolate among the Gentiles was oriented toward the salvation of Israel.*

This is a crucial point. Paul's Law-free mission among the Gentiles was not an apostasy from Israel.[127] He simply shared with the messianic community he joined the vision that Isaiah's prophecy of the last days, in which Gentiles would look to Israel and be converted morally, was being fulfilled in their midst. One important theme in Romans, a letter written to a congregation in which sympathy with oppressed Israel had become a theological and social liability, is that the gospel of God's justice is—*must be*—"for the Jew first, and also for the Greek" (Rom. 1:16).[128] Correspondingly, the Spirit that pants in labor to bring forth the redemption of the whole creation (Rom. 8:22–23) convulses Paul in personal agony for the salvation of his people, the Jews (Rom. 9:1–5). The climax of this section of Romans—in the opinion of many scholars, the climax of the whole letter—is Paul's apocalyptic pronouncement that it is through the salvation of the Gentiles that God will save "all Israel" (Rom. 11:25–36).[129]

In the mid-40s, Paul declared before the Jerusalem apostles that he had already resolved to "remember the poor" in his mission among the Gentiles (Gal. 2:10). This may have meant a commitment from the beginning of his apostolate to the poor among the Jerusalem congregation;[130] it clearly meant this, at least, in the early 50s, as he wrote letters to congregations in Achaia and Italy (1 Cor. 16:1–4; 2 Cor. 8–9; Rom. 15:26–28).[131]

The collection for Jerusalem was more than a financial contribution, however, and Paul did more than organize a relief fund.[132] The congregations he established in Roman provinces represented the "nations" of the earth, so that Paul could claim to have "secured the obedience of the nations [*ta ethnē*] . . . from Jerusalem as far round as Illyricum" (Rom. 15:18–19). In his frenetic activity in Asia, Macedonia, Achaia, and Italy he intended to organize a caravan of the "firstfruits" of the nations, holy gentile men and women marching into Jerusalem in fulfillment of the prophetic scenario of the last days (Isa. 2:2–4, 12:3, 25:6–8, 60:3, 66:18; Jer. 16:19; Mic. 4:1–3; Zech. 8:20–23). Paul understands this work as an act of worship. He is "a sacred minister [*leitourgōn*] of Christ Jesus to the Gentiles, doing priestly service [*hierourgōn*] for the gospel of God, so that the offering [*prosphora*] of the Gentiles may be acceptable, sanctified by the Holy Spirit" (Rom. 15:14–16). He thus fulfills Isaiah's prophecy that at the last days the "gifts of the Gentiles" will be brought to Israel (Isa. 66:18–20).[133]

Even if Johannes Munck has gone too far in declaring that Paul believes himself to be "the one on whom the arrival of the Messianic age depends,"[134] he has shown that the apostle conceives his work in the broadest terms: "The apostle's mission to the Gentiles is itself the way in which God is intervening for Israel's salvation."[135] Paul asks the Christians in Rome to pray for his presentation of sanctified Gentiles, and their gifts of money, in Jerusalem—he anticipates opposition from the "faithless in Judea" (Rom. 15:25–32). He intends the collection, that is, as the concrete expression of the vision he articulates earlier in the letter. He has undertaken his apostolate to the Gentiles so as to make Israel jealous (Rom. 11:13–14). This eschatological scenario is not, Paul insists, his own invention. He reveals to the Romans an apocalyptic mystery (11:25), the otherwise inscrutable will of God (11:33–35), that it is precisely through the ingathering of "the full number of the nations" that God intends to save "all Israel" (11:25–26).

Clearly, then, Paul conceives his apostolate to the Gentiles as an indirect way of "evangelizing" the Jews, and particularly his compatriots in Judea. (We must understand that word, which has gained unfortunate connotations in Christian parlance, in the way Paul intends it: He announces the good news of God's decisive action on Israel's behalf.)[136]

Paul has not dissolved Israel's covenant in a sea of theological universalism.[137] It is more accurate to say that Paul shares with Jewish covenantal theology the assumption that God intends Israel to fulfill the role of an obedient humanity and, thereby, God's purposes for all creation; for the ultimate horizon of the covenant is all humanity. If the Messiah recapitulates the history of Israel's covenant, he thereby also brings the history of creation itself to a climax.[138]

Paul does understand the covenant's fulfillment in a paradoxical way, a nonnationalistic way, however, just because his vision is shaped by the resurrection of Jesus. Despite his fervent affirmations of God's continuing purpose toward Israel, he says nothing explicit about the Roman shadow-regime in Judea, perhaps because he now considers it irrelevant.

The one possible exception to this generalization is Rom. 9:30–10:4, where Paul describes "Israel's misstep" (Lloyd Gaston); perhaps here he has the Judean regime specifically in view. Paul writes,

> What shall we say then? That Gentiles who did not pursue justice came upon justice, the justice that is a matter of trust; but that Israel, ardently pursuing a law of justice, did not lay a finger on that law. Why? Because not from trust, but from works. They stumbled over a stone that makes people stumble, as it is written: "I will lay in Zion a stone of stumbling," "a rock that will make them fall," and "the one who trusts in it [en autō] will not be put to shame." Brothers, my heart's desire and prayer to God is their salvation. For I testify to their zeal for God, but it is not an informed zeal: for being ignorant of God's justice, but being zealous for their own, they did not submit to the justice of God.

As Romans 9–11 has been rediscovered in the post-Holocaust context, these verses have attracted considerable attention.[139] Interpreters are now generally agreed that Paul does not mean to describe the attitude of works-righteousness that Luther opposed in the sixteenth century. It is increasingly held instead that here Paul is opposing an exclusivistic attitude in Israel that wants to hold onto "God's justice" as a privilege "for Jews and Jews only" (N. T. Wright).[140] The "Jewish failure" on this view is a refusal to recognize the inclusivity that Paul proclaims as his gospel: "The righteousness of God for Gentiles, which is the goal of the Torah, has now been manifested, and it is the failure of Israel to acknowledge this which is what Paul holds against them" (Lloyd Gaston).[141] This interpretation is consistent with the "new perspective on Paul," which identifies his quarrel with Judaism as a critique of a narrowly ethnocentric or ritualistic exclusivism.

Significantly, however, that is not what Paul goes on to criticize. (In fact references to Gentiles, or to preaching to Gentiles, do not occur in 10:1–21). Paul declares that "Christ is the end of the Torah" (10:4), but that phrase is as ambiguous in Greek as it is in English: Does "end" here mean the termination of the Torah, or the goal toward which it leads? The argument that follows (Rom. 10:5–8), juxtaposing different scriptural texts in good midrashic fashion, makes the meaning clear.[142] Christ is the *goal* of Torah, for Paul shows through the juxtaposition of two passages from the Torah (Lev. 18:5; Deut. 30:12) that fulfilling what the Torah requires is a matter of believing in the messiah. It is wrong to seek to "bring the messiah down" (from heaven) or to "bring the messiah up from the abyss," that is, from the dead, simply because God has already sent the messiah, Jesus, as Lord, and has raised him from the dead: believing this brings salvation (Rom. 10:9–13).

Israel's pursuit of "their own justice" means, quite simply, pursuing God's justice, the vindication of God's purposes for Israel, in ignorance of the Messiah's appearance. The undertaking is represented as absurd;[143] but Paul does not say that Israel is wrong to expect God's vindication of the covenantal promises, or that Israel has pursued this fulfillment for themselves alone. He says that they have pursued the right goal, using the right tool, the Torah, but without recognizing that goal when they came across it—or in Paul's words, when they fell over it. Unable to recognize the Messiah (understandably, as we have seen!), they are in effect pursuing a phantasm of God's justice instead.

But perhaps we can say more about "Israel's misstep" in this passage. Paul begins his quotation from Deuteronomy 30 with a phrase that actually comes from Deuteronomy 9, "Do not say in your hearts . . . " The conflation of passages may simply be an accident of memory, for in Deuteronomy 30 Moses also warns Israel against a false attitude; but the connection may be more profound.[144] In each passage Israel is warned against assuming a particular attitude once they arrive in the promised land. The attitude prohibited in Deuteronomy 30 is despair; the attitude prohibited in Deuteronomy 9, on the other hand, is the presumption that "it is because of my righteousness that the Lord has brought me in to possess this land." Significantly the focus in Deuteronomy is not the individual's existential standing before God, but the people's fate in the land. The verbal resonances between Deuteronomy 9 and Romans 10 ("my righteousness," "their own righteousness") suggests that Paul perceives a "failure" on Israel's part similar to that envisioned in Deuteronomy 9. The people have mistakenly sought to achieve their well-being in the land through their own efforts rather than accepting God's initiative.

Given the political dimension of Paul's own "conversion," it is reasonable to suggest that what Paul finds "wrong" in Israel's conduct is the persistence in an endeavor he has abandoned—namely, striving to secure Judea's future through the precarious balance of power vis-à-vis Rome.

I want to distinguish here between the Judean nationalism that Fredriksen finds missing in Paul's thought, on the one hand, and God's integrity to the covenant with Israel that so clearly constrains his apostolate, on the other. Romans was written by an apostle who had surrendered one particular approach to the Judean nationalist cause and who now confronted a peculiar strain of anti-Semitism within the gentile church of Rome.

The distinction may be important in our own day, when Paul's legacy is caught up in highly charged theological and political debates that effectively trap the apostle between the Holocaust and the Intifada. Since the Holocaust, Christian churches have moved from a dawning awareness and repentance of their complicity in Nazi violence and anti-Semitism to the affirmation, especially after 1967, that *the survival of the Jews as a people is a theological value in its own right*—a startling innovation, given the preceding twenty centuries of Christian theology.[145] In order to counteract the disastrous anti-Jewish legacy of the past, Christian theologians have emphasized Paul's affirmation of Israel's covenant, sometimes going to the dubious extreme of describing two separate "covenants" for Jews and for Gentiles. What Paul says about Israel in Romans 9–11 has been reexamined, and the new consensus, that Paul was concerned to defend the integrity of God's covenant with Israel, has played an enormously important role in the theological discussion.[146]

In more recent decades, however, some churches have become increasingly reluctant to lend theological support to the State of Israel, especially since Israel's invasion of Lebanon and the Palestinian Intifada in the 1980s.[147] Paul's prominence in ecclesiastical affirmations of Israel has meant that some persons sympathetic with the plight of the Palestinians under Israeli occupation have found themselves at apparent cross-purposes with this aspect of Paul's apostolic witness.

Not surprisingly, it often proves easier to ignore these tensions than to confront them and deal with them honestly and sympathetically. Jewish liberation theologian Marc Ellis notes that in interfaith dialogue today Christians are often asked not only "to cleanse their tradition of anti-Judaic elements and to set a course that recognizes and affirms both their biblical patrimony and contemporary Jewish history as authentic in and of itself," but to affirm their commitment to the state of Israel as well. "Within this framework, from the Jewish side, it makes perfect sense to equate criticism of Israel with anti-Jewishness. From the Christian side it makes perfect sense to question whether a Christian critique of Israel is in fact anti-Jewish." Ellis characterizes this situation as an "ecumenical deal," involving "a demand on the Jewish side and silence on the Christian side, with both postures becoming increasingly difficult to maintain."[148]

What we have seen about Paul's understanding of his apostolate suggests that it is wrong to force a choice between "the universalistic strand or the nationalistic one" in his thought.[149] Paul readily affirmed both (see Rom. 1:16; 11:28–32). He never surrendered his hope for his people, but he became convinced that that hope would find fulfillment in a way many of his contemporaries in Judea had failed to recognize. Paul's work among the Gentiles was driven by the conviction that he was participating in God's liberative purposes *for Israel.* He continued to pursue as an apostle of Jesus Christ the same goal that he had served as a Pharisee and a persecutor of the church, namely, "the revelation of the liberation of the children of God" (Rom. 8:21). His "conversion" changed not his goal but the strategy he would now adopt to reach that goal; the apocalypse of the crucified Messiah convinced Paul that God did not work through the balance of terror through which successive empires exacted their will.

That insight has usually been obscured by a theological preoccupation with Paul's "debate with Judaism," a preoccupation that we have seen to be grossly exaggerated and misunderstood. Tragically it is only after the horror of the Holocaust that we are able to see the contours of Paul's apostolate more clearly. Once we recognize the political dimension of his conversion and apostolate, his relevance for theology in the age of the Intifada comes to light as well.

Paul came to disown the political "realism" he once had embraced. Indeed, we must admit, in the grisly final years of the twentieth century after Jesus' birth, that Paul's vision of the resurrected Lord proved to be profoundly "unrealistic." We cannot say whether history would have been different if Paul had outlived Nero's purge of undesirables in Rome, or if gentile converts had not set themselves busily to adapting his vision to a new strategy of accommodation to the empire; or if his fellow Jews in Judea had had more of an opportunity to hear out the message of the messianic movement. Rome was impatient: The client aristocracy it had created in Judea had failed to win the people's support,[150] and knowing no response more efficient than suppression, Rome sealed the desperate fate of the country with fire and sword.

Paul fervently believed the Messiah would return within his lifetime (1 Thess. 4:15–17; 1 Cor. 15:51–52). But his gospel is "unrealistic" in other ways than the mere miscalculation of the apocalyptic time.[151] In the vision of the crucified Messiah, he met a God different from the God of Death who finds worship in the blood of his enemies. The announcement of God's compassionate solidarity with the crucified people—the proclamation that, in the words of Martin Luther King, Jr., "the universe bends toward justice"—is no more "realistic" today, and the pressure to substitute the seductive "realism" of imperial theology is almost irresistible. The present world empire is no more patient with disruptive clients (Manuel Noriega, Saddam Hussein, Siad Barre); its only lessons have been in increasing the magnitude and efficiency of suppression and in the control of popular opinion.

By the grace of God, men and women nevertheless continue to live out the power of the resurrection even within the realm of Death, decked out in the splendor of the current world empire and to defy the thunderous threats of death, trusting themselves to a God who gives life to the dead. Those men and women are Paul's true legacy today.

The reconstruction of the logic of Paul's conversion that I have offered here must meet an immediate practical test. It was Paul's audacious claim that he advanced the cause of Israel's liberation through his apostolate to the Gentiles. We turn next to examine the practical strategy of that apostolate. How did Paul incarnate his liberative vision in his work in the gentile cities of the Roman Empire?

6

Apostolic Praxis:
Living out the Dying of Jesus

The picture of Paul that emerges from the preceding two chapters is markedly different from the way he is often represented. I have argued that Paul's visionary encounter with the crucified and risen Jesus shattered the fine calculus of sacred violence that had driven him to persecute the churches in Judea and Syria. As a consequence, in Robert Hamerton-Kelly's words, "he went over to the side of the victim. Instead of continuing the crucifixion he joined the crucified."[1]

Further, Paul refused to cherish this vision as a private apocalypse. He was compelled to announce its world-transforming import. God had revealed an astonishing alternative course to Israel's liberation, indeed to the redemption of all creation: a path wholly separate from the futile political realism to which he had previously dedicated his energies. Paul now was "slave" and "priest" to a God who had begun to vindicate the oppressed through the nonviolent power of resurrection. His apostolate among the Gentiles was informed by this vision, from beginning to end. The congregations he helped to establish across the northeastern arc of the Mediterranean were the firstfruits of a redeemed humanity, sanctifying the nations to God's holy and liberative purposes.

This new picture of Paul must yet survive the acid test of praxis. If Paul could "think globally" of God's liberation of an oppressed creation, did he also "act locally," in his daily endeavors among his congregations, in consonance with that vision? Did the concrete decisions expressed in his letters reveal a coherent and liberative strategy?

As we have seen, Paul's interpreters have routinely answered no. Since Paul anticipated the imminent return of the Messiah and the glorious liberation of the messianic age, we are told, he considered efforts to ameliorate social injustices a waste of time, like "tinkering with the engines on a sinking ship" (John Ziesler). Indeed Paul went further, encouraging conformity to the structures and institutions of

Roman society, however unjust, in the interim before the return of Christ (Albert Schweitzer); thus, surprisingly to some, "social conservatism and apocalyptic enthusiasm . . . seem to coincide" in his thought (J. Christiaan Beker).[2] Since he was preoccupied with the survival and stability of "his" churches, and particularly with his grand vision of harmony between Jew and Gentile, he subordinated concern for equality and justice within the ekklesia to this "missionary concern." The result, Elaine Pagels writes, was "a double standard":

> to continue observing kosher laws is to deny "the freedom for which Christ died," but to continue observing social, political and marital laws and conventions remains acceptable, even commendable. Although the "new humanity" has transformed the entire relationship between Jews and Gentiles, Paul does not allow it to challenge the whole structure of the believers' social, sexual, and political relationships.[3]

On these premises, the resulting impression of Paul's ethic is of "something like a religious accommodation to the social sphere" (J. Christiaan Beker); or again, of a "realistic" assessment of limited options, an "energy calculus" that moved Paul to "postpone commitment to the concrete sociopolitical cause" (Juan Luis Segundo); or of the "moderate social conservatism" of "love-patriarchalism," which purchased the new sect's survival and cohesion at the cost of challenging social structures (Gerd Theissen); or even of Paul's paradoxical acceptance of a level of "good violence" that is "necessary for most of the world," "holding society together until the truth [of nonviolence] can be made known," an order of sacred violence to which "there is no practical alternative at present" (thus Robert Hamerton-Kelly subverts his own nonviolent reading of Paul's theology).[4]

These are distortions of Paul's thought and work. We have already seen that the common perception of Paul's "social conservatism" is based largely on 1 Cor. 7:17–24, a passage long misread as Paul's appeal for Christians to "remain in their situation" or "worldly status," however desperate their circumstances. That reading reflects the unacceptable influence of the pseudo-Pauline writings (see chapter 2) and neglects the argumentative context of 1 Corinthians 7. Read in that context, this passage simply does not support generalizations about Paul's ethic of the status quo.

Another text that has long served as evidence of Paul's "social conservatism," the exhortation to "be subject to the governing authorities" in Rom. 13:1–7, has proven just as toxic in recent history, providing cover for fascist, racist, and militarist regimes around the world as it has served to muzzle Christian resistance. These verses have "caused more unhappiness and misery in the Christian East and West than any other seven verses in the New Testament by the license they have given to tyrants, and the support for tyrants the Church has felt called on to offer as a result" (J. C. O'Neill); and in the process they have poisoned our perception of Paul. These verses convinced Paula Fredriksen that Paul's vision "shrinks the significance of contemporary politics. . . . He thus minimized the political aspects of this messianic movement." These verses led J. Christiaan Beker to speak of Paul's "religious accommodation to the social sphere." These verses revealed to Robert G. Hamerton-Kelly Paul's acceptance of "good violence," if only at a level that is "absolutely necessary." These verses have proven to be perhaps "the most influential part of the New Testament on the level of world history" (Ernst Bammel)—and arguably the most disastrous.[5]

As with 1 Cor. 7:17–24, the power these verses have been given to determine the shape of "Paul's ethics" is out of all proportion to their role in the context of Romans. Their influence on our perceptions of Paul has nevertheless become so great that, for better or worse, any attempt to recover the "liberating Paul" stands or falls with the interpretation of Rom. 13:1–7. Paul's intention in these verses is far from self-evident, however, as the disarray in recent scholarship indicates. Examining this passage in its context will be a crucial task later in this chapter.

The principal reason to doubt the usual generalizations about Paul's "social conservatism" is that they fail to do justice to much broader patterns in Paul's letters. After all, we should doubt that Paul routinely deferred questions of justice and equality for the sake of his own idiosyncratic apostolic vision, once we recall that he risked his apostolate itself to persuade a slaveholder to release his slave (Philem. 8–14). We should doubt that Paul glossed over disparities between rich and poor in order to preserve a superficial harmony across the congregation, once we recall that he challenged the Corinthians to abandon their eucharistic assemblies if they could not feed the hungry in their midst (1 Cor. 11:33–34). We should doubt that Paul's gospel was a purely "spiritual" matter, socially and politically innocuous, once we recall the efforts of the Nabatean king Aretas IV to arrest Paul in Damascus (2 Cor. 11:32–33) and the apparent regularity with which Paul was hauled before civic magistrates, thrown into Roman prisons, and condemned as a menace to public order (Philem. 1, 9, 13; Phil. 1:7, 12–14, 16; 4:14, 1 Thess. 2:2; 1 Cor. 4:9; 2 Cor. 1:8–9, 6:5, 11:23).[6]

Why did Paul so consistently provoke this response if his gospel was as unpolitical as many interpreters suggest? Could the Roman authorities have detected in Paul's words and actions a real threat to the social order? Was his praxis in fact more engaged with sociopolitical reality than conventional readings have allowed us to recognize?

Just here an objection is raised. May we appropriately speak of Paul's "political engagement" at all? J. Christiaan Beker points the issue when he writes that although Paul's understanding of the church suggests "a revolutionary impact on the values of the world," his ethic apparently "does not struggle with the issue of the empirically possible versus the religiously necessary, and [he] does not wrestle with strategies for political and social action."[7]

But surely those are very modern questions. They would have seemed quite curious to a first-century Pharisee whose understanding of "the empirically possible" was grounded in the conviction that God had raised a man crucified by Rome from the dead. It is true that Paul did not concern himself with "strategies" for bringing about the reign of God, the *basileia tou theou,* for he was convinced that *God* would bring about the world's liberation, and very soon (Rom. 8:18–25; 13:11–14). But this does not mean that he was indifferent to social and political action: quite the contrary, if we consider how he insisted on reciting his arrest record to establish his apostolic credentials!

We properly ask, not what Paul expected Christians to achieve in the political forum (which after all was the nearly exclusive domain of the powerful),[8] but what contours he expected their life together to assume as they lived in anticipation of God's coming triumph.

Given that Paul's letters have the character of persuasion, that is, that they were meant to accomplish something,[9] we should regard them as the instruments, applied in very specific situations, of a broader apostolic praxis. That praxis evidently had a clear strategic goal: the "sanctification" of gentile converts (1 Thess. 4:3; Rom. 15:16), and the formation of assemblies (*ekklēsiai*) of the sanctified (1 Cor. 1:2). Further, as Beker rightly insists, that praxis also had a cosmic horizon: the apocalyptic triumph of God.[10] The question at the heart of our inquiry, then, is, What political shape does Paul expect his readers' lives to take as they "wait with patience" for the liberation of creation?

THE IDEOLOGICAL CONTEXT: THE THEOLOGY OF EMPIRE

As we have seen in previous chapters, one obstacle to a political reading of Paul is our own tendency to interpret him in narrowly "religious" terms, primarily by way of contrast with Jewish "theology" or "soteriology." The political edge to Paul's proclamation and exhortation stands in sharper relief if we shift our angle of vision to include another prominent, yet often neglected, aspect of the ekklesia's immediate environment: the eschatology of Roman propaganda, prevalent in "a time when the gospel according to Augustus held the world spellbound" (historian of early Christianity Dieter Georgi).

As evidence of this imperial theology, Georgi points us to the propagandists of the Augustan age, Horace and Virgil, and of course Augustus himself, as well as other texts from the time of Nero (the propagandizing poetry of Calpurnius Piso, Calpurnius Siculus, Statius, the Einsiedeln eclogues),[11] to which we may add the mute testimony of coins, art, and sacred architecture. The picture that emerges from this evidence is of an intense "realized eschatology" (Georgi) through which Rome taught its subjects to celebrate the Roman order as the coming of a golden age of peace and security, the Pax Augusta.

Walter Wink reminds us that an empire is, by its very nature, "a system in a permanent crisis of legitimation," held together by force. It therefore requires propaganda to convince people "that they benefit from a system that is in fact harmful to them, that no other system is feasible, that God has placed the divine imprimatur on this system and no other." Classical historian Richard Gordon points out that a legitimating ideology functions not only, not even primarily, "as a mask consciously employed to deceive social subordinates"; it also acts as an "unconscious veil distorting the image of social reality within [a] class and sublimating its interest basis," representing "a social fact—that is, imperialism"—in "the guise of fate and piety."[12]

The veil obscuring the harsh realities of Roman imperialism was an ideology of the "peace and security" the gods had achieved in and through Rome. As early as 63 B.C.E., Pompey invaded Judea under the banner of "peace and security" (*met' eirēnēs . . . meta asphaleias pollēs: Psalms of Solomon* 8:18). But "peace and security," *pax et securitas,* was supremely the achievement of Augustus, as he was himself eager to declare in the *Acts of the Divine Augustus,* a solemnly self-serving text published throughout the empire. Thrice during his principate, the emperor boasted, the senate had proclaimed "peace, secured through victory, throughout the whole domain of the Roman people on land and sea," ordering the sacred arch of Janus Quirinus closed (*Res Gestae Divi Augusti* 13). Virgil explained this ritual action in a passage from the Aeneid, that piece of revisionist propaganda that read Roman glory back into the days of Homeric legend. Jupiter had prophesied that in the days of Augustus, "wars shall cease and the rough ages soften; hoary Faith [*Fides*] and Vesta, Quirinus with his brother Remus, shall give laws. The gates of war, grim with iron and close-fitting bars, shall be closed; within, impious Rage, sitting on savage arms, his hands fast bound behind with a hundred brazen knots, shall roar in the ghastliness of bloodstained lips" (*Aeneid* 1:291–296). A propagandist in Nero's day, Calpurnius Siculus, would praise the same cosmic victory over the vanquished and bound enemy, "impious War" (*Eclogue* 1:45–54).

The Augustan gospel celebrated a "peace secured through victory," for "the *Pax Romana* was usually imposed on the peoples by means of warfare." Augustus had "pacified" Gaul, Spain, Germany, Ethiopia, Arabia, and Egypt through force of arms; accordingly the senate erected the altar to the Peace of Augustus on the hill of Mars, god of war (*Res

Gestae 26). As Ernst Bammel succinctly observes, "Everywhere that Rome makes an appearance, the provision of peace and security is made to justify the loss of autonomy and more than compensate for all the initial terrors."[13]

The subjection of other peoples extended the reach of the Roman elite. As G. E. M. de Ste. Croix notes, "The intensely practical Roman governing class ruled because that was the best means of guaranteeing the high degree of exploitation they needed to maintain." Within its sphere of effectiveness, Roman law preserved the property rights of the wealthy. Not surprisingly, following Augustus's "pacification" of nations, "the inbuilt disposition of Roman law to respect and favour the propertied classes became more explicitly institutionalized during the Principate." De Ste. Croix echoes historian A. H. M. Jones's verdict: "There was one law for the rich and another for the poor."[14]

But that is the view from outside, or better, from the underside of the empire. To a prosperous Roman like Virgil, on the other hand, the accession of Augustus fulfilled ancient and sacred promises of the glory of Rome; his triumph was nothing less than the climax of universal history, the fulfillment of the divine will. Virgil proclaimed Augustus as the "son of a god," come to restore "the golden age" of humanity (*Aeneid* 6:791–795). With Augustus's accession, Justice (Astraea, the Roman version of the Greek Dikē) returned to rule over the earth. Augustus brought nothing less than the transformation of the cosmos, the fulfillment of the universe's history: "The reign of Saturn returns; now a new generation descends from heaven on high." Under Augustus, "the iron brood shall first cease and a golden race spring up throughout the world" (*Eclogue* 4:4–10).

Thus Virgil reversed the ancient world-chronology of Hesiod, who had lamented that humanity's original golden age had degenerated into the present age of iron (*Works and Days* 106–201). No, said Virgil, the divine Augustus had brought the iron age to an end and inaugurated the age of gold! So the cosmos was renewed, "the great line of the centuries begins anew"; Saturn, who ordered the ages of the cosmos, renewed his reign.

Aelius Aristides, praising imperial Rome in the second century, repeated these themes, lauding the unprecedented "order" achieved by the Caesars ("in everyday life and in the state there is clear light of day"), the justice accomplished through Roman law, the piety that washed through the world now that "faith has been found at the altars of the gods." Indeed, "the whole earth is arrayed like a paradise" (*Eulogy of Rome* 103). Had Hesiod been a true seer, Aristides told Caesar, "he would have lamented those who had been born before your time" (106).

These same themes resound in the poetry of Calpurnius Siculus, in the age of Nero. Saturn reigned in Latium, "Fair peace [*Pax*] shall come," peace "knowing not the drawn sword" (*Eclogue* 1:55–64). "Laws shall be restored, right [*Ius*] will come in fullest force"; the "age of oppression" would cease (1:70–74). Contemporary with Calpurnius Siculus, the Einsiedeln eclogues proclaimed "the story of the universe," now at its zenith (*Eclogue* 1:22–31), and celebrated the happy union of piety and peace. Now that villagers "offer their yearly vows and begin the regular altar-worship, temples reek of wine, the hollow drums resound to the hands," no one could deny "to these times the realms of gold. The days of Saturn have returned with Justice the Virgin"; now the farmboy "marvels at the sword hanging in the abode of his fathers," an inscrutable relic of a bygone age (2:18–32).

The last words were penned during the bloody decade in which Judean resistance to the Roman occupation broke out into full-scale war.

But revolts on the frontiers, or riots in Alexandria or Judea, did not trouble the propagandists. Writing in 30 c.e., an official chronicler of Rome praised, first, the incomparable divine benefits achieved by Augustus, for throughout the world

> there is nothing that man can desire from the gods, nothing that the gods can grant to a man, nothing that wish can conceive or good fortune bring to pass, which Augustus on his return [to Rome] did not bestow upon the republic, the Roman people, and the world. The civil wars were ended after twenty years, foreign wars suppressed, peace restored, the frenzy of arms everywhere lulled to rest; validity was restored to the laws, authority to the courts, and dignity to the senate. . . . Agriculture returned to the fields, respect to religion, to mankind freedom from anxiety. (Velleius Paterculus, *History of Rome* 89:1–4)

The poet proceeded to describe Augustus's "pacification" of other peoples (90:1–4), the events of subsequent years deserving mention only as they affected "the perpetual security and the eternal existence of the Roman empire" (103:4).

None of these authors apparently regarded their perspective as parochially "Roman." "Let *all* the peoples rejoice," Calpurnius Siculus exulted; nowhere in the world is there "any woman who, dangerous in her motherhood, gives birth to an enemy" of Rome, declared the Einsiedeln author. Velleius Paterculus proclaimed that Augustus had brought the provinces "to such a condition of peace, that whereas they had never before been free from serious wars, they were now . . . exempt even from brigandage." Only the most perverse of the empire's beneficiaries would have remained ungrateful.

Nor were these the cynical sentiments of a few well-subsidized court propagandists. The small but prosperous elite in each of Rome's client cities evidently found the imperial "gospel" inviting. Indeed, a famous honorary inscription from Priene, near Ephesus (9 b.c.e.), praises him "who has brought war to an end and has ordained peace" so that "for the world, the birthday of the god" (that is, the divine Augustus) "is the beginning of the gospel [*euangelion*] of peace."

Rome moved quickly to integrate local aristocracies into the twin grids of piety and economic benefaction. According to historian Richard Gordon, depictions of the emperor as priest in monumental carving, statuary, and on coins, served as pervasive political propaganda, inviting provincial aristocracies to identify through their piety with the power of Rome.[15] New elites were incorporated within a complex but well-defined web of patronage relationships that allowed power and wealth to flow increasingly toward Rome, where the Caesars posed as the supreme benefactors of a global household (the *oikoumenē*). Within this system, the most important social determinants for behavior and perception concerned one's place within the chain of patronage relationships.[16] As G. E. M. de Ste. Croix observes,

> Under the Principate . . . such political influence as the lower classes had had soon largely disappeared, and the ways in which patronage could be valuable to a great man changed. With the virtual cessation of election from below, and indeed the gradual drying up of all initiative from below, as political authority became concentrated in the hands of the Emperor, the new role of patronage assumed great importance.[17]

Much like "trickle-down" economics in our own day, the patronage system effected a massive evaporation of wealth toward the upper strata while masquerading as the generous "benefaction" of the rich for the poor. But the main purpose of such philanthropy "is not to relieve poverty," Richard Gordon observes. "Part of the function of philanthropic gestures is to register and naturalize the inequalities of the social system in each community, just as the emperors' patronage and generosity marshals and orchestrates the overall hierarchy of the system as a whole."[18]

Holland Hendrix has shown that Thessalonika, to take one example, secured its "freedom" from Roman subjugation (it remained immune from tribute, if no less dependent economically) by developing an elaborate cultus honoring Augustus. Roman benefactors received official civic recognition and the imperial pantheon of Rome was incorporated into the official worship of the city (a temple to Augustus was built; Augustus's head replaced Zeus's head on the city's coinage). The result was a thorough integration of Roman and local cults into a sacred pyramid of civic worship, the imperial cult assuming priority.[19]

The Corinthians were no less eager to render praise to Rome, erecting altars and inventing cults to honor the imperial family and to celebrate the emperors' birthdays, accessions, and triumphs, adding imperial games to the schedule of Isthmian games and observing not one but two cycles of artistic competitions to rehearse the virtues and beneficence of the emperors. The careers of individual Achaians illustrate how the imperial cult proved an effective way for Rome to co-opt the local aristocracies and thus neutralize potential opposition. Such examples serve to explain "why the imperial cult was strongly promoted in first-century Corinth" (John K. Chow).[20]

The message of the Augustan gospel was clear. Justice and peace, the gifts of the gods, were now being made manifest on earth in the order and security imposed by Rome, whose subjects were invited to respond with gratitude, awe, and loyalty.

How did Paul's apostolic praxis respond to this imperial program?

COMMUNITIES OF DISCERNMENT

Paul repeatedly calls the Christian ekklesia to a mutual discernment, asking them to "distinguish what really matters" (Phil. 1:10), to "resist conformity to this world and be transformed by the renewal of your minds, that you may prove what is the will of God" (Rom. 12:2). As J. Louis Martyn remarks, this apocalyptic discernment is a matter of "knowing what time it is" (Rom. 13:11).[21] In the context of imperial propaganda, we might expect such discernment inevitably to have involved what we would call "political consciousness-raising," or what Mark Chmiel has called an ideological intifada, a throwing off of imperial illusions.[22]

For Paul, the rhapsodies about a "golden age" are a fraud. There is only "this present evil age" (Gal. 1:4), a "crooked and perverse generation" (Phil. 2:15), the age of the earth's "bondage to decay" (Rom. 8:21), an age that is "passing away" (1 Cor. 7:31), the present "night" of stupor and drunkenness (1 Thess. 5:7), an age subject to impending divine wrath (1 Thess. 1:10, Rom. 5:9). These conventional phrases derive from Jewish apocalypticism, of course; why should we imagine that there is anything expressly political about them? Does Paula Fredriksen's generalization about Jesus' message, that "the nature of apocalyptic is political," apply to Paul's apocalyptic discernment as well?[23]

Discerning the Lie: "Peace and Security"

The answer is clearly yes, in light of Paul's explicit denial in 1 Thessalonians of the slogan at the heart of Augustan propaganda, "Peace and security" (in Greek, *eirēnē kai asphaleia*):

Just as people are saying "peace and security," then sudden destruction will come upon them, as labor pains come upon a pregnant woman; and there will be no escape. But you, brothers and sisters, you are not in the dark, so that day might sneak up on you like a thief. For you are children of light and of the day; we are not of the night, or of darkness. So then: let us not sleep, as others do, but let us be on the watch and keep our wits about us. (1 Thess. 5:3-6)

Here "the words 'peace and security'—and therefore that for which they stand, the Pax Romana—clearly stand on the side of night and darkness" (Klaus Wengst). The pretensions of imperial propaganda are torn away (Ernst Bammel); this is nothing less than "a frontal attack on the *Pax et Securitas* programme of the early Principate" (Karl P. Donfried). "If the two Letters to the Thessalonians stood alone," W. H. C. Frend writes, "we might suspect that the Christians were in fact guilty of harboring disloyal and antisocial thoughts toward their contemporaries. Paul's attack on the watchwords of the time *Pax et Securitas* is bitter."

Frend promptly relinquishes this insight, however, in view of the "triumph of the moderate" in Rom. 13:1-7. But why should Romans 13 be given such control over the interpretation of this strident passage from 1 Thessalonians, particularly since a much more critical stance toward "the rulers" is attested elsewhere in Paul's letters?[24]

Karl P. Donfried asks whether there are "elements in the proclamation of Paul and his co-workers in Thessalonica which might have been perceived as . . . politically inflammatory." Some of the letter's distinctive vocabulary—the rule (*basileia*) of God (2:12), the language of royal visits (*parousia, apantēsis,* 4:15-17), the very term gospel (*euangelion*)—"could be understood or misunderstood in a distinctly political sense."[25] But surely "misunderstanding" on this point is unlikely, given Paul's incisive remarks about "those who proclaim 'peace and security.'" Rather than prudently retreating from potential "misunderstanding" through some quick and circumspect qualifications, Paul seizes the opportunity to press home his frontal attack on the false peace of the empire.

Discerning the Lie: "Justice and Faith"

Paul's ideological intifada comes to clearest expression in Romans. Ironically, however, it has been obscured by centuries of Christian interpretation that have read the letter as a dogmatic treatise on Christian salvation. We must bear in mind that Paul wrote the letter to Christians in the heart of the Roman Empire, at a time when the antijudaism rife in imperial circles had begun to infect the church as well.[26] Paul appeals to the Christians of Rome to throw off the mental shackles of the empire's theology, to resist conformity to the world and embrace the transformation of their minds, and to come at last to share in God's compassionate purposes toward humanity, and more particularly toward the covenant people Israel.

He begins by announcing that "the justice of God [*dikaiosynē tou theou*] is now being revealed, from faithfulness to faithfulness" (Rom. 1:17). Christian readers who have assumed that Paul is talking here about the way God imputes righteousness to individuals, his doctrine of "justification by faith" in its supposed opposition to Jewish works-righteousness, have been hard pressed to explain why that theme intrudes so abruptly into a letter to gentile Christians.[27] But we are now increasingly aware that the phrase "the justice of God" meant much more to Paul than God's justification of unrighteous individuals (the *iustificatio impii*). The *dikaiosynē tou theou* is God's justice; the phrase speaks "of the God who brings back the fallen world into the sphere of his legitimate claim" (Ernst Käsemann). The justice of God is God's integrity, faithfulness to God's own being and purposes. Those purposes, according to the broad sweep of the biblical tradition, are the redemption of the creation and the fulfillment of the covenant with Israel (which has the redemption of creation as its horizon).[28]

Further, we better understand what Paul is doing in Romans 1 when we recall that "justice" (*dikaiosynē*) and "faith" (*pistis*) were not only "theological" terms from the Greek Bible; in contemporary Greek inscriptions they corresponded to the Latin *ius* and *fides,* the lifeblood of Augustan propaganda. Augustus had restored the faith of the Roman people; "Faith" was inscribed on his coinage. Justice was one of Augustus's characteristics, proclaimed in the *Res Gestae* (34) and recognized by senatorial decree; as a god, Ovid solemnized, Justice was "enshrined" in Augustus's mind (*Ex Ponto* 3:6:23–29).[29]

Paul was not the only Jew in a position to dispute the vaunted claims of Roman justice. The commentary on Habakkuk found among the Dead Sea Scrolls (1QpHab, routinely dated to the late first century B.C.E.) speaks heatedly of the "Kittim," that is, the Romans,[30] who are "quick and valiant in war, causing many to perish" (2:12–13); who "advance [through mountains] and valleys to strike and plunder the cities of the earth" (3:1); who "ravage many lands" and "slay many people by the sword—youths, grown men, the aged, women and children, and have no pity on the fruit of the womb" (6:10–12). The book of Habakkuk had declared of the "Chaldeans" that "their justice and grandeur proceed from themselves" (1:7). "This concerns the Kittim," the Dead Sea commentary announces, "who inspire all the nations with fear. All their evil plotting is done with intention, and they deal with all the nations in cunning and trickery" (3:4–5).

Astonishingly, the dominant theological tradition has devoted considerable attention to possible parallels in the scrolls to Paul's doctrine of justification by faith; no comparisons are made with the Habakkuk commentary's opposition of God's justice to the injustice radiating from Rome and its hirelings in Jerusalem.[31]

While the commentary reflects the immediate experience of Roman military brutality in Judea, Paul writes, perhaps a century later, to an audience in the imperial capital tempted to identify with Rome's perspective on its victims. From the very beginning of Romans, Paul is engaged in a mortal struggle to decide who shall declare what "justice" is. He opposes God's justice to the forces that militate against God's purposes: human rebellion (1:18–32); the dominion of Sin and Death that took human rebellion as its foothold (5:12–21) and captured God's creation, subjecting it to "futility" and "corruption" (8:20–21); Israel's apparent failure to recognize God's mysterious plan for the world's redemption (Romans 9–10); and finally, at the argumentative climax of the letter, the arrogance of gentile Christianity (Romans 11). In this last passage, Paul is concerned not that the arrogance of the Gentiles might obstruct God's purposes (for that is in his eyes impossible) but that their boast will exclude the Gentiles from the fulfillment of those purposes (11:21).

Paul cannot expect the Christians of Rome to give up their boast until they discern the lie at the heart of imperial policy. So he begins the letter by condemning the rampant injustice and wickedness of this age, "the impiety [*asebeia*] and injustice [*adikia*] of mortals who by their injustice suppress the truth" and thus provoke the wrath of God (1:18). God's justice is manifest (not, as Caesar proclaims, in the pomp of imperial ceremony or the solemnity of official decrees, but) in the royal proclamation (*euangelion*) of the crucified Messiah (1:16–17).

As Juan Luis Segundo observes, in Romans 1 *injustice,* "the generic sin against all that is due to any human being," holds first place as "the mechanism of enslavement to sin"; *impiety,* on the other hand, is the consequent "shackling of truth," a "mechanism on the level of consciousness or conscience." In Paul's thought,

> the desire for idolatry is not the mainspring of this attitude or behavior. The self-deception that draws the human being from worship of the *super*human to worship of the unworthy *infra*human is a *means* for something else: i.e., injustice. That is what the desires of the human heart are really aiming at. In the idolatry depicted by Paul the real intention of human beings is to justify, on the basis of the divine, the dehumanized relations they want to have with other human beings.[32]

Paul declares that the effort of the wicked to mystify injustice through religion is manifest first as idolatry (1:19–22), a connection made by the Habakkuk commentary as well.[33] But where the Dead Sea document speaks of the military ravages of the Kittim, Paul proceeds to describe how the syndrome of injustice and idolatry among the wicked produces "impurity, the dishonoring of their bodies among themselves," that is, sexual perversion (1:24–27). Homosexual acts are particularly in view, between women (1:26) and between men (1:27).

Why does sexual abuse play so important a role in Paul's indictment of injustice?

These verses from Romans 1 exercise an inordinate influence today in public debate over the rights of gays and lesbians and in ecclesiastical controversies over the place of gays and lesbians in the church.[34] But this passage cannot be read as Paul's "theology of homosexuality." Despite the currency of views that Paul has settled on "homosexual practice" as "a sign of humanity's alienation from God the creator," "symptomatic of the one sickness of humanity as a whole" (New Testament scholar Richard Hays), we should doubt, first of all, that the perversions Paul describes can be readily translated into our categories of "homosexual practice," let alone homosexual orientation. The ancient world simply did not recognize the latter.[35] We should also doubt that Paul is thinking in such abstract terms as "humanity's alienation from God the creator," for he speaks more restrictively of "those human beings who through their injustice suppress the truth."

In Paul's world, sexuality was readily perceived as a medium of power. Sexual penetration normally rehearsed the prerogative the freeborn male enjoyed over the bodies of others.[36] Robin Scroggs observes that homosexual activities in the Greco-Roman environment generally took place within relationships characterized by inequalities of power: the use of prostitutes, the abuse of slaves, and pederasty. Neither did Jewish writers show any awareness of *mutual* homosexual relationships between adults. Scroggs concludes that "the homosexuality the New Testament opposes is the pederasty of the Greco-Roman culture; the attitudes toward pederasty and, in part, the language used to oppose it are informed by the Jewish background."[37]

Romans 1 simply doesn't provide an adequate foundation for theological reflection on homosexuality. (It certainly does not justify the antagonism gays and lesbians face as they seek housing, employment, civil rights, and even full participation in the life of the church.) Scroggs sensibly concludes,

> The basic model in today's Christian homosexual community is so different from the model attacked by the New Testament that the criterion of reasonable similarity of context is not met. The conclusion I have to draw seems inevitable: *Biblical judgments against homosexuality are not relevant to today's debate.* They should no longer be used in denominational discussions about homosexuality, should in no way be a weapon to justify refusal of ordination, *not because the Bible is not authoritative,* but simply because it does not address the issues involved.[38]

Of course, that judgment about the relevance of the biblical material is not enough in itself to inform our current ecclesiastical conversation. The heterosexual majority within the church must also learn to listen with discernment to the experience of gay and lesbian Christians in our midst, and especially to their experience of the Spirit.[39]

But our immediate interest in this passage from Romans lies in another direction. What is Paul trying to achieve in Romans 1? He speaks of acts of sexual humiliation ("the dishonoring of their bodies," 1:24); but why concentrate upon sexually abusive behavior at just this point in the letter?

On the premise that Hellenistic Jewish literature provides the closest background for Paul's remarks, particularly in connecting idolatry and sexual immorality (*porneia*) as characteristic "abominations" of the gentile world (Wisdom of Solomon 12–13), commentators have routinely regarded Rom. 1:18–32 as a subtle "trap" set for the Jew. But this reading is improbable, for it implies that the gentile Christian readers to whom the letter is addressed (1:6, 13–15) are in effect sitting out this portion of the letter as Paul maneuvers to trap a hypothetical Jewish listener![40]

To the contrary, the force of Paul's argument here must depend on the moral revulsion he can expect from pagan converts in Rome, for, as Wayne A. Meeks has shown, the attack on "judging" in Rom. 2:1–6 is the basis for Paul's more specific appeal for gentile Christians to show consideration toward the sensibilities of Jews (Rom. 14:1–15:13).[41] On what basis could Paul expect such a response?

I think the answer is to be found in observing that at the very time Paul wrote, the sexual outrages of recent emperors had scandalized practically everyone in the capital. The relevant facts can be summarized quickly.

When Tiberius had retired to Capri, he had stocked the island with male and female sex slaves, procured from throughout the empire for their talent in "every imaginable unnatural act"; the emperor especially liked to watch threesomes, according to the historian Suetonius (*Tiberius* 43). His successor, Gaius Caligula, had horrified Rome not only through his monstrous claims to self-deification, in Rome and elsewhere (recall that he almost brought on war in Judea by ordering his statue erected in the Temple), but also through his sexual predation. Not satisfied by his incestuous relationships with his sisters (Suetonius, *Gaius* 24), he had routinely pulled the wives of dinner guests from his table, noisily raped them in nearby rooms, then returned to the table to criticize his victims' performance. He had submitted sexually to men, even—the Roman mind boggled—to "foreign hostages" (36). Rather than contribute his own funds for building projects, he had launched an imperial brothel, serviced (under what duress we can only imagine) by the wives and sons of Rome's nobility (41).

The conspirators who assassinated Caligula included an officer he had sexually humiliated, who stabbed the emperor repeatedly in the genitals (56–58). "Men imposing shame on men," Paul writes, "and receiving in their own bodies the penalty for such deviance" (Rom. 1:27).[42]

Caligula's assassination, and the relative moral gravity ensuing with the reign of Claudius, had brought welcome relief to many in Rome. But Paul wrote Romans during the reign of Claudius's successor, the tyrant Nero, whose rapes of Roman wives and sons, brothel-keeping, incest with his mother, and sexual submission to various men and boys prompted his tutor, the philosopher Seneca, to conclude that Nero was "another Caligula" (Suetonius, *Nero* 26–29).

Surely it is reasonable to suppose, against this context, that by juxtaposing the senselessness of pagan idolatry with a lurid depiction of sexual perversion Paul sought to evoke for his readers the moral bankruptcy of the imperial house itself. Indeed, his description of the depraved continues: "Filled with all manner of injustice, evil, greed, wickedness, full of avarice, murder, factiousness, deceit, malice, they trade in lies and slanderers, they outrage God; insolent, arrogant, boastful, devising evil, dishonoring parents, without conscience or feeling, without compassion or mercy" (Rom. 1:29–31). As a description of conventional gentile morality, the passage is an inexcusable exaggeration (which Christian commentators occasionally recognize and seek to excuse nonetheless by refering to Paul's "radical" and "apocalyptic" perspective).[43] As a description of the horrors of the imperial house, however, Paul's words actually seem restrained.

Paul's repudiation of the imperial pretension to justice, and of the imperial slander of its victims, is nowhere more evident than in Romans. His target from the letter's beginning is not the false religiosity of an individual in the abstract, or of the Jew as the paradigm of "religious humanity," despite the tireless labors of Christian exegetes to prove that it is. Paul's target is the arrogant pretense at the spiritual core of the empire, that the "golden age" of the gods' favor is at hand; that the world is awash in piety and the benevolent justice of Augustus and his successors; and that those who suffer within this sacred order are pernicious rebels, whom the gods have justly abandoned to their fate.

The letter's message to the Roman congregation is clear: *The justice of God is not what the empire calls justice.* Those who have been baptized into Christ are to understand themselves as "demobilized" from the Roman order, having left the "dominion of sin" behind. While others suppress the truth in the service of injustice and violate one another's bodies in unspeakable acts, Christians are to yield their bodies to God "as instruments [*hopla,* 'weapons'] of justice" (6:13–14). They must practice an ideological intifada, refusing to be coerced into conformity with the world and allowing their minds to be transformed (12:1–2).

COMMUNITIES OF RESISTANCE

Paul's shorter letters of exhortation show that the repudiation of imperial illusion to which he called his audiences was costly. For Paul's converts to have "turned to God from idols" (1 Thess. 1:9) required their refusal to participate in the intricate web of local cults that gave sacred legitimation to the empire. They now belonged to a different realm, the "kingdom [*basileia*] of God" (2:12). Everyday routines sacralizing the Roman city were repudiated. Further, "old ties of kinship were dissolved, and a new, fictive kinship was established. This all seemed terribly subversive to the basic institutions of society" (Wayne A. Meeks). Christians risked the ostracism of their neighbors; further, they also may have become targets of suspicion from pagans sworn to report cases of disloyalty to the empire (E. A. Judge).[44]

No wonder, then, that Paul reminds the Thessalonians that he proclaimed the word with "courage," "in the face of great opposition" (2:2), and that they received it "in much affliction" (1:6). No wonder that he reminds them how he warned them in advance, as he does again in this letter, that "such affliction is to be expected" (3:3–4), and that he sent Timothy to urge them "not to be moved by these afflictions" and to be reassured of their resolve (3:2–3). No wonder that he makes such an intensely emotional appeal now for their continued fidelity—"we live, if you stand fast" (3:8)—and declares his constant prayer for their steadfastness (3:10–13).

The consequences for Paul and for those who share his vision will be grave; yet Paul also holds out the ultimate promise of vindication before God at the *parousia* of Christ (4:13–18). This is "a section of critical importance for 1 Thessalonians," Karl P. Donfried argues, for those who have "fallen asleep" are most probably the victims of extreme persecution.[45] The Thessalonians must understand they are not alone in the radical new *basileia* to which they are now committed. "Visibly they are a tiny club gathering cautiously in someone's house in Thessalonica," Wayne A. Meeks writes, "but Paul is teaching them that 'really' their troubles are part of a comprehensive pattern of God's activity in and for the world." Paul emphasizes their sharing in a "brotherhood" that extends beyond the city, throughout Macedonia, Achaia, and beyond (1:8–9).[46] He commends their solidarity with this international movement, a solidarity they have expressed in material aid for "the saints" (4:9–10; see 2 Cor. 8:1–5). They must understand that their affliction is also shared by others. Paul first suffered "shameful treatment" in Philippi (2:2).

In Philippians, too, Paul addresses "the need to understand the social situation of the Christian community in the Greco-Roman *polis* in the light of the persistent fact of persecution" (Pheme Perkins).[47] He writes from prison, perhaps in Ephesus, where he has been put on "charges of civic disturbance," very possibly similar to the riots described in Acts (16:16–24, 17:1–9, 19:23–41) but carrying, at any rate, the threat of a death sentence (1:20). Perkins suggests both that "this disturbance may have been fairly widespread," including the Philippians (1:28–30) as well as the Thessalonians, and that "the reason for this disturbance and persecution was probably related to [Christian antagonism to] the imperial cult." Paul writes to make it clear to the Christians of Philippi that his sitting in a Roman jail is not a failure, but shows the advance of his gospel (1:12). Perceiving his imprisonment aright should lead them to even greater boldness (1:14).[48] Paul reminds the Philippians that they have a heavenly "commonwealth" or "citizenship," a politically loaded word (*politeuma,* 3:20). The sense of the phrase is not "that heaven as such is the homeland of Christians to which they, as perpetual foreigners on earth, must strive to return," but rather that their life on earth is to be governed by the heavenly commonwealth. They are to be "converted" to a new way of life, here and now, within the confines of the *polis* (Andrew Lincoln).[49]

The obedient self-emptying and consequent exaltation of Christ (2:6–11) is the "governing metaphor" in Philippians, through which Paul argues that "conversion implies an 'emptying' analogous to that of Christ." For himself this emptying has meant giving up the privileges of belonging to the Jewish *politeuma* (3:4–11) and renouncing the privileges of Roman citizenship as well.[50] He is in prison as a slave of Christ (1:1) and thus is "sharing in the sufferings of Christ" (3:10).

The Philippians as well must "remain vulnerable to suffering that results from their confession that Christ is *kyrios.*" Indeed, this radical vulnerability in the world is one of the most striking characteristics of Pauline praxis. In a time when Rome officially recognized the right of Jews, alone in the Empire, to honor Caesar by prayers to their own solitary God in his behalf, Paul steadfastly urges the Philippians (and other congregations) to resist those—probably gentile converts to Christianity—who advocate the protective camouflage of a Judaizing way of life: "Look out for the dogs, the evil-workers, those who mutilate the flesh" (3:2); "enemies of the cross of Christ, their end is destruction" (3:18–19). As Pheme Perkins contends, it was a concern to evade the suspicion of neighbors in the Roman colony, "not a concern about the conditions of righteousness before God, that motivated the 'dogs' in Philippians 3 to advocate circumcision and kosher observance."

John Barclay's study of Paul's ethics in Galatians describes the Judaizers in that congregation in similar terms. In Galatia as well, Paul seeks to solidify the Christian community as an alternative to the *politeuma* of the synagogue, *not because he is an apostate from Judaism,* but because (as we have seen in chapter 5) the ultimate horizon of his apostolate among the Gentiles is an apocalyptic "evangelization" of Israel. He struggles against the timidity of those gentile converts who would rather acquiesce in the religious roles dictated by their society than live out the challenge of the gospel. In Galatians as well, Paul's own vulnerability to the penalties Rome exacted on his person inheres in his proclamation of Christ: "I bear on my body the marks of Jesus" (Gal.

6:17). He appeals to the Galatian Christians to stand fast, even in the face of persecution, and to refuse to seek refuge in the Jewish *politeuma* by "living like a Jew." Instead he calls them to join him in a new reality, "a new creation" (6:15), even if this means taking a stand with the crucified (6:12, 14).[51]

We cannot read these exhortations to steadfastness in the face of persecution in purely religious terms, as if they reflected Rome's unenlightened suppression of "false belief," for then we should have to explain why the usual Roman practice of tolerance for a variety of religions—extended even to the exclusively monotheistic Jewish faith— should not have applied in this case. Neither can we explain these exhortations in purely sociological terms, as if they expressed a simple sectarian impulse toward separation from "the world."[52] We cannot shrug off these exhortations as the apostle's surprised reaction when his converts have met unexpected hostility from their neighbors. Paul takes pains to remind each congregation that he prepared them for this struggle in advance; he, and they, knew full well that resisting the empire's claims on their loyalties and their bodies would cost them dearly.

COMMUNITIES OF SOLIDARITY WITH THE CRUCIFIED

The radical vulnerability to which Paul calls his converts is crucially significant for the ekklesia's formation. The cross is "the foundation of the new [Pauline] community," Robert Hamerton-Kelly declares, but this does not mean that Paul "merely founds another 'sect of the Cross.'"[53] The congregations of the crucified are established in a reality other than the sacred violence upon which human community is so often founded. René Girard writes that "since the truth about violence will not abide in the community, but must inevitably be driven out, its only chance of being heard is when it is in the process of being driven out, in the brief moment that precedes its destruction as the victim. The victim therefore has to reach out at the very moment when his mouth is being shut by violence."[54]

For Paul, Robert Hamerton-Kelly declares, "the antidote to sacred violence is identification with the victim." Thus in his apostolic activity Paul deliberately takes his stand in the place of the victim. Paul's sufferings reveal the very heart of apostolic existence, for the apostles imitate the crucified Christ in his self-emptying (2 Cor. 8:9; Phil. 2:5–11). Writing to the Corinthians, Paul explicitly identifies the apostles as "the scapegoats of the world, the noxious waste of all things, until now" (1 Cor. 4:13). "Suffering is an integral part of the apostolic ministry" described in 2 Corinthians, not because of the inherent value of suffering as such, but because "reconciliation can take place only through knowledge of the mechanism of the scapegoat."[55]

The church as well is "the body of the victim and so the target rather than the source of sacred violence." Its rites, baptism and the Eucharist, "are essentially rites of identification of the victim," for baptism is a dying with Christ, specifically to the dominion of death (Romans 6), and the Eucharist is the "proclamation of the Lord's death until he comes" (1 Cor. 11:26).[56]

Scholars recognize Paul's solemn declaration in Gal. 3:28 as a formula used by his congregations at baptism: "As many of you as were baptized into Christ have clothed yourself with Christ. There is no longer Jew or Greek, there is no longer slave or free, there is no longer male and female; for all of you are one in Christ Jesus."[57] Indeed, Paul's exhortations constantly appeal to his audiences to "remember your baptism" (see 1 Cor. 6:1–11; Romans 6, 8:12–17; Gal. 3:26–4:6).

Wayne A. Meeks observes that Paul's exhortations are saturated with metaphorical references to aspects of the baptism ritual: "nudity, symbolic death, rebirth as a child, abolition of distinctions of role and status." The "abolition of distinctions of role and status" is characteristic of the moment in initiation rites when individuals cross a ritual threshold from one way of being to another. Within a small, homogeneous society, when the change is from one status to another—from boy to man, for example, or from single to married—the threshold stage is temporary. The intense sense of a common humanity gives way once the ritual transition is accomplished and the participants move smoothly into a new status within the continuing social order. But "baptism in early Christianity was different from that," Meeks writes. Joining a community that rehearsed its distinctiveness from "the world," Christian initiates were plunged into a permanent "threshold" state. "The ekklēsia itself, not just the initiates during the period of their induction, is supposed to be marked by sacredness, homogeneity, unity, love, equality, humility, and so on."

The Pauline congregations experienced considerable tension between this ideal of community and the normal structures of the larger society, perhaps inevitably, since "the Christians continue to live in the city and to interact with its institutions, and besides, they still carry some of its structures in their minds and in the houses where they meet." Nevertheless the sense of community experienced in baptism, "in which divisions of role and status are replaced by the unity of brothers and sisters in the new human, ought to be visible, in Paul's intention, in the [Lord's] Supper." It is that meal, as Paul intends it to be understood in 1 Corinthians 11, that allows the intensely communal feeling of the threshold experience to "linger in [the congregation's] daily life."[58]

Paul understood baptism and the Lord's Supper as moments that revealed with intense clarity the Christian's ongoing participation in the body of Christ, at once crucified and alive again (Rom. 6:3–4; 1 Cor. 11:26). His vision of the transformed body of Jesus, still bearing the marks of crucifixion yet raised, living, radiant, no longer subject to death, had changed the way he had looked upon the bodies of the Jewish messianists whom he previously had persecuted. For Paul, the body of Christ became a "condensed symbol" conveying at once all the power of Roman imperialism concentrated upon a single human body *and* the archetypal experience of Israel's oppression by foreign powers (N. T. Wright).[59] Convinced of the terrible necessity of violence, Paul had replicated Rome's violence against Israel in his own persecution of his brothers and sisters. In the light of his vision of the crucified and risen Jesus, however, the mirage of the necessity of violence had evaporated. For this reason, the symbolism of the body of Christ never allowed Paul to mystify oppression or to escape into mystical rapture; neither did it allow a "realistic" acceptance of the oppression perpetrated by the "rulers of this age."

From the point of his conversion on, the holiness of bodies infused with the same "Spirit of holiness" that had raised Jesus from the dead (Rom. 1:4) was more real to Paul than the iron that had pierced Jesus' body and that now continued to shackle the bodies of his followers. In the holiness of their bodies precisely as they continued in vulnerability to suffering, the baptized were an anticipation of the glorious liberation of all creation (Rom. 8:18–24).

In the words of historian Peter Brown, Paul was "a man whose whole body ached for the great change that might soon come upon it. He lived his life poised between revelation and resurrection":

> In Paul's letters, we are presented with the human body as in a photograph taken against the sun: it is a jet-black shape whose edges are suffused with light. Perishable, weak, "sown in dishonor," "always carrying the death of Jesus" in its vulnerability to physical risk and to bitter frustration, Paul's body was very much an "earthen vessel." Yet it already glowed with a measure of the same spirit that had raised the inert body of Jesus from the grave: "so that the life of Jesus may be manifested in our mortal flesh."[60]

In encouraging a cruciform vulnerability to the world, Paul envisions Christian existence "as a living out of the nonviolent life of the divine victim in the world of sacred violence," in Robert Hamerton-Kelly's words;[61] in Paul's own, the "showing-forth of the Lord's death" (1 Cor. 11:26), the "carrying about in our bodies the dying of Jesus, so that the life of Jesus may also be manifested in our bodies" (2 Cor. 4:10). The ekklesia, Hamerton-Kelly suggests, is a "new community of non-acquisitive and nonconflictual agape love," "founded on the possibility of nonrivalrous mimesis."[62] Appeals for harmony, mutual regard, and affection within the ekklesia are deliberately opposed to the values of rivalry that saturate the surrounding culture. "Let no one seek his own advantage, but rather the advantage of the other" (1 Cor. 10:24); "I bid all of you to think of yourselves no more highly than appropriate, but think with sober judgment. . . . Love one another with brotherly affection; compete with one another in showing honor" (Rom. 12:3, 10); "be of the same mind, having the same love, being of full accord" (Phil. 2:2–4); "let us have no self-conceit, no mutual provocation or envy" (Gal. 5:26). These values also extend to outsiders: "may the Lord make you increase and abound in love for one another and for all people" (1 Thess. 3:12); "let us do good to all people" (Gal. 6:10); "so far as it is in your power live peaceably with everyone" (Rom. 12:18).

But we must press behind this rhetoric to ask how these values of mutuality and "solidarity with the victim" were to be incarnated. Did Paul's rhetoric have any contact with the actual dynamics of exploitation and oppression in his age?

We should note, first of all, that Paul does not leave community values of mutuality and solidarity in the abstract. The "brotherly love" the Thessalonians show one another (1 Thess. 4:9) is shared "throughout all of Macedonia" (4:10); such specificity suggests financial or material aid, as 2 Cor. 8:2–4 confirms. Further, the collection "for the poor among the saints in Jerusalem" (Rom. 15:25–27) not only has a particular eschatological significance for Paul (as we saw in chapter 5);[63] it also expresses "solidarity with them and all others" (*koinōnia eis autous kai eis pantas,* 2 Cor. 9:13).

But can we say more? Given the fact that Paul's letters do not outline a program of social transformation, is there any evidence that the apostle's rhetoric has any contact with the realities of socioeconomic exploitation and oppression?

I note, first of all, that Paul was perfectly aware of operating in the midst of an elaborate social grid of patron-client relationships. Recent scholarship has shown that patronage embedded inequalities of power and privilege in a logic of reciprocal obligation, serving to distribute power "from the top down," the "top" being of course the emperor.[64] Peter Marshall has shown that Paul's refusal to accept the obligations implied by aid from the elite of Corinth provoked their animosity, and the rhetoric of "enmity" in 2 Corinthians.[65] Significantly, although Paul accepts the patronage of those more closely his peers (Phoebe of Cenchrae is his *prostasis,* Rom. 16:1–2), he refuses to submit to the patronage of the powerful in Corinth, not because he fears a diminution of his personal prestige, but because, in his eyes, the truth of the gospel itself is at stake. It is Christ who speaks in him, who "was crucified in weakness but lives by the power of God; for we are weak in him, but in dealing with you we shall live with him by the power of God" (2 Cor. 13:3–4). Apparently the power that raised the crucified Jesus from the dead must not be laundered into the currency of Roman honor.[66]

Paul offers no analysis of class conflict, but was he unaware of its reality? In a society where wealth consisted "above all in the ownership of land, and in the control of unfree labor," the assets that above all "enabled the propertied classes to exploit the rest of the population," Paul's congregations (with the conspicuous exception of Corinth) were probably drawn from the ranks of small, independent artisans and merchants, people who "neither exploited the labor of others (outside their own families) to any appreciable extent nor were they exploited to any marked degree, but lived not far above subsistence level," forming "a kind of intermediate class, between exploiters and exploited." More usually, however, they were "only too likely to be exploited."[67] It is true that in his letters to audiences from this class, Paul says nothing categorical about either slavery or land ownership. On the other hand, it is telling that Paul can, by carefully crafted rhetoric, urge Onesimus's master to renounce his prerogatives over his slave (Philemon). Further, as I argued in chapter 2, the way he refers without elaboration to the "duty" he could "command" of the slaveowner (Philem. 8) strongly suggests that his formation of the ekklesia already included definitive, if not comprehensive, teaching concerning the exploitation of others.

If we conceive of "class" in terms of relationships of power, we will understand that being a slave was a matter of legal status, but not necessarily of class. In other words, many exploited people were slaves, but not all slaves were exploited to the same degree. Thus, although "the people of Paul's culture did have, contrary to many modern assumptions, a concept of class conflict," according to Dale B. Martin, it would be anachronistic to expect that these same people would "place slavery unproblematically on one side of the class dichotomy." As we have seen, Paul uses terms that refer to class relations ("the powerful" [hoi dynamoi], "the nothings" [hoi mē ontes], "the haves" [hoi echontes], "the have nots" [hoi mē echontes]: 1 Cor. 1:26–29; 11:18–22).[68] It is quite conceivable, therefore, that although Paul never formulated an attack on the legal category of slavery as such, he did not hesitate to condemn the sort of exploitation to which many slaves were subjected.

It is no less significant that Paul urges the Thessalonians not to exploit or defraud each other in business (en tō pragmati, 1 Thess. 4:6), and that he urges them to "live quietly, mind your own affairs, work with your hands . . . so that you may command the respect of outsiders, and be dependent on no one" (4:11–12, RSV). The reason Paul says he wants the Thessalonians to work with their own hands is so they will not rely on the labor of others (hina . . . mēdenos chreian echēte).[69] The "quietism" Paul encourages is not withdrawal from the sphere of public life (he in fact hopes Christians will "command the respect of outsiders"),[70] but withdrawal from the public frenzy of exploitation (hyperbainein kai pleonektein, 4:6). Paul is obviously no social analyst;

but he can recognize, and rejects on principle, the exploitation of the labor of others.[71]

Similarly it would be anachronistic to look to Paul for an anticipation of the modern feminist critique of patriarchal culture. Nevertheless I notice that Paul exhorts the men of Thessalonica to avoid sexually exploitative behavior (*porneia*) and to "control their bodies" (1 Thess. 4:3–4, RSV margin). That, of course, is a translator's gentle euphemism; Paul is more candid. "Manage your 'tools' with holiness and honor," he commands, employing a double entendre as effective in Greek as in English.[72] Against the contours of an abusive culture of male domination, Paul dramatically restricts the "reign of the phallus" to the bounds of holiness and honor.[73]

On the positive side, Paul's letters provide considerable evidence for the active leadership of women in the congregations to which he wrote and suggest that Paul's normal relationships with women were characterized by mutuality and respect. The only causes for hesitation in this regard are, first, the poisonously patriarchal interpolation in 1 Cor. 14:33–35 and the pseudepigraphic Ephesians or 1 Timothy, none of which can rightly be taken as evidence of Paul's views; and, second, two other passages in 1 Corinthians, namely chapter 7 (to which we return momentarily), and 11:2–16. Both these passages are notoriously difficult to interpret, particularly given their character as only one half of a conversation (to put the matter generously). But aspects of 1 Corinthians 7 can be described as "a frontal assault" on the patriarchal ethos of the age (Elisabeth Schüssler Fiorenza); and whatever else the discussion of head coverings in 11:2–16 is meant to accomplish, at any rate it clearly recognizes the authority (*exousia*) of charismatic women to lead the congregation in prayer and prophecy. If not a "feminist," Paul was clearly not the misogynist the Pauline tradition quickly made him.[74]

These exegetical "samples" are not incidental aspects of Paul's thought. The sustained argument in 1 Corinthians and in Romans will show us that Paul made "solidarity with the victim" the criterion of life together. As I suggested in chapter 3, there is reason to believe Paul recognized and taught what some Latin American bishops would later call the preferential option for the poor. "God chose what is foolish in the world to shame the wise," he writes to the Corinthians; "God chose what is weak in the world to shame the strong, God chose what is low and despised in the world, even things that are not, to bring to nothing things that are" (1 Cor. 1:27–28). That logic, revealed in the resurrection of the crucified (1:17–25), was also evident in Paul's formation of an alternative ekklesia—the term routinely referred to a "public assembly" within a Roman colony[75] —composed of the low-born, the uneducated, and the powerless (1:26). Such a congregation forfeits its very being, Paul insists, when the poor go hungry or are held in contempt

(11:20–22). Thus he urges the Christians of Rome, "Make your way with the oppressed" (tois tapeinous synapagomenoi, Rom. 12:16).

As Luise Schottroff writes, an orientation toward the the poor as "the primary representatives of the people of God is clear in the writings of Paul . . . . If one considers that Roman society oriented itself in all of its politics and economy to the interests of the wealthy (plousioi), the explosive power of the Christian faith becomes clear."[76]

We should expect the ethos of discernment, resistance, and solidarity to which Paul called his congregations to encounter the most resistance among those Christians who stood to lose the most. The tension between the dominant Roman culture and the "heavenly citizenship" Paul sought to promote is most evident in the more extended letters to the Corinthians, which provide our most intimate data regarding life in the early ekklesia, and in Romans.

CHALLENGING THE IDEOLOGY OF PRIVILEGE: 1 CORINTHIANS

Because it provides tantalizing glimpses into social realities in the Pauline ekklesia, 1 Corinthians has attracted a great deal of attention from interpreters applying social scientific methods and models. While earlier investigations of the letter often relied on identifying the distinct programs of the "parties" referred to in 1:10–13 (F. C. Baur, C. K. Barrett), or on reconstructing a religio-historical background such as Gnosticism (Walter Schmithals) or "Hellenistic-Jewish syncretism" (Dieter Georgi) behind the Corinthian "heresy,"[77] more recent studies emphasize the social basis for the tensions within the Corinthian assemblies. The "factions" referred to in 1:10–13 now appear to reflect different estimations among the Corinthians of Paul alongside other Christian leaders, involving a preference for the more rhetorically skilled Apollos and an unwillingness on the part of some to submit their affairs to Paul's arbitration.[78] Paul's discussion of sexuality and marriage (1 Corinthians 5–7) is now accounted for in terms of ascetic impulses in early Christianity rather than on the dubious premise of rampant libertinism in Corinth.[79]

Studies by E. A. Judge, Gerd Theissen, and Wayne A. Meeks have established that many of the problems Paul addresses have arisen from social stratification within the Corinthian ekklesia.[80] As Theissen argues, if in 1 Cor. 1:26 "Paul says that there were not many in the Corinthian congregation who were wise, powerful, and well-born, then this much is certain: there were some. . . . If the actual number of such people was small, their influence must be accorded all the more import."[81]

We can reconstruct the events that led to the crisis Paul addresses with some confidence. Paul responds to the troubling oral report from

"Chloe's people" (1:10–13) by reminding the Corinthians of his activity in founding their congregation (1:13–17) and asserting his exclusive authority over them as apostle, the one who "planted" them (3:6–9) and "laid their foundation" (3:10–15), their "father" (4:14–15).[82] He repeatedly distinguishes the priority of his work from the secondary but no less valid work of Apollos ("I planted, Apollos watered"; "I laid the foundation, others have built upon it"). Paul is careful not to criticize his "co-worker" Apollos (3:9), although his name stands over one of the "slogans" in 1:12. Apparently the problem to which Paul refers with these slogans has to do not with any error or inadequacy on Apollos's part, but with the Corinthians' evaluation of his significance.[83]

Combined with Paul's strenuous insistence that he baptized only a few of the Corinthians at the first (1:14–17)—he is careful, of course, to point out that he baptized enough—these observations suggest the sequence of events that provoked 1 Corinthians. After Paul established a small congregation by baptizing a few individuals of modest means ("not many . . . wise, powerful, well-born"), along with their households, he left, satisfied that he had thus produced the "firstfruits of Achaia" (16:15). Subsequently Apollos came to Corinth, and his powerful public speaking (compare Acts 18:24–28) made a much stronger impression among the ranks of the privileged in the colony. Apollos baptized a number of higher-status Corinthians ("I planted, Apollos watered"), so that the resulting congregation was a combination of "Paul's people" and "Apollos's people" (and perhaps a few others who belonged to neither contingent: those "of Cephas" and those "of Christ"), in which Apollos's converts exercised a disproportionate influence by virtue of their status within the colony.

On this reconstruction, the divisions Paul attributes to the slogans "of Paul" and "of Apollos" actually center on emerging tensions between the social perceptions and strategies of two groups: the relatively lower-status "charter members" of the congregation and the more recent converts of Apollos whose wealth, power, and status have subtly introduced new standards and expectations for community life.[84]

As Theissen and others have shown, the resulting social tensions explain a range of problems that Paul discusses in 1 Corinthians. Disputes over food sacrificed to "idols," for example, and meals in the sacred precincts of pagan temples (1 Corinthians 8, 10) reflect social stratification within the ekklesiai. Offending others by eating consecrated meat would have been a regular possibility only for the wealthier classes who would be invited to banquets in temples and would be the usual customers for meat in the marketplace. In contrast, those from the lower classes ate meat infrequently, and then only at "public distributions of meat which were always organized around a ceremonial occasion." As a result, the rich and the poor perceived idol meat differently: The rich looked on it with relative indifference; to the poor, "it belonged to a sacred time segregated from the everyday world. It had a 'numinous' character." Theissen further points out that "restrictions on meat sacrificed to idols were barriers to communication" in the *polis;* an upper-class Corinthian like Erastos, the city treasurer (Rom. 16:23), "could have jeopardized his public position had he rejected all invitations where 'consecrated meat' might have been expected."[85] Higher-status Christians in Corinth would have heard Paul's injunctions as an infringement on their accustomed privileges.[86]

The "knowledge" of the "strong" in Corinth (8:4; 10:23) served to rationalize for higher-status Christians their own social expectations as responsible Roman citizens. Cultural codes for acknowledging status in a heavily stratified society underlie the practices that Paul considers abuses at the Lord's Supper (11:17–34). Comparisons with private and cultic meals in Paul's day show that higher-status individuals would normally expect more and better food than lower-status persons who might be present. The same expectations had come to dictate the conduct of the Lord's Supper as well, in such a way that lower-status Christians were disadvantaged and even went hungry.[87]

Similar tensions are evident behind Paul's defensive comments regarding his own lack of rhetorical skill (1:17; 2:1–5). The elite may have valued rhetorical skill highly, particularly if they were engaged in litigation against each other in pagan courts (6:1–8), the arena where citizens competed with each other for honor as much as for money.[88]

Differences in social location may also determine tensions regarding charismata in the assembly. Dale B. Martin has observed that in various cultures "esoteric speech acts" normally function as indicators of high status and has argued that glossolalia functioned in this way in Corinth as well. On the other hand, Wayne A. Meeks has observed that glossolalia provides access to a form of power that "does not usually flow only in the normal channels of authority created by society, with its roles and statuses." That suggests that glossolalia provided an alternative means to achieve status through speech for those untrained in rhetoric.[89]

Discerning and Resisting the Ideology of Privilege

Interpreters have frequently spoken of a group of "pneumatics" who practiced a spiritual elitism in Corinth. Paul's repeated qualifications of certain general principles throughout the letter (e.g., "all things are lawful for me," 6:12, 10:23; "food is meant for the stomach and the stomach for food," 6:13; "it is well for a man not to touch a woman," 7:1; "all of us possess knowledge," 8:1, namely, that "an idol has no real existence," and "there is no God but one," 8:4) suggest that Paul is quoting slogans current among the Corinthians. The editors of the Revised Standard Version have consequently set many of these phrases within quotation marks in the text of the letter.

One of Gerd Theissen's key insights has been that the "knowledge" (*gnōsis*) celebrated in Corinth was neither a particular religio-historical tradition (there is no need to search for the roots of "Gnosticism in Corinth," for example), nor an abstract philosophy of human nature, but a pragmatic rationale for moving comfortably across the boundaries of the Christian assembly; a rationale, moreover, dictated by the requirements for full participation in the sacralized public life of a Roman colony.[90]

Significantly Paul refuses to debate the ideology of the Corinthian elite in exalted abstractions. In each case, Paul seems to affirm the "slogan" on principle, only to renounce it in practice. He insists, again and again, that behavior must be determined not by high-sounding principles of freedom and autonomy, but by the needs of one's brothers and sisters in the concrete situation. From the point of view of the letter's rhetoric, it is somewhat misleading to say that Paul "shares and approves" the elite knowledge of the "strong" in Corinth and "affirms [their] intellectual position" (Wayne A. Meeks),[91] for in each case it is Paul's concern to circumscribe the theoretical validity of *gnōsis* within the practical constraints of life together. "All things are permitted me, but not all things are beneficial" (6:12). "All of us have knowledge: knowledge puffs up; but love builds up" (8:1). "We all know that an idol is no real thing, and that there is no God but one. . . . But watch out: do not let your freedom somehow present a scandal to the weak" (8:4, 9). As Antoinette Clark Wire points out, Paul's apparent agreement really serves to restrict the freedoms of the strong; what appears a qualification of principle "turns to be a reversal in terms of advised conduct. . . . The result is limitation."[92]

Paul exposes the "knowledge" of the elite as a rationale for indifference. Measuring the ideology of *gnōsis* against the requirements of love, Paul finds it wanting, and rejects it as a basis for practice.

There is nothing oblique in Paul's confrontation with "the powerful" in Corinth (*hoi dynatoi,* 1:26), those who benefit from the grid of power relations imposed by Rome. He mocks the vaunt of those who wish to be regarded as benefactors, ready to exchange increments of wealth for debts of honor: "Who sees anything distinctive about you? What do you have that you were not given? If you were given it, why do you boast as if it were not a gift?" (4:7). His ironic taunt in 4:8 reflects the comfortable lives of some in Corinth: "Already you are filled! Already you are rich! Without us, you are already ruling!" The congregation is filled with self-satisfaction, which Paul assails as "boasting" and "being inflated" (4:6, 19). This is the satisfaction of the well-off, which has smothered the discontent and longing of the poor or, as Paul names them, "the foolish," "the vulnerable," "the ill-born," "the nothings," "the contemptible," "the have-nots" (1:27–28; 11:22).

He gasps at their observance of status distinctions at the common meal: "I hear there are divisions among you, and I almost believe it. For there actually has to be discrimination in your meetings, so that, if you please, 'the elite' may stand out from the rest!"[93] His rebuke is withering. "Do you despise the church of God and hold the have-nots in contempt? What do you expect me to say; shall I congratulate you in this? I certainly will not!" (11:22). At last he exclaims, "When you come together to eat, wait for one another—if anyone is hungry, eat at home—so you do not come together to be condemned!" (11:31).

Astonishingly some interpreters take the outburst "eat at home!" as a sincere proposal on the apostle's part. It is, Gerd Theissen assures us, a workable compromise "which asks that the wealthy have their private meal (*idion deipnon*) at home, so that in the Lord's Supper (*kyriakon deipnon*) the norm of equality can prevail"[94] —the "norm of equality," we are to understand, having nothing to do with the difference between hunger and satiety. But how can anyone miss the acid irony dripping from the apostle's voice? He has already made it clear that the disparity between their separate meals (*idion deipnon*) disqualifies their eating together as the Lord's Supper (11:20–21). Are we really to understand that Paul now encourages the further privatization of the meal? Hardly! His response is a humiliating sarcasm for any who would display their status in the quality of food they are served at the common meal: "eat at home" (where no one can see what you eat)![95]

This is not prudent rhetoric. First Corinthians is filled with blunt talk, forcing the audience to see their social reality in light of the cross of Jesus (2:1–13). The letter may convey the "rhetoric of reconciliation," as Margaret M. Mitchell argues, but Paul has framed this rhetoric of reconciliation within an apocalyptic indictment of the "rulers of this age" who crucified Jesus (2:6–8) and who will be defeated by Jesus' messianic triumph in the near future (15:23–28). Paul's strategy, Mitchell writes, is to criticize "the norms and values of human politics which the Corinthians are mirroring by their factionalism." But we must recognize that this "human politics" wore a specifically Roman face in Corinth and that Paul chose to strip away this facade with the proclamation of the cross.[96]

At the same time Paul appeals for the unity of the Christian ekklesia, he calls them away from (the literal meaning of *ekklēsia*) the blithe consensus of the *polis*. It is the error of the Corinthian elite, from Paul's perspective, to have failed to recognize how incompatible these loyalties are. Thus Paul calls for an end to "factions" within the congregation yet also calls Christians to identify with what must appear to their neighbors as a particularly suspicious "faction" on the civic landscape, the rival ekklesia of the crucified Jesus.[97] The social order itself is under assault in 1 Corinthians. From now on, members of the ekklesia are to live within the city as resident aliens, whatever their imputed rank or status within the civic order. "Let those who do business live as those who have no possessions; those who profit from the world, as those who gain nothing from it. For the order of this world is disintegrating" (1 Cor. 7:30–31).

This is not the Stoic ethic of internalized indifference (*apatheia*). The practical cost to the elite will be high. Paul calls on them to relinquish the honor of superior treatment at the congregational sacred meal, an act with potentially revolutionary consequences beyond the boundaries of the ekklesia should it become known—as it did by the time of Celsus (second century c.e.)—that rich and poor, powerful and weak, free citizens and slaves are reclining at the same meal.[98] They are to abandon litigation in the courts, their primary recourse within the civic order for regaining the honor due them, even at the cost of sustaining economic or social "injury" (6:7–8). They must publicly censure and exclude from the assembly a sexual offender who may have been tolerated up to this point precisely on account of his status within the city.[99] In short, they must take conspicuous actions to renounce the privileges granted them within the city's sacred order of honor and power.

In 1 Corinthians Paul goes beyond a general repudiation of idolatry (compare 1 Thess. 1:10) to address the specific cultic responsibilities that would normally be expected of the elite in a Roman city. He categorically prohibits ritual meals in pagan shrines (1 Cor. 8:1–6; 10:14–22) and circumscribes conduct at private meals where idol meat could be expected. Higher-status Christians who followed his advice would have made themselves painfully conspicuous by their refusal to participate in these routine observances.[100]

Paul also proscribes one of the most widely recognized gestures of Roman piety when he insists that men may not cover their heads in prayer in the Christian ekklesia, as a Roman would normally do when he came before the gods of the city. Paul declares that this ordinary gesture dishonors their "head," who is Christ (11:2–16).

This passage has been read since the time of Tertullian, at least, as concerned with *women's* head-coverings, and thus as a restraint on women's freedoms (and an expression of Paul's fundamentally patriarchal perspective). But the argument of these verses has proven almost impenetrable on that assumption, as witness the abundance of competing and mutually contradictory interpretations.[101] Since what is supposed to be the burden of Paul's argument in the passage, that women ought to have their heads covered in public, is something he assumes his audience already recognizes as "proper" and "natural" (11:13–15), his supposed argument appears particularly inept ("the logic is obscure at best and contradictory at worst," declares Robin Scroggs; "tortuous and opaque," agrees Ross Shepard Kraemer).[102] It has proven just as difficult to explain why Paul, who clearly endorses the women's right to pray and prophesy in the assembly, should apparently want to subordinate them symbolically to a masculine hierarchy; or why, for their part, women who had supposedly thrown off such head coverings in an enthusiastic gesture of equality in the Spirit would be persuaded by Paul's supposed counterarguments about "propriety."[103]

Just what does Paul intend to accomplish in this passage? Because his instructions regarding men and women are set side by side, connected with the simple conjunction *de* ("and" or "but") rather than a stronger conjunction, it is not self-evident which way his argument flows. That his comments concerning women take up more space than those concerning men has usually been taken to indicate that women are the target of his rhetoric. But that assumption is unnecessary and in fact generates the very difficulties that continue to vex interpreters.[104] If we look instead to the order of Paul's argument, we observe that he wants the Corinthians to know, first of all, that "the head of every man is Christ" (11:3); and that the practical consequence of this teaching is, first of all, that "any man who prays or prophesies with his head covered dishonors his head," that is, Christ (11:4).[105]

That gesture on the part of a pious man was common enough, indeed ubiquitous, in Roman religion. Pulling his toga up over his head (in Latin, praying *capite velato;* in Greek, perhaps, *kata kephalēs echōn*)[106] was "the iconographic mark of a sacrificant presiding over a specifically Roman ritual," whether the emperor, a Roman priest, or a layman (Richard Gordon). This, several scholars have recently argued, is the most plausible context for the practices addressed by Paul in 1 Cor. 11:4.[107] This suggestion, which reverses the more conventional reading of the passage as restricting women's behavior, also arrives at a clearer logic. Paul discusses accepted cultural norms concerning hair (11:13–15) and women's head adornment in public (11:5–6), not because he wants to impose his own cultural standards (Jewish? Greek? Roman?) on the Corinthian women, but in order to establish a principle he regards as basically uncontroversial: that customs of head adornment bring honor or dishonor to one's social "head." Once it is established, he may then apply this principle to the gestures of men in prayer. Whatever he means by reference to "the angels" or to "authority" on the woman's head (11:10), the subordination of women is not his concern, as 11:8–9 and 11–12 clearly indicate.[108]

The thrust of Paul's argument is rather that for a man to adopt in the ekklesia a gesture recognized throughout the empire as the sign of *pietas,* and thus to emulate the emperor's own virtue, would dishonor the man's head, since that "head" is Christ (11:4)—the one whom Caesar's subordinate in Judea had crucified. The cross of Jesus is not named explicitly, of course; Paul apparently considers it sufficient to bring the significance of the head-covering gesture and the "headship" of Christ into juxtaposition, expecting the inappropriateness of praying *capite velato* then to become obvious.

Assuming the context of Roman men praying *capite velato,* David Gill concludes that (male) "members of the social elite within the church—

the *dynatoi* and the *eugeneis* (1:26)—were adopting a form of dress during worship which drew attention to their status in society." More important, the symbolic context of the head-covering gesture within the imagery of imperial piety suggests that the issue at stake goes beyond social stratification within the congregation. Corinthian images of both Augustus and Nero worshiping with their heads covered invited the onlooker to identify with the pyramid-like network of favoritism that channeled wealth and power upward to the emperor, even to feel awe and reverence before the sacred trappings of piety in which the imperium was cloaked.[109] Paul declares such reverence incompatible with the headship of Christ.

The spiritual program of the elite allowed them fuller participation in the cultic life of the city. Despite their sloganeering of "freedom" in which "all things are permitted," the effect within the ekklesia was (if we can trust Paul's argument at all!) to reinforce a very real barrier of material inequity and status discrepancy. Confident that "an idol is no real thing," the rich can attend the meals in pagan shrines that their civic responsibilities require, scandalizing their brothers and sisters for whom "idol meat" means only an ostentatious rehearsal of the benefaction of the city's gods. Enthusiasm for the life of the spirit has taken the form of encouraging rhetorical eloquence in the assembly, clearly the prerogative of an educated elite, something to which others may respond with a counter-barrage of glossolalia. Representing their wealth as God's blessing, the elite posture as the benefactors of the community and hold Paul in contempt when he rejects their patronage.

For the upper classes, there may have been a "free-market in honor" in the decades after Augustus (Antoinette Clark Wire). But there were relatively few Horatio Algers in Roman society (as there were in Horatio Alger's day);[110] there were numerous slaves like the protagonist in Apuleius' *The Golden Ass,* who finally escapes from a series of misadventures only through the intervention of a powerful patron, the god Isis.[111] "People with no influence became the victims of the competition for wealth. Peasants and slaves who worked the land bore on their bodies the force exerted by both taxes and rents."[112] Then—as in our own day, when treaties camouflage massive transnational exploitation and profiteering as a "Free Trade Agreement"—the rhetoric of "freedom" seems especially to have served the interests of the privileged.[113] The urgency of Paul's rhetoric, on the other hand, suggests that in his eyes, the poor of the Corinthian ekklesia are "free" only to endure the contempt of the "spiritual," and their neglect.

A Holy Solidarity with Those Not Yet Free

As we have seen, Paul's interpreters have routinely based generalizations about Paul's social ethic on 1 Corinthians 7, and especially on the "rule" in 7:17–24, "let everyone remain in the calling to which you were called." As a consequence, asking how "eschatological radicalism" and "social conservatism" relate in Paul's thought has usually meant asking how Paul's admonition to "remain," usually taken to mean "remain in your condition" (7:17–24), relates to his apocalyptic announcement that "the appointed time has grown short . . . the form of this world is passing away" (7:29–31). Albert Schweitzer collapsed the two attitudes into a single ethic, Paul's "theory of the *status quo*," according to which the expectation of imminent liberation *required* that no action be taken to improve circumstances now. Vincent Wimbush perceives "some awkwardness" on Paul's part as he endorses the Corinthians' radicalism yet qualifies it with the rule, "remain." Wimbush concludes that Paul uses eschatological language only because it expresses an indifference to worldly structures that Paul wants to promote among the Corinthian ascetics. Antoinette Clark Wire reads the passage as Paul's effort to rein in the emancipatory energies of holy women in Corinth. In her view, the more egalitarian aspects of 1 Corinthians 7 are mere concessions, calculated to leverage the holy women back into more conventional marital roles and thus save the congregation from *porneia*.[114]

But we have just seen a different struggle going on in 1 Corinthians. Paul confronts a theological rationale that allows wealthier Christians to negotiate the grid of patronage relationships with indifference to the poor; further, he contends against the ritual sacralization of that network in the civic cults. Can we make sense of 1 Corinthians 7 in the context of this struggle?

Whether or not Paul's declarations of an ascetic ideal are his quotations of slogans current among the Corinthians, he clearly assumes that ideal is not controversial.[115] At issue are sexual or marriage relationships that could be seen as falling short of the ascetic ideal. For some of the Corinthians, freedom from constraint is the highest value, and this means that asceticism is always preferable to sexual contact. *On principle*, then, "it is good for a man not to touch a woman."[116] But this principle has apparently raised questions among the Corinthians themselves.[117] Paul addresses real anxieties when he touches on marriage to a pagan spouse (Will my spouse be saved? 7:14, 16; Are my children holy? 7:15), and betrothals that predate entry into the Christian community (Do I dishonor my fiancée if I do not marry her? 7:36–38).

Given what we have seen about the Corinthian situation, we should not be surprised to discover that differences in socioeconomic status underlie tensions regarding sexual and marital relations as well. The congregation's "boast" concerning the immoral man in 5:1, for example, or the possibility, suggested by 6:15–17, that men in the church have gone to prostitutes, may have less to do with a principled libertinism than with the congregation's reluctance to challenge the personal conduct of some members of their congregation. One plausible explanation (though there is no way to prove this) is that the person(s) in question were members of the city's elite.[118]

Further, the anxieties about sexual liaisons—whether to withdraw from sexual relations within marriage (7:1), whether to divorce the spouse (7:10–16), whether to marry (7:25–40)—seem to arise from options considered by the relatively well off. The married, Paul says, "are anxious about worldly affairs," while the unmarried are free to pursue the "affairs of the Lord" (7:33–34). Apparently these are people whose time—and labor—are their own. With regard to these verses, early church historian Peter Brown speaks of wealthy, "cultivated" and "argumentative" householders in the Roman colony. "Leisured and sufficiently wealthy [to be] in a position to change the tenor of their lives from top to bottom," they engaged in "daring experiments in social living," particularly by undoing "the elementary building blocks of conventional society," that is, renouncing sexual life in marriage.[119]

But what about the unleisured, those whose circumstances tie them to nonbelieving husbands, fathers, or masters? Their anxieties regarding relationships across the community boundary (7:12–16, 36–38, 39) may reflect the disdain shown them by their social superiors within the church, who are at liberty to reshape their intimate lives around a spiritual ethic of autonomy and self-sufficiency. Paul's obvious enthusiasm for the celibate ideal (7:1, 7) may have aggravated those tensions: Are sexual liaisons as such to be avoided by the truly holy?[120]

Significantly, Paul argues that both abstinence and sexual contact within marriage are acceptable alternatives to engaging in immoral acts (*porneias*, 7:2), that is, sinning; either is preferable to being tempted to sin through lack of self-control or through "being aflame with passion" (7:5, 9). He thus concludes that those who marry and engage in sexual relations—with "self control" (7:37)—"do not sin" (7:28, 36); both celibacy and sexual activity in marriage are acceptable (one "does well," the other "does better"). Sexual activity within marriage, even if these are marriages with "nonbelievers," is acceptable. It is even desirable as a bulwark against immorality (*porneia*, 7:1-2).

The threat of *porneia* disappears after 7:1-2, however.[121] Paul clearly prefers celibacy, but only for those who enjoy the "gift" (*charisma*) of being able to exercise self-control (*enkrateia*) as celibates; he clearly assumes this route is not available or appropriate for everyone. The apostle seeks to defuse the volatile issue of sexuality by insisting that his preference for celibacy is not to be taken as an absolute rule for all Christians.

In light of this, the "rule" in 7:17-24, that everyone "remain in the calling to which God has called you" (7:17, 20), is manifestly not a general "rule of the status quo" that Paul applies to various specific situations; he does not even apply such a rule in this part of 1

Corinthians! In context these verses simply explain why Paul has encouraged celibate living, given that (as Paul is chiefly concerned to argue here) sexual relations, even with nonbelieving spouses, are not in fact sinful. In effect, the "rule" of "remaining in your calling" is the same as the "calling to peace" that discourages Christians from disputing a divorce from an unbelieving spouse (7:15); it hardly binds the Christian individual to a particular social status.

One's "calling" into Christ is not the same as one's standing in society; but one's social location is not a matter of indifference. The calling to holiness brings one into the sphere of God's lordship and thus moves one toward liberation. As Paul says in Galatians, "For freedom Christ has set us free; stand fast therefore, and do not submit again to a yoke of slavery" (5:1). The argument in 1 Corinthians prevents the elite of Corinth from identifying their own superiority to the powerless as a sign of God's preference. True, God has called a church in which the "educated, powerful, and well-born" are to be found (1:26), but there are "not many of these," and their presence does not define the church. It is rather the presence of the simple, the powerless, the low and despised, the "nothings" of the world (1:27-28), that is the sign of God's calling. True, some in the congregation can reasonably claim to be "satisfied" and "rich" and to "rule" (4:8-10); but since they enjoy these privileges alone, they are farther from God's call than the men and women whose poverty and harassment from the civil authorities defines their apostolate. It is the embodied sharing of Christ's fate rather than the possession of privilege or power that marks the church (11:26).

The bodies of the powerless, too, are holy, even though the labor of their bodies may belong to others within the structures of society. Yet this affirmation does not mean that Paul acquiesces in imbalances of power and privilege within that society. The bodies of the poor are holy, though not yet free; their holiness is nevertheless the guarantee of their coming freedom (Rom. 8:9-17).

CONFRONTING THE IDEOLOGY OF POWER (ROMANS)

We return at last to Romans, the letter that holds the potential to make or break any case for a "liberating Paul." As we have seen in previous chapters, this letter has enjoyed inordinate influence in Pauline interpretation on the premise, first, that it represents a summary of Paul's gospel. Recent suggestions that the letter was occasioned by particular circumstances in Rome, or in Paul's own apostolic mission, have modified, but not overthrown that premise.[122] Second, at least since the time of Luther the letter has been read as Paul's effort to address the relation of the Christian gospel to Judaism (and to Jews). Interpretation in the shadow of the Holocaust has changed the contours of that interpretation—Paul is increasingly perceived as criticizing Jewish "ethnocentrism" or "exclusivism" rather than "works-right-eousness"—but that he was primarily engaged in a "debate with Judaism" remains an almost universal premise.[123]

The net effect of these assumptions has been to locate the center of gravity in Paul's doctrine of salvation (or, alternatively, of "being in Christ") and consequently to push any ethical or social concern to the periphery of Paul's thought. As a consequence, the sheer mass of the "Paul" generally perceived in Romans threatens to eclipse the vision of a liberating Paul that I have sketched in previous chapters.

But not only are these assumptions hotly disputed in current research on Romans; I have already argued that they are in fact serious misapprehensions of Paul's purposes in that letter.[124] Paul writes in order to wrest from the empire the right to declare where justice is to be discerned. He calls the Christians of Rome to abandon the futility and senselessness of an unjust age (Rom. 1:18–32), an age "under the power of sin" and devoted to violence, an age that stands, Paul declares, under the indictment of the Torah:

> "Their throat is an open grave,
> they use their tongues to deceive";
> "The venom of asps is under their lips."
> "Their mouth is full of curses and bitterness."
> "Their feet are swift to shed blood,
> in their paths are ruin and misery,
> and the way of peace they do not know."
>
> (3:13–17)

Paul exhorts the baptized of Rome to throw off the coercive power of this age and to be so transformed in their thinking that they may offer themselves in holiness to God (12:1–2; 6:12–14). In fact the letter is built around this ideological intifada.[125]

The transformation Paul has in mind requires that specific perceptions and specific loyalties be changed. The burden of Paul's rhetoric in this letter is to change the way gentile Christians in Rome look upon Jews. These gentile Christians are not theological abstractions but flesh-and-blood residents of Rome, almost certainly accustomed to hearing Jews regularly denigrated in public discourse as at once avaricious and wretched, misanthropic and eager to proselytize; barbarous, lecherous, smelling of strange foods and personal habits.[126] In Roman eyes the Jews had proven themselves unsuitable as servants and as subjects.[127] Their resistance to anti-Jewish apartheid in Greek Alexandria had led to deadly riots that the emperor Claudius had called a war. There were "tumults" in Rome itself during Claudius's reign.[128] Romans knew well the antisemitic slanders of the Jews' enemies in Egypt,[129] and the overblown scandals involving Jewish charlatans in Rome itself,[130] and therefore Jewish writers such as Philo and Josephus were compelled in the following decades to answer these obscene slanders in the most dignified terms. And Romans knew, of course, that the homeland of the Jews was a seething cauldron of sedition.

The gentile Christians of Rome knew some Jews much more intimately, for certainly there were in the Roman churches Jews who had been expelled from the city under Claudius but had returned under Nero's rescript. These would have appeared a wretched lot: dispossessed, without sufficient food (for they insisted stubbornly on restricting their diets to the meager kosher food available), without adequate shelter (Juvenal would later write that the public parks had been "taken over" by Jewish indigents), forbidden by Roman law to gather in the streets.[131] To the opprobrium of public disgust the Gentiles of the Christian churches were in a position to add a theological judgment as well, what must have seemed to them a "theological fact" (Daniel Fraikin):[132] Just as God had punished Israel of old for its rebellion, so the human flotsam washing through Rome was evidence of God's judgment in their own time. Israel had fallen (compare Rom. 3:3, 9:6). The Jews' stubborn loyalty to their Torah was the foolish obstinacy of a doomed race.

The burden of Paul's argumentation throughout Romans is to move these gentile Christians away from a theology that scapegoats the Jews as the victims of God, as well as of Rome, to embrace an ethos of solidarity with them. The climax of the letter's argument is reached when Paul solemnly warns the Gentiles not to imagine in their conceit that they have replaced the Jews in God's favor. Despite all empirical evidence, it is God's mysterious will yet to save all Israel (11:13–32). That warning is channeled into the admonition to sober self-assessment in Romans 12 and the much more specific exhortation to the "strong," that is, gentile Christians, to defer to the "weak," that is, Jews, at common meals (14:1–15:13).[133]

The coherence and force of Paul's argumentation, then, is visible precisely in an assault on gentile Christian boasting and an appeal for gentile Christian solidarity with Israel.[134] This appeal is not based simply on the apocalyptic "mystery" of Israel's miraculous salvation (11:25); it is grounded in the necessity for Christians to resist conformity to this world (12:1–2). Thus Paul's vision is more than an apocalyptic dream of ethnic harmony: It is a vision of justice, centered on the resurrection of the crucified Messiah. "We who are powerful [*hoi dynatoi*] ought to make up the deficiencies of the powerless [*hoi astheneis*], and not satisfy ourselves . . . for Christ did not please himself; but as it is written, 'the reproaches of those who reproached you fell on me'" (15:1, 3).

The Theological Offense of Romans 13:1–7

In the midst of these chapters we strike the reef that threatens to capsize every Christian liberative project: the exhortation to "be subordinate to the governing authorities" in Rom. 13:1–7.

The terrible offense of these lines for us today arises from our own agonizing awareness, in the shadow of Auschwitz, and with our ears ringing with the screams from My Lai, Sharpesville, Sabra and Shatila, El Mozote, or Jean-Rabel, of how readily we acquiesce in the alibis our governments offer for murder and massacre. We know how monotonously this Pauline plea for the status quo has been mingled with those screams in our consciousness. These seven verses from Romans "have caused more unhappiness and misery in the Christian East and West than any other seven verses in the New Testament by the license they have given to tyrants," as they "have been used to justify a host of horrendous abuses of individual human rights" (J. C. O'Neill).[135] But the fault has not been Paul's. For that flood of suffering, each generation must bear its own responsibility.

We also recognize that whatever thin camouflage this passage has provided for Nazism, Apartheid, or the relentless pressure of American imperialism, some Christian witnesses have torn away in order to expose to each generation its own complicity in violence. In our age, it is the destiny of these words from Paul to be bound up again and again with a *status confessionis,* a crisis in which the very confession of Christ is at stake. Any exegesis that proceeds in blithe oblivion of this fact proceeds at the greatest spiritual peril.

This passage is deeply troubling; but there is more to our offense than horror at the violence of our age. We are also shocked that Paul could speak so positively of Rome in his own time, apparently so oblivious to the brutality around him. As Joseph Klausner wrote in 1939,

> When one considers all the shameful deeds of oppression, the murders and extortions, of the Roman government in every place where the hand of its authority reached, and particularly in the lands and provinces where Paul lived and travelled, one cannot escape a feeling of resentment and protest against this recital of praise for the tyranny of Caligula and Nero, or of Gessius Florus. One is forced to see in it flattery of the rulers.[136]

James Kallas agrees, yet goes even further: "Paul could not have ascribed such an exalted status to Rome without being not only hypocritical and servile, but untrue to his whole theological position."[137] Kallas and others offer pointed arguments that these verses from Romans 13 are dramatically out of line with the rest of Paul's thought and must be regarded as an interpolation. Absent here is any sense of the "estrangement of the world from God" (compare 2 Cor. 4:4, Gal. 1:4, 1 Cor. 7:31), or of the imminent expectation of the end of the age (compare the immediate context, Rom. 13:8, 11–12!). Absent here is any awareness that the "authorities" are arrayed against God (compare the "rulers" of 1 Cor. 2:6–8). Elsewhere Paul encouraged submission to the undeserved suffering meted out by a corrupt order (see Rom. 12:14); here that world order seems to win a contented endorsement. Indeed, the apocalyptic insight "profoundly engrained in the very substance of Pauline logic," that innocent suffering in this world is a sharing in the fate of Jesus, is missing entirely here.

Kallas concludes simply that "this is not Paul," and cites the textual disturbances involving Romans 14, 15, and 16 as evidence that "*something* has happened to the closing chapters of this epistle."[138]

But there is no significant evidence of textual disruption around these seven verses.[139] Despite Kallas's compelling observations that "this is not Paul" as he writes in other letters, I believe we must give some account of how these words nevertheless came from his pen.

The Historical Problem of Romans 13:1–7

This passage is so incongruous with other aspects of Paul's thought that we cannot read it straightforwardly as "Paul's theology of the state." Although it can hardly be construed as a text "by which Paul calls the authorities themselves to account" (against Stanley E. Porter),[140] neither is there any warrant for inflating these verses into a statement of Paul's "political realism" in which he required "living *within* the political system even if that meant living to a large extent in the terms laid down by that system" (James D. G. Dunn).[141] With an eye to other texts where Paul's view of the reigning authorities is much more sharply critical (e.g., 1 Thess. 5:3–11; 1 Cor. 15:24–26), Ernst Bammel rightly declares Rom. 13:1–7 "just as much a foreign body when seen from the general viewpoint of Pauline theology as it is evidence for an exceptional case when viewed historically"; he concludes that "in an account of the Pauline view of the state, Romans 13 must be given its place rather in a side aisle than in the nave."[142] In a more recent article, Rebecca DeNova has even maintained that "most modern scholars are agreed that this passage neither establishes an agenda for 'blind obedience,' nor a theology of political power, as they were not part of Paul's agenda,"[143] although (like many declarations of scholarly consensus) this conclusion may be rather premature.[144]

In a number of recent studies, interpreters justifiably reluctant to accept the passage as a Pauline theology of the state have tried to identify the specific historical circumstances that elicited Paul's admonition here, and thus in effect to circumscribe the passage's significance. While illuminating, none of these studies alone has proven sufficient to explain why this exhortation appears just here in the letter to Rome.

Ernst Käsemann saw in the passage a challenge to a form of Christian "enthusiasm" that "in virtue of heavenly citizenship views authorities with indifference or contempt."[145] But the category of "enthusiasm" is so vague, and the social phenomenon so unsubstantiated for Rome (Käsemann relied on generalizations from the Corinthian correspondence in describing "enthusiasm" in Rome), that this argument has not won support.[146]

Two other approaches have met with wider approval by virtue of their greater precision. One approach looks to Tacitus's reference (*Annals* 13:50) to public unrest in Rome around 58 C.E. protesting the corruption of the agencies responsible for tax farming in Italy.[147] G. Friedrich, O. Pöhlmann, and P. Stuhlmacher have argued that Paul writes with regard to this very specific situation, urging Christians not to engage in public disturbances, but to submit to paying their taxes.[148] This hypothesis has proven attractive to a number of interpreters,[149] but it has been criticized by others for finding no explicit support in the text.[150] It is further weakened if, with a number of scholars, we take the phrase in 13:6, *dia touto gar kai phorous teleite,* as an indicative ("this is also the reason you pay taxes") rather than an imperative ("for this reason, you must even pay taxes!").[151]

Marcus Borg has argued that the passage must be set "within the context of Jewish nationalism." Noting a series of parallels throughout Rom. 12:14–21 to Synoptic traditions in which Jesus repudiated "the path of armed national resistance," Borg concludes that similar anti-Roman sentiments must have been abroad among the Jews of Rome as well; he appeals for corroboration to Suetonius's reference to "tumults" during the time of Claudius.[152] I find no reason to doubt that Jews in Rome were sympathetic with the nationalist struggle in Judea.[153] In fact what Paul says earlier in this letter, and in the immediately preceding verses where Paul anticipates both persecution from the ekklesia's enemies and eschatological vindication by God (12:14, 17–21), could hardly be expected to have a calming effect on the subjects of the empire! Nevertheless there is no more direct indication in the letter that Paul sought to rein in anti-Roman agitation among the Jews of Rome.[154]

Although these studies have increased our understanding of the historical context in which Romans was written, none satisfactorily explains why Paul would have responded to the specific situation in Rome with just this argument. Indeed, the subtle effect of either theory—agitation over taxation or Jewish militancy against Rome—is only to raise the question of Paul's rhetorical competence most acutely. We have to wonder, in the first place, whether restive members of the ekklesia, tempted to rebellion (13:2) by the exorbitant abuses of the tax gatherers, really would have had their minds changed by platitudes about magistrates serving the good and punishing only the bad (13:3, 4). Or would these verses really have carried weight "in a situation in which the authorities were held to be 'the sons of darkness' at war with 'the sons of light,' not to speak of the oppressors and pollutants of the land God gave his children" (J. I. H. McDonald)?[155]

Further, on either reconstruction we are left wondering about Paul's own perceptions and motives. If he is intimately aware of tax abuses in Italy, perhaps through the additional burden imposed on his friends Prisca and Aquila,[156] how can he speak so blithely of the benevolence, or at least the benignity, of the authorities? If he is addressing anti-Roman agitation on the part of Jews in Rome, do his arguments here imply so thorough an alienation from the Jewish cause that he might rightly be described as an apostate and a renegade? If Paul's goal is purely pragmatic, isn't his praise of the rulers effusive? If on the other hand we imagine him speaking from a coherent theological standpoint, aren't we thrown back onto the conventional reading of the passage as a more or less global "theology of the state" or as Paul's articulation of the "requirements" of Christian spirituality, "the inevitable outworking of the Christian grace of humility"?[157]

This passage stubbornly resists integration with the argument of the rest of the letter. Unfortunately, right though they are in principle, recent attempts to relate 13:1–7 with the overarching concern in the rest of Romans—the relation between Jews (or Jewish Christians) and gentile Christians—too often have miscarried because of the same misconceptions of the letter's purposes that I have discussed.

On Marcus Borg's view, for example, the question Paul addresses in Rom. 13:1–7 is at heart a question about *Jewish* boasting: "Does Israel have some special claim on God's grace which commits God to preserving their particularity and separateness, that is, their nationhood?" This is, of course, the agenda Christian interpreters have usually perceived in the "debate with Judaism" in Romans 1–4. Borg shares that perception, declaring that in the earlier part of Romans "those features to which first-century Judaism commonly pointed as signs of God's special favour are systematically reviewed and reinterpreted in such a way as to nullify their national significance." The message Borg finds in Romans 1–11, that "Israel has no special claim on God's grace," becomes the basis for Paul to insist in Rom. 13:1–7 that whatever obligation the gentile Christians in Rome feel toward Israel, that obligation "cannot encompass participation in their cause against Rome."[158]

I doubt that is the message of Romans. As we have seen, the mood Paul confronts among the gentile Christians of Rome is hardly an unrestrained tide of sympathy with the Jews in the capital city, let alone in Judea!

Borg not only reads the theology of Romans through the lens of Ephesians, declaring that "salvation for Paul is fundamentally corporate and involves the reconciliation of Jew and Gentile into one body"; he concludes that for Paul, "the Roman government contributes to this work of Christ ('your good') to the extent that it restrains the perpetuation of that particularity which partially produced the hostility," namely, "Israel's cause."[159] By Rome's "contribution" Borg apparently means the expulsion of thousands of Jews from their homes and the imposition of martial law in the streets; such measures, we are given to understand, are in harmony with Paul's gospel, which sees only the benefit for the gentile-Christian majority ("your good"). But this flies in the face of Paul's agonized appeal in Romans 9–11.

James D. G. Dunn offers a different explanation of Rom. 13:1–7. We must take account of the "political realities confronting the Christian groups in Rome," meaning the dreadful risk gentile Christians ran of being identified with Jews in the wake of the Claudian expulsion, and of "Paul's attempt to redraw the boundaries of the redefined people of God" in "nonethnic terms." The apostle cautions the ekklesia to be subordinate to the ruling authorities, Dunn writes, in order to avoid putting "the political status of the new congregations at risk."[160] He thus provides "a theology of the orderly state, of good government," as a sort of safe conduct pass for the Christians of Rome.

But it was the gentile church of Rome, not Paul, that was going about "redrawing the boundaries of the people of God in nonethnic terms"—as Dunn himself recognizes: "Whatever [Paul] might claim about Gentiles being grafted into the olive tree of Israel, the political reality was that the new congregations were in process of shedding the identity of ethnic Israel, and the sociological reality was that the believers in Jesus as the Christ were breaking down or ignoring the very boundaries which had given the Jews their distinctiveness and thus their protection." Apparently Dunn would have us believe this was a development Paul was concerned to accelerate, in order to protect gentile members of the ekklesia from the harassment Jews must expect to endure.

But this is not what Romans is about. If Rom. 13:1–7 really belongs to this letter, we should read these verses as part of an argument addressed to a church in which the gentile Christian's inclination to dispossess the Jew, politically as well as theologically, has provoked the apostle's concern. That much is evident from the letter's climax in chapter 11.

It is the emerging theological consensus of gentile Christianity, not the "dangerous" view of an embattled Jewish minority, that Paul confronts here.[161] What sense can we make of Rom. 13:1–7 in that context?

An Exhortation against Rivalry

The historical treatments just discussed finally prove unsatisfactory because they have not gone far enough. They have identified very specific historical circumstances that might have provided points of contact for these seven verses, either as an exhortation to pay taxes (13:7) or to renounce the revolutionary cause in Judea (13:2), but they have not connected these historical circumstances with an adequate view of what Paul is trying to do in the rest of the letter.

The very specificity of these proposals is also their weakness. If we ask more broadly about the precarious position Jewish communities usually held in the Roman diaspora, we can see just how volatile these factors could be in combination. In this regard, Luise Schottroff is right to suggest that seeking a precise "historical situation" is less appropriate than a "life context" for the passage.[162]

Only twenty years before Paul penned this letter, the Jewish population of Alexandria—the largest concentration of Jews in the world outside of Judea—had suffered a dreadful pogrom. The emperor Augustus had earlier set the scene for catastrophe by confirming the Jews' long-held (and much resented) privileges at the same time he imposed a capital tax (*laographia*) on noncitizens, including the Jews. Wealthier segments of the Jewish population lobbied for citizenship. They were rebuffed in a furious campaign of antisemitic propaganda that left scars still evident today.

After Caligula came to power, it became known that the Jews of Alexandria declined to offer the worship the emperor increasingly demanded. The city's Greek citizenry also knew that the Roman governor, Flaccus, stood in the emperor's disfavor. Playing on the governor's fear, they channeled their resentment of Rome, whom they could not resist directly, into fury against Rome's "protégés the Jews, who were at hand and far more vulnerable" (Mary Smallwood).[163] Yielding to their fury, Flaccus allowed the desecration of synagogues, deprived the Jews of their civic rights, moved them into a ghetto, confiscated their property, and arrested members of the Jewish council. These moves whipped the Alexandrian Greeks into a frenzy of "pillaging, destruction, beatings, torture, and murder" (John G. Gager).[164]

Looking back upon the horror after Flaccus's execution and Caligula's assassination, the emperor Claudius spoke frankly of "the war against the Jews." Claudius imposed a truce, commanding the Alexandrians "not to dishonor any of [the Jews'] customs in their worship of their god." But he refused to grant the Jews citizenship, insisting to the contrary that they be content with the advantages they already enjoyed in "a city not their own." He evidently held the Jews responsible for the pogrom, for he prohibited them from receiving Jews from Roman Syria (where Caligula's insanity had almost brought on another catastrophe) and threatened, "If they disobey, I shall proceed against them as fomenting a common plague for the whole world."

Two aspects of this violent episode are important for our purposes. First, we see how readily even an established Jewish population could become the scapegoats of other groups resentful of Roman domination. As Gager observes regarding the leaders of the pogrom in Alexandria, "Their own anti-Semitism had its roots not in hatred of Jews as such but in nationalistic and violent anti-Romanism."[165] We know the Jewish community of Rome was even less organized and thus more vulnerable, as the expulsions under Tiberius (19 C.E.) and Claudius (49 C.E.) demonstrate.[166] As Dunn observes, in Rome as elsewhere "Jews, by reason of their special privileges, above all in the matter of taxation (the unique provisions regarding the temple tax), would have been in an especially sensitive position," as is illustrated by the antagonism of Cicero and others.[167]

Second, we observe that the propaganda war begun in Alexandria was continued in Rome itself, as both Alexandrian and Jewish delegations sued for vindication before Caligula (Philo, *Embassy to Gaius*). Not only did the anti-Jewish slanders of Chaeremon or Apion find a ready audience in Rome, they flourished there, requiring Josephus to address them decades later in his *Against Apion*.

As in Alexandria, so in Rome. A constant current of anti-Semitism would have led Paul to expect that any popular outcry against exploitive taxes might be deflected onto the most vulnerable population in the city: the Jewish refugees, who come directly into view in Rom. 14:1–15:13. Ironically, the Jews were often perceived as the undeserving beneficiaries of official largesse. They appear in hostile pagan writings as the ancient equivalents of Ronald Reagan's mythical "welfare queens." Note that Paul urges the ekklesia to "welcome the weak" at common meals (15:1) by appealing to the example of Christ, who bore the insults of others (15:3) and "became the servant of the circumcision" (15:8).

The curious combination in 13:1–7 of pragmatism (13:2, 4b) and idealism regarding the authorities (4a, 6) is not meant to "propound philosophically grounded theories concerning the essence of the state," for Paul is not a teacher of philosophy (Luise Schottroff).[168] Paul means simply to keep members of the ekklesia from making trouble in the streets. He wants to deflect his audience from private resentments and from the calculation of one's just deserts, for these are the spiritual roots of scapegoating violence against the poor; and to impel them rather toward mutual compassion and striving for the common good.

I doubt that Paul's suggestions that the authority is already the "servant of God on your behalf for the good" (13:4) and that one pays taxes precisely because "the authorities are ministers to God, diligently attending to the same thing" (13:6) constitute his evaluation of government in the abstract or government officials in particular. These arguments are mere rhetorical commonplaces, meant only to focus the audience's attention on the discernment of "the good" (compare 12:1–2) which finds expression in recognizing one's obligations to others (12:3–13). Thus the obligations of 13:7—to give taxes and revenue, and respect and honor, as due—yield naturally to the over-arching obligation to "owe no one anything but mutual love" (13:8).

If Paul's remarks in 13:1–7 address specific historical circumstances in Rome, they do so in such a way as to extend to those circumstances the more general ethos Paul has encouraged in the preceding verses: an ethos of mutual accommodation and harmony within the ekklesia (12:3–13) and an ethic of nonretaliation toward enemies without (12:14–21). As Gordon Zerbe has shown, the wider context of Romans 12 and 13 involves the theme of nonrivalrous love (*agapē anypokritos*, 12:9) and "the apocalyptic conflict between the aeons of good and evil" (12:19–20; 13:11–13). The apostle entertained no illusions that efforts to live peaceably with all (12:18) would "effect a change in the abuser" or achieve "the conversion and reconciliation of opponents." Never-theless Paul encourages the "unilateral readiness" to pursue peace, in the conviction that this is "the proper conduct with which one battles evil, the method by which Christians gain ultimate victory" *through God's vindication.*[169]

Within this context, Paul's exhortation to be subordinate to the authorities (13:1–7) focuses the ethic of nonretaliation on a potentially volatile situation. Just as Christians are to "live peaceably with all," leaving vindication to God (12:18–20), and thus to "overcome evil with good" (12:21), so they are to "do good" within the city (13:3), cooperating with the authorities as they "diligently pursue the same goal" (13:6). They are not to take the righting of wrongs into their own hands by opposing the present "disposition" (*diatagē*) of earthly power, *since God's redisposition of the powers is imminent anyway* (13:11–14).

There is no "theology of the state" here, beyond the conventional prophetic-apocalyptic affirmation that God disposes the rise and fall of empires and gives the power of the sword into the hands of the ruler (13:1, 4).[170] That the authorities are made "servants of God" (13:4) no more implies divine approval of their actions than do the biblical affirmations that Assyria is "the rod of God's anger" (Is. 10:5), for the king of Assyria also will be "punished for his haughty pride" (10:12); or that Nebuchadnezzar of Babylon is "God's servant" (Jer. 27:6), at least "until the time of his own land comes" (27:7). So with Rome. The present disposition of the authorities (*diatagē*, 13:2) in which they are "put in their place" by God (*tetagmenai hypo theou*) is not permanent, as the apocalyptic assurance of 13:11–14 makes clear;[171] there is hardly a hint here of a "general truth of creation" (against Robert H. Stein).[172] Although Paul does not dwell here as he does elsewhere (1 Cor. 15:24–26) on the apocalyptic destruction of "every rule and authority and power," his saying that the authority "bears the sword" as "the servant of God to execute wrath on the evildoer" (13:4) must not be allowed to eclipse the affirmation in 12:19–21 that judgment and wrath belong to God alone.

Paul's purpose is not to enjoin unqualified obedience to the authorities. On that premise we should have to explain the sudden reversal on the part of the man who reveled in the consequences of his disobedience in 2 Cor. 2:14–16. Luise Schottroff points out that Paul prohibits "resistance" (*antitassesthai*) here but commands "resistance" (*mē syschēmatizesthai*) in 12:2; she reasonably concludes that "the word 'resist' in Rom. 13:2 must have a very concrete meaning, not a general meaning."[173]

Paul encourages subordination to the authorities (*hypotassesthai*, 13:1). Although in our own time these words have been torn from their context and inflated into a call for absolute obedience to governments, even (and without any exegetical warrant whatsoever) into an apostolic endorsement of warmaking, their meaning was far more circumscribed for the earliest Christian generations who heard them. As Luise Schottroff observes, just these verses from Romans were taken up by the Christian martyrs of the second century as an integral part of their declarations of loyalty at the moment of execution.

The aged bishop of Smyrna, Polycarp, provides our earliest evidence for this use of Paul's legacy, though he clearly depends on an earlier tradition. Polycarp declares before the proconsul who will sentence him a moment later to death in the arena that "we have been taught to show appropriate honor to the principalities and powers ordained of God, if that does not compromise us" (*The Martyrdom of Polycarp* 10). Similar protestations of innocence appear in Scilla, in North Africa, around 180 C.E. An African Christian named Speratus proclaims, "We have never done evil to anyone and have in no manner worked for the cause of injustice: we have never cursed, we have rather been thankful when we were mistreated; therefore we give honor to Caesar"; another, Donata, cries out, "Honor Caesar as Caesar, but fear God!" (*Acts of the Scilitan Martyrs* 2, 9). Yet another, Apollonius, declares that Jesus

> taught us to tame our anger, to moderate our desires, to bridle our cravings, to banish sadness, to be peaceable, to increase in love, to lay aside vanity, not to permit ourselves to be carried away with vengeance toward those who offend us, to despise death on the basis of a legal sentence, not because one has done wrong, but by bearing it patiently, additionally to obey the laws of Caesar and to honor him; however, to worship and adore God alone, the only immortal one.[174]

Of course, Jesus is not recorded in our New Testament as having taught these things; but this is a fair rendition of Paul's admonitions in Romans 12–13.

The pattern is hardly accidental. As Schottroff writes, "The requirement and/or the declaration of loyalty belongs together with persecution," in a tradition reaching back to the Jewish martyrs under the Greek tyrant Antiochus Epiphanes. In this context, "Rom. 13:1–7 loses its apparently singular character and becomes a link in the long chain of declarations of loyalty of the members of subjugated peoples toward Rome"; indeed, K. H. Schelkle declares these verses from Romans 13 "a requisite for the martyr apology."[175]

The real puzzle of these lines for us today, therefore, is not that they provide an inadequate program for direct action in resisting repressive governments. After all, no one in the early church conceived even the extreme witness of martyrdom as an instrument for political change.[176] The puzzle is rather our own willingness to yield to the deadly purposes of the empire's functionaries the very phrases that were first found on the lips of martyrs.

That we should allow these verses to thwart even the most modest inquiries into our government's complicity in repression and murder is a staggering betrayal, not only of the oppressed, but also of the holy man who traced his apostolate from city to city with his own blood. Only the arrogant presumptions of our own privilege have allowed us to hear these verses as a sacred legitimation of power.

Perhaps the greatest irony of Paul's legacy in our day is just this: that we cannot hear the blow of the executioner's sword, let alone the sharp-edged proclamation that brought that blow down upon the apostle's neck, above the chorus of imperial acolytes around us who hymn these verses as a magic charm to protect the policies and the profits of the already rich. Those of us who live in the heart of the empire would do well to surrender these verses to those who stand in the place of the martyrs today and accord them the right to interpret the apostle's words, for Paul was one of them.

LIBERATING PAUL

We return at last to the question with which we began: What do we do with Paul?

As we have seen, that question is very much alive in academic circles today. In the last twenty years, the profoundly different climate in theology after the Holocaust, and the impact of the discovery of the Dead Sea Scrolls, have ushered in such dramatic changes that New Testament scholars now routinely speak of a "new perspective on Paul" or of a "paradigm shift" in Pauline studies.[177] One consequence is that many assumptions that could be taken for granted two decades ago are now in doubt or are already regarded as obsolete. John Gager quotes Lloyd Gaston, author of the groundbreaking study *Paul and the Torah*

(1987), on one aspect of this sudden upheaval in scholarship: "I suddenly find that I have great difficulty in reading the standard literature on Paul: why do other interpreters miss the obvious while spending much time on matters not in the text at all? I find that I cannot even trust such 'objective' works as lexica on some points. It's almost paralyzing when it comes to writing, for so little can be assumed and all must be discussed."[178]

Here Gaston is reacting in particular to the still tenacious assumption that "the real opponent of the Apostle Paul is the pious Jew" (Ernst Käsemann).[179] I have argued in the preceding chapters that a similar set of assumptions about Paul's social conservatism continues to hold Pauline studies in thrall. Those assumptions are also beginning to crumble, however. Just as the "new perspective on Paul" has begun to erode long-held tenets about the center of Pauline theology, feminist biblical interpreters have shown that the Pauline churches were far more egalitarian, and far more committed to the full leadership of women of Spirit, than the canon, or traditional biblical scholarship, had previously allowed us to imagine.[180]

Perhaps surprisingly, the epochal emergence of Latin American liberation theology, which occasioned a dramatic political reinterpretation of Jesus, has not ushered in a corresponding new understanding of Paul. The grounds for such a reinterpretation are nevertheless clear. After all, at the heart of the New Testament stands the cross on which Jesus of Nazareth was tortured and executed as an enemy of Rome. The cross, in its nakedly political singularity, is at the heart of Paul's proclamation as well.

The cross showed Paul the extent of the violence he was willing to tolerate, even to promote, in order to maintain the balance of power vis-à-vis Rome. In this light, the vision of the crucified Jesus raised from the dead could only have brought to an end the world in which Paul had lived: "*I have been crucified to the world and the world to me.*" Paul's conversion to the cause of the crucified, and the theology of the cross that flows from it, are thus profoundly political.

What can *this* Paul say to us today?

My answer to that question is tied up with two constant and vivid impressions that have accompanied my work on this book.

The first impression has been of the immediate reactions of friends and colleagues when I have spoken of "a liberative reading of the apostle Paul." Some have responded with embarrassed silence, no doubt questioning my critical faculties. Others have voiced their doubts: "But there's nothing political about Paul!" Still others have assumed (naturally enough, given the standard portrayal of Paul in many churches) that my work would be a swift and merciless indictment: "Paul is a chauvinist and an egotistical jerk. What more is there to say?"

But in the eyes of a few others I have seen the immediate spark of recognition, and I have heard a sudden urgency in their voices, as if to say, "Yes, it's about time." About time the "slave of Christ" was wrested away from the theology of privilege. About time the man who celebrated his partnership with women prophets, deacons, and apostles was unshackled from the machinery of the patriarchal church. About time the martyr's voice was heard again over the din of imperial apologetics.

Significantly, no one has been at a loss for an opinion. Paul continues to attract a great deal of emotion for many of us today, whether that has meant our frustration, our anger, or a troubled loyalty.

A second impression has been of the continuing deadliness of my nation's global war against the poor, what Jack Nelson-Pallmeyer calls the confessional situation of our age.[181] In Haiti alone, as many as 5,000 men, women, and children have been murdered by the army and civilian attachés since the 1991 coup that drove president Jean-Bertrand Aristide into exile. The mutilated corpses of activists, lawyers, and ordinary people who dared to speak out for reform appear in the streets of Port-au-Prince with dreadful regularity. My nation's response has been to force Haitian refugees back to Haiti in direct violation of U.S. and international law; to pressure Aristide to surrender his rightful power to the officers who deposed him, officers whom Central Intelligence Agency officials have hailed as Haiti's "best hopes for democracy"; and to work behind Aristide's back to arrange a coalition government that would shut him out.

The war against the poorest people in our hemisphere continues to enrich the U.S. corporations that profit from cheap Haitian labor. In 1993, fifty companies, enjoying exemptions from the economic embargo against Haiti, actually increased their exports of manufactured goods from that country by a staggering 63% while the average Haitian factory worker's pay plummeted to 14 cents an hour. U.S. policy toward Haiti seem crystal clear: to deter the threat of real democracy at any cost, and thus to guarantee ever higher profits for U.S. businesses.

What has the apostle Paul to say to us in this confessional situation?

Much, I think. While the Gospels tend to turn our attention back to the "sacred history" of Jesus in Judea, Paul bids us look around and discern the body of Christ in our own world: the body offered to God as a living sacrifice, no longer at the disposal of the powers of injustice but mobilized for God's justice; vulnerable, wounded, bleeding, bearing the marks of Jesus' death, carrying about in human flesh the death Jesus suffered. Paul calls on us to recognize the body of Christ starving, struggling, bleeding, being crucified again in El Salvador, in Somalia, in Los Angeles, and in Port-au-Prince. It is Paul who insists we seek the body of Christ precisely in the have-nots who are pushed away from our eucharistic meals. It is Paul who insists we "make our way in the company of the oppressed."

But we may learn more from Paul than a heightened awareness of the injustice and misery around us or a deepened resolve to alleviate them. Action and contemplation must go hand in hand.

"We are inundated by the cries of an entire creation," Walter Wink writes: "the millions now starving to death each year, the tortured, the victims of sexual abuse and battering, the ill." Our electronic media and our scientific discoveries have made us "so interconnected with all of life that we cannot help but be touched by the pain of all that suffers. . . . How much more, then, those who have deliberately opened their hearts as one family in God?" Yet this openness carries a tremendous risk: "We human beings are far too frail and tiny to bear all this pain. . . . For us to be this open and vulnerable to both the pain of the world and the anguish of God is unendurable, unless it is matched with a precise sense of divine vocation."[182]

Wink finds that sense of divine vocation in Paul's words to the Romans: "God's Spirit is actually praying for us in those agonizing longings which cannot find words" (8:26–27). We are called to "give speech to the Spirit's groanings within us," to "articulate these agonizing longings and let them pass through us to God." To act, of course, as well; but to act without calculating beforehand whether our efforts will produce the desired results—for often they cannot.

Wink appeals to Mahatma Gandhi, who insisted that "we must never accept evil, even if we cannot change it." As a man of faith, Gandhi believed that even if we cannot change it, evil will nevertheless be changed. I find the same confidence in the apostle Paul, who found in the radiant fact of Jesus' resurrection the assurance that "nothing in all creation shall separate us from the love of God in Christ Jesus our Lord" (Rom. 8:39). "The transcendent power belongs to God and not to us," he assured the Corinthians, who had found reason to doubt the value of Paul's ministry after he had been arrested one too many times. "We are afflicted in every way, but not crushed; perplexed, but not driven to despair; persecuted, but not forsaken; struck down, but not destroyed; always carrying in the body the death of Jesus, so that the life of Jesus may also be manifested in our bodies" (2 Cor. 5:8–10).

Hearing Paul's word to us today requires critical discernment, of course. Antoinette Clark Wire has shown that Paul understood his own experience, his loss of privilege and status, as the way of God revealed in the cross. He nevertheless enjoyed more prestige and power than many of the women and men in his congregations. When they have been directed against the aspirations of those traditionally excluded from the common table, Paul's words have helped to forge the chains of oppression up to our own day. But heard rightly, Paul's message could not be more appropriate for some of us, Christians of the First World, who (if we are honest) find ourselves in the place of the Corinthian elite, privileged, comfortable, spiritually content, confident that all we possess we deserve. Or in the place of the gentile Christians of Rome, eager to celebrate our own relative safety as the blessing of God and ready enough (though with proper regret, to be sure) to acknowledge God's judgment on the victims of empire in our cities and in our history.

Having our world mediated to us by the bland technicians of consent on the evening news, we need to practice the ideological intifada Paul urged in Romans 12: "Do not be conformed to this world, but be transformed by the renewing of your minds!" In different ways, men who confront the just claims of feminism and First-World citizens awash in a sea of consumption that drains life from the poor of the Two-Thirds World need to hear the "theology of relinquishment" (Elisabeth Schüssler Fiorenza) that calls to us from Paul's letters to Corinth and to Rome.[183] Aware of the war waged, in our name and for our sake, against the poor, we must yield to his appeal for solidarity with the oppressed. We must answer his call for resistance to the sacred routines legitimating the course of empire.

Once we understand the world of privilege in which Paul moved as the world to which he spoke on behalf of the poor, we may discover ourselves in his letters. We may even rediscover Paul as the apostle of liberation for the First World. The result, I think, will be revolutionary; or as the apostle himself might put it, "nothing less than life from the dead."

Notes

1. Paul in the Service of Death

1. Francis Le Jau, *The Carolina Chronicle of Dr. Francis Le Jau, 1706–1717*, ed. Frank W. Klinberg (Berkeley: University of California Press, 1956); cited in *A Documentary History of Slavery in North America*, ed. Willie Lee Rose (New York: Oxford University Press, 1976), pp. 27–36.

2. Rosemary Radford Ruether and Rosemary Skinner Keller, eds., *Women and Religion in America, Vol. 2: The Colonial and Revolutionary Periods. A Documentary History* (San Francisco: Harper & Row, 1983), chap. 4.

3. See Claude Lanzmann, *Shoah: An Oral History of the Holocaust: The Complete Text of the Film* (New York: Pantheon, 1985); Martin Gilbert, *The Holocaust: A History of the Jews of Europe during the Second World War* (New York: Henry Holt, 1985), pp. 502, 693–694, 770–771.

4. David Stoll, *Is Latin America Turning Protestant? The Politics of Evangelical Growth* (Berkeley and Los Angeles: University of California Press, 1990), p. 192; Vicki Kemper, "In the Name of Relief: A Look at Private U.S. Aid in Contra Territory," *Sojourners* 14:9 (1985), pp. 12–20.

5. Jack Nelson-Pallmeyer, *War against the Poor: Low-Intensity Conflict and Christian Faith* (Maryknoll: Orbis, 1989).

6. Stoll, *Is Latin America Turning Protestant?* pp. 198–203.

7. The phrase comes from the renunciations spoken in the Baptismal Covenant in *The Book of Common Prayer* of the Episcopal Church (New York: Seabury, 1979), p. 302.

8. Cited in *Advice among Masters: The Ideal in Slave Management in the Old South*, ed. James O. Breeden (Westport, CT: Greenwood Press, 1980), pp. 224–238.

9. *The Confessions of Nat Turner, the Leader of the Late Insurrection in Southampton, Va., as Fully and Voluntarily Made to Thomas R. Gray* (Richmond: Thomas R. Gray, 1832); cited in Rose, ed., *A Documentary History*, pp. 122–134.

10. Cited in "Gabriel's Attempted Uprising," in Rose, ed., *A Documentary History*, pp. 107–114.

11. Discussed in Rose, ed., *A Documentary History*, pp. 115–121. At the conclusion of a trial in which some thirty-five blacks were condemned to death, the mayor of Charleston wrote a public letter reassuring the citizens that the

public safety had been restored and that at no time had there been any real danger, the slaves having amassed no weapons beyond a few tools. The mayor was understating the situation. Henry Aptheker calculates that more than five hundred pike heads, bayonets, and daggers had been collected or manufactured (*American Negro Slave Revolts* [New York: International Publishers, 1969]); Howard Zinn observes that "the trial record itself, published in Charleston, was ordered destroyed soon after publication, as too dangerous for slaves to see" (*A People's History of the United States* [New York: Harper & Row, 1980], p. 169).

12. Cited in Breeden, ed., *Advice among Masters*, p. 225.

13. Mary Daly, *The Church and the Second Sex* (New York: Harper & Row, 1968), p. 38.

14. For discussion of this commonplace as the background of early Christian attitudes, see David L. Balch, *Let Wives Be Submissive: The Domestic Code in 1 Peter*, Society of Biblical Literature Monograph Series 26 (Chico: Scholars, 1981), pp. 1–121.

15. The story is recounted in *Witness: Writings of Bartolomé de las Casas*, ed. George Sanderlin (Maryknoll: Orbis, 1992).

16. Pablo Richard, "1492: The Violence of God and the Future of Christianity," in *1492–1992: The Voice of the Victims*, ed. Leonardo Boff and Virgil Elizondo (London: SCM Press, 1990).

17. Betty A. DeBerg, *Ungodly Women: Gender and the First Wave of American Fundamentalism* (Minneapolis: Fortress, 1990).

18. Susan Faludi, *Backlash: The Undeclared War against American Women* (New York: Crown, 1991), p. 233.

19. R. Emerson Dobash and Russell Dobash, *Violence against Wives* (New York: Free Press, 1979), chap. 3.

20. Joanne Carlson Brown and Carole R. Bohn, eds., *Christianity, Patriarchy, and Abuse: A Feminist Critique* (New York: Pilgrim, 1989).

21. Susan Brooks Thistlethwaite, "Every Two Minutes: Battered Women and Feminist Interpretation," in *Feminist Interpretation of the Bible*, ed. Letty M. Russell (Philadelphia: Westminster, 1985), p. 104; Elisabeth Schüssler Fiorenza, "The Will to Choose or to Reject: Continuing Our Critical Work," ibid., p. 130; interview with Chung Hyun-Kyung, *Episcopal Life*, April 1992, p. 3.

22. Raul Hilberg, *The Destruction of the European Jews*, 3 vols. (New York: Holmes & Meier, 1985).

23. For a few significant examples, see Rosemary Radford Ruether, *Faith and Fratricide* (New York: Seabury, 1974); Alan Davies, ed., *Anti-Semitism and the Foundations of Christianity* (New York: Paulist, 1979); Peter Richardson and D. Granskou, eds., *Anti-Judaism in Early Christianity*, vol. 1 (Waterloo, Ontario: Wilfried Laurier, 1986); Lloyd Gaston, *Paul and the Torah* (Vancouver: University of British Columbia Press, 1987); William S. Campbell, *Paul's Gospel in an Intercultural Context* (Frankfurt am Main: Peter Lang, 1991); Sydney Hall III, *Christian Anti-Semitism and Paul's Theology* (Minneapolis: Fortress, 1993).

24. Martin Luther, "On the Jews and Their Lies," cited by Gilbert, *The Holocaust*, p. 19.

25. Ernst Christian Helmreich, *The German Churches under Hitler: Background, Struggle, and Epilogue* (Detroit: Wayne State University Press, 1979), pp. 343–344.

26. *Church and Society—A Testimony of the Dutch Reformed Church*

(Bloemfontein, Netherlands: NGK Sendingpers, 1987). Biblical scholar Winsome Munro discusses the document in her essay "Romans 13:1–7: Apartheid's Last Biblical Refuge," *Biblical Theology Bulletin* 20:4 (1990), pp. 161–168.

27. *The Kairos Document: Challenge to the Church*, rev. 2d ed. (Braamfontein: Skotaville Publishers; and Grand Rapids: Eerdmans, 1986); reprinted in *Kairos: Three Prophetic Challenges to the Church*, ed. Robert McAfee Brown (Grand Rapids: Eerdmans, 1990), p. 29.

28. *Kairos Central America: A Challenge to the Churches of the World* (New York: Circus Publications, 1988), reprinted in Brown, ed., *Kairos*, p. 90.

29. *The Road to Damascus: Kairos and Conversion* (Washington, D.C.: Center for Concern, 1989), reprinted in Brown, ed., *Kairos*, p. 129.

30. L. Francis Bouchey, Roger Fontaine, David Jordan, Lt. Gen. Gordon Sumner, and Lewis Tambs, ed., *A New Inter-American Policy for the Eighties* (Washington, D.C.: Council for Inter-American Security, 1981), p. 20. For incisive critiques of the document, see Nelson-Pallmeyer, *War against the Poor*, and Noam Chomsky, *Deterring Democracy* (New York: Verso, 1991).

31. Besides running battles in the pages of *Christianity & Crisis* and *Sojourners*, the efforts of IRD members are evident, for example, in Michael Novak's "The Case against Liberation Theology," *New York Times Magazine*, October 21, 1984, and *Will It Liberate?* (Mahwah, N.J.: Paulist, 1986).

32. Ross Gelbspan, *Break-ins, Death-threats, and the FBI: The Covert War against the Central America Movement* (Boston: South End Press, 1991).

33. Stoll, *Is Latin America Turning Protestant?* p. 325; Kemper, "In the Name of Relief."

34. René de Visme Williamson, "The Theology of Liberation," *Christianity Today* 19:22 (1975), pp. 1049–1055; George W. Knight III, "Can a Christian Go to War?" *Christianity Today* 20:4 (1975), pp. 192–195. The myopia of these essays—the active participation of *American* Christians in coordinating and training repressive armies and equipping them with M-16s, landmines, and helicopter gunships with air-to-surface missiles is not in view—mirrors the log-in-the-eye vision of charismatic superpatriot Ollie North, mastermind of illegal weapons-supply operations to the Contras, who (referring to Christians in the ranks of the Nicaraguan Sandinistas) solemnly intoned that "Jesus Christ never advised anyone to pick up a rifle."

35. See now Ramsey Clark, *The Fire This Time: U.S. War Crimes in the Persian Gulf War* (New York: Thunder's Mouth Press, 1993).

36. See Mark Danner's exposé, "The Truth of El Mozote," in *The New Yorker*, December 6, 1993.

37. Chomsky, *Deterring Democracy*, chaps. 4 ("Problems of Population Control") and 12 ("Force and Opinion"). The model of the U.S. propaganda system is developed in Edward S. Herman and Noam Chomsky, *Manufacturing Consent: The Political Economy of the Mass Media* (New York: Pantheon, 1988).

38. The term "love patriarchalism," inspired by Ernst Troeltsch (see *The Social Teaching of the Christian Churches*, vol. 1, trans. Olive Wyon [New York: Macmillan, 1931], pp. 69–89), has gained new currency through the work of Gerd Theissen; see *The Social Setting of Pauline Christianity: Essays on Corinth*, trans. John Schütz (Philadelphia: Fortress, 1983).

39. James D. G. Dunn, "The New Perspective on Paul," *Bulletin of the John*

Rylands Library 65 (1983), pp. 95–122; John G. Gager, *The Origins of Anti-Semitism* (New York: Oxford University Press, 1981).

40. Christine E. Gudorf, *Victimization: Examining Christian Complicity* (Philadelphia: Trinity Press International, 1992), pp. 1–10.

2. The Canonical Betrayal of the Apostle

1. Werner Georg Kümmel's *Introduction to the New Testament* (rev. ed., trans. Howard Clark Kee [Nashville: Abingdon, 1975]). Kümmel's work may inspire trust among more anxious readers because he sets out *both* sides of authenticity questions and often reaches conservative conclusions. Norman Perrin's *The New Testament: A Student's Introduction*, 3d ed. by Dennis Duling (New York: Harcourt Brace Jovanovich, 1993) reaches more negative conclusions.

2. Richard Bauckham's observations about the requirements of a pseudepigraphic letter ("Pseudo-Apostolic Letters," *Journal of Biblical Literature* 107:3 [1988], esp. pp. 474–478) are relevant here.

3. Victor Paul Furnish's survey of the issues is admirably judicious: "Colossians," *Anchor Bible Dictionary*, vol. 1, pp. 1090–1096.

4. For an overview of text-critical issues, see William O. Walker, Jr., "Text-Critical Evidence for Interpolations in the Letters of Paul," *Catholic Biblical Quarterly* 50:4 (1988), pp. 622–631. Antoinette Clark Wire rightly observes that the text-critical evidence for an interpolation at 1 Cor. 14:34–35 is not conclusive, since the verses are present (albeit in different places) in every manuscript of the letter. Her argument for the authenticity of the passage (*The Corinthian Women Prophets: A Reconstruction through Paul's Rhetoric* [Minneapolis: Fortress, 1990], pp. 229–232) is tied to her analysis of the rhetoric of the whole letter and is addressed later in this chapter.

5. Birger Pearson's case for an interpolation is convincing ("1 Thessalonians 2:13–16: A Deutero-Pauline Interpolation," *Harvard Theological Review* 64 [1971], pp. 79–94). Counterarguments that the passage "works" in its present context and that the "wrath" that has come upon the Jews is a reference to the cross (Karl P. Donfried, "Paul and Judaism: 1 Thessalonians 1:13–16 as a Test Case," *Interpretation* 38:3 [1984], pp. 242–253) are not to the point of Pearson's argument.

6. James Kallas, "Romans xiii:1–7: An Interpolation," *New Testament Studies* 11 (1965), p. 369; see also Winsome Munro, *Authority in Paul and Peter: The Identification of a Pastoral Stratum in the Pauline Corpus and 1 Peter*, Society for New Testament Studies Monograph Series 45 (Cambridge: Cambridge University Press, 1983).

7. See Schüssler Fiorenza, *In Memory of Her: A Feminist Theological Reconstruction of Christian Origins* (New York: Crossroad, 1988), pp. 47–48, 175–184; Mary Rose D'Angelo, "Women Partners in the New Testament," *Journal of Feminist Studies in Religion* 6:1 (1990), pp. 65–86.

8. William O. Walker, "The Burden of Proof in Identifying Interpolations in Pauline Letters," *New Testament Studies* 33 (1987), p. 615; see also Winsome Munro, "Interpolation in the Epistles: Weighing the Probability," *New Testament Studies* 36 (1990), pp. 431–443.

9. Discussing the relation between men and women in Ephesians, Johnson refers to "the author's willingness to contradict—not simply reinterpret—Paul's understanding." See her article on "Ephesians" in *The Women's Bible Commentary*, ed. Carol A. Newsom and Sharon H. Ringe (Louisville: Westminster/John Knox Press, 1992), p. 341.

10. Luke Timothy Johnson, *The Writings of the New Testament: An Interpretation* (Philadelphia: Fortress, 1986), p. 357.

11. Ibid., p. 257.

12. Johnson, "Ephesians," p. 338.

13. J. Christiaan Beker, *Heirs of Paul: Paul's Legacy in the New Testament and in the Church Today* (Minneapolis: Fortress, 1991), p. 126.

14. This is, for example, the fundamental flaw in Margaret MacDonald's otherwise excellent study, *The Pauline Churches: A Socio-historical Study of Institutionalization in the Pauline and Deutero-Pauline Writings*, Society for New Testament Studies Monograph Series 60 (Cambridge: Cambridge University Press, 1988).

15. Hans von Campenhausen, *The Formation of the Christian Bible*, trans. J. A. Baker (Philadelphia: Fortress, 1972), p. 181.

16. Dennis R. MacDonald, *The Legend and the Apostle: The Battle for Paul in Story and Canon* (Philadelphia: Westminster, 1983), pp. 14–15. An English translation of the *Acts of Paul and Thekla* is provided in *The New Testament Apocrypha, Volume 2: Writings Related to the Apostles; Apocalypses and Related Subjects*, rev. ed. by Wilhelm Schneemelcher, English trans. ed. Robert McL. Wilson (Louisville: Westminster/John Knox Press, 1992), pp. 213–270. On the historical reality behind the *Acts of Paul and Thekla*, see also *Semeia 38: The Apocryphal Acts of Apostles*, ed. Dennis R. MacDonald (Atlanta: Scholars, 1986).

17. David Efroymson shows that in the works of Marcion's orthodox opponents, Justin, Irenaeus, and Tertullian, "the God of the Hebrew Bible was 'salvaged' for Christians precisely by means of the anti-Judaic myth" ("The Patristic Connection," in *Anti-Semitism and the Foundations of Christianity*, ed. Alan T. Davies [New York: Paulist, 1979], p. 101).

18. For a compelling survey of how the Gnostics read Paul, see Elaine H. Pagels, *The Gnostic Paul: Gnostic Exegesis of the Pauline Letters* (Philadelphia: Fortress, 1975).

19. Leander E. Keck, *Paul and His Letters* (Philadelphia: Fortress, 1979), pp. 94–95.

20. For example, James E. Crouch allows 7:20 to govern his interpretation of 7:21: *The Origin and Intention of the Colossian Haustafel*, Forschungen zur Religion und Literatur des alten und neuen Testaments 109 (Göttingen: Vandenhoeck & Ruprecht, 1972), pp. 124–125.

21. The New American Bible translates, quite expansively, "even supposing you could go free, you would be better off making the most of your slavery." The New International Version, in contrast, offers "although if you can gain your freedom, do so"; similarly, the Jerusalem Bible gives "if you should have the chance of being free, accept it." The Revised Standard Version reads, "but if you can gain your freedom, avail yourself of the opportunity," supplying in a footnote the alternative "make use of your present condition instead"; that arrangement was reversed in the New Revised Standard Version. The New English Bible reads "if a chance of liberty should come, take it," putting the

alternative into a footnote, "even if a chance of liberty should come, choose rather to make good use of your servitude"; the Revised English Bible continues that practice.

In a monograph devoted to this single verse, S. Scott Bartchy notes two other possibilities for completing the phrase: "by all means, keep the commands of God" (supplying *tais entolais theou,* following the immediately preceding phrase in v. 20 and paralleling an idiom in Josephus), or "by all means, live according to your calling [in Christ]" (supplying *tē klēsē,* following the rule in vv. 17, 20, and 24): *Mallon Chrēsai: First Century Slavery and 1 Corinthians 7:21,* Society of Biblical Literature Dissertation Series 11 (Missoula: Scholars, 1973), pp. 156–157.

22. Bartchy, *Mallon Chrēsai,* pp. 135–137; Gregory W. Dawes, " 'But if you can gain your freedom' (1 Corinthians 7:17–24)," *Catholic Biblical Quarterly* 52:4 (1990), p. 684, n. 17.

K. L. Schmidt cites the observations of a number of scholars that "the unnecessary sense of *externa conditio* [imputed to the word *klesis*] has been invented"; that "it is hard to see why the word should have at [1 Corinthians] 7:20 a different sense from 1:26," where it means "calling to be Christians"; and that "the sense of calling as a state is ruled out elsewhere in the NT." Schmidt rejects as "untenable" the suggestions that just here Paul was "boldly coining a word" or "adopting a rare and mostly popular usage" otherwise unknown to modern lexicographers (s.v. "*kaleō ktl,*" *Theological Dictionary of the New Testament* 3:491, n. 1).

23. Allan Callahan, "A Note on 1 Corinthians 7:21," *Journal of the Interdenominational Theological Center* 17:1–2 (1989–90), p. 111.

24. Gordon Fee, *First Corinthians,* New International Commentary on the New Testament (Grand Rapids: Eerdmans, 1987), p. 309. Similarly, Wolfgang Schrage writes, "The state in which [Christians] were called is the state, assigned by God, in which they are to be tested and endure" (*The Ethics of the New Testament,* trans. David E. Green [Philadelphia: Fortress, 1988], p. 233).

25. Dawes, " 'But if You Can Gain Your Freedom.' "

26. Schmidt, loc. cit.

27. Hans Conzelmann, *First Corinthians: A Commentary on the First Epistle to the Corinthians,* trans. James W. Leitch, Hermeneia (Philadelphia: Fortress, 1975), p. 127 and n. 27.

28. Peter Richardson, *Paul's Ethic of Freedom* (Philadelphia: Westminster, 1979), p. 41.

29. Crouch, *Origin and Intention of the Colossian Haustafel,* p. 125.

30. John Ziesler, *Pauline Christianity,* rev. ed. (New York: Oxford University Press, 1990), p. 126.

31. E. P. Sanders, *Paul,* Past Masters (New York: Oxford University Press, 1991), p. 107 (emphasis added).

32. Leander E. Keck, *Paul and His Letters* (Philadelphia: Fortress, 1979), p. 94; J. Paul Sampley, *Walking between the Times: Paul's Moral Reasoning* (Philadelphia: Fortress, 1991), p. 113 (emphasis added).

33. Richardson, *Paul's Ethic of Freedom,* p. 41.

34. David Schroeder, "Die Haustafeln des neuen Testaments (ihre Herkunft und theologischer Sinn)," diss. Hamburg, 1959; Crouch, *Origin and Intention of the Colossian Haustafel.*

35. See Crouch, *Origin and Intention of the Colossian Haustafel,* pp. 122–125.

36. Conzelmann, *First Corinthians,* p. 126.

37. J. Christiaan Beker, *Paul the Apostle: The Triumph of God in Life and Thought* (Philadelphia: Fortress, 1980), pp. 325–327.

38. Calvin J. Roetzel, *The Letters of Paul: Conversations in Context,* 2d ed. (Atlanta: John Knox, 1982), p. 137.

39. Amos Jones, Jr., *Paul's Message of Freedom: What Does It Mean to the Black Church?* (Valley Forge: Judson Press, 1984), p. 38.

40. For a sampling of recent discussion, see F. Forrester Church, "Rhetorical Structure and Design in Paul's Letter to Philemon," *Harvard Theological Review* 71 (1978), pp. 17–33; N. T. Wright, *The Epistles of Paul to the Colossians and to Philemon* (Grand Rapids: Eerdmans, 1986); Norman Peterson, *Rediscovering Paul: Philemon and the Sociology of Paul's Narrative World* (Philadelphia: Fortress, 1985); Peter Lampe, "Keine 'Sklavenflucht' des Onesimus," *Zeitschrift für die neutestamentlichen Wissenschaft* 1/2 (1985), pp. 135–137; Sara Winter, "Methodological Observations on a New Interpretation of Paul's Letter to Philemon," *Union Seminary Quarterly Review* 39 (1984), pp. 203–212, and "Paul's Letter to Philemon," *New Testament Studies* 33 (1987), pp. 1–15; J. Duncan M. Derrett, "The Functions of the Epistle to Philemon," *Zeitschrift für die neutestamentlichen Wissenschaft* 79 (1988), pp. 63–91; John M. G. Barclay, "Paul, Philemon and the Dilemma of Christian Slave-Ownership," *New Testament Studies* 37:2 (1991), pp. 161–186; Clarice J. Martin, "The Rhetorical Function of Commercial Language in Paul's Letter to Philemon (Verse 18)," in *Persuasive Artistry: Studies in New Testament Rhetoric in Honor of George A. Kennedy,* ed. Duane F. Watson, Journal for the Study of the New Testament Supplement 60 (Sheffield: Sheffield Academic Press, 1991), pp. 321–337; Brian Rapske, "The Prisoner Paul in the Eyes of Onesimus," *New Testament Studies* 37:2 (1991), pp. 187–203; John G. Nordling, "Onesimus Fugitivus: A Defense of the Runaway Slave Hypothesis in Philemon," *Journal for the Study of the New Testament* 41 (1991), pp. 97–119.

41. John Knox, *Philemon among the Letters of Paul* (Nashville: Abingdon, 1959); Winter, "Methodological Observations," "Paul's Letter to Philemon." This suggestion gains some support from the epithet, applied to Archippus, of "fellow soldier" (*systratiōtēs*), which occurs in ancient papyrus letters of request.

42. Winter, "Paul's Letter to Philemon"; Martin, "The Rhetorical Function"; Nordling, "Onesimus Fugitivus"; Rapske, "The Prisoner Paul."

43. J. B. Lightfoot, *Saint Paul's Epistles to the Colossians and to Philemon,* rev. ed. (London: Macmillan & Co., 1879), pp. 301–329.

44. Wright, *Epistles,* p. 166; Rapske, "The Prisoner Paul," p. 192.

45. Derrett, "Functions of the Epistle to Philemon."

46. A convenient introduction to the ancient Greek and Roman systems of rhetoric and their relevance for New Testament study is George A. Kennedy's *New Testament Interpretation through Rhetorical Criticism* (Chapel Hill: University of North Carolina Press, 1984). The emphasis in much recent research on the logic of argumentation owes as much to Chaim Perelman and L. Olbrechts-Tyteca, *The New Rhetoric: A Treatise on Argumentation* (Notre Dame: Univer-

sity of Notre Dame Press, 1965); see now Burton L. Mack, *Rhetoric and the New Testament* (Minneapolis: Fortress, 1990).

47. I find these observations telling against Winter's argument that Onesimus could not have been absent from his master without his master's knowledge and consent.

The question whether the slave is a runaway (*fugitivus*) or seeks a mediator to represent him to his angered master (an *amicus domini*) is misconstrued to the extent that these are legal categories used by the state to determine whether slaves found apart from their masters should be prosecuted. The more appropriate question is what Onesimus sought from Paul, for he must have come to be in Paul's company by design (so Rapske, "The Prisoner Paul"). This does not mean, however, that Onesimus must have sought only to be reconciled to his master as a penitent slave (against Rapske). Whatever Onesimus expected from Paul is finally secondary to what Paul in fact envisions as the appropriate resolution of Onesimus's situation.

48. Peterson, *Rediscovering Paul,* pp. 133, 135.

49. "For a slave to run away was itself a form of theft" (Barclay, "Paul, Philemon," p. 165, n. 15; so also Peterson, *Rediscovering Paul,* p. 73). Roman law referred to a runaway slave as a "thief of himself," *sui furtum facere* (*Digest of Justinian* 47:2:61, cited by Nordling, "Onesimus Fugitivus," p. 115).

50. Thus Paul in effect puts Onesimus's master in the position of having to choose *not* to act like the "unforgiving debtor" in Jesus' parable (Matt. 18:23–35).

51. S. Scott Bartchy, "Not a Runaway after All: The Case of Onesimus, Philemon, and Paul," presented to the Pauline Epistles Section at the Annual Meeting of the Society of Biblical Literature in November 1991. I am grateful to Professor Bartchy for kindly sharing a copy of this paper with me. See also his articles on "Slavery (Greco-Roman)" and "Philemon, Epistle to" in the *Anchor Bible Dictionary.*

52. Peterson, *Rediscovering Paul,* pp. 135, 290.

53. Dale B. Martin, "Ancient Slavery, Class, and Early Christianity," *Fides et Historia* 23:2 (1991), pp. 105–113.

54. Barclay, "Paul, Philemon," pp. 182–185.

55. MacDonald, *Pauline Churches,* pp. 44, 104.

56. Crouch, *Origin and Intention of the Colossian Haustafel,* pp. 124–125.

57. Callahan, "A Note on 1 Corinthians 7:21."

58. Callahan reads the simple conditional clause in 7:21 so that it no longer refers to a hypothetical possibility in the indeterminate future—"if you can become free"—but to an actual possibility in the Corinthian congregation: "if you can be(come) free [which you can be]." The particle *ei* indicates a real condition (see the Blass-DeBrunner-Funk *Grammar,* sect. 371); the aorist tense of *genesthai* indicates a change in status at one point in time, not necessarily the indefinite future (we should then expect a conditional sentence with *ean* and the subjunctive).

Callahan renders the following injunction (*mallon chrēsai*) "then act like it," translating *chrēsai* as "behave" or "conduct oneself" as in 2 Cor. 1:17 (his article mistakenly refers to 2 Cor. 7:17). The Bauer-Arndt-Gingrich-Danker *Lexicon* cites 2 Cor. 1:17 as an example of *chraomai,* meaning "*act, proceed, with dative of the characteristic shown*"; the dative, *eleutheria,* would in this case have to be supplied (as it would under the conventional readings already discussed).

This translation of the phrase removes the difficulty, already perceived by S. Scott Bartchy, that since the master, not the slave, made the decisions concerning manumission, "it would have been rather pointless for anyone to have advised [the slave] to choose to be manumitted (i.e., 'take freedom')" (*Mallon Chrēsai,* pp. 104–114); but we should on Callahan's reading expect an adverb to supplement the verb ("behave *accordingly*").

Callahan argues that Paul's advice to the person called as a slave "not to worry about it" is addressed, not to a slave's anxiety about continuing slave status, but to a possible "relapse" on the part of manumitted freedpersons "into considering themselves or allowing others to consider them as still in some way slaves, no doubt an important interdiction in a society which never allowed the freedman to forget his origins."

The net effect of this reading correlates well with what we have seen to be the overall argument in 1 Corinthians 7: One's previous social status does not determine the contours of one's obedience to God.

59. See Schüssler Fiorenza, *In Memory of Her,* pp. 208–218; most recently, J. Albert Harrill, "Ignatius, *Ad Polycarp* 4:3 and the Corporate Manumission of Christian Slaves," *Journal for Early Christian Studies* 1:2 (1993), pp. 107–142. Harrill argues that Ignatius's letter "addresses a clearly specific economic procedure and, therefore, cannot be used as a proof text that the early church was generally opposed to the manumission of Christian slaves" (p. 107). Despite evidence of Christian manumission and redemption practices, Harrill observes, rightly, that "ancient Christians did not hold abolitionist tendencies," although I find no basis for the following generalization that Christians "considered slavery a natural, integral part of human civilization" (p. 130).

60. Rapske, "The Prisoner Paul," pp. 197–202.

61. By "rhetorical situation" I mean "previous stages in the discussion" as these constrain the possibilities of rhetoric: see Perelman and Olbrechts-Tyteca, *The New Rhetoric*; Lloyd Bitzer, "The Rhetorical Situation," *Philosophy and Rhetoric* 1 (1968), pp. 1–14; Scott Consigny, "Rhetoric and Its Situations," *Philosophy and Rhetoric* 7 (1974), pp. 175–186.

62. Antoinette Clark Wire, *Corinthian Women Prophets;* Elisabeth Schüssler Fiorenza, "Rhetorical Situation and Historical Reconstruction in 1 Corinthians," *New Testament Studies* 33 (1987), pp. 386–403.

63. Wire writes that "the women's silencing is not a parenthetical matter but the turning point in his argument concerning the spiritual" (*Corinthian Women Prophets,* p. 155); "the women's speech is the heart of the alternative spiritual authority to his own" (p. 156). Schüssler Fiorenza admits the plausibility of Michel Bünker's argument that "the intended or inscribed audience against whom Paul argues are the few members of the community of high social status and considerable education who have caused the party strife in Corinth" (*Briefformular und rhetorische Disposition im 1. Korintherbrief* [Göttingen: Vandenhoeck & Ruprecht, 1983]); but she finally rejects that argument, because Paul's "'veiled hostility' and appeal to authority in the so-called women's passages [i.e., 1 Cor. 11:2–16 and 14:34–35] indicate, however, that he does not include women of high social and educational status in this appeal" ("Rhetorical Situation," p. 399).

64. Schüssler Fiorenza, *In Memory of Her*, p. 232.

65. Ibid., p. 232; Wire, *Corinthian Women Prophets*, p. 157.

66. Wire, *Corinthian Women Prophets*, p. 4; compare the remark of Scott Consigny that a speaker who fails to take into account the constraints of the rhetorical situation "may rightly be dismissed as ineffective and irrelevant" ("Rhetoric and Its Situations," p. 178).

67. Schüssler Fiorenza, *In Memory of Her*, p. 225.

68. Paul "prepares women to concede [i.e., submit to] marriage where a man requires it in practice by validating unequivocally in theory their decision [i.e., celibacy] and its motivation" (*Corinthian Women Prophets*, p. 94).

69. Schüssler Fiorenza, *In Memory of Her*, p. 216.

70. Ibid., p. 230.

71. See *Corinthian Women Prophets*, pp. 149–152. Wire's arguments are, first, that the marginal gloss in scenario (a) "would have been very early, probably on the original letter either by the writer, an amanuensis, or possibly by the first person to copy the letter." Of the earliness of the textual alteration there is no doubt; but since our earliest extant manuscript of the letter dates from a century after the autograph, there is no reason why the marginal gloss would have to have been as early as the autograph. It would only have to be the archetype of all extant manuscripts of the letter, not of all copies actually produced.

Her second argument is simply that the second scenario—omission and restoration of the verses in a different location—is plausible insofar as all manuscripts showing that variation can be traced to a single archetype. But of course these observations would relate to either scenario equally.

3.   The Mystification of the Apostle Paul

1. See the discussion of these phrases from Hans Conzelmann, Peter Richardson, and James E. Crouch in chapter 2.

2. Walter Wink, *Engaging the Powers: Discernment and Resistance in a World of Domination* (Minneapolis: Fortress Press, 1992), pp. 73–78.

3. References: Tarsus: Acts 21:39, 22:3; Roman citizenship: 16:35–39, 22:25–29, 23:27; education at the feet of Gamaliel (I), a figure Luke clearly expects his readers to recognize more readily than Paul: 22:3; oratorical skill: 13:13–43; his being out of place in the countryside: 14:8–18 (in a rural environment so uncivilized that the population does not even speak Greek, Paul and his companion, Barnabas, "scarcely restrained the people from offering sacrifice to them," a scene calculated to amuse the urban reader); upper-class audiences: 13:4–12, 17:16–34, 18:8, 24:1–23, 26:1–32.

4. E. A. Judge, *The Social Pattern of the Christian Groups in the First Century: Some Prolegomena to the Study of New Testament Ideas of Social Obligation* (London: Tyndale Press, 1960).

5. Wayne A. Meeks, *The First Urban Christians: The Social World of the Apostle Paul* (New Haven: Yale University Press, 1983), p. 61.

6. Richard J. Cassidy, *Society and Politics in the Acts of the Apostles* (Maryknoll: Orbis, 1987), p. 118.

7. Gerd Lüdemann, *Paul, Apostle to the Gentiles: Studies in Chronology,*

trans. E. Stanley Jones (Minneapolis: Fortress, 1984), pp. 11–18; see also Vernon K. Robbins, "The Social Location of the Implied Author of Luke-Acts," in *The Social World of Luke-Acts: Models for Interpretation*, ed. Jerome H. Neyrey (Peabody: Hendrickson, 1991), pp. 305–332.

8. Adolf Deissmann, *Light from the Ancient East: The New Testament Illustrated by Recently Discovered Texts of the Graeco-Roman World* (London: Hodder & Stoughton, 1910), p. 144.

9. See Hans Dieter Betz, "The Problem of Rhetoric and Theology according to the Apostle Paul," in *L'Apôtre Paul: Personnalité, style et conception du ministère*, ed. A. Vanhoye (Leuven, 1986), pp. 16–48.

10. The argument of Wilhelm Wüllner, "The Sociological Implications of 1 Corinthians 1:26–28 Reconsidered," *Studia Evangelica* 6 (1973), pp. 666–72, and "Tradition and Interpretation of the 'Wise-Powerful-Noble' Triad in 1 Corinthians 1:26," *Studia Evangelica* 7 (1982), pp. 557–562.

A considerable body of literature is now available on the social class of the early Christians. For readily accessible recent surveys and bibliographies, see Susan R. Garrett's article on "Sociology (Early Christianity)" in the *Anchor Bible Dictionary;* Richard Rohrbaugh, "Methodological Considerations in the Debate over the Social Class Status of Early Christians," *Journal of the American Academy of Religion* 52:3 (1984), pp. 519–546; Daniel J. Harrington, "Second Testament Exegesis and the Social Sciences: A Bibliography," *Biblical Theology Bulletin* 18:2 (1988), pp. 77–85; Richard Rohrbaugh and David Balch, *Early Christianity in Its Social Environment*, Library of Early Christianity (Philadelphia: Westminster, 1986).

11. Judge, *Social Pattern*, p. 60.

12. Gerd Theissen, *Social Setting of Pauline Christianity*, p. 69.

13. Meeks, *First Urban Christians*, pp. 53–55; Antoinette Clark Wire, *Corinthian Women Prophets*, pp. 62–71.

14. Rohrbaugh, "Methodological Considerations," pp. 531–537.

15. Ibid., pp. 542–543.

16. Wire, *Corinthian Women Prophets*, p. 62.

17. Ramsay MacMullen, *Roman Social Relations 50 B.C. to A.D. 284* (New Haven: Yale University Press, 1974), p. 89; see also Abraham Malherbe, *Social Aspects of Early Christianity*, 2d ed. (Philadelphia: Fortress, 1983), pp. 84–91.

18. Stanley K. Stowers, "Social Status, Public Speaking and Private Teaching: The Circumstances of Paul's Preaching Activity," *Novum Testamentum* 26:1 (1984), pp. 59–82.

19. Meeks, *First Urban Christians*, p. 65.

20. References: 1 Cor. 9:15–19; compare 2 Cor. 2:17 and 1 Thess. 2:9; Bengt Holmberg specifies that "only when Paul has left a church he has founded does he accept any money from it, in order to stress the fact that it has the character of support in his continued missionary work" (*Paul and Power: The Structure of Authority in the Primitive Church as Reflected in the Pauline Epistles* [Philadelphia: Fortress, 1978], p. 91).

21. Peter Marshall, *Enmity in Corinth: Social Conventions in Paul's Relations with the Corinthians* (Tübingen: J. C. B. Mohr [Paul Siebeck], 1987); Margaret M. Mitchell, *Paul and the Rhetoric of Reconciliation: An Exegetical Investigation of the Language and Composition of 1 Corinthians* (Tübingen: J. C. B. Mohr [Paul Siebeck], 1991).

22. Ronald Hock, *The Social Context of Paul's Ministry: Tentmaking and Apostleship* (Philadelphia: Fortress, 1980).

23. Anthony J. Saldarini, *Pharisees, Scribes, and Sadducees in Palestinian Society: A Sociological Approach* (Wilmington: Michael Glazier, 1988), p. 139.

24. Holmberg, *Paul and Power*, p. 91; Dale B. Martin, *Slavery and Salvation: The Metaphor of Slavery in Pauline Christianity* (New Haven: Yale University Press, 1990), pp. 122–124. Similarly, E. A. Judge observes that Paul refers to his "occasional periods of manual labor" only "in order to establish a point of honor, as his advertisement of it admits. Normally he expected to be supported at the charges of the groups who enjoyed his religious leadership" (*Social Pattern*, p. 58).

On the other hand, when Judge writes that Paul's "constant sensitivity to the humiliations he suffered from time to time"—as for example when Paul complains that "we are made as the filth of the world, and are the off-scouring of all things unto this day" (1 Cor. 4:13)—"is certainly not the complaint of a person to whom social affronts were normal. On the contrary, they are felt as indignities he ought not to have been subjected to," one wonders whether the ancient world in fact included any class of people who considered social affronts normal and would have felt that they *should* be subjected to indignities. Such observations tell us less about Paul's social perceptions than about those of the modern observer.

25. Theissen, *Social Setting*, p. 104.

26. Ernst Troeltsch, *The Social Teaching of the Christian Churches*, vol. 1, trans. Olive Wyon (New York: Macmillan, 1931; German original 1912), pp. 69–79.

27. Albert Schweitzer, *The Mysticism of Paul the Apostle*, trans. William Montgomery (New York: Henry Holt & Company, 1931; German original 1929), pp. 193–195, emphasis added.

28. Here the work of British cultural anthropologist Mary Douglas has been enormously influential. See her *Natural Symbols: Explorations in Cosmology*, rev. ed. (New York: Penguin, 1973).

29. Wire, *Corinthian Women Prophets*, pp. 66–67.

30. Ibid., p. 67 (emphasis added).

31. Ibid., pp. 69–71.

32. Ibid., pp. 69–70.

33. Ibid., pp. 66–67.

34. Ibid., p. 9. Wire admits that these women are usually not in view in the letter: in her words, they "are often hidden within a generic address, only occasionally spoken about, and still less often spoken to" (p. 3).

35. This last move has been widely criticized as the chief flaw in an otherwise carefully argued book. See reviews by Jeffrey S. Siker and Margaret M. Mitchell (*Religious Studies Review*, 19:4 [1993], pp. 305–311); Robin Scroggs (*Journal of Biblical Literature* 111:3 [1992], pp. 546–548); and Barbara E. Reid (*Catholic Biblical Quarterly* 54:3 [1992], pp. 594–596).

36. Wire, *Corinthian Women Prophets*, p. 192.

37. Ibid., pp. 193–195; Marshall, *Enmity in Corinth*.

38. Eating idol meat would have been a problem only for members of the higher classes who could routinely expect to be invited to dinners where such meat was served (see "The Strong and the Weak in Corinth: A Sociological

Analysis of a Theological Quarrel," chapter 3 in *Social Setting of Pauline Christianity*). I will take up Theissen's arguments in chapter 6.

39. Theissen, *Social Setting of Pauline Christianity*, pp. 107–110.

40. MacDonald, *The Pauline Churches*, pp. 2–5, 8.

41. Ibid., pp. 42–43, 104.

42. A. S. Peake, "The Quintessence of Paulinism," *Bulletin of the John Rylands Library* 4 (1917–18), pp. 285ff. F. F. Bruce took it as the title of his chapter on Ephesians in *Paul: Apostle of the Heart Set Free* (Grand Rapids: Eerdmans, 1977), pp. 424–440, citing G. B. Caird's judgment that the writing, "if not by Paul, is a masterly summary of Paul's theology by a disciple who was capable of thinking Paul's thoughts after him" (*The Apostolic Age* [London, 1955], p. 133). More recently Andrew Lincoln has characterized Ephesians as presenting "the logic of [Paul's] position in an unqualified fashion," in contrast to the more occasional, and thus more "dialectical," thought of Romans ("The Church and Israel in Ephesians 2," *Catholic Biblical Quarterly* 49 [1987], p. 612).

43. A. Lindemann, *Die Aufhebung der Zeit* (Gütersloh: Güterslöher Verlagshaus Gerd Mohn, 1975), p. 253; J. Christiaan Beker, *Paul the Apostle*, p. 343.

44. In Romans 9–11 Paul is "attempting to salvage some remnant of racial privilege for the historic Israel" (F. W. Beare, *St. Paul and His Letters* [Nashville: Abingdon, 1962], p. 97); he "gives expression to the emotional interest in national hopes which his estrangement fom his nation had not destroyed" (C. H. Dodd, *The Epistle of Paul to the Romans* [New York: Harper & Row, 1932], p. 151). More recently Robert Hamerton-Kelly has written that "the most portentous instance" of Paul's failure to "break free of the coils of sacred violence" is "his clinging to the category of election with regard to the role of Israel in the plan of salvation," the result of "powerful personal factors," of "nostalgia overwhelming his judgment" (*Sacred Violence: Paul's Hermeneutic of the Cross* [Minneapolis: Fortress, 1992], pp. 11–12).

45. Barth, *Epistle to the Romans*, p. 40; Ernst Käsemann, "Justification and Salvation History in the Epistle to the Romans," in *Perspectives on Paul*, trans. Margaret Kohl (Philadelphia: Fortress, 1971), p. 72.

46. Günther Bornkamm, *Paul*, trans. D. M. G. Stalker (New York: Harper & Row, 1971), pp. 94–95.

47. F. C. Baur, *Paul the Apostle of Jesus Christ*, vol. 1, trans. Eduard Zeller (London and Edinburgh: Williams & Norgate, 1876), pp. 308–313.

48. Walter Schmithals, *Der Römerbrief als historisches Problem* (Gütersloh: Güterslöher Verlagshaus Gerd Mohn, 1975), pp. 7–8.

49. Krister Stendahl, "The Apostle Paul and the Introspective Conscience of the West," *Harvard Theological Review* 56 (1963), pp. 199–215; reprinted in *Paul among Jews and Gentiles* (Philadelphia: Fortress, 1976), pp. 78–96; Käsemann, "Justification and Salvation History."

50. Rudolf Bultmann, *Theology of the New Testament*, vol. 1, trans. Kendrick Grobel (New York: Charles Scribner's Sons, 1951), p. 187.

51. Ibid., pp. 190, 279.

52. See Georg Strecker, "Befreiung und Rechtfertigung," in *Rechtfertigung: Festschrift für Ernst Käsemann*, ed. J. Friedrich, W. Pöhlmann, and P. Stuhlmacher (Tübingen: J. C. B. Mohr [Paul Siebeck], 1976), pp. 479–508; Dieter Lührmann, "Christologie und Rechtfertigung," in the same volume, pp. 351–63.

James D. G. Dunn, though eager to promote "the new perspective on Paul," admits that the declaration in Galatians 2:15 ("a man is not justified by works of law . . . in order that we might be justified by faith in Christ") is "evidently something Jewish, something which belongs to Jews 'by nature' "; on this point "Paul is wholly at one with his fellow Jews in asserting that justification is *by faith*," Dunn nevertheless promptly insists that in this same verse, Paul attacks Jewish "racial" or "nationalistic" exclusivism, which Dunn then describes as a "basic Jewish self-understanding": "The New Perspective on Paul," *Bulletin of the John Rylands Library* 65 (1983), pp. 95–122.

53. Hans-Joachim Schoeps, *Paul: The Theology of the Apostle in the Light of Jewish Religious History*, trans. Harold Knight (Philadelphia: Westminster, 1961); George Foot Moore, *Judaism in the First Three Centuries of the Christian Era: The Age of the Tannaim*, 3 vols. (Cambridge: Harvard University Press, 1927–1930); E. P. Sanders, *Paul and Palestinian Judaism: A Comparison of Patterns of Religion* (Philadelphia: Fortress, 1977).

54. *Paul and Palestinian Judaism*, pp. 552–553.

55. Heikki Räisänen, *Paul and the Law* (Philadelphia: Fortress, 1983), pp. 258–261.

56. In his review of recent works by James D. G. Dunn and John Ziesler, proponents of the "new perspective on Paul," Thomas Deidun shows that attempts to do justice to the "new perspective" and at the same time make his conversion relevant for Christian theology too often allow "practically all the old Lutheran demons" of Jewish self-justification and works-righteousness "to return unabashed to the Judaism which Sanders had by all accounts meticulously swept and put in order" ("James Dunn and John Ziesler on Romans in New Perspective," *Heythrop Journal* 33 [1992], pp. 79–84).

57. This line of explanation appears in James D. G. Dunn, "New Perspective"; John G. Gager, *The Origins of Anti-Semitism;* Lloyd Gaston, *Paul and the Torah* (Vancouver: University of British Columbia Press, 1987); Richard B. Hays, " 'Have We Found Abraham to Be Our Forefather According to the Flesh?' A Reconsideration of Rom. 4:1," *Novum Testamentum* 27 (1985), pp. 77–98; George Howard, "Romans 3:21–31 and the Inclusion of the Gentiles," *Harvard Theological Review* 63 (1970), pp. 223–33; Richard Longenecker, *Eschatology and the Covenant: A Comparison of 4 Ezra and Romans 1–11* (Sheffield: JSOT Press, 1991); Räisänen, *Paul and the Law;* Sanders, *Paul and Palestinian Judaism;* idem, *Paul, the Law, and the Jewish People* (Philadelphia: Fortress, 1983); and Francis Watson, *Paul, Judaism, and the Gentiles: A Sociological Approach* (Cambridge: Cambridge University Press, 1986).

58. Thus Lloyd Gaston writes, "Paul's major concern *I take to be* the justification of the legitimacy of the Gentile mission" (*Paul and the Torah*, p. 6). Gaston's essay "For *All* the Believers: The Inclusion of Gentiles as the Ultimate Goal of Torah in Romans" (pp. 116–134) demonstrates the theme's presence in Romans, but not that it is the "goal" of Romans.

59. Gaston, "Paul and the Torah"; William S. Campbell, *Paul's Gospel in an Intercultural Context: Jew and Gentile in the Letter to the Romans* (Frankfurt am Main: Peter Lang, 1991).

60. One initially attractive alternative is to imagine that Paul conceived of *two* covenants, one for Jews through Torah and another, parallel covenant for Gentiles through Christ (Franz Rosenszweig, *The Star of Redemption* [New

York: Holt, Rinehart & Winston, 1971]; Gaston, *Paul and the Torah*, pp. 7, 21, et passim; Gager, *Origins of Anti-Semitism*, pp. 194–195, et passim). This view is rightly rejected as exegetically unsupportable.

61. Campbell, *Paul's Gospel*, p. 112, p. 99 (citing Jakob Meuzelaar, *Der Leib des Messias* [Assen: Van Gorcum, 1961], p. 86).

62. Hamerton-Kelly, *Sacred Violence*, pp. 60, 76.

63. Johannes Munck, *Paul and the Salvation of Mankind*, trans. Frank Clarke (Atlanta: John Knox Press, 1959).

64. Gaston, *Paul and the Torah*, pp. 22–23.

65. Ibid., p. 4. To the same point, Gaston asks "what would happen to interpretation if one were to start from the premise that Paul knew at least as much about 'covenantal nomism' and Jewish 'soteriology' as does E. P. Sanders?" (p. 65).

Gaston's questions have been taken up by Gager in a chapter on "Reinventing Paul" in *Origins of Anti-Semitism;* by Campbell, *Paul's Gospel in an Intercultural Context;* by Peter Tomson, *Paul and the Jewish Law: Halakha in the Letters of the Apostle to the Gentiles* (Assen: Van Gorcum; Philadelphia: Fortress, 1990); and in my own work, *The Rhetoric of Romans: Argumentative Constraint and Strategy and Paul's Debate with Judaism*, Journal for the Study of the New Testament Supplement 45 (Sheffield: Sheffield Academic Press, 1990).

66. See Rosemary Radford Ruether, *Faith and Fratricide* (New York: Seabury, 1974); Gager, *Origins of Anti-Semitism;* Alan Davies, ed., *Anti-Semitism and the Foundations of Christianity* (New York: Paulist, 1979); Peter Richardson and D. Granskou, eds., *Anti-Judaism in Early Christianity, Vol. 1: Paul and the Gospels* (Waterloo, Ontario: Wilfried Laurier, 1986).

67. Richardson, *Paul's Ethic of Freedom*, pp. 41–42.

68. This perception of Paul, which (as we have observed) is a mystification of the apostle, can frustrate the efforts of liberation theologians to find resources in Paul's writings for the liberative project. Thus Juan Luis Segundo finds himself unable to use the "political key" to understand Paul in the way he had used that same key to illuminate the historical Jesus of the Synoptic Gospels. To the contrary, Segundo (citing 1 Cor. 7:21) declares that Paul's view of social issues "seems to put him poles apart from Jesus' commitment to the poor. Paul counsels slaves to remain such!" Equally convinced that the heart of Paul's theology was more or less systematically laid out in Romans 1–8, Segundo felt obliged to focus on those chapters, using an "anthropological" key that (among other things) transposed "Law" into structures of societal obligation and coercion ("Paul's Key and Latin America Today," in *The Humanist Christology of Paul*, vol. 2 of *Jesus of Nazareth Yesterday and Today;* ed. and trans. John Drury [Maryknoll: Orbis, 1986], pp. 161–182).

Segundo's procedure is a valiant attempt to make the best of what we should regard as obsolete assumptions. I hope to show in the following chapters that there are, in fact, much more valuable resources for human liberation in Paul's thought and work.

Segundo's treatment also sets an undesirable precedent by making a straightforward correlation of the Jewish Law with the sociological dynamics of oppression. See Elizabeth Schüssler Fiorenza's warnings against salvaging the Christian biblical tradition for the liberation project by scapegoating Judaism as the oppressive "background": *In Memory of Her*, pp. 105–110.

69. J. B. Lightfoot, *Saint Paul's Epistle to the Galatians* (London: Macmillan, 1865), p. 49; Bruce, *Paul, Apostle of the Heart Set Free*, pp. 325–326; C. E. B. Cranfield, *The Epistle to the Romans*, vol. 2 (Edinburgh: T. & T. Clark, 1975), pp. 816–817. On historical and rhetorical-critical issues involved in discussions of the letter's occasion, see Elliott, *Rhetoric of Romans*, Introduction and chap. 1.

70. See the essays collected in K. P. Donfried, ed., *The Romans Debate*, 2d ed. (Peabody: Hendrickson Publishers, 1991).

71. Beker, *Paul the Apostle*, pp. 11–12; on Romans, see pp. 59–108.

72. I have elaborated these arguments in *Rhetoric of Romans*, pp. 69–104. See also L. Ann Jervis, *The Purpose of Romans: A Comparative Letter Structure Investigation*, Journal for the Study of the New Testament Supplement 55 (Sheffield: JSOT Press, 1991), on the argumentative character of the letter opening and closing.

73. Victor P. Furnish, *Theology and Ethics in Paul* (Nashville: Abingdon, 1968), pp. 105–106.

74. Bultmann, *Theology*, 1:72–73, 105–106; see my *Rhetoric of Romans*, pp. 94–104, 277–283.

75. Hendrikus Boers, "The Problem of Jews and Gentiles in the Macro-Structure of Romans," *Svensk Exegetisk Årbosk* 47 (1982), pp. 184–196; William S. Campbell, "Romans III as a Key to the Structure and Thought of the Letter," *Novum Testamentum* 23 (1981), pp. 22–40, reprinted in *The Romans Debate*, 2d ed., pp. 251–264; see also Campbell, *Paul's Gospel in an Intercultural Context*, pp. 1–24.

76. Oscar Romero, "The Political Dimension of the Faith from the Perspective of the Option for the Poor" (February 2, 1980), in *Liberation Theology: A Documentary History*, ed. Alfred T. Hennelly (Maryknoll: Orbis, 1990), pp. 292–303.

77. "Declaration on Human Development and Christian Salvation," in *Liberation Theology: A Documentary History*, pp. 205–219.

78. "Opening Address at the Puebla Conference" (January 28, 1979), in *Liberation Theology: A Documentary History*, pp. 225–232.
Celebrating a Eucharist in Sandinista Nicaragua a few years later, the pope again relied on the Paul of the Pastorals to warn that the unity of the church is threatened when "the powerful factors which constitute and maintain it—faith itself, the revealed word, the sacraments, obedience to the bishops and to the Pope, the sense of vocation and mutual responsibility in Christ's mission in the world—are relegated to a position inferior to earthly considerations, unacceptable ideological commitments, temporal options, even concepts of the church which supplant the true one." See "Unity of the Church" (March 4, 1983), in *Liberation Theology: A Documentary History*, pp. 329–334.

79. "Instruction on Certain Aspects of the 'Theology of Liberation'" (August 6, 1984), in *Liberation Theology: A Documentary History*, pp. 393–414.

80. "Evangelization, Liberation, and Human Promotion," in *Liberation Theology: A Documentary History*, p. 234.

81. David Bosch, "Paul and Human Hopes," *Journal of Theology for South Africa* 67 (1989), pp. 3–16.

82. Clodovis Boff and George V. Pixley, *The Bible, the Church and the Poor*, trans. Paul Burns (Maryknoll: Orbis, 1989), pp. 54, 56.

83. Ignacio Ellacuría, "The Political Nature of Jesus' Mission," in *Faces of Jesus: Latin American Christologies*, p. 80.

84. The 1980s and 1990s have seen the publication or reprint of several biographies of Niebuhr, anthologies of his essays, and studies of his thought: Charles C. Brown, *Niebuhr and His Age: Reinhold Niebuhr's Prophetic Role in the Twentieth Century* (Philadelphia: Trinity Press International, 1992); idem, ed., *A Reinhold Niebuhr Reader: Selected Essays, Articles, and Book Reviews* (Philadelphia: Trinity Press International, 1992); Robert McAfee Brown, ed., *The Essential Reinhold Niebuhr: Selected Essays and Addresses* (New Haven: Yale University Press, 1986); Richard W. Fox, *Reinhold Niebuhr: A Biography* (New York: Pantheon, 1985); Richard Harries, ed., *Reinhold Niebuhr and the Issues of Our Time* (Grand Rapids: Eerdmans, 1986); Charles W. Kegley, *Reinhold Niebuhr: His Religious, Social, and Political Thought*, rev. ed. (New York: Pilgrim, 1984); Larry Rasmussen, ed., *Reinhold Niebuhr: Theologian of Public Life* (New York: Harper & Row, 1989); Ronald H. Stone, *Professor Reinhold Niebuhr: A Mentor to the Twentieth Century* (Louisville: Westminster/John Knox Press, 1992); idem, *Reinhold Niebuhr: Prophet to Politicians* (University Press International, 1981 [reprint]).

On the evaluation of liberation theology from the perspective of Niebuhr's "Christian realism," see Thomas G. Sanders, "The Theology of Liberation: Christian Utopianism," *Christianity and Crisis* 33 (September 17, 1973), pp. 167–173; Dennis McCann, *Christian Realism and Liberation Theology: Practical Theologies in Creative Conflict* (Maryknoll: Orbis, 1981); McGovern, *Liberation Theology and Its Critics*, pp. 55–58; and Craig L. Nessan, *Orthopraxis or Heresy: The North American Theological Response to Latin American Liberation Theology* (Atlanta: Scholars, 1986), esp. pp. 223–339.

85. See Robert McAfee Brown, "Reinhold Niebuhr: His Theology in the 1980s," *Christian Century* 103:3 (January 22, 1986), pp. 66–68.

Brown, a student of Niebuhr at Union Theological Seminary and editor of *The Essential Reinhold Niebuhr*, has written or edited a number of books introducing liberation theology themes to North American audiences (*Theology in a New Key: Responding to Liberation Themes* [Philadelphia: Westminster, 1978]; *Making Peace in the Global Village* [Philadelphia: Westminster, 1981]; *Unexpected News: Reading the Bible with Third World Eyes* [Philadelphia: Westminster, 1984]; *Kairos: Three Prophetic Challenges to the Church* [Grand Rapids: Eerdmans, 1990]; and *Gustavo Gutiérrez: An Introduction to Liberation Theology* [Maryknoll: Orbis, 1990]).

86. Brown, *The Essential Reinhold Niebuhr*, pp. xxi-xxii; see also John C. Bennett, "Niebuhr's Ethic: The Later Years," *Christianity & Crisis* 42:6 (April 12, 1982), pp. 91–95; Ronald Preston, "Reinhold Niebuhr and the New Right," in *Reinhold Niebuhr and the Issues of Our Time*, ed. Richard Harries (Grand Rapids: Eerdmans, 1986), pp. 88–104.

87. *Christianity and Crisis*, July 21, 1952, p. 97; *Radical Religion*, Spring 1939, p. 11.

88. Reinhold Niebuhr, "Why the Christian Church Is Not Pacifist," in *The Essential Reinhold Niebuhr*, pp. 102–119.

89. It is in the spirit of this "religious fact" that Niebuhr commended the consciences of bomber crews who refused to receive Communion before taking off to drop bombs on German cities, but gently urged them nevertheless to

accept the sacrament as "the peace of divine forgiveness, mediated to the contrite sinner who knows that it is not in his power to live a sinless life on earth" ("The Bombing of Germany," in *Love and Justice: Selections from the Shorter Writings of Reinhold Niebuhr*, ed. D. B. Robertson [Gloucester: Peter Smith, 1976], pp. 222–223).

90. Edward T. Oakes, S.J., in *America*, May 30, 1992, p. 448.

91. Paul Merkley, *Reinhold Niebuhr: A Political Account* (Montreal: McGill-Queen's University, 1975), chap. 14.

92. Reinhold Niebuhr, "American Hegemony and the Prospects for Peace," in *Annals of the American Academy of Political and Social Science* (1962).

93. Jack Nelson-Pallmeyer, "Wise as Serpents, Gentle as Doves? The Challenge to Nonviolence in the Face of Pleas for Intervention," *Sojourners* 22:3 (April 1993), p. 11.

94. On the question of the "effectiveness" of nonviolence, John Howard Yoder's comments are to the point. Yoder criticizes the widespread assumptions that "the relationship of cause and effect [in history] is visible, understandable, and manageable, . . . that we are adequately informed to be able to set for ourselves and for all society the goal toward which we seek to move it, . . . that effectiveness in moving towards these goals which have been set is itself a moral yardstick." Against these assumptions, Yoder cites Niebuhr's own doctrine of "irony": "that when men try to manage history, it almost always turns out to have taken another direction than that in which they thought they were guiding it" (*The Politics of Jesus* [Grand Rapids: Eerdmans, 1972], pp. 234–236).

There is no better index of that irony than the miserable failure of a century of war and militarism to secure peace and justice for its intended beneficiaries.

95. Bill Kellermann, "Apologist of Power: The Long Shadow of Reinhold Niebuhr's Christian Realism," *Sojourners* (March 1987), pp. 14–20; Noam Chomsky, "Reinhold Niebuhr," *Grand Street* 6:2 (Winter 1987), pp. 197–212.

96. Michael Novak, another of Niebuhr's students and a prolific author for the American Enterprise Institute, has called Niebuhr "The Father of Neoconservatives" (*National Review*, May 11, 1992, pp. 39–42).

In Novak's view, a "realistic" appraisal of the global economy shows that Latin American misery is the result of laziness (Novak's euphemism is "the Spanish ethos"), not of North American management of Latin American economies ("investment"), which alone should be credited for what improvements Latin American countries have seen in their living standards. The century-old role of the U.S. military in securing national and international corporate interests throughout Latin America and the Caribbean plays no significant role in Novak's analysis, presumably being irrelevant to the dictates of "realism." Rather "realism" should lead us to recognize the U.S. policy of exploitation by force of Latin American resources (his euphemism is "democratic capitalism") as the only genuine "liberation theology for North America." Latin Americans who fail to appreciate the benefits flowing to their countries from a benign neighbor to the North, or who claim to perceive structural conflicts between the interests of the wealthy to the North and the wretchedly poor masses to the South ("class struggle"), are by definition dupes of Marxist ideology. See Michael Novak, *Liberation South, Liberation North* (Washington: American Enterprise Institute, 1981); *The Spirit of Democratic Capitalism* (New York: Simon & Schuster, 1982); *Will It Liberate? Questions about Liberation Theology* (New York:

Paulist, 1986); *Human Rights and the New Realism: Strategic Thinking in a New Age* (Freedom House, 1986); *The Catholic Ethic and the Spirit of Capitalism* (New York: Maxwell MacMillan, 1993).

97. Theodore R. Weber, "Christian Realism, Power, and Peace," in *Theology, Politics, and Peace,* ed. Theodore Runyon (Maryknoll: Orbis, 1989), p. 58.

98. J. Christiaan Beker, *The Triumph of God: The Essence of Paul's Thought* (Minneapolis: Fortress, 1990), pp. x, 124.

99. Tomson, *Paul and the Jewish Law,* p. 56.

100. Gustavo Gutiérrez, *A Theology of Liberation* (Maryknoll: Orbis, 1973), p. 300.

101. J. Christiaan Beker, "The Method of Recasting Pauline Theology: The Coherence-Contingency Theme as Interpretive Model," in Kent H. Richards, ed., *Society of Biblical Literature 1986 Seminar Papers* (Atlanta: Scholars, 1986), p. 597.

102. On rhetorical criticism in New Testament studies, see Kennedy, *New Testament Interpretation through Rhetorical Criticism;* Mack, *Rhetoric and the New Testament;* on the question of Paul's possible rhetorical training, Betz, "The Problem of Rhetoric and Theology according to the Apostle Paul."

103. Examples in English of the application of Perelman and Olbrechts-Tyteca's methodology in *The New Rhetoric* include Wire, *Corinthian Women Prophets,* and Elliott, *Rhetoric of Romans.*

104. Wire, *Corinthian Women Prophets,* p. 10.

105. Albert Schweitzer, *The Quest of the Historical Jesus: A Critical Study of Its Progress from Reimarus to Wrede* (New York: Macmillan, 1968), p. 399.

106. Earlier scholarship on the historical Jesus articulated the criterion of dissimilarity as dissimilarity "to characteristic emphases of both ancient Judaism and early Christianity" (for example, Norman Perrin, *The New Testament: An Introduction,* 2d ed. [New York: Harcourt Brace Jovanovich, 1982], p. 405). But see the following note.

107. With regard to historical Jesus research, E. P. Sanders describes a "convincing historical depiction of Jesus" as one that "sets him firmly in Jewish history"; he thus considers the "double" criterion of dissimilarity—which filters out material from the tradition of Jesus' sayings that resembles the self-definition of the early churches *or* the perspective of early Judaism—"inadequate" (*Jesus and Judaism* [Philadelphia: Fortress, 1985], pp. 5, 14). Paula Fredriksen similarly speaks of a "modified criterion" of dissimilarity and a more recent approach to the historical Jesus related positively to knowledge of first-century Judaism (*From Jesus to Christ* [New Haven: Yale University Press, 1988], pp. 6, 96).

108. Gaston, *Paul and the Torah,* passim.

109. Tomson's review of research on Paul critiques three widespread assumptions, namely, that "(1) the center of his thought is a polemic against the Law; (2) the Law for him no longer had a practical meaning; and (3) ancient Jewish literature is no source for explaining his letters." Those assumptions are mistaken, as Schweitzer already saw. Tomson, *Paul and the Jewish Law,* pp. 1–19.

110. Perelman and Olbrechts-Tyteca, *The New Rhetoric,* p. 45; Chaim Perelman, *The Realm of Rhetoric,* trans. W. Kluback (Notre Dame: University of Notre Dame Press, 1982), pp. 9, 11.

111. Segundo, *The Humanist Christology of Paul,* p. 6.

112. Ibid., pp. 161–182.

113. Elisabeth Schüssler Fiorenza, "The Ethics of Interpretation: De-Centering Biblical Scholarship," *Journal of Biblical Literature* 107:1 (1988), pp. 3–17.

114. Robert McAfee Brown, "Reflections of a North American: The Future of Liberation Theology," in *The Future of Liberation Theology: Essays in Honor of Gustavo Gutiérrez,* ed. Marc H. Ellis and Otto Maduro (Maryknoll: Orbis, 1989), pp. 491–501.

115. Brown, *Kairos: Three Prophetic Challenges to the Church,* pp. 143–151; Nelson-Pallmeyer, *War against the Poor,* pp. 73–88.

116. Carter Heyward, "Doing Theology in a Counterrevolutionary Situation," in *The Future of Liberation Theology,* pp. 397–409.

117. Beker, *Paul the Apostle,* pp. 325–327.

118. Juan Luis Segundo, "Two Theologies of Liberation," in *Liberation Theology: A Documentarty History,* p. 356.

119. Or "poor": the Greek word *tapeinois* is one of several routinely used throughout the Septuagint, particularly in the Psalms, for the "poor and oppressed" who cry to God for deliverance.

120. Susan Griffin, *A Chorus of Stones: The Private Life of War* (New York: Doubleday, 1992).

121. Alice Miller, *For Your Own Good: Hidden Cruelty in Child-Rearing and the Roots of Violence,* trans. Hildegarde and Hunter Hannum (New York: Farrar Strauss Giroux, 1983).

122. "Biographers say that the miracle of Paul's vision on the road to Damascus had been repeated, that a mortal soul had been caught up in an experience of the divine that sublimated worldly traits into an overwhelming desire to offer himself to God" (Arnaldo Fortini, *Francis of Assisi,* trans. Helen Moak [New York: Crossroad, 1981], pp. 188–189). Fortini suggests that this momentous experience was specifically a conformation to Paul's martyrdom.

4. Paul and the Violence of the Cross

1. Beker declares that "the cross is Paul's most succinct interpretation of the death of Christ and functions as its specific apocalyptic hermeneutic" (*Paul the Apostle,* p. 199).

2. Robert Hamerton-Kelly calls this verse a "summary of the Pauline *kērygma*" (*Sacred Violence,* p. 72, n. 19).

3. Beker, *Paul the Apostle,* p. 207.

4. Martin Hengel, *Crucifixion,* trans. John Bowden (London: SCM Press, 1977); reprinted with *The Son of God* and *The Atonement* in *The Cross of the Son of God* (London: SCM Press, 1986). Citations are from the reprint edition.

5. Ibid., pp. 125–137.

6. Cited by G. E. M. de Ste. Croix, *The Class Struggle in the Ancient Greek World, from the Archaic Age to the Arab Conquests* [Ithaca: Cornell University Press, 1981], p. 409.

7. Ibid., pp. 138–142.

8. South African President DeKlerk's government was compelled at last to admit the continued activities of the notorious "Civilian Cooperations Bureau,"

which the African National Congress has long accused of covert death squad activity. A pathologist accused police of "systematic" torture and murder of prisoners in custody.

Israeli Defense Minister Moshe Arens called a press conference to advertise the activity of similar groups ostensibly targeting "Palestinian terrorists," but accused by eyewitnesses of shooting two Palestinian youths in the back as they painted anti-Israeli slogans on a wall (Associated Press, May 11, 1992). The chief of police in Jerusalem described the beating death of a young Palestinian in custody as consistent with "routine police procedure."

A physician from Los Angeles reports that on the average, three or four persons of color are brought into the County Hospital jail ward beaten "as badly as [Rodney] King, or worse," each night; hospital personnel see blacks and Hispanics who have been beaten to death, often by police, "once or twice a month" (*Newsday*, April 23, 1993). In Chicago a police commander was at last dismissed for brutality after more than sixty accusations that he and colleagues had coerced confessions from black prisoners through beatings and electric shock (*Zeta*, May 1993).

9. Beker, *Paul the Apostle*, p. 206 (citing Josephus, *War* 5:44:9).

10. Americas Watch, *El Salvador's Decade of Terror: Human Rights since the Assassination of Archbishop Romero* (New Haven: Yale University Press, 1991).

11. Rigoberta Menchú, *I, Rigoberta Menchú* (Boston: Verso, 1981).

12. Amy Willentz, *The Rainy Season: Haiti Since Duvalier* (New York: Simon & Schuster, 1989), pp. 347–355; Jean-Bertrand Aristide, *In the Parish of the Poor* (Maryknoll: Orbis, 1990).

13. On these massacres see Zinn, *A People's History of the United States*; on the continuity of imperialist violence in this hemisphere over the last five centuries, see Noam Chomsky, *Year 501: The Conquest Continues* (Boston: South End Press, 1993).

14. Aristide, *In the Parish of the Poor*, p. 53.

15. On "fear as a cultural and political construct" in terrorist states see *Fear at the Edge: State Terrorism and Resistance in Latin America*, ed. Juan E. Corradi, Patricia Weiss Fagen, and Manuel Antonio Garretón (Berkeley and Los Angeles: University of California Press, 1992); on state terrorism as a cornerstone of U.S. foreign policy, Jack Nelson-Pallmyer, *War against the Poor.*

16. The effectiveness of the School of the Americas is evident from the accomplishments of its graduates, as documented by the United Nations "Truth Commission" in its report on violence in El Salvador.

17. A less enchanted view of the Pax Romana comes from the Marxist historian de Ste. Croix. The cessation of war was "made inevitable by the exhaustion of Italian manpower . . . too many Italians had been fighting for too long" (*Class Struggle in the Ancient Greek World*, p. 358).

18. Ibid., p. 355.

19. Richard A. Horsley, *Jesus and the Spiral of Violence: Popular Jewish Resistance in Roman Palestine* (San Francisco: Harper & Row, 1987), pp. 20–29; he cites Dom Helder Camara, *Spiral of Violence* (London: Sheed & Ward, 1971), pp. 29–31.

20. Klaus Wengst, *Pax Romana and the Peace of Jesus Christ*, trans. John Bowden (Philadelphia: Fortress, 1987), pp. 52–53.

21. Richard Horsley, *Jesus and the Spiral of Violence*, p. 29.

22. See K. R. Bradley, *Slaves and Masters in the Roman Empire: A Study in Social Control* (New York: Oxford University Press, 1987); Orlando Patterson, *Slavery and Social Death: A Comparative Study* (Cambridge: Harvard University Press, 1982).

23. The standard reference is L. Robert, *Gladiateurs dans l'Orient grec* (1940).

24. See Paul Duff, "Processions," *Anchor Bible Dictionary*, vol. 5, ed. David Noel Freedman (New York: Doubleday, 1992), pp. 469–493.

25. See de Ste. Croix's discussion of "Class Struggle on the Ideological Plane," in *Class Struggle in the Ancient Greek World*, chap. 7; on the emperor cult, Duncan Fishwick, "The Development of Provincial Ruler Worship in the Western Roman Empire," *Aufstieg und Niedergang der römischen Welt* II:16:2, ed. H. Temporini and W. Haase (Berlin and New York: DeGruyter, 1972ff.), pp. 1201–1253.

26. Sanders addressed the Annual Meeting of the Society of Biblical Literature in San Francisco, November 1992; he published related comments in *Reflections* 87:1 (1992), pp. 4–12.

27. James W. Douglass, *The Nonviolent Coming of God* (Maryknoll: Orbis, 1991), p. 12.

28. De Ste. Croix, *Class Struggle in the Ancient Greek World*, p. 344.

29. Chomsky, *Year 501*, p. 7.

30. Walter Wink, *Engaging the Powers: Discernment and Resistance in a World of Domination* (Minneapolis: Fortress, 1992), pp. 100–101.

31. Gilbert, *The Holocaust*, passim.

32. Fredriksen, *From Jesus to Christ*, pp. 109, 115–123.

33. Ibid., p. 121.

34. Ibid., pp. 214–215.

35. See Jon Sobrino, *Christology at the Crossroads: A Latin American Approach*, trans. John Drury (Maryknoll: Orbis, 1978), chap. 11.

36. Horsley, *Jesus and the Spiral of Violence*, p. 319.

37. Schüssler Fiorenza, *In Memory of Her*, p. 135.

38. Wink, *Engaging the Powers*, pp. 109–110.

39. See Fredriksen, *From Jesus to Christ*, chaps. 7 and 8; Burton L. Mack, "The Innocent Transgressor: Jesus in Early Christian Myth and History," *Semeia* 33 (1985), pp. 135–165.

A few other crucial observations make the point. The Jerusalem crowd's preference for Barabbas, a murderous rebel (*lestes*, Mark 14:7), over Jesus, an innocent man (14:14), allows the later conflict between Rome and the *lestai* to be encapsulated in the events leading to Jesus' death; the Temple's destruction forty years later is signaled at the moment Jesus dies on the cross (15:38). Matthew makes the logic explicit: Jesus pronounces his Pharisaic opponents guilty of "all the innocent blood shed on earth" from the foundation of the world (23:35) and pronounces God's punishment on the Jews of Jerusalem (23:36–39); a few chapters later, the Jews accept the curse, crying out, "His blood be on our heads and the heads of our children!" (27:25).

40. Fredriksen, *From Jesus to Christ*, pp. 182–183, 104.

41. See especially Rudolf Bultmann, *The History of the Synoptic Tradition*, rev. ed., trans. John Marsh (New York: Harper & Row, 1963), pp. 1–7.

42. Mack, "The Innocent Transgressor," p. 150.

43. Girard's theory is set out in *Violence and the Sacred*, trans. Patrick Gregory (Baltimore: Johns Hopkins University Press, 1977); *The Scapegoat*, trans. Yvonne Freccero (Baltimore: Johns Hopkins University Press, 1986); and *Things Hidden from the Foundation of the World*, with J. M. Oughourlian and G. Lefort (Palo Alto: Stanford University Press, 1987); see also Robert G. Hamerton-Kelly, ed., *Violent Origins: Walter Burkert, René Girard, and Jonathan Z. Smith on Ritual Killing and Cultural Formation*, (Palo Alto: Stanford University Press, 1987).

For applications of Girard's theory in biblical studies, see especially *René Girard and Biblical Studies*, *Semeia* 33 (1985); Raymund Schwager, *Must There Be Scapegoats?* trans. Maria L. Assad (San Francisco: Harper & Row, 1987); James G. Williams, *The Bible, Violence, and the Sacred: Liberation from the Myth of Sanctioned Violence* (San Francisco: Harper San Francisco, 1991); and Hamerton-Kelly, *Sacred Violence*. The *Bulletin of the Colloquium on Violence and Religion*, published in Innsbruck, Austria, lists several hundred bibliographical items on Girard's thought.

44. Girard, *The Scapegoat*, p. 100.

45. See on these issues Lloyd Gaston, *No Stone on Another: Studies in the Significance of the Fall of Jerusalem in the Synoptic Gospels* (Leiden, Netherlands: E. J. Brill, 1970); Rosemary Radford Ruether, *Faith and Fratricide: The Theological Roots of Anti-Semitism* (New York: Seabury, 1974); Fredriksen, *From Jesus to Christ*, chap. 8; Burton L. Mack, *A Myth of Innocence: Mark and Christian Origins* (Philadelphia: Fortress, 1988).

46. This insistence on the "revelatory" character of the Gospels, emerging in *Things Hidden from the Foundation of the World* and *The Scapegoat* and reiterated in the Foreword to Williams, *The Bible, Violence, and the Sacred*, is tempered by Girard's admission that it is our recent *history*, the naked violence of the twentieth century, that "mediates" this revelation to us today (see the final chapter of *Things Hidden from the Foundation of the World*).

47. Girard, in Hamerton-Kelly, ed., *Violent Origins*, p. 143; *The Scapegoat*, pp. 106, 109.

48. Observing Jesus' imputation to the Pharisees of "all the blood of the prophets shed from the foundation of the world," Lucien Scubla asks, "How can one fail to recognize here the selfsame illusion that is the product of the victimage mechanism and the cause of its efficacy?" See "The Christianity of René Girard and the Nature of Religion," in *Violence and Truth: On the Work of René Girard*, ed. Paul Dumouchel (London: Athlone Press, 1988), pp. 160–171.

Burton Mack hails Girard's hermeneutic as "the most startling reading of early Christian texts since Bultmann's announcement of a program for their demythologization," but proposes that we "take seriously Girard's theory in general . . . and use it to read the gospels not as unique texts, but as myths generated by social conflict, just as Girard has done with all his other extrabiblical texts" ("The Innocent Transgressor," p. 148). James Williams, an enthusiastic advocate of Girard's program, nevertheless departs from Girard in admitting that "sacrificial language still has a strong hold" in the Gospels (*The Bible, Violence, and the Sacred*, p. 188). And Walter Wink, who relies on Girard's theory in discussing the nonviolent significance of the cross, nevertheless insists that "the idea of the sacrificial, expiatory death of Jesus is far more pervasive in the New Testament than Girard acknowledges" (*Engaging the Powers*, p. 153).

49. Girard, in the Foreword to Williams, *The Bible, Violence, and the Sacred*, p. viii.

50. Sobrino, *Christology at the Crossroads*, pp. 371–374.

51. Wink, *Engaging the Powers*, p. 148.

52. Ibid., pp. 148–149. On the problem of distorted christologies in Latin American Christianity see the essays collected in Bonino, ed., *Faces of Jesus*; Leonardo Boff, *Passion of Christ, Passion of the World: The Facts, Their Interpretation, and Their Meaning Yesterday and Today*, trans. Robert R. Barr (Maryknoll: Orbis, 1987); Jon Sobrino, *Jesus in Latin America* (Maryknoll: Orbis, 1987).

53. Segundo, *Humanistic Christology of Paul*, p. 1.

54. Ernst Käsemann, "The Saving Significance of Jesus' Death in Paul," p. 49.

55. Characteristically, Paul speaks of the death of Jesus in terms that we must call mythical; that is, he interprets Jesus' death consistently within narrative schemes in which the protagonist in that death is God, who has "sent Jesus out" (as a scapegoat? *exapostellein*, Gal. 4:4, 6) or "surrendered" Jesus (*paradidonai*, Rom. 8:32) or "offered" Jesus (as a sacrifice, *prothetein*, Rom. 3:25); or else, Jesus, who offers himself (Gal. 1:4, 2:20). The initiative, the purpose, in every case is God's: the cross manifests God's love (Rom. 5:8), God's justice (Romans 3:25), God's power (1 Cor. 2:18). If the confession that Christ died "for us" (1 Thess. 5:10; Rom. 5:8, 8:32; 2 Cor. 5:21) can involve several different metaphors—the paschal lamb (1 Cor. 5:7), the scapegoat (Gal. 4:4–6), or a ransom (Rom. 8:32), the tradition Paul has received from Christian predecessors confesses that Christ died "for our sins" (1 Cor. 15:3; also Rom. 4:25), even as an expiatory sacrifice provided by God "on our behalf" (*hilastērion*, Rom. 3:25; *hamartia* = "sin-offering," 8:3, 2 Cor. 5:21), so that "we are justified in his blood" (Rom. 3:25; 5:9).

On the atoning significance of Jesus' death in Paul, a theme "too frequent to be ignored," see Hengel, *The Cross of the Son of God*, pp. 189–263. Käsemann observes that although "Paul was familiar with the idea of sacrifice [and] he used it without scruple," nevertheless "the Pauline texts provide no basis" for "the old view of the vicarious punishment of Christ" ("The Saving Significance of Jesus' Death in Paul," pp. 42–43). Hamerton-Kelly discusses "The Cross and the Category of Sacrifice" from a Girardian perspective in *Sacred Violence*, pp. 77–81. On the scapegoat and ransom metaphors, see Daniel Schwarz, "Two Pauline Allusions to the Redemptive Mechanism of the Crucifixion," *Journal of Biblical Literature* 102:2 (1983), pp. 259–268. Recently Bradley McLean has announced "The Absence of an Atoning Sacrifice in Paul's Soteriology" (*New Testament Studies* 38 [1992], pp. 531–553), basing his argument on Jacob Milgrom's studies of the levitical sacrificial system; but Milgrom's studies leave a few significant questions unanswered (see the discussion and bibliography provided by Gary Anderson, "Sacrifice and Sacrificial Offerings (OT)," *Anchor Bible Dictionary*, 1:870–886). For a recent argument that *hamartia* in fact means "sin-offering," see N. T. Wright, *The Climax of the Covenant: Christ and the Law in Pauline Theology* (Edinburgh: T. & T. Clark, 1991), pp. 220–225. On the atoning significance of the martyr's death (as in 4 Maccabees) as the source of early Christian thinking, Paul's in particular, on Jesus' death, see John S. Pobee, *Persecution and Martyrdom in the Theology of Paul*, Journal for the Study of the New Tetament Supplement 6 (Sheffield: JSOT Press, 1985); Sam K. Williams, *Jesus' Death as Saving Event: The Background and Origins of a Concept* (Missoula: Scholars, 1975); on Greco-Roman concepts as the background, David Seeley, *The Noble Death: Greco-Roman Martyrology and Paul's Concept of Salvation*, Journal for the Study of the New Testament Supplement 28 (Sheffield: Sheffield Academic Press, 1989).

56. "If Christ's death saves us from the wrath of God (Rom. 5:9); if Jesus was sent by God as a sin offering (1 Cor. 15:3; Rom. 8:3, NRSV margin); if Christ is a paschal lamb sacrificed on our behalf (1 Cor. 5:7), it would appear that God's wrath must indeed be appeased. Paul has apparently been unable fully to distinguish the insight that Christ is the end of sacrificing from the idea that Christ is the final sacrifice whose death is an atonement to God. And Christianity has suffered from this confusion ever since" (*Engaging the Powers*, pp. 153–154).

57. Rita Nakashima Brock, *Journeys By Heart: A Christology of Erotic Power* (New York: Crossroad, 1988); Ruether, *Faith and Fratricide*; Gudorf, *Victimization*; Brown and Bohn, eds., *Christianity, Patriarchy, and Abuse*.

58. G. F. Moore, *Judaism in the First Three Centuries of Christianity: The Age of the Tannaim*, 3 vols. (Cambridge: Harvard University Press, 1927–1930); Anderson, "Sacrifice and Sacrificial Offerings (OT)"; Joseph Fitzmyer, *Paul and His Theology: A Brief Sketch* (Englewood Cliffs: Prentice-Hall, 1967), p. 65.

59. References: Moore, *Judaism*; C. G. Montefiore, *Judaism and St. Paul: Two Essays* (London, 1914); H. J. Schoeps, *Paul: The Theology of the Apostle in the Light of Jewish Religious History*, trans. Harold Knight (Philadelphia: Westminster, 1961); Samuel Sandmel, *The Genius of Paul* (New York, 1958); Maccoby, *Paul and Hellenism*. For a convenient summary of issues, see Sanders, *Paul and Palestinian Judaism*, pp. 1–11.

60. Fredriksen, *From Jesus to Christ*, p. 173.

61. Hyam Maccoby, *The Mythmaker: Paul and the Invention of Christianity* (San Francisco: Harper San Francisco, 1987), p. 50; see also his *Paul and Hellenism* (Philadelphia: Trinity Press International, 1991); and John G. Gager's review of *The Mythmaker* in *Jewish Quarterly Review* 79:2–3 (October 1988– January 1989), pp. 248–250.

62. De Ste. Croix, *The Class Struggle in the Ancient Greek World*, p. 432.

63. George V. Pixley, *God's Kingdom* (Maryknoll: Orbis, 1981), p. 100.

64. Thus Shaye Cohen summarized a common perception of Paul in a lecture on "Judaisms at the Time of Jesus," at the Jay Phillips Symposium of the Center for Jewish-Christian Learning in St. Paul, Minnesota (April 19, 1993).

65. Paul "excised the nationalist context and content" of the life and death of Jesus "and presented a scheme of salvation in the cosmopolitan idiom of Hellenism. He thus minimized the political aspects of the messianic movement while presenting his message in terms already meaningful to his Gentile audience" (Paula Fredriksen, *From Jesus to Christ*, p. 173).

On the so-called mystery religions, see Marvin W. Meyer, "Mystery Religions," *Anchor Bible Dictionary* 4:941–945, and the bibliography there; on their influence on early Christianity, Bousset, *Kyrios Christos*, and Maccoby, *Paul and Hellenism* (strongly influential); A. J. M. Wedderburn, *Baptism and*

Resurrection (Tübingen: Mohr-Siebeck, 1987), and Jonathan Z. Smith, *Drudgery Divine: On the Comparison of Early Christianities and the Religions of Late Antiquity* (Chicago: University of Chicago Press, 1990) (their influence is not decisive).

66. Ernst Käsemann represents an important Protestant tradition when he writes that "the Reformers were indisputably right when they appealed to Paul for their understanding of evangelical theology as a theology of the cross" ("The Saving Significance of Jesus' Death in Paul," p. 32).

67. Representative views can be found in Fitzmyer, *Paul and His Theology*, pp.36–38; Käsemann, "The Saving Significance of Jesus' Death in Paul," and "Justification and Salvation History in the Epistle to the Romans."

68. Sölle addresses in particular the triumph of "kerygmatic neoorthodoxy" over theological liberalism in continental theology: see her *Political Theology*, trans. John Shelley (Philadelphia: Fortress, 1974), pp. 19–39; on similar issues in Latin America, Bonino, ed., *Faces of Jesus*.

69. See, for example, Käsemann's celebrated *theological* response (in "Justification by Faith and Salvation History in the Epistle to the Romans") to Stendahl's *historical* inquiry in "Paul and the Introspective Conscience of the West."

70. For Rudolf Bultmann, for example, Paul's theology, "which is more or less completely set forth in Romans," is "at the same time, anthropology," and "Paul's christology is simultaneously soteriology" (*Theology of the New Testament*, vol. 1, p. 191).

71. This logic is almost obligatory among Christian commentators: at Rom. 1:18–3:20, W. Sanday and A. C. Headlam declare, "St. Paul has just stated [in 1:16–17] what the Gospel is; he now goes on to show the necessity for such a Gospel. The world is lost without it" (*A Critical and Exegetical Commentary on the Epistle to the Romans*, 5th ed., International Critical Commentary [Edinburgh: T. & T. Clark, 1902], p. 40). The artificiality of this logic has been pointed out recently by Richard Hays ("Psalm 143 and the Logic of Romans 3," *Journal of Biblical Literature* 99 [1980], pp. 107–115).

72. A particularly noteworthy example is Ernst Käsemann, *Commentary on Romans*, trans. Geoffrey W. Bromiley (Grand Rapids: Eerdmans, 1983), passim.

73. Under the heading "the holistic comparison of patterns of religion," Sanders proposes to compare "*how getting in and staying in are understood*," or what "a systematic theology classifies under 'soteriology.'" He cavils only at the "connotations" of the term soteriology (*Paul and Palestinian Judaism*, p. 17).

74. Ibid., p. 432.

75. Ibid., pp. 474–511.

76. J. Christiaan Beker, "Paul's Theology: Consistent or Inconsistent?" *New Testament Studies* 34 (1988), pp. 364–377; Dunn, "The New Perspective on Paul."

77. Along with Sanders's sketch, see the more extensive treatment in Heikki Räisänen, *Paul and the Law* (Philadelphia: Fortress, 1986).

78. Francis Watson, *Paul, Judaism, and the Gentiles: A Sociological Approach* (Cambridge: Cambridge University Press, 1986); see William S. Campbell's response, "Did Paul Advocate Separation from the Synagogue?" *Scottish Journal of Theology* 41 (1988), pp. 1–11. Räisänen at length argues that it was

"in the course of his work among Gentiles" that Paul became "internally alienated from the ritual aspects of the law"; it was only "under the pressure of events" (the Antioch crisis) that Paul turned the question of the law "into a question of soteriology" in order to justify "a global rejection of the law" (*Paul and the Law*, pp. 256–263).

79. Mack seeks to correlate different symbolizations of Jesus with different group configurations, on a rather positivistic model of form-criticism developed by Helmut Koester and James M. Robinson in *Trajectories through Early Christianity* (Philadelphia: Fortress, 1971). For Mack, Paul's letters reveal "the astounding practices of the Jesus people in northern Syria," astounding because they cannot be explained in continuity with the origins of the movement in Jerusalem or elsewhere. His letters "are to be read with a very critical eye"; his account of the gospel "might be overly dramatized," and his gospel itself "his own construction"; his reports of his former persecution of the church and of his conversion are to be held in deepest suspicion; all are "obvious signs of an unstable, authoritarian person" (*A Myth of Innocence*, p. 98).

80. Maccoby, *The Mythmaker*, p. 15.

81. Beker, "Paul's Theology: Consistent or Inconsistent?"

82. Wright, *The Climax of the Covenant*, p. 259.

83. Stendahl, *Paul among Jews and Gentiles*, p. 3.

84. Paul refers rather frequently to the "teaching" he expects Christians to remember and hold fast to (*tēn didachēn*, Rom. 16:17; *typon didachēs*, Rom. 6:17; *tas paradoseis*, 1 Cor. 11:2; *ton logon akoēs tou theou*, 1 Thess. 2:13). For a concise discussion of Paul's contact with the Jesus tradition, see Fitzmyer, *Paul and His Theology*, pp. 32–34, and the bibliography there.

85. Fredriksen, *From Jesus to Christ*, chaps. 3, 9.

86. Käsemann, "The Saving Significance of Jesus' Death in Paul," p. 36; see now the discussion in Wright, *The Climax of the Covenant*, chap. 4.

87. Charles B. Cousar, *A Theology of the Cross: The Death of Jesus in the Pauline Letters* (Minneapolis: Fortress, 1990), p. 26.

88. Luke 23:13, 35; 24:20; Acts 4:8–10, 26; 13:27–28; John 7:26. See Wink, *Naming the Powers*, p. 40.

89. Bultmann sees in the passage an allusion to the gnostic redeemer myth (*Theology of the New Testament*, 1:175, 181). See also Conzelmann, *First Corinthians*, p. 61; Gerhard Delling, "*archōn*," *Theological Dictionary of the New Testament*, ed. Gerhard Kittel, trans. G. W. Bromiley (Grand Rapids: Eerdmans, 1964), 1:488–489; Martin Dibelius, *Die Geisterwelt im Glauben des Paulus* (Göttingen: Vandenhoeck & Ruprecht, 1909), p. 89 (cited by Wink, *Naming the Powers,* p. 40).

90. C. Colpe, *Die religionsgeschichtliche Schule: Darstellung und Kritik ihres Bildes vom gnostischen Erlösermythus* (Göttingen: Vandenhoeck & Ruprecht, 1961); a similar presentation in English, depending in part on Colpe's work, is Edwin Yamauchi, *Pre-Christian Gnosticism: A Survey of the Proposed Evidences* (Grand Rapids: Eerdmans, 1973); and now see Simone Pétrement, *A Separate God: The Christian Origins of Gnosticism*, trans. Carol Harrison (San Francisco: Harper San Francisco, 1990). Birger Pearson's demonstration that Paul used terms like *pneumatikoi* and *psychikoi* differently from later Gnostics was also decisive in undermining the "Gnostic" interpretation of 1 Corinthians: see *The Pneumatikos-Psychikos Terminology in 1 Corinthians: A Study in the*

Theology of the Corinthian Opponents of Paul in Its Relation to Gnosticism (Missoula: Scholars, 1973).

91. See E. Elizabeth Johnson, "The Wisdom of God as Apocalyptic Power," in *Faith and History: Essays in Honor of Paul W. Meyer*, ed. John T. Carroll, Charles H. Cosgrove, and E. Elizabeth Johnson (Atlanta: Scholars, 1990), pp. 137–148.

92. Judith Kovacs, "The Archons, the Spirit, and the Death of Christ: Do We Really Need the Hypothesis of Gnostic Opponents to explain 1 Cor. 21:6–16?" in *Apocalyptic in the New Testament: Essays in Honor of J. Louis Martyn*, JSNT Supplement 24, ed. Joel Marcus and Marion L. Soards (Sheffield: JSOT Press, 1989).

93. See Paul D. Hanson, A. Kirk Grayson, John J. Collins, and Adela Yarbro Collins, "Apocalypses and Apocalypticism," *Anchor Bible Dictionary*, 1:279–282. For issues in recent scholarship see the essays in John J. Collins, ed., *Apocalypse: The Morphology of a Genre*, *Semeia* 14 (1979); David Hellholm, ed., *Apocalypticism in the Mediterranean World and the Near East: Proceedings of the International Colloquium on Apocalypticism, Uppsala, August 12–17, 1979* (Tübingen: Mohr-Siebeck, 1983); Adela Yarbro Collins, *Early Christian Apocalypticism: Genre and Social Setting*, *Semeia* 36 (1986); and a judicious synthesis, John J. Collins, *The Apocalyptic Imagination: An Introduction to the Jewish Matrix of Christianity* (New York: Crossroad, 1987).

94. Kovacs, "The Archons, the Spirit, and the Death of Christ," pp. 224–225.

95. Jon Sobrino discusses the tension between the "eschatologization" of Jesus' death and its historical significance as a death taking place among the poor: *Jesus in Latin America*, pp. 39–40.

96. Between his accounts of these incidents in Judea and Samaria, Josephus narrates two "scandals" in Rome that reveal a similar disposition toward Roman order. First, a senator's wife was seduced with the connivance of the staff at a temple of Isis; Tiberius crucified the temple staff and the maidservant of the seduced woman but banished the seducer (who was after all a Roman citizen). "Such," Josephus concludes, "were the insolent acts of the priests in the temple of Isis" (18:65–80). Again, when another senator's wife was bilked by Jewish conmen, Tiberius exiled the whole Jewish population of Rome, empressing four thousand able-bodied Jewish men into a military campaign on Sardinia—to suppress popular "brigandage," Suetonius tells us (*Tiberius* 36)—and "punishing" any who refused; this, Josephus concludes, resulted from "the wickedness of four men" (18:81–84).

97. Hamerton-Kelly, *Sacred Violence*, p. 82.

98. Ibid., p. 84.

99. Bultmann, *Theology of the New Testament*, 1:298.

The reluctance to give the apocalyptic view of the Powers due weight is obvious in Bultmann's program of "demythologization," of course. Bultmann declared that "the mythological eschatology is untenable [that is, for the modern reader] for the simple reason that the parousia of Christ never took place as the New Testament expected ("The New Testament and Mythology," in *Kerygma and Myth*, ed. H. W. Bartsch [New York: Harper & Row, 1961], p. 5). Bultmann and his followers also insisted that Paul's theology of the Powers in 1 Corinthians 2:6–8 was both uncharacteristic of the apostle's own thought and completely separate from the "word of the cross," which represented the genius of Paul's theology in demythologizing apocalyptic and Gnostic mythologies into "believing self-understanding" (Bultmann, *Theology of the New Testament*, 1:293). Elizabeth Johnson declares Bultmann "the most influential scholar in this devaluation of Pauline apocalyptic eschatology" (*The Function of Apocalyptic and Wisdom Traditions*, pp. 10–12).

100. Beker, *Paul the Apostle*, pp. 189–190.

101. On the translation of the dative (*tō nomō*) see Elliott, *Rhetoric of Romans*, pp. 243–245.

102. Beker, *Paul the Apostle*, p. 168.

103. Beker declares that "the author of Colossians interprets Paul correctly on this point," citing Col. 2:15 and Eph. 1:20–22: Ibid., p. 190.

104. On Paul's visionary experience see James D. Tabor, *Things Unutterable: Paul's Ascent to Paradise in Its Greco-Roman, Judaic, and Early Christian Contexts* (Lanham: University Press of America, 1986); Alan F. Segal, *Paul the Convert: The Apostolate and Apostasy of Saul the Pharisee* (New Haven: Yale University Press, 1990), chap. 2.

105. See Segal's discussion and bibliography, loc. cit.

106. Klyne Snodgrass, "Justification by Grace—to the Doers: An Analysis of the Place of Romans 2 in the Theology of Paul," *New Testament Studies* 32 (1986), pp. 72–93.

107. To the same point Hamerton-Kelly declares that 1 Corinthians 2 reveals the crucifixion as the essence of the mystery of God's plan of salvation (*Sacred Violence*, p. 82).

108. Kovacs, "Archons, the Spirit, and the Death of Christ," pp. 224–225.

109. Wink, *Naming the Powers,* pp. 6–11.

110. Wink, *Engaging the Powers,* p. 3; *Naming the Powers,* pp. 104–113.

111. Wink, *Engaging the Powers,* p. 10.

112. Wink, *Naming the Powers,* p. 60.

113. Wink, *Engaging the Powers,* p. 140.

114. Gene Sharp, *The Politics of Nonviolent Action,* 3 vols. (Boston: Porter Sargent, 1973).

115. Wink, *Engaging the Powers,* p. 140.

116. Ibid., pp. 141–142.

117. What Wink describes as the logic of Colossians and Ephesians is clearly argued in 4 Maccabees, an essay demonstrating the sovereignty of "devout reason" over the emotions by rehearsing the martyrdoms of faithful Jews on the orders of Antiochus Epiphanes. The author of 4 Maccabees is concerned precisely with the psychology of coercion, "those emotions that hinder one from justice, such as malice, and those that stand in the way of courage, namely anger, fear, and pain" (1:4). The Torah, given to human reason, is an exact antidote to the psychology of coercion, for even the kosher laws teach "self-control" (1:17, 31–35), and the laws of regard for the poor teach the suspension of "natural" greed (2:6–9). Their minds formed by the Torah, the martyrs were thus able to resist the king's coercion and to "conquer the tyrant" and "purify their native land" (1:11).

Since Colossians and Ephesians do not dwell on Jesus' resistance to coercion in the manner of 4 Maccabees, I remain unconvinced that this is the meaning of their theology of the cross.

118. Wink leaves open the possibility that Colossians is authentic in *Naming the Powers* (p. 8); in *Engaging the Powers,* he speaks without qualification of "Paul" writing the letter (e.g., p. 66).

119. Wink, *Engaging the Powers,* p. 140.

120. Wink demythologizes Eph. 6:12 as referring to *"the interiority of earthly institutions or structures or systems,"* not just the personalistic level; that is, to "the inner *and* outer manifestations of political, economic, religious, and cultural institutions" (*Engaging the Powers,* pp. 77–78). The analytical concept is powerful, but I am not convinced this is what Ephesians means when it speaks of "heavenly powers, not flesh and blood."

121. Beker, *Paul the Apostle,* p. 196.

122. Cited in Jon Sobrino, *Archbishop Romero: Memories and Reflections,* trans. Robert R. Barr (Maryknoll: Orbis, 1990), p. 49.

123. Mark Danner, "The Fall of the Prophet" (third in a series), *The New York Review of Books,* December 2, 1993, p. 53.

124. Wink, *Engaging the Powers,* p. 141.

125. Heyward, "Doing Theology in a Counterrevolutionary Situation," p. 404.

126. Regarding the Jesus tradition in the Synoptic Gospels, Paula Fredriksen writes that "the evolving evangelical emphasis on realized eschatology saved Christian tradition from the embarrassments of its apocalyptic past while enhancing the spiritual prestige and value of the church. . . . A realized eschatology, in other words, so explains away the difficulty of the continuing delay of the End that it fails the criterion of dissimilarity: the provenance of such a teaching, according to this reasoning, must be the post-resurrection church" (*From Jesus to Christ,* p. 101).

127. De Ste. Croix, *Class Struggle in the Ancient Greek World,* p. 432 (on the language of the Magnificat).

128. Wink relies (*Naming the Powers,* pp. 61–62) on Beker's judgment that 1 Corinthians 2 is "less central" for Paul's apocalyptic theology than Romans (*Paul the Apostle,* pp. 189–190). If, as Beker writes, for Paul "the death of Christ now marks the defeat of the apocalyptic power alliance," the cosmic *fait accompli* of Col. 1:16 no longer seems so remote. But as we have seen, Beker's preference for the theology of Romans over 1 Corinthians is vulnerable to criticism (Kovacs).

Wink also suggests that if the early Christians spoke of the powers already under Christ's feet, "we might see here an expression of the everyday experience of the early Christians that demons could be and were being cast out, the sick healed, compulsive and obsessive behavior changed, harmful and violent ways of living rectified, new meaning and joy being poured into life" (*Naming the Powers,* pp. 59–61, 63). I point out that when Paul himself spoke of these realities, he never spoke of vanquished powers. He spoke, instead, of the "demonstration of the Spirit and of power" (1 Cor. 2:4) and of the "manifestation of the Spirit" in the assembly, evident in gifts of healing, the working of miracles, prophecy, the discernment of spirits, glossolalia and the interpretation of glossolalia (12:7–10).

129. On the mythic background of "powers" language, see Wink, *Naming the Powers,* pp. 13–35.

130. Romans 8:35 "refers not simply to hardships, such as 'famine' (RSV) but to things done to us by 'someone' (*tis*) who wants to 'separate us from the love of Christ.'" "Nakedness" (*gymnotēs*) does not mean that the Christian walks around naked; "he or she is prevented by economic sanctions or persecution from being able to buy adequate clothing." "In short, every sanction that the state, religion, the economic system, the courts, police, the army, public opinion, mob action, or peer pressure can bring to bear to enforce our complicity in the great defection from God has been robbed of its power" (Wink, *Naming the Powers,* p. 48).

131. Aristide, *In the Parish of the Poor,* p. 46.

132. On the rhetorical connection between Romans 8 and 9, usually not recognized by commentators, see Elliott, *Rhetoric of Romans,* pp. 253–270.

133. See Wolfgang Wiefel, "The Jewish Community in Ancient Rome and the Origins of Roman Christianity," in *The Romans Debate,* 2d ed. by Karl Donfried (Peabody: Hendrickson Publishers, 1991); see my discussion in *Rhetoric of Romans,* pp. 43–59. On Palestine under "The Roman Procurators A.D. 44–66," see *The History of the Jewish People in the Age of Jesus Christ,* vol. 1, ed. Geza Vermes, Fergus Millar, Matthew Black, and Pamela Vermes (Edinburgh: T. & T. Clark, 1973), pp. 455–470.

134. Wink, *Engaging the Powers,* pp. 297–317.

135. Elliott, *Rhetoric of Romans,* loc. cit.

136. On the metaphor of triumphal procession see Paul Brooks Duff, "Apostolic Suffering and the Language of Processions in 2 Corinthians 4:7–10," *Biblical Theology Bulletin* 21:4 (1991), pp. 158–165; idem, "Metaphor, Motif, and Meaning: The Rhetorical Strategy behind the Image 'Led in Triumph' in 2 Corinthians 2:14," *Catholic Biblical Quarterly* 53:1 (1991), pp. 79–92.

137. Hamerton-Kelly, *Sacred Violence,* p. 85.

138. See especially Beker, *Paul the Apostle,* pp. 194–198; 205–208.

139. "The concept of the atoning, sacrificial death of a human being comes to Jewish-Hellenistic Christianity by way of Diaspora theology" (Beker, *Paul the Apostle,* p. 203).

140. See the references in note 55 above. McLean argues that since in the Greek Scriptures *hilastērion* never meant anything other than the "mercy seat" on the ark of the covenant, it is inappropriate to translate the term "expiatory sacrifice" in Rom. 3:25 ("Absence of an Atoning Sacrifice," p. 545); he suggests, rather, "the place or means where expiation takes place," citing 4 Macc. 17:22, where the blood of the martyrs provides expiation (*hilastērion*) and "preserves Israel." Williams finds the parallels in 4 Maccabees more cogent than the often-presumed biblical antecedents pertaining to the sacrificial cultus of the Temple (*Jesus' Death as Saving Event*; see also Seeley, *The Noble Death*). Schwarz discusses a possible allusion to the scapegoat ritual in Gal. 4:4 ("Two Allusions").

141. On "The Dogmatic Debate: Anselm and the 'Classical' View of the Atonement," see Beker, *Paul the Apostle,* p. 208; also Käsemann, *Commentary on Romans,* pp. 91–101.

142. Rom. 3:21–31 stands "in sharp antithesis to the depicted hopelessness of mankind" that precedes (ibid., p. 91). Sanday and Headlam declare that after

Rom. 1:16–17, "St. Paul has just stated what the Gospel is; he now goes on to show the necessity for such a Gospel. The world is lost without it" (*The Epistle to the Romans*, p. 40). On this and the following points, consensus is so widespread that documentation is almost superfluous.

143. Käsemann, *Commentary on Romans*, p. 34. Similarly Bultmann, *Theology of the New Testament*, 1:227; C. E. B. Cranfield, *Romans*, 1:103.

144. Bultmann, *Theology of the New Testament*, 1:227; Käsemann, *Commentary on Romans*, pp. 101–105 ("polemical development").

145. Käsemann, *Commentary on Romans*, p. 78.

146. Bultmann, *Theology of the New Testament*, 1:279, 281.

147. Elliott, *Rhetoric of Romans*, chap. 1. Compare the results of Ann Jervis, *The Purpose of Romans*, and Jeffrey A. Crafton, "Paul's Rhetorical Vision and the Purpose of Romans: Toward a New Understanding," *Novum Testamentum* 32:4 (1990), pp. 317–339.

148. Elliott, *Rhetoric of Romans*, pp. 108–119.

149. Stanley K. Stowers, *The Diatribe and Paul's Letter to the Romans* (Chico: Scholars, 1981), p. 112.

150. Jouette Bassler, *Divine Impartiality: Paul and a Theological Axiom* (Chico: Scholars, 1982), pp. 123–137.

151. Elliott, *The Rhetoric of Romans*, pp. 119–127.

152. See Stanley K. Stowers, "Paul's Dialogue with a Fellow Jew in Romans 3:1–9," *Catholic Biblical Quarterly* 46 (1984), pp. 709–710.

153. John Gager remarks that the principles articulated in Rom. 2:12–13 were "presumably taken for granted by most of Paul's Jewish contemporaries" (*Origins of Anti-Semitism*), pp. 214–217. Regarding the privileges listed at 2:17–24, Käsemann notes that "the Jew was summoned to all this by the Old Testament" (*Commentary on Romans*, p. 69). Sanders considers that "the best way to read 1:18–2:29 is as a synagogue sermon. It is slashing and exaggerated, as many sermons are, but its own natural point is to have its hearers become better Jews" (*Paul, the Law, and the Jewish People*, p. 129).

154. Assuming that 2:17–20 is designed as an iron-tight indictment of the Jew, Sanders declares the argument "not convincing: it is internally inconsistent and it rests on gross exaggeration" (*Paul, the Law, and the Jewish People*, p. 125). Räisänen finds the presumed logic of indictment behind Rom. 3:9 "a blatant non-sequitur . . . simply a piece of propagandist denigration" (*Paul and the Law*, pp. 100–101). See my "Excursus: Romans 1–4 as a 'Debate with Judaism' " in *Rhetoric of Romans*, pp. 167–223.

155. Stowers, *The Diatribe*, p. 153.

156. Moore, *Judaism*, 1:508. Moore cites *mishna Yoma* 8:8–9: "If anyone says to himself, 'I will sin, and repent, and I will sin and repent,' no opportunity is given him to repent." Similarly E. P. Sanders observes that "the idea of being privileged as children of Abraham may have been abused, but abuses were criticized by the rabbis themselves" (*Paul and Palestinian Judaism*, p. 87).

157. Elliott, *Rhetoric of Romans*, pp. 132–141.

158. William S. Campbell, "Romans III as a Key to the Structure and Thought of the Letter," *Novum Testamentum* 23 (1981), pp. 22–40; reprinted now both in Donfried, ed., *The Romans Debate*, 2d ed., and in Campbell, *Paul's Gospel in an Intercultural Context*.

159. Elliott, *Rhetoric of Romans,* pp. 225–235.

160. Ibid., pp. 43–59; Wiefel, "The Jewish Community in Ancient Rome"; Peter Lampe, *Die Stadtrömischen Christen in den ersten beiden Jahrhunderten: Untersuchungen zur Sozialgeschichte* (Tübingen: Mohr-Siebeck, 1987).

161. See Gager, *The Origins of Anti-Semitism,* pp. 63–88.

162. So H. W. Bartsch, "Die antisemitischen Gegner des Paulus im Römerbrief," in W. Eckert et al., eds., *Antijudaismus im Neuen Testament?* (Munich: Kaiser, 1967); idem, "Die historische Situation des Römerbriefes," *Studia Evangelica* 4 (1968), pp. 282–291). Josephus reports that while Felix was procurator of Judea (in 52–60 c.e.), Jewish priests sent under arrest to Caesar were able to observe *kashrut* only by subsisting on figs and nuts (*Life,* 3). See Elliott, *Rhetoric of Romans,* pp. 51–55.

163. Wright, *Climax of the Covenant,* p. 234.

164. So rather than opposing Jews to Gentiles, God's mysterious action has as its goal fulfilling "the promises to Abraham, promises which declared *both* that [God] would give [Abraham] a worldwide family *and* that his own seed would share in the blessing" (ibid., p. 236).

165. "Paul could see that, in Rome, the temptation would always be for a largely gentile church to downplay or forget its Jewish roots. But if the church heeds his argument, such a possibility will never be realized" (ibid., p. 251).

166. Elliott, *Rhetoric of Romans,* pp. 277–299; Wright, *Climax of the Covenant,* pp. 252–253; Campbell, *Paul's Gospel in an Intercultural Context.*

167. It is not as evident as Robert G. Hamerton-Kelly suggests that Paul's language in Rom. 3:21–26 is an "inversion" of sacrifice (*Sacred Violence,* pp. 80–81). The argument that when Paul spoke of "the wrath of God" he meant to refer to "the effects of sacred violence in the human world" (pp. 81, 100–101) is particularly unconvincing, although of course as a modern demythologization this may make sense.

168. Elliott, *Rhetoric of Romans,* pp. 239–244; Joyce A. Little, "Paul's Use of Analogy: A Structural Analysis of Romans 7:1–6," *Catholic Biblical Quarterly* 46 (1985), pp. 82–90.

169. "The 'men of the Torah' are those who for their salvation rely on the works of the Torah" (Hans Dieter Betz, *Galatians: A Commentary on Paul's Letter to the Churches in Galatia* [Philadelphia: Fortress, 1979], p. 144). Betz's comment is, of course, only illustrative of a far more widespread viewpoint among interpreters.

170. See Räisänen, *Paul and the Law,* pp. 94–96.

171. Bultmann, *Theology of the New Testament,* 1:259–269.

172. Sanders, *Paul and Palestinian Judaism,* pp. 157–180; 298–305; Wright, *Climax of the Covenant,* p. 145.

173. Taking these objections seriously (though without rethinking the basic premise that Paul means this to be an argument from plight to solution) has led some scholars to the conclusion that Paul's thought actually moves in the reverse direction to what he writes here (e.g., Sanders, *Paul, the Law, and the Jewish People,* pp. 17–27). This evacuates the declaration that "Christ redeemed us from the curse of the law" (Gal. 3:13; 4:4–5) of any prior significance; it is merely a secondary rationalization of a conclusion Paul has already reached on other grounds, namely, that salvation is only available through Christ. Others

have sought to restrict the "plight" in view here to the situation of gentiles alone, since gentiles are clearly the audience of Galatians (Gaston, *Paul and the Torah*, pp. 64–79); but this merely compounds the exegetical difficulties.

174. Robert G. Hamerton-Kelly goes even farther, arguing that Judaism in Paul's day was in fact "a structure of sacred violence" which Paul saw exposed in the cross. Paul understood the crucifixion as "the work of the Mosaic Law in its role as an instrument of the primitive Sacred operating through the sacrificial system" (*Sacred Violence*, p. 63). See my review of this work in *Forum* 9:1–2 (1994).

175. Sanders, *Paul, the Law, and the Jewish People*, p. 19; against the approach taken by Betz, *Galatians*.

176. Christopher D. Stanley, "A Fresh Reading of Galatians 3:10–14," *New Testament Studies* 36 (1990), p. 488. Stanley is not sure whether or not the "troublemakers" who have come onto the Galatian scene from outside insist that the Gentiles take on the full obligations of the Torah (p. 490), but of course their motives are less relevant to a rhetorical analysis than the motives of the Galatian Christians themselves. In this regard, Sanders's comment (*Paul, the Law, and the Jewish People*, p. 19) that Paul opposes the view "that Gentiles must accept the law *as a condition* of or as a basic requirement for membership" is hardly to the point; the Galatians are already "members." Galatians 3:3 suggests rather that their goal is progress toward "perfection" (*epiteleisthē*).

177. This crucial understanding of "Judaizers" as distinct from Jews and proselytes is Gaston's correct and indispensable insight (*Paul and the Torah*, pp. 25–26); see also Gager, *Origins of Anti-Semitism*, passim.

178. Sanders detects here a "policy of gradualism" on the part of Paul's opponents, "a policy which was probably not unique among Jewish missionaries" (*Paul, the Law, and the Jewish People*, p. 29). In light of the rhetorical-critical approach proposed by Stanley, it is more appropriate to look to the motives of the Galatians considering circumcision, not the "opponents" (whose position is even more difficult to reconstruct). John Barclay looks to "the precariousness of their social position as Christians," suggesting that circumcision might "regularize their position in relation to the rest of Galatian society" (*The Obedience of Faith: A Study of Paul's Ethics in Galatians*, Studies of the New Testament and Its World [Edinburgh: T. & T. Clark, 1988], pp. 58, 60); while he doubts that 5:3 indicates either ignorance or lack of commitment on the Galatians' part (p. 62), he thinks they may have been "somewhat naive" about it (p. 64).

179. Gaston, *Paul and the Torah*, p. 30; "Paul's argument is not against circumcision (or Judaism) as such, but for adult Gentiles to circumcise themselves would mean seeking to earn something and thus deny God's grace" (p. 90).

180. Wright's qualification (ibid., p. 144) of Stanley's argument (op. cit.).

181. Against Sanders, loc. cit.

182. Wright, *The Climax of the Covenant*, pp. 140–141.

183. Ibid., p. 151.

184. For this reason, Wright's reference to the "inability of the Torah to give the blessing which had been promised" (p. 147) seems inconsistent with his main argument. It is not so much that the Torah *could not*, because of some fatal

flaw, serve as the channel of blessing, but that in the actual course of Israel's history it *has not* done so.

Similarly, the syllogism he constructs:

a. Israel as a whole is under the curse if they fail to keep Torah;

b. Israel as a whole failed to keep Torah;

c. therefore Israel is under the curse,

seems to reverse the logic of his argument on p. 141 and to suggest that Paul had some prior conviction concerning whether or not Israel had kept the Torah. At the most, (b) would be a "suppressed premise" for Paul. But Wright's own argument suggests a different syllogism:

a. Israel as a whole is under the curse if they fail to keep Torah;

b. but given the "publicly observable fact" that Israel is still under the curse,

c. it must be the case that Israel as a whole has failed to keep Torah.

185. Ibid., p. 152.

186. Horsley, *Jesus and the Spiral of Violence,* p. 139.

187. On the phrase "the righteousness of God," see Manfred Brauch's appendix in recent scholarship in Sanders, *Paul and Palestinian Judaism,* pp. 523–542. Käsemann showed that the phrase has its background in Jewish apocalypticism and refers to God's "salvation-creating power" ("The Righteousness of God in Paul"); Hays finds the same background already in the Bible ("Psalm 143 and the Logic of Romans 3"). Against Käsemann, I doubt Paul's use of the phrase is directed against Jewish covenant theology (see Wright, *The Climax of the Covenant,* p. 234).

188. See Beker, "The Faithfulness of God and the Priority of Israel in Paul's Letter to the Romans," *Harvard Theological Review* 79 (1986), pp. 10–16.

189. Wright, *The Climax of the Covenant,* p. 261.

190. Sobrino, *Jesus in Latin America,* p. 31.

5. *The Apocalypse of the Crucified Messiah*

1. Seyoon Kim, *The Origin of Paul's Gospel,* Wissenschaftliche Untersuchungen zum neuen Testament 2/4, 2d ed. (Tübingen: Mohr-Siebeck, 1986).

2. Stendahl, "Call Rather Than Conversion," *Paul among Jews and Gentiles,* pp. 7–23.

3. Beker, *Paul the Apostle,* pp. 6–7.

4. Beker describes a tension in the history of scholarship between views of Paul as a mystic and as a dogmatic theologian. He nevertheless insists that "It would be an error to oppose experience and thought, as if we have to choose between them," for in Paul's apostolic call "both experience and thought cohere" (ibid.).

5. J. Christiaan Beker, "The Method of Recasting Pauline Theology: The Coherence-Contingency Scheme as Interpretive Model," in Kent Richards, ed., *Society of Biblical Literature 1986 Seminar Papers* (Atlanta: Scholars, 1986), p. 597, reprinted in Bassler, ed., *Pauline Theology;* see also *Paul the Apostle,* pp. 15–16.

6. See Hendrikus Boers's remarks, "The Foundations of Paul's Thought: A Methodological Investigation—The Problem of the Coherent Center of Paul's

Thought," *Studia Theologica* 42 (1988), pp. 55–68. Boers participated with Beker in the 1986 Society of Biblical Literature seminar on Pauline theology, where this paper was originally delivered.

7. Segal, *Paul the Convert,* p. 34.

8. Ibid., pp. 38–52.

Sources for ancient Jewish apocalyptic mysticism include the "Angelic Liturgy" text from Qumran (Carol Newsom, *Songs of the Sabbath Sacrifice: A Critical Edition,* Harvard Semitic Studies 27 [Atlanta: Scholars, 1985]) to biblical pseudepigrapha (James H. Charlesworth, ed., *The Old Testament Pseudepigrapha,* 2 vols. [Garden City: Doubleday, 1983–1985]) and the hekhalot literature (Peter Schaefer, Margaret Schlueter, and Hans Georg Von Mutius, eds., *Synopse zur Hekhalot-Literatur* [Tübingen: Mohr-Siebeck, 1981]). For discussion see Christopher Rowland, *The Open Heaven: A Study of Apocalyptic in Judaism and Early Christianity* (New York: Crossroad, 1982); Alan F. Segal, "Heavenly Ascent in Hellenistic Judaism, Early Christianity, and Their Environments," *Aufstieg und Niedergang der römischer Welt,* II:23:2, pp. 1332–1394; and the essays collected in Hellholm, ed., *Apocalypticism in the Mediterranean World and the Near East.*

9. Ibid., pp. 34, 40, 48.

10. Ibid., pp. 36–39; 58. Several features connect Paul's report (see also Gal. 1:16–17) with the apocalyptic and merkabah traditions: the ambiguity about where, exactly, the ecstatic voyager is ("in the body" or "out of the body"?); a specific heavenly topography to which the ecstatic travels ("the third heaven," "Paradise"); the experience of a call; the vision of the supernatural figure present with God (identified by Paul as Christ, God's Son); and the prohibition against revealing publicly what one has seen in ecstasy.

On the background of the passage see also Tabor, *Things Unutterable.* Tabor reads 2 Corinthians 12 as narrating a two-stage journey, "the third heaven" being a level inferior to Paradise (= the seventh heaven), where the throne of God is (pp. 115–121).

11. Ibid., pp. 36–37. See also Lüdemann, *Paul, Apostle to the Gentiles,* pp. 30–31, n. 5; Tabor, *Things Unutterable,* p. 115.

12. Segal, *Paul the Convert,* pp. 59, 69.

13. Ibid., p. 123.

14. Ibid., pp. 58–61, 117.

15. Ibid., pp. 134, 148.

16. Ibid., p. 123.

17. Fredriksen, *From Jesus to Christ,* p. 145. Her argument is set forth more fully in "Judaism, the Circumcision of Gentiles, and Apocalyptic Hope: Another Look at Galatians 1 and 2," *Journal of Theological Studies* 42:2 (1991), pp. 541–542.

18. Fredriksen, *From Jesus to Christ,* pp. 146, 107–108; so also Sanders, *Paul and Palestinian Judaism,* pp. 479–480 (against W. D. Davies, *Torah in the Messianic Age and/or the Age to Come,* Society of Biblical Literature Monograph 7 [Philadelphia: Scholars, 1952]); Räisänen, *Paul and the Law,* pp. 236–240.

Robert Hamerton-Kelly holds that the first followers of Jesus spontaneously perceived in the ritual markers of Judaism "the same violence" that had killed Jesus, and thus identified the cross as standing for "the inclusion of those that the Law excludes." On Hamerton-Kelly's view, the early community understood the "scandal of the cross" in this way, and consequently abandoned circumcision, kosher laws, and the Sabbath: just this was the scandal that attracted Paul's persecution (*Sacred Violence*, p. 72).

There is simply no evidence anywhere in the New Testament that the earliest congregations drew such a conclusion.

19. In Martin Hengel's view, the Hellenists "called for the eschatological abolition of Temple worship and the revision of the law of Moses in the light of the true will of God" (*Acts and the History of Earliest Christianity* [London: SPCK, 1979], pp. 72–73; see also *The Cross of the Son of God*, p. 66; and especially *Between Jesus and Paul: Studies in the Earliest History of Christianity*, trans. John Bowden [London: SCM, 1983]). Consequently Paul "persecuted the Jewish Christian hellenists in Jerusalem because he saw what was most holy in Israel threatened by their proclamation and their conduct" (*The Pre-Christian Paul*, trans. John Bowden [Philadelphia: Trinity Press International, 1991], p. 80).

20. Fredriksen, *From Jesus to Christ*, loc. cit.; Räisänen, *Paul and the Law*, pp. 251–256; Watson, *Paul, Judaism, and the Gentiles*, pp. 25–28. Räisänen believes the Hellenists had a distinctive theology, but what the Hellenists' supposed "laxity as regards the ritual Torah" involved, he admits, "we cannot say" (p. 252). Watson notes the inconsistency of accepting the accusations against Stephen in Acts 8 as authentic, but rejecting Luke's insistence that these are false accusations (p. 26). Other scholars perceive an extensive scholarly fabrication in the appeal to "Hellenists" in Acts 6:1: see Jonathan Goldstein, "Jewish Acceptance and Rejection of Hellenism," in E. P. Sanders, ed., *Jewish and Christian Self-Definition, vol. 2: Aspects of Judaism in the Greco-Roman Period* (Philadelphia: Fortress, 1981), pp. 64–87; Maccoby, *The Mythmaker*, pp. 72–81 ("Paul and Stephen").

21. Fredriksen, *From Jesus to Christ*, p. 108; Räisänen, *Paul and the Law*, pp. 245–248.

22. In Hengel's view, Paul reveals in Gal. 3:13 "not only his present experience of mission but the personal offence which he had taken to the message of the crucified Messiah as a Pharisaic scribe on the basis of his understanding of the Torah" (*The Pre-Christian Paul*, pp. 83–84).

23. Räisänen rightly insists that "Paul never suggests that it was the *law* that condemned Jesus or brought him to the cross" (*Paul and the Law*, p. 249). Neither would it have made sense for Paul to draw such a conclusion on his own: "It is by no means obvious that the idea of a person bearing the curse of others should logically lead to the idea that the law which entailed the curse must be abolished, just as the destiny of the OT scapegoat did not lead to the idea of an abolition of the Torah" (p. 250).

24. Fredriksen observes that "in no Jewish writing of this period, Paul's included, do we find crucifixion itself taken to indicate a death cursed by God or by the Law" (*From Jesus to Christ*, p. 147). On the contrary, "the rabbis apparently associate this Roman mode of execution with an event of great positive significance for their religion: the binding of Isaac" (p. 148, citing Genesis Rabbah 56:3). Other Jewish citations of Deuteronomy 21 (for example, 11QTemple 64) refer to criminals "cursed" not because they are "hanged on a tree," but because of the crimes that led to their execution; this is the sense of the text in Torah as well.

25. For the excavation report, V. Tzaferis, "Jewish Tombs at and near Giv'at ha-Mivtar, Jerusalem," *Israel Exploration Journal* 20 (1970), pp. 18–32; "The Ossuary Inscriptions from Giv'at ha-Mivtar," *Israel Exploration Journal* 20 (1970), pp. 33–37. See Joseph Fitzmyer's discussion of the discovery, "Crucifixion in Ancient Palestine, Qumran Literature, and the New Testament," *Catholic Biblical Quarterly* 40:4 (1978), pp. 493–513.

26. Fredriksen, *From Jesus to Christ,* p. 148. Tuckett, too, declares it "inherently unlikely that all victims of crucifixion would have been ipso facto regarded as divinely cursed by the pre-Christian Paul" ("Deuteronomy 21:23 and Paul's Conversion," pp. 347–348).

27. Ibid., p. 147. This principle, increasingly recognized among scholars now, suggests that Galatians 2 cannot explain Paul's persecution of the Judean churches; see also Sanders, *Paul, the Law, and the Jewish People,* p. 25; Tomson, *Paul and the Jewish Law,* pp. 229–230.

28. Räisänen, *Paul and the Law,* p. 249; Wright, *The Climax of the Covenant,* p. 152.

29. Fredriksen, *From Jesus to Christ,* p. 149; see also Shaye Cohen, "Crossing the Boundary and Becoming a Jew," *Harvard Theological Review* 82:1 (1989), pp. 13–33.

The heated debate over the existence of "Godfearers" centers around the interpretation of the evidence. That gentile sympathizers existed, and were recognized as "God-fearers" in various places in the Diaspora, now appears beyond doubt (see J. Andrew Overman, "The God-Fearers: Some Neglected Features," *Journal for the Study of the New Testament* 32 [1988], pp. 17–26); but that they enjoyed a specific halakic status as "semi-proselytes" has rightly been refuted (John Nolland, "Uncircumcised Proselytes?" *Journal for the Study of Judaism* 12 [1981], pp. 173–194).

30. Ibid., pp. 150–151.

31. Tomson, *Paul and the Jewish Law,* pp. 230–236, citing Yehezkel Cohen, "The Attitude towards the Non-Jew in Halakha and Reality in the Period of the Tannaim," Ph.D. diss., Hebrew University, 1975 (in Hebrew).

Fredriksen suggests that if Jews were willing to eat with Gentiles under certain conditions, we should also expect that the sorts of Gentiles involved in the Antioch congregation—Gentiles familiar with Jewish sensitivities, in fact probably sympathetic with them—would be willing to accede to those conditions for the sake of table fellowship. Gentile Judaizers were most often identified by their observance of dietary restrictions, the Sabbath, and the festivals ("Judaism, the Circumcision of Gentiles, and Apocalyptic Hope," pp. 541–542).

32. Tomson, *Paul and the Jewish Law,* pp. 228–229; citing Gedalyahu Alon, "The Levitical Uncleanness of Gentiles" and "The Bounds of the Laws of Levitical Cleanness," in *Jews, Judaism and the Classical World: Studies in Jewish History in the Times of the Second Temple and the Talmud* (Jerusalem: Magnes, 1977), pp. 146–189 and 190–234.

33. Tomson, *Paul and the Jewish Law,* p. 228.

34. Robert Hamerton-Kelly insists that Saul the Pharisee represented a violently xenophobic form of Judaism characterized by "zeal," that is, "zealous Jewish persecution for the sake of strict observance of the ritual requirements of

the Law" (*Sacred Violence,* p. 71). But this view of Paul's "zeal" as violent enforcement of the halakah is only as valid as the presumption that the Jewish Christians before Paul had consciously violated halakah, a premise we have found to be baseless.

35. Fredriksen, *From Jesus to Christ,* p. 151.

36. Fredriksen, "Judaism, the Circumcision of Gentiles, and Apocalyptic Hope," p. 547.

37. Fredriksen, *From Jesus to Christ,* pp. 150–151.

38. Hengel, *The Zealots,* chapter IV, "Zeal"; similarly Rhoads, *Israel in Revolution,* p. 85; Horsley, *Jesus and the Spiral of Violence,* pp. 127–128; and Hamerton-Kelly, *Sacred Violence,* pp. 72–77.

39. Fredriksen, "Judaism, the Circumcision of Gentiles, and Apocalyptic Hope," p. 556; *From Jesus to Christ,* p. 154.

40. See Fredriksen, *From Jesus to Christ,* p. 119, and the discussion in chapter 3 above.

41. Fredriksen, "Judaism, the Circumcision of Gentiles, and Apocalyptic Hope," pp. 556–557.

42. Ibid., p. 558.

43. In Fredriksen's view, Paul transposed the significance of the messiah "from the historical to the cosmic plane"; "through the originally political vocabulary of liberation, he praises a reality that is utterly spiritual." He "minimized the political aspects of the messianic movement while presenting his message in terms already meaningful to his Gentile audience" (*From Jesus to Christ,* p. 173).

But how could the Pharisee obsessed with suppressing the early Christian movement on political grounds have become the apostle dedicated to a spiritual, apolitical gospel? What was the content of Paul's vision that could have led to such a change? Like Segal, Fredriksen answers, "we cannot say"; the answers lie "beyond historical examination, in his personality and in his own view of his call" (pp. 158–159, 166).

44. Horsley, *Jesus and the Spiral of Violence,* pp. 143–144.

45. John J. Collins' remarks relating the genre "apocalypse," "apocalyptic" thinking and the question of "apocalyptic movements" are valuable in this regard (*The Apocalyptic Imagination,* chap. 1). Declaring a writing "apocalyptic" suggests that "it frames its message within the view of the world characteristic of the genre," but hardly determines what that message is.

46. Martin Goodman, *The Ruling Class of Judaea: The Origins of the Jewish Revolt against Rome A.D. 66–70* (Cambridge: Cambridge University Press, 1987), pp. 90–91.

47. See Horsley, "Apocalyptic Orientation and Historical Action," in *Jesus and the Spiral of Violence,* pp. 129–145. Horsley's discussion is necessarily general, given his premise that "so far as we know, none of the Jewish resistance movements produced any literature; at least none is extant" (p. 132); but see below.

48. Martin Goodman, "Opponents of Rome: Jews and Others," in Loveday Alexander, ed., *Images of Empire,* Journal for the Study of the Old Testament Supplement 122 (Sheffield: Sheffield Academic Press, 1991), p. 224.

49. Horsley, *Jesus and the Spiral of Violence,* p. 88. On the motives of

Jewish resistance to the census see Martin Hengel, *The Zealots: Investigations into the Jewish Freedom Movement in the Period from Herod I until 70 A.D.*, trans. David Smith (Edinburgh: T. & T. Clark, 1989), pp. 127–141.

50. Hengel, *The Zealots*, p. 91.

51. Ibid., pp. 90–145.

52. Ibid, p. 122. Where the manuscripts read "the bloodshed [*phonou*] that would be involved," Hengel prefers the conjecture "the trouble [*ponou*] that would be involved." Louis Feldman accepts the text of the manuscripts ("bloodshed"), but only because he believes (on the basis of *Antiquities* 18:6) that Judas advocated slaughter anyway (*Antiquities*, vol. 9, p. 7 note b). On the probable meaning of "bloodshed" here see the discussion that follows in the text.

53. Hengel, *The Zealots*, pp. 123–124, 143.

54. Martin Hengel, *Victory over Violence* (Philadelphia: Fortress, 1973), pp. 31–32; cited by Horsley, *Jesus and the Spiral of Violence*, pp. 77–78.

55. Ibid., pp. 143–144.

56. See Morton Smith, "Zealots and Sicarii: Their Origin and Relation," *Harvard Theological Review* 64 (1971), pp. 1–19; Goodman, *The Ruling Class of Judaea*, pp. 94–95.

57. Horsley declares that "none of [Hengel's description of guerrilla action by Judas and his followers] is historically true; there is simply no extant evidence to support any of these assertions" (*Jesus and the Spiral of Violence*, p. 78).

58. The same identification appears in Schürer, *History of the Jewish People*, 1:381, and in Louis H. Feldman, *Josephus: Antiquities*, vol. 9 (Cambridge: Harvard University Press, 1981), p. 5.

59. See Horsley, *Jesus and the Spiral of Violence*, pp. 78–89. As David M. Rhoads points out, if Josephus had known the two figures were the same "it would have been to his advantage, given his bias against revolutionaries, to make that explicit" (*Israel in Revolution*, p. 51). Goodman concludes "that Judas did teach some novel ideas in A.D. 6, or at least revive some long-buried ancient notions, but that he founded no sect and that his philosophy was of marginal effect in the increasingly violent confrontation in Judaea" (*The Ruling Class of Judaea*, p. 96).

60. Martin Goodman declares that "the failure of Josephus in his detailed narrative of first-century Palestine to ascribe any clear-cut blame to the religious ideologues of whom he disapproved should be taken as evidence that such ideologues were not responsible for most of the unrest" ("Opponents of Rome," p. 223).

61. Goodman, *The Ruling Class of Judaea*, pp. 94–95.

62. Rhoads, *Israel in Revolution*, p. 57.

63. Horsley, *Jesus and the Spiral of Violence*, pp. 79; 83. As to the claim that Judas called for *apostasis* (also Acts 5:37), Horsley points out that the word "has a meaning both broader and a good deal more ambiguous than the English 'rebellion' or 'revolt.'" He cites the RSV translation of Acts 5:37, that Judas "drew away some of the people after him" (p. 80).

64. The primary testimonies are *Antiquities* 18:4–5, 23–25; *War* 2:118. Hengel analyzes the elements of the Fourth Philosophy against biblical and Jewish backgrounds: *The Zealots*, pp. 90–140.

65. So *War* 2:118. Later revolutionaries are described as descendants of Judas "who upbraided the Jews for recognizing the Romans as masters when

they already had God": *War* 2:433 (Menahem); *Antiquities* 20:102 (Jacob and Simon); *War* 7:253 (Eleazar: but here opposition to those who consented to Roman rule is attributed to sicarii "in those days": the days of Eleazar?).

66. Hengel, *The Zealots*, pp. 90–110, 122–127.

67. Horsley, *Jesus and the Spiral of Violence*, p. 86.

68. Ibid., pp. 77–89.

69. See Gene Sharp's discussion in *The Dynamics of Nonviolent Action*, pp. 456–458.

70. "Syria, Phoenicia, and Cilicia" (4:2) were combined within a single province between 20 and 54 C.E.; perhaps Caligula's threat to the Temple in 41 is reflected in 4:4–14. See Elias Bickerman, "The Date of Fourth Maccabees," in *Louis Ginzberg Jubilee Volume* (New York: American Academy for Jewish Research, 1945), pp. 105–112.

71. Daniel J. Harrington finds no reason the text could not be written before the war of 66–70, and prefers a date "around the time of Jesus" (*The Old Testament Pseudepigrapha*, vol. 2, p. 299); D. Mendels opts for a date between 44 and 66 C.E. ("Pseudo-Philo's *Biblical Antiquities*, the 'Fourth Philosophy,' and the Political Messianism of the First Century C.E.," in J. H. Charlesworth, J. Brownson, M. T. Davis, S. J. Kraftchick, and A. F. Segal, eds., *The Messiah: Developments in Earliest Judaism and Christianity* [Minneapolis: Fortress, 1992], p. 266 n. 1).

72. Mendels, "Pseudo-Philo's *Biblical Antiquities*," pp. 267, 269.

73. George W. E. Nickelsburg, "Good and Bad Leaders in Pseudo-Philo's *Liber Antiquitatum Biblicarum*," in Nickelsburg and John J. Collins, ed., *Ideal Figures in Ancient Judaism: Profiles and Paradigms*, Septuagint and Cognate Studies 12 (Chico: Scholars, 1980), pp. 49–66.

74. Saul M. Olyan, "The Israelites Debate Their Options at the Sea of Reeds: *LAB* 10:3, Its Parallels, and Pseudo-Philo's Ideology and Background," *Journal of Biblical Literature* 110:1 (1991), p. 85.

75. The story amplifies the people's eagerness to secure their own ruler like Kenaz the warrior, "a man who may free us from our distress" (49:1); but Elkanah, upon whom the lot falls, declines. Instead God provides a prophet, Samuel (chaps. 50–51), who declares (in an expansion of 1 Samuel 8) that "the time has not yet come for the ascendancy of a king of the house of David" (56:1–3). Mendels concludes that "although our author has messianic hopes (like many Jews at the time), he seems to be against a messiah in the present" ("Pseudo-Philo's *Biblical Antiquities*," p. 274).

76. Kenaz prays for the power to defeat the Amorite army singlehanded: "I will fight your enemies in order that they and all the nations and all your people may know that the Lord saves not by means of a huge army or by the power of horsemen" (27:7); the lesson is driven home after his triumph while the Israelite army slept: "for among men a great number prevails, but with God, whatever he has decided" (27:12).

77. Suicide was not only a consideration in the revolutionary period, however, as Hengel shows: *The Zealots*, pp. 262–265.

78. Against Olyan, "The Israelites Debate Their Options," pp. 84–85.

79. Rightly Mendels, "Pseudo-Philo's *Biblical Antiquities*," p. 271.

80. R. B. Wright gives "the widest limits for dating" as 125 B.C.E. to mid-first century C.E.; "narrow limits would be about 70 to 45 B.C.E., with the caveat that

the undatable psalms may have been earlier or later and the collection as a whole was certainly later" (*Old Testament Pseudepigrapha*, 2:640–641).

81. Horsley, *Jesus and the Spiral of Violence*, pp. 61–62.

82. See John Howard Yoder, "The Possibility of Nonviolent Resistance," in *The Politics of Jesus*, pp. 90–93; André Trocmé, *Jésus-Christ et la révolution non-violente* (Geneva: Labor et Fides, 1961), pp. 124ff.

83. In addition to *Jesus and the Spiral of Violence* see Richard A. Horsley, "Popular Messianic Movements around the Time of Jesus," *Catholic Biblical Quarterly* 46 (1984), pp. 471–495; and "'Like One of the Prophets of Old': Two Types of Popular Prophets at the Time of Jesus," *Catholic Biblical Quarterly* 47 (1985), pp. 435–463.

84. R. A. Horsley, "'Messianic' Figures and Movements in First-Century Palestine," in Charlesworth et al., eds., *The Messiah*, p. 283.

85. Rhoads, *Israel in Revolution*, pp. 83–84.

86. Hengel, *The Zealots*, p. 91.

87. Morton Smith has argued that Josephus wrote the *Antiquities* to point the Romans toward cooperation with the Pharisees in Judea: "Palestinian Judaism in the First Century," in Moshe Davis, ed., *Israel: Its Role in Civilization* (New York: Harper & Row, 1956); see esp. pp. 81–84. In contrast, Steve Mason argues that Josephus's portrayal of the Pharisees is usually negative and that they are represented as pursuing their own political power through religious scrupulosity (*Flavius Josephus on the Pharisees* [Leiden, Netherlands: E. J. Brill, 1991]; *Josephus and the New Testament* [Peabody: Hendrickson Publishers, 1992], pp. 131–148).

88. Hengel, *The Zealots*, p. 144.

89. Cecil Roth, "The Pharisees in the Jewish Revolution of 66–73," *Journal of Semitic Studies* 7 (1962), pp. 63–80.

90. Ibid., p. 78.

91. Schürer, *History of the Jewish People*, vol. 2, p. 394.

92. Jacob Neusner, *The Rabbinic Traditions about the Pharisees before 70*, 3 vols. (Leiden, Netherlands: E. J. Brill, 1971); the results of that study are presented in *From Politics to Piety* (Englewood Cliffs: Prentice-Hall, 1973).

93. Gedalyahu Alon, "The Attitudes of the Pharisees to Roman Rule and the House of Herod," in *Jews, Judaism and the Classical World: Studies in Jewish History in the Times of the Second Temple and Talmud*, trans. Israel Abrahams (Jerusalem: Magnes, 1977), p. 34. For a methodical critique of Neusner's work see Anthony J. Saldarini, *Pharisees, Scribes and Sadducees in Palestinian Society: A Sociological Approach* (Wilmington: Michael Glazier, 1988); idem, "Pharisees," *Anchor Bible Dictionary*, vol. 5, pp. 289–303.

94. Saldarini, *Pharisees, Scribes and Sadducees in Palestinian Society*, p. 214; chap. 10 provides an extensive response to Neusner's work.

95. Saldarini, *Pharisees, Sadducees, and Scribes*; Horsley, *Jesus and the Spiral of Violence*.

96. Horsley, *Jesus and the Spiral of Violence*, pp. 69–70.

97. Ibid., p. 43.

98. Ibid., pp. 22, 45–47.

99. For this understanding of the doctrine see also Schürer's *History of the Jewish People*, vol. 2, p. 394. The translation "providence" is unfortunate, evoking as it does later Christian debates over the role of "free will" in an

individual's salvation. It is important to recognize in contrast that Josephus is describing the role of human initiative and divine plan in human history.

100. See Gabriele Boccaccini, *Middle Judaism: Jewish Thought 300 B.C.E. to 200 C.E.* (Minneapolis: Fortress, 1991), pp. 141–149.

101. Boccaccini, *Middle Judaism,* p. 145.

102. J. Louis Martyn, "Apocalyptic Antinomies in Paul's Letter to the Galatians," *New Testament Studies* 31 (1985), p. 418.

103. Jürgen H. C. Lebram, "The Piety of the Jewish Apocalyptists," in Hellholm, ed., *Apocalypticism in the Mediterranean World and the Near East,* pp. 171–210.

104. See Hengel, *The Zealots,* chap. 5, "The Zealots as an Eschatological Movement."

105. Smith, "Palestinian Judaism in the First Century," pp. 74–75; cited by Neusner, *From Politics to Piety,* pp. 147–148.

106. Mason, *Josephus and the New Testament,* p. 47.

107. *The Fathers according to Rabbi Nathan,* trans. Judah Goldin (New Haven: Yale University Press, 1955), pp. 35–37.

108. Neusner, *From Politics to Piety,* pp. 144–145.

109. Maccoby, *The Mythmaker,* p. 48.

110. On the (remote) biblical precedent for the Fourth Philosophy's views, see Hengel, *The Zealots,* pp. 90–99.

111. See Michael Stone, "Reactions to Destructions of the Second Temple: Theology, Perception and Conversion," *Journal for the Study of Judaism* 12:2, pp. 195–204; Anthony J. Saldarini, "Varieties of Rabbinic Response to the Destruction of the Temple," in Kent H. Richards, ed., *Society of Biblical Literature 1982 Seminar Papers* (Chico: Scholars, 1982), pp. 437–458; Robert Kirschner, "Apocalyptic and Rabbinic Responses to the Destruction of 70," *Harvard Theological Review* 78:1–2 (1985), pp. 27–46.

112. On the problem of Christian interpolation in the passage and a sensible reconstruction of Josephus's text, see Schürer, *History of the Jewish People,* 1:62–63; John P. Meier, "Jesus in Josephus: A Modest Proposal," *Catholic Biblical Quarterly* 52:1 (1990), pp. 76–103.

113. As we saw in chapter 4, this is the likely background against which some Jews began to think of Jesus' death as atoning; some scholars have argued that this belief could have *preceded* belief in Jesus' death as the death of the messiah.

114. Fredriksen, *From Jesus to Christ,* p. 168.

115. See chapter 3 above.

116. Fredriksen, *From Jesus to Christ,* p. 134; on the concept, Leon Festinger, Henry W. Reicken, and S. Schachter, *When Prophecy Fails: A Social and Psychological Study of a Modern Group That Predicted the Destruction of the World* (New York: Harper & Row, 1956); applied to earliest Christianity, John G. Gager, *Kingdom and Community: The Social World of Early Christianity* (Englewood Cliffs: Prentice-Hall, 1975), pp. 40–44.

117. Hamerton-Kelly, *Sacred Violence,* pp. 183, 82.

118. So Hamerton-Kelly can affirm that Judaism had its own "antidotes to sacred violence" (ibid., p. 65). Unfortunately he does not develop this insight. See my review of *Sacred Violence* in *Forum* (forthcoming).

119. Ibid., pp. 12, 67–68, 125.

120. Ibid., p. 75.

121. Such a theological calculus is explicit in the pseudepigraphic *Testament of Asher* (in the *Testament of the Twelve Patriarchs*), where "evil action" done to achieve a "good result" is declared "good on the whole" (6:3).

122. On the period of God's nonintervention see Lebram, "The Piety of the Apocalyptists," passim.

123. Wright, *The Climax of the Covenant*.

124. Käsemann, "The Saving Significance of Jesus' Death in Paul," p. 41; the reference is to the blessing of God as "the one who gives life to the dead" in the Eighteen Benedictions.

125. Hamerton-Kelly, *Sacred Violence*, pp. 11–12, 120–139. This particularly unfortunate *and inaccurate* aspect of Hamerton-Kelly's work was discussed at the May 1992 Colloquium on Violence and Religion, where similar discussions in Jerusalem were reported.

126. On this point Hamerton-Kelly's treatment is particularly insightful (ibid., pp. 180–182).

127. Paula Fredriksen has decisively demonstrated this in *From Jesus to Christ*, pp. 165–170.

128. See William S. Campbell, "The Freedom and Faithfulness of God in Relation to Israel," *Journal for the Study of the New Testament* 13 (1981), pp. 27–45; J. C. Beker, "The Faithfulness of God and the Priority of Israel in Paul's Letter to the Romans," *Harvard Theological Review* 79:1–3 (1986), pp. 10–16.

129. See Campbell's thorough rethinking of Romans along these lines in *Paul's Gospel in an Intercultural Context*.

130. So Johannes Munck understood it (*Paul and the Salvation of Mankind*, pp. 287–288); John Knox, on the other hand, recognizes "plenty of evidence in Paul's letters that the churches were expected to care for their poor" but insists that "such passages cannot be cited to prove that there was a custom of sending money to *Jerusalem*" (*Chapters in a Life of Paul*, pp. 36–40).

131. See now Dieter Georgi, *Remembering the Poor* (Nashville: Abingdon, 1992).

132. See Johannes Munck, *Paul and the Salvation of Mankind*, chaps. 2, 10.

133. See Arland Hultgren, *Paul's Gospel and Mission* (Philadelphia: Fortress, 1985), pp. 125–150. It bears note that Paul no longer understands these "gifts" as the return of the dispersed Jews but as Gentiles themselves.

134. So Munck interprets the "restrainer" of 2 Thess. 2:6–7 as indicating Paul, who "holds back" the eschatological day as he completes the evangelization of the nations (*Paul and the Salvation of Mankind*, pp. 36–42).

135. Ibid., p. 46.

136. The verb *euangelizesthai* refers in ordinary Greek usage to royal announcements, the self-aggrandizement of kings; the Septuagint uses the word in Isaiah to describe the heralds of God's sovereign action among the nations. These connotations are never lost in the New Testament writings; the substitution of a strictly "spiritual" sense for "evangelizing" is a later development.

137. That insight is elusive. Despite her demonstration that Paul's apostolate among Gentiles is consistent with Jewish eschatological traditions, Paula Fred-

riksen goes on to contend that Paul *has* diverged from Jewish thought on a crucial point, namely by renouncing the "particularity" of Jewish eschatology. "We search in vain to find Paul praising the future Jerusalem or the eschatological Temple. . . . What place has the land of Israel, the city of Jerusalem, the walls of the Temple—in brief, the *realia* of Judaism—in such an expansive and inclusive vision? . . . In brief, *Paul denationalizes Jewish restoration theology*" (ibid., p. 172).

138. N. T. Wright has shown this to be the background of Paul's Adam-christology, and the indispensable covenantal context of his thought (*Climax of the Covenant*).

139. For issues of translation and exegesis see esp. the perceptive essay by Paul W. Meyer, "Romans 10:4 and the 'End' of the Law," in J. L. Crenshaw and S. Sandmel, eds., *The Divine Helmsman: Essays Presented to Lou Silberman* (New York: KTAV, 1980), pp. 59–78; and Richard Hays, *Echoes of Scripture in the Letters of Paul*, pp. 73–83.

140. Wright, *The Climax of the Covenant*, p. 241, where Wright claims having introduced this interpretation, now widely accepted by other scholars.

141. Gaston, *Paul and the Torah*, p. 142.

142. On the logic of the midrash here see Wright, *The Climax of the Covenant*, pp. 244–246; Richard Hays, *Echoes of Scripture in the Letters of Paul*, loc. cit.

143. Hays, *Echoes of Scripture in the Letters of Paul*, p. 79.

144. So Hays, *Echoes of Scripture in the Letters of Paul*, pp. 78–79.

145. For texts and discussion see *The Theology of the Churches and the Jewish People: Statements by the World Council of Churches and Its Member Churches*, edited and with commentary by Allan Brockway, Paul van Buren, Rolf Rendtorff, Simon Schoon (Geneva: World Council of Churches Publications, 1988); on a similar development in Roman Catholic teaching, Eugene Fisher, "Interpreting *Nostra Aetate*," *Conservative Judaism* 38:1 (1985), pp. 7–20; "The Holy See and the State of Israel: The Evolution of Attitudes and Policies," *Journal of Ecumenical Studies* 24:2 (1987), pp. 191–211.

146. See most recently Sydney Hall III, *Anti-Semitism and Paul's Theology* (Minneapolis: Fortress, 1993).

147. *The Theology of the Churches*, pp. 170–173.

148. Marc Ellis, "Jews, Christians, and Liberation Theology: A Response," in *Judaism, Christianity, and Liberation: An Agenda for Dialogue*, ed. Otto Maduro (Maryknoll: Orbis, 1991), pp. 141–142.

149. The dilemma is beautifully illustrated in the transcript of a conversation between Palestinian theologian Naim Ateek and members of the Ecumenical Theological Research Fraternity in Israel in *Immanuel* 22/23 (1989); see also *People, Land, and State of Israel*, pp. 102–119; Naim Ateek, *Justice and Only Justice: A Palestinian Theology of Liberation* (Maryknoll: Orbis, 1989).

150. Goodman, *The Ruling Class in Judaea*.

151. Beker points out, in contrast to an "unfortunate" preoccupation with the question of chronology, that Paul can simultaneously "contemplate a universal mission and yet live in terms of apocalyptic imminence"; "for Paul the issue is primarily not one of chronological reckoning but one of theological necessity" (*Paul the Apostle*, pp. 177–181).

6. Apostolic Praxis: Living out the Dying of Jesus

1. Hamerton-Kelly, *Sacred Violence*, p. 82.

2. Ziesler, *Pauline Christianity*, pp. 124–126; Beker, *Paul the Apostle*, p. 326. Schweitzer's discussion of the "theory of the *status quo*" in Paul's thought has been extremely influential: *The Mysticism of Paul the Apostle*, pp. 187–196, 310–314.

3. Elaine Pagels, "Paul and Women: A Response to Recent Discussion," *Journal of the American Academy of Religion* 42 (1974), p. 545; cited by Beker, ibid., p. 324.

4. Beker, *Paul the Apostle*, p. 326; Segundo, *The Humanist Christology of Paul*, pp. 164–165; Theissen, *The Social Setting of Pauline Christianity*, pp. 106–110, 139–140; Hamerton-Kelly, *Sacred Violence*, pp. 76, 154.

5. J. C. O'Neill, *Paul's Letter to the Romans* (London: Penguin, 1975), p. 209; Fredriksen, *From Jesus to Christ*, p. 173; Beker, *Paul the Apostle*, p. 326; Hamerton-Kelly, *Sacred Violence*, pp. 154–155; Ernst Bammel, "Romans 13," in *Jesus and the Politics of His Day*, ed. Ernst Bammel and C. F. D. Moule (Cambridge: Cambridge University Press, 1984), p. 365.

6. On Philemon, see the discussion in chapter 2 above, and in Peterson, *Rediscovering Paul*; on 1 Corinthians 11, see the discussion in chapter 3 and below; on Paul's journey "to Arabia" being something other than a private mystical retreat, see Knox, *Chapters in a Life of Paul*, pp. 55–56.

7. Beker, *Paul the Apostle*, pp. 318, 326.

8. As Sir Moses Finley points out, political assemblies were quite restricted in the range of activities to which they could attend; the masses exercised their influence "not through participation in the formal machinery of government, through its voting power, but by taking to the streets, by agitation, demonstration and riots" (*Politics in the Ancient World* [Cambridge: Cambridge University Press, 1983], p. 91).

9. Tomson writes that "the basic coherence of Paul's thought is not in any particular theological theme but in the organic structure of practical life" (*Paul and the Jewish Law*, pp. 55–58, 265); Beker argues that "Paul seems more interested in persuasion, emotional appeal and moral exhortation in his letters than in the academic pursuit of coherence and consistency of thought" ("The Method of Recasting Pauline Theology," p. 597).

10. *Paul the Apostle*, p. 19.

11. See Dieter Georgi, "Who Is the True Prophet?" *Christians among Jews and Gentiles: Essays in Honor of Krister Stendahl on His Sixty-Fifth Birthday*, ed. George W. E. Nickelsburg and George W. MacRae (Philadelphia: Fortress, 1986), pp. 100–127; idem, *Theocracy in Paul's Praxis and Theology*, trans. David E. Green (Minneapolis: Fortress, 1991). The ancient texts on which Georgi relies are available in the Loeb Classical Library from Harvard University Press: *Virgil: Eclogues, Georgics, Aeneid I-VI*, rev. ed., with English translation by H. Rushton Fairclough (1978); *Velleius Paterculus: Compendium of Roman History; Res Gestae Divi Augusti*, with English translation by Frederick W. Shipley (1955); *Minor Latin Poets*, with English translation by J. Wight Duff and Arnold M. Duff (1954).

12. Wink, *Engaging the Powers*, p. 93; Richard Gordon, "From Republic to Principate: Priesthood, Religion, and Ideology," in *Pagan Priests: Religion and*

Power in the Ancient World, ed. Mary Beard and John North (Ithaca: Cornell University Press, 1990), p. 192.

13. Bammel, "Romans 13," pp. 375, 376; Wengst, *Pax Romana,* pp. 11–19.

14. De Ste. Croix, *Class Struggle in the Ancient Greek World,* pp. 327–331; citing A. H. M. Jones, *The Later Roman Empire 284–602; A Social, Economic, and Administrative Survey,* 3 vols. (University of Oklahoma Press, 1964).

15. Richard Gordon, "The Veil of Power: Emperors, Sacrificers and Benefactors," in *Pagan Priests,* pp. 199–234.

16. On patronage and the ethos of benefaction see de Ste. Croix, *Class Struggle in the Ancient Greek World,* pp. 364–366; Frederick Danker, *Benefactor: Epigraphic Study of a Greco-Roman and New Testament Semantic Field* (St. Louis: Clayton, 1982); L. Michael White, ed., *Social Networks in the Early Christian Environment: Issues and Methods for Social History,* Semeia 56 (Atlanta: Scholars, 1992).

17. De Ste. Croix, *Class Struggle in the Ancient Greek World,* p. 342.

18. Gordon, "The Veil of Power," p. 229.

19. Holland Hendrix, "Thessalonicans Honor Romans" (Harvard Divinity School, Th.D. thesis, 1984); discussed in Karl P. Donfried, "The Cults of Thessalonica and the Thessalonian Correspondence," *New Testament Studies* 31 (1985), pp. 336–356.

20. John K. Chow, *Patronage and Power: A Study of Social Networks in Corinth,* Journal for the Study of the New Testament Supplement 75 (Sheffield: JSOT Press, 1992), pp. 38–64; on the "romanization" of Corinth under Augustus and his successors, see also Meeks, *First Urban Christians,* pp. 47–48.

21. On the apocalyptic theme of "knowing what time it is" see Martyn, "Apocalyptic Antinomies."

22. Chmiel, "On Chomsky, Language, and Liberation."

23. Fredriksen, *From Jesus to Christ,* pp. 124–125.

24. Wengst, *Pax Romana,* pp. 76–78; Bammel, "Romans 13," p. 378; Donfried, "The Cults of Thessalonica," p. 344; W. H. C. Frend, *The Early Church* (Philadelphia: Fortress, 1965), pp. 29–30.

25. Donfried, "The Cults of Thessalonica," p. 344.

26. See the discussion in chapter 5; Bartsch, "Die antisemitische Gegner"; Gager, *The Origins of Anti-Semitism.*

27. Paul indicates in Rom. 15:28–29 that he wants to win the support of the Roman church as he faces "unbelievers in Judea"; he says nothing about these "unbelievers" in the letter opening, however. Some interpreters assert that the letter's actual readers have completely dropped out of sight in Romans 2 so that Paul can address his imaginary opponents, "the Jews"; others describe Paul as concealing his real agenda out of timidity. See Jacob Jervell, "The Letter to Jerusalem," in Donfried, ed., *The Romans Debate,* pp. 53–64; Knox, *Romans,* pp. 358–363; Käsemann, *Commentary on Romans,* p. 390. On the problem of the letter's "double character" see Kümmel, *Introduction to the New Testament;* Schmithals, *Der Römerbrief;* Elliott, *Rhetoric of Romans.*

28. Käsemann, *Commentary on Romans,* p. 29 et passim. For a brief history of interpretation of the phrase *hē dikaiosynē tou theou* see Manfred Brauch, "The 'Righteousness of God' in Recent Interpretation," in Sanders, *Paul and Palestinian Judaism,* pp. 523–542; also Käsemann, "The Righteousness of God in Paul," in *New Testament Questions of Today,* pp. 168–182; Sam K. Williams,

"The 'Righteousness of God' in Romans," *Journal of Biblical Literature* 99 (1980), pp. 260ff.; Richard Hays, "Psalm 143 and the Logic of Romans 3," *Journal of Biblical Literature* 99 (1980), pp. 107–115.

29. Georgi, *Theocracy in Paul's Praxis and Theology,* pp. 81–96.

30. On this identification see Geza Vermes, *The Dead Sea Scrolls in English,* 3d ed. (New York: Doubleday, 1992), pp. 28–29; A. Dupont-Sommer, *The Essene Writings from Qumran,* trans. G. Vermes (Gloucester, MA: Peter Smith, 1973), pp. 341–346.

31. Walter Grundmann, "The Teacher of Righteousness of Qumran and the Question of Justification by Faith in the Theology of the Apostle Paul," *Révue de Qumran* 2 (1960), pp. 237–259; now in Jerome Murphy-O'Connor and James H. Charlesworth, eds., *Paul and the Dead Sea Scrolls* (New York: Crossroad, 1990), pp. 85–114.

32. Segundo, *The Humanist Christology of Paul,* pp. 28–29.

33. The Habakkuk commentary juxtaposes the distinctive Roman practice of "sacrificing to their standards" with Roman dominion "over all the peoples year by year, ravaging many lands" (6:1ff).

34. Victor P. Furnish, *The Moral Teaching of Paul* (Nashville: Abingdon, 1979), pp. 73–78; Robin Scroggs, *The New Testament and Homosexuality: Contextual Background for Contemporary Debate* (Philadelphia: Fortress, 1983); Richard Hays, "Relations Natural and Unnatural: A Response to John Boswell's Exegesis of Romans 1," *Journal for Religious Ethics* 14:1 (1986), pp. 184–219; idem, "Awaiting the Redemption of Our Bodies," *Sojourners* 20:6 (1991), pp. 17–21. I am particularly grateful to Jeffrey Siker for sharing with me a draft of his article "Homosexual Christians and Gentile Inclusion: Confessions of a Repenting Heterosexist," to be published in *Theology Today.*

35. Hays, "Relations Natural and Unnatural," pp. 189–190; the question is treated at length by Scroggs, *The New Testament and Homosexuality.*

Historian John Boswell writes that "Roman society almost unanimously assumed that adult males would be capable of, if not interested in, sexual relations with both sexes. It is extremely difficult to convey to modern audiences the absolute indifference of most Latin authors to the question of gender" (*Christianity, Social Tolerance, and Homosexuality: Gay People in Western Europe from the Beginning of the Christian Era to the Fourteenth Century* [Chicago: University of Chicago Press, 1980], p. 73).

It was expected, for example, that adolescent boys would experiment sexually with male and female partners before settling down to a proper marriage and thus yielding to "the inexorable claims of the city" (see Peter Brown, *The Body and Society: Men, Women, and Sexual Renunciation in Early Christianity* [New York: Columbia University Press, 1988], pp. 5–32). Consequently most references in ancient Greek and Latin literature to homosexual acts are to acts performed by men whom *we* would be tempted to describe as heterosexual, that is, men eventually married to women, yet also resorting on occasion to sex with male and female prostitutes or slaves (ibid., p. 23).

Brown observes that what pagan moralists in Paul's day found most troubling and condemned as "unnatural" was a citizen's willingness to submit, that is, to "play the female role," with a man his social equal: "No free man should allow himself to be so weakened by desire as to allow himself to step out of the ferociously maintained hierarchy that placed all free men, in all their dealings, above women and slaves" (ibid., p. 30). Similarly Boswell notes that "a male who voluntarily adopted the sexual role of the powerless partook of the inferior status they occupied" (*Christianity, Social Tolerance, and Homosexuality*, pp. 74–75). This, not homosexuality as such, is the apparent concern in the passages Hays cites, read in context ("Relations Natural and Unnatural," pp. 192–194).

36. The "reign of the phallus" in classical Athens dictated that boys became men through ritualized sodomy. On the other hand, "a mutual sex relationship between two adult men of approximately the same age and social standing negates the use of sex as the underpinning of a power structure. . . . It is probably for that reason, and not because it is 'unnatural,' or breaks the link between sex and procreation, that true male homosexuality is usually censured, as in the case of classical Athens" (Eva Keuls, *The Reign of the Phallus: Sexual Politics in Ancient Athens* [New York: Harper & Row, 1985], pp. 276–277). Closer to Paul's day, a Roman lawyer would defend his client, a freedman, from ridicule for submitting to his former master sexually by declaring that such "sexual service is an offense for the freeborn, a necessity for the slave, and a duty for the freedman" (cited by Boswell, *Christianity, Social Tolerance, and Homosexuality*, p. 78).

37. Scroggs argues that the terms Paul uses in 1 Cor. 6:9 should not be rendered "homosexuals"; they more likely refer to male prostitutes and their customers, or perhaps to pederasts and "the morally dissolute" (*The New Testament and Homosexuality*, pp. 62–65; 84; 101–109). See also Boswell, *Christianity, Social Tolerance, and Homosexuality*, pp. 341–353; David F. Wright, "Homosexuals or Prostitutes? The Meaning of *ARSENOKOITAI* (1 Cor. 6:9, 1 Tim. 1:10)," *Vigiliae Christianae* 38 (1984), pp. 125–153; and the response by William L. Petersen, "Can *ARSENOKOITAI* Be Translated by 'Homosexuals'? (1 Cor. 6:9; 1 Tim. 1:10)," *Vigiliae Christianae* 40 (1986), pp. 187–191.

38. Scroggs, *The New Testament and Homosexuality*, p. 127 (emphasis in original).

39. Jeffrey S. Siker, "Homosexual Christians and Gentile Inclusion." In this regard Siker cites Chris Glaser's *Uncommon Calling: A Gay Man's Struggle to Serve the Church* (San Francisco: Harper & Row, 1988).

40. Thus Hays, who sees a "rhetorical trap" for the Jew in 1:18–2:1, concedes that "this suggests that Paul's purpose in Romans 1:26–27 is not to provide moral instruction for Roman Christians" ("Relations Natural and Unnatural," p. 195). See my discussion of the exegetical issues involved in *Rhetoric of Romans*, pp. 108–127.

41. See Wayne A. Meeks, "Judgment and the Brother: Romans 14:1–15:13," in *Tradition and Interpretation in the New Testament: Essays in Honor of E. Earle Ellis*, ed. G. F. Hawthorne and O. Betz (Grand Rapids: Eerdmans, 1987), esp. pp. 290–292.

42. The same pattern is evident in the Habakkuk pesher, where we read that the Wicked Priest's corruption, his extortion of his own people, and his defilement of the Temple are punished by "horrors of evil diseases" in his "body of flesh" (9:1).

43. At Rom. 1:18–32 Käsemann remarks on the "blackness of the picture which leaves hardly any place for a consideration of authentic religiosity, presents the general depravity of humanity without differentiation, and demon-

strates it by the most abhorrent perversions," resulting in a picture that "does not do justice to Gentile religion as a whole" and "appears distorted" (*Commentary on Romans*, pp. 34, 46, 49). By frequent references to Paul's "apocalyptic" perspective, Käsemann practically make this distortion appear a theological virtue.

44. Wayne A. Meeks, "Social Functions of Apocalyptic Language in Pauline Christianity," in Hellholm, ed., *Apocalypticism*, p. 691; E. A. Judge, "The Decrees of Caesar at Thessalonica," *Reformed Theological Review* 30 (1971), pp. 2–7; Donfried, "The Cults of Thessalonica," pp. 344–345, 350.

45. Donfried, "The Cults of Thessalonica," p. 349, following F. F. Bruce, *The Acts of the Apostles* (Grand Rapids: Eerdmans, 1951), pp. 327–328.

46. Meeks, "Social Functions of Apocalyptic Language," p. 692. On the international "reference group" of the Pauline ekklesia see idem, "The Circle of Reference in Pauline Morality," in Abraham Malherbe, David L. Balch, Everett Ferguson, and Wayne A. Meeks, eds., *Greeks, Romans, and Christians: Essays in Honor of Abraham Malherbe* (Minneapolis: Fortress, 1990), pp. 305–317; on the intimate "family" language in the Pauline congregations, idem, *First Urban Christians*, pp. 85–89; on these same questions related specifically to women in the Pauline churches, Ross Shepard Kraemer, *Her Share of the Blessings: Women's Religions among Pagans, Jews, and Christians in the Greco-Roman World* (New York: Oxford University Press, 1992), chap. 10.

47. Pheme Perkins, "Philippians: Theology for the Heavenly Politeuma," in *Pauline Theology I: Thessalonians, Philippians, Galatians, Philemon*, ed. Jouette M. Bassler (Minneapolis: Fortress, 1991), pp. 89–104.

48. Stanley K. Stowers, "Friends and Enemies in the Politics of Heaven: Reading Theology in Philippians," in *Pauline Theology*, pp. 105–121.

49. Andrew Lincoln, *Paradise Now and Not Yet* (Cambridge: Cambridge University Press, 1981), pp. 193, 63; cited by Stowers, "Friends and Enemies."

50. Perkins, "Philippians," p. 92.

51. Ibid., pp. 92–94 (Perkins cites Joachim Gnilka, *Der Philipperbrief* [Freiburg: Herder, 1968], pp. 186–189, 206); Barclay, *The Obedience of Faith*. On the "agitators" in Galatia as Jewish Christians seeking "to consolidate the [Christian] community within Judaism" see Fredriksen, *From Jesus to Christ*, pp. 165–170.

52. Meeks, *First Urban Christians*, chap. 3.

53. See Hamerton-Kelly, *Sacred Violence*, pp. 85–86.

54. Girard, *Things Hidden from the Foundation of the World*, p. 218.

55. Hamerton-Kelly, *Sacred Violence*, pp. 175–178; see also John Pairman Brown, "Inversion of Social Roles in Paul's Letters," *Novum Testamentum* 33:4 (1991), pp. 303–325. On scapegoat rituals in Greek religion see Walter Burkert, *Greek Religion*, trans. John Raffan (Cambridge: Harvard University Press, 1985), pp. 82–84.

56. Hamerton-Kelly, *Sacred Violence*, pp. 68–71, 179–180.

57. Kraemer, *Her Share of the Blessings*, p. 141.

58. Meeks, *First Urban Christians*, pp. 157–161. The most important anthropological studies of ritual on which Meeks depends are Arnold van Gennep, *The Rites of Passage*, trans. M. B. Vizedom and G. L. Caffee (Chicago: University of Chicago Press, 1960), and Victor Turner, *The Ritual Process: Structure and Antistructure* (Ithaca: Cornell University Press, 1977).

59. Wright, *The Climax of the Covenant;* see chapter 5 above.

60. Brown, *The Body and Society,* pp. 46–47.

61. Hamerton-Kelly, *Sacred Violence,* p. 69.

62. Ibid., pp. 69, 180.

63. Munck, *Paul and the Salvation of Mankind;* Georgi, *Remembering the Poor.*

64. See Gordon, "Veil of Power"; Chow, *Patronage and Power;* de Ste. Croix, *Class Struggle,* pp. 364–366.

65. Marshall, *Enmity in Corinth.*

66. Chow, *Patronage and Power,* pp. 167–190.

67. De Ste. Croix, *Class Struggle in the Ancient Greek World,* pp. 32–33; see Rohrbaugh, "Methodological Considerations," p. 541, and Meeks, *First Urban Christians,* chap. 2.

68. Martin, "Ancient Slavery, Class, and Early Christianity," p. 111.

69. On *chreia* as "use, service," see the Liddell-Scott *Lexicon.*

70. Malherbe, *Paul and the Thessalonians,* pp. 105–106.

71. Malherbe shows that Paul's language here "was commonly used in the first century to describe the contemplative life in opposition to an activism that was described as meddlesomeness" (*polypragmosynē*) (*Paul and the Thessalonians,* pp. 95–107). A crucial difference between the Pauline praxis and the ideal of "the quiet life" (*hēsychia*) described by the Stoics or Epicureans, however, is that "the Thessalonians were to spend their time in manual labor," which "was held in low esteem and unlikely to commend them to persons of some social standing." Malherbe concludes, in part by relying on 2 Thessalonians, that Paul faces "a tendency among converts to abandon their jobs": he is "dealing with manual laborers who have a tendency not to live quietly but to interfere in other people's business." Paul thus seeks to distance the Christian community from public stereotypes of Cynic idleness and of Epicurean misanthropy.

"Meddlesomeness" and "idleness" are prominent in 2 Thessalonians (see 3:6), which Malherbe considers genuine (p. 99); but there is no evidence that they are issues in 1 Thessalonians.

72. See the Bauer-Arndt-Gingrich-Danker *Lexicon.*

73. Karl P. Donfried suggests the translation, "gain control over" the phallus ("The Cults of Thessalonica," pp. 341–342). The phrase "reign of the phallus" comes from Eva Keuls, *The Reign of the Phallus.*

74. See the judicious treatment of issues in Schüssler Fiorenza, *In Memory of Her,* pp. 168–184; 205–236.

75. Meeks, *First Urban Christians,* pp. 93–94.

76. Luise Schottroff, "'Give to Caesar what Belongs to Caesar and to God what Belongs to God': A Theological Response of the Early Christian Church to Its Social and Political Environment," in Willard Swartley, ed., *The Love of Enemy and Nonretaliation in the New Testament* (Louisville: Westminster/John Knox, 1992), p. 249.

77. F. C. Baur's essay, "Die Christuspartei in der korinthischen Gemeinde" (*Tübinger Zeitschrift* 4 [1831], pp. 61–206), has never been published in English translation; some of its assumptions are represented, however, by C. K. Barrett (*A Commentary on the First Epistle to the Corinthians* [New York: Harper & Row, 1968]; "Cephas and Corinth," in *Essays on Paul*). On the "Ideological Reconstruction of the Corinthian Conflict," see the survey by Wire, *The*

Corinthian Women Prophets, pp. 206–208; Walter Schmithals, *Gnosticism in Corinth* (Nashville: Abingdon, 1971); Dieter Georgi, *The Opponents of Paul in 2 Corinthians* (Philadelphia: Fortress, 1986).

78. Munck, "The Church without Factions: Studies in 1 Corinthians 1–4," in *Paul and the Salvation of Mankind,* pp. 135–167; Dahl, "Paul and the Church at Corinth according to 1 Corinthians 1:10–4:21," in *Studies in Paul,* pp. 40–61; Meeks, *First Urban Christians,* pp. 117–118.

79. See Vincent Wimbush, *Paul the Worldly Ascetic: Response to the World and Self-Understanding according to 1 Corinthians 7* (Macon: Mercer University Press, 1987); O. Larry Yarbrough, *Not Like the Gentiles: Marriage Rules in Paul's Letters* (Atlanta: Scholars, 1985); Wire, *Corinthian Women Prophets.*

80. Judge, *Social Pattern of Christian Groups;* idem, "The early Christians as a Scholastic Community"; idem, "St. Paul and Classical Society"; Meeks, *First Urban Christians;* Theissen, *Social Setting of Pauline Christianity,* and esp. "The Sociological Interpretation of Religious Traditions: Its Methodological Problems as Exemplified in Early Christianity," pp. 175–200.

81. Theissen, *Social Setting of Pauline Christianity,* p. 72.

82. Several recent scholars have challenged the assumption that Paul is "reminding" the Corinthians of his authority; rather, his assertion of authority is a bold innovation in his relationship with the Corinthian church. See Wire, *Corinthian Women Prophets,* passim; Schüssler Fiorenza, "The Rhetorical Situation in 1 Corinthians"; Elizabeth Castelli, *A Discourse of Power* (Louisville: Westminster/John Knox, 1992).

83. Munck, "The Church without Factions."

84. Similarly Wire suggests there may have been individuals in the Corinthian congregation who "will be new converts who first heard of Paul from others" (*Corinthian Women Prophets,* p. 46). Her reconstruction of the community's history is also based on her supposition that a single group, the Corinthian women prophets, have themselves moved from lower status (1:26) to higher status within the ekklesia (pp. 44–46). But this judgment depends on a prior assumption that the women prophets are the primary addressees of the letter (for example, she declares that "their ears are shaping his mouth throughout" the letter, p. 55), an assumption I do not share.

85. See Theissen, *Social Setting of Pauline Christianity,* pp. 127, 130; Chow, *Patronage and Power,* pp. 154–166; Meeks, *First Urban Christians,* p. 98.

86. Curiously, Theissen goes on to argue that Paul only "mitigates the tension" between higher and lower classes when he advises the Corinthians (10:23–25) to "eat whatever is sold in the meat market without raising any question on the ground of conscience" (*Social Setting of Pauline Christianity,* p. 139). "The factual privileges of status enjoyed by the higher strata are preserved. For example, private meals with consecrated meat continue to be allowed in principle (10:23ff). Nor is participation in cultic meals excluded in principle. All that is prohibited is disturbing a weak person by doing so."

But Paul *does* exclude cultic meals in principle: "I do not want you to be partners with demons. You cannot drink the cup of the Lord and the cup of demons. You cannot partake of the table of the Lord and the table of demons" (10:19–22). (The conditional sentence in 8:10, "if anyone sees you, a person of knowledge, at table in an idol's temple," is hypothetical.) As for private meals in the homes of non-Christians, Christians are not to balk at consecrated meat *unless* someone at the meal mentions the meat's origin. Once the associations with idolatry are explicit—once the food is linked to the beneficence of the city's gods—the Christian is obligated to abstain. This is not a matter of deference to "the weak" but a matter of witness to the unbeliever (10:27–29).

87. Theissen, *Social Setting of Pauline Christianity*, pp. 145–174; Chow, *Patronage and Power*, pp. 94, 110–112; R. Alastair Campbell, "Does Paul Acquiesce in Divisions at the Lord's Supper?" *Novum Testamentum* 33:1 (1991), pp. 61–70.

88. On this point Munck's arguments are decisive ("The Church without Factions"); see also Chow, *Patronage and Power*, pp. 75–80.

89. I am grateful to Dale Martin for a copy of his paper, "Tongues of Angels and Other Status Indicators," first presented at the 1992 Annual Meeting of the Society of Biblical Literature and soon to be published. Meeks's arguments are presented in *First Urban Christians*, pp. 119–120. As he points out, it is not clear how glossolalia could have been restricted as the possession of a privileged few; it is a behavior that can be learned (p. 149), more easily than the rules of ancient rhetoric, and since Paul expects it usually to be unintelligible to others (1 Cor. 14:2–11, 16), it can be simulated easily enough. Further, Paul suggests unrestrained glossolalia contributes to "disorder" (*akatastasia*, 14:33) in which authority is undifferentiated; this would be an effective way to disrupt the strategies of prestige through rhetorical skill that were apparently favored by the elite (1:17; 14:8). It would seem that glossolalia could have functioned as a sort of antirhetorical solvent to the prestige of the elite within the ekklesiai.

90. Theissen, *Social Setting of Pauline Christianity*, pp. 134–137.

91. Meeks, *First Urban Christians*, pp. 98, 160.

92. Wire, *Corinthian Women Prophets*, pp. 13–14.

93. On this translation see Campbell, "Does Paul Acquiesce in Divisions at the Lord's Supper?" pp. 69–70.

94. Meeks, *First Urban Christians*, p. 159, citing Theissen, *Social Setting of Pauline Christianity*, pp. 313–314; Wire, *Corinthian Women Prophets*, p. 16.

95. Campbell, "Does Paul Acquiesce in Divisions at the Lord's Supper?" Clearly the conditional clause, "if anyone is hungry," is also ironic: otherwise Paul would be guilty of the same contempt of which he accuses the Corinthian elite (11:21–22). Here he addresses not the have-nots but the elite, who can, if they wish, take their fill in their own homes; their "hunger" is mere appetite.

96. Margaret M. Mitchell, *Paul and the Rhetoric of Reconciliation: An Exegetical Investigation of the Language and Composition of 1 Corinthians* (Tübingen and Louisville: J. C. B. Mohr [Paul Siebeck] and Westminster/John Knox, 1992).

97. Paul adopts a term that in koine Greek routinely referred to "the voting assembly of citizens of a free Greek city" (Meeks, *First Urban Christians*, pp. 93–94).

98. See Origen, *Contra Celsus*, 3:44, 55. By "potentially revolutionary implications" I refer to the sort of consequences other scholars have recognized with regard to Philemon (see chapter 2 above). N. T. Wright and B. M. Rapske, for example, express concern that Paul's mission would come under profound suspicion from the local householders if it became known that he advocated the release of a fugitive slave (Wright, *Epistles*, p. 166; Rapske, "The Prisoner Paul,"

p. 192.). Paul's instruction concerning the Lord's Supper in Corinth would attract similar concerns, I suggest, as second- and third-century criticisms of Christian subversiveness indicate (on which see Robert Wilken's discussion in *The Christians as the Romans Saw Them* [New Haven: Yale University Press, 1984]).

99. "If the spiritual and immoral man was also a rich patron in the church, he would certainly have a better chance of being approved by the church. For who would want to dishonor a powerful patron?" (Chow, *Patronage and Power,* pp. 139–140).

100. Theissen, *Social Setting of Pauline Christianity,* p. 130; so also Meeks, *First Urban Christians,* p. 98.

101. For recent treatments and bibliography, see Wire, "Appendix 8: Women's Head Covering," in *Corinthian Women Prophets,* pp. 220–223; Ross Shepard Kraemer, *Her Share of the Blessings,* pp. 146–149.

102. Robin Scroggs declares that "today no real sense can be made out of the whys of the logic, why the head covering, why such a 'symbol' is necessary" ("Paul and the Eschatological Woman," *Journal of the American Academy of Religion* 40 [1972], p. 301); see also Kraemer, *Her Share of the Blessings,* p. 146; Wire, *Corinthian Women Prophets,* p. 157.

103. Wire contends that Paul means to "rein in" these women, and consequently she must argue that Paul's rhetoric has lost its cogency at just this point: He seems "to misgauge the women prophets." The subordination of women Paul supposedly seeks "could not be defended on the basis of the common baptism into Christ or the common good"; his desperate appeal to "church tradition" in 14:34–35 shows that "either Paul underestimates the depth of his opposition in Corinth," or else his "sharp challenge and threat" are "signs of insecurity." "The stonewalling here could also show that he senses he cannot get further by rational appeals" (*Corinthian Women Prophets,* pp. 153–158).

But assuming that at this point Paul has become "completely incompetent" at persuasion surrenders the operating assumption of rhetorical criticism, as Wire herself articulates it: "to argue is to gauge your audience as accurately as you can at every point, to use their language, to work from where they are in order to move them toward where you want them to be."

In fact Wire concedes that her "subordinationist" reading of 11:2–16 depends on the construction of chapters 11–14 (p. 121). On the authenticity of the latter passage, see her excursus, pp. 149–152; on the premise of rhetorical criticism, see p. 3.

Ross Shepard Kraemer accepts the view that 14:34–35 is an interpolation and concludes, rightly, that it is "unnecessary to discuss them further in any reconstruction" of the Corinthian situation (*Her Share of the Blessings,* p. 149). Kraemer argues that while Paul may wish to impose a grid of "classification and hierarchy, here according to gender" in 11:2–16, he clearly "has no interest in curbing women's ritual activity—their praying and prophesying are givens" (p. 147).

104. Richard Oster points out, with some irony, that commentators routinely consider the address to men only a rhetorical foil for the "real" address to women ("When Men Wore Veils to Worship," pp. 482–484). Conzelmann, for example, declares that "the parallelisms between vv. 4 and 5 express the fundamental equality of rights although it is only the *woman's* conduct that is at issue" (*First Corinthians,* p. 184, n. 35).

105. That the order of Paul's statement in 11:2 is not the expected order of the hierarchy he describes (that is, God, Christ, man, woman) has puzzled commentators; it may in fact indicate the target of his argument, that is, that "the head of a man is Christ."

106. The phrase is an unusual circumlocution for "veil," as Jerome Murphy-O'Connor notes ("Sex and Logic in 1 Corinthians 11:2–16," *Journal of Biblical Literature* 42 [1980], pp. 483–484); but (against Murphy-O'Connor) it is just as unlikely a circumlocution for "long hair." It would be a reasonable way of describing the gesture of covering one's head with one's garment (see Richard Oster, "When Men Wore Veils to Worship: The Historical Context of 1 Corinthians 11:4," *New Testament Studies* 34 [1988], pp. 481–505).

107. Gordon, "The Veil of Power," p. 202; Oster, "When Men Wore Veils," pp. 496–501; David W. J. Gill, "The Importance of Roman Portraiture for Head Coverings in 1 Corinthians 11:2–16," *Tyndale Bulletin* 41:2 (1990), pp. 245–260. Gordon cites H. Freier, *Caput Velare* (diss. Tübingen, 1966), pp. 26–29. The gesture reflects "a public role which is in principle no different from the role of every *paterfamilias* who sacrifices to the Lares in his own house" (Gordon, op. cit., p. 266). See also S. K. Price, *Rituals and Power: The Roman Imperial Cult in Asia Minor* (Cambridge: Cambridge University Press, 1984), chap. 7.

108. Scroggs, "Paul and the Eschatological Woman"; Morna D. Hooker, "Authority on Her Head: An Examination of 1 Corinthians 11:10," *New Testament Studies* 10 (1963–64), pp. 410–416.

The statements in 11:5–6 are to be taken hypothetically; that is, they do *not* address women in Corinth who are eager to pray with their heads uncovered. On that rather common assumption, interpreters have been compelled to explain how Paul should expect these women to submit to his view that such behavior is as "shameful" as going about unshaven; and to explain how, if the women do not already see things Paul's way, Paul can assume in 11:13–14 that they do.

109. Gill, "The Importance of Roman Portraiture," p. 258; Gordon, "The Veil of Power." On the standardization of imperial images as a function of propaganda, see Price, *Rituals and Power,* pp. 172–177.

110. Zinn, *A People's History of the United States,* chap. 15.

111. Luther H. Martin, *Hellenistic Religions* (New York: Oxford University Press, 1987).

112. Wire, *Corinthian Women Prophets,* p. 191; the same point is made more forcefully by de Ste. Croix, *Class Struggle in the Ancient Greek World,* p. 349.

113. See in particular de Ste. Croix's discussion of "libertas" as the legitimation of "the rule of a class and the perpetuation of privilege" (*Class Struggle in the Ancient Greek World,* pp. 366–370).

114. Schweitzer, *Mysticism of the Apostle Paul,* pp. 187–194; Wimbush, *Paul the Worldly Ascetic,* pp. 14–17; Wire, *Corinthian Women Prophets,* pp. 72–97.

115. Wire rightly points out that "there is little evidence of Paul answering written questions"; she suggests rather that "Paul is not answering questions but questioning answers" (*Corinthian Women Prophets,* p. 80).

116. Wire argues that Paul's horror at a scandalous episode of immorality (*porneia,* 5:1) leads him to restrict the freedoms of holy, ascetic women in order

to protect the church from even more immorality (*Corinthian Women Prophets*, p. 74; on the motives of the men, p. 81). In her view, Paul has no hope of persuading the immoral men in the church to refrain from immorality, "but he can hope to have shocked their actual or potential spouses" by invoking the threat of *porneia* infecting the body of Christ. Paul hopes thus to persuade the women ascetics "to give up what they have gained through sexual abstinence in order that the community and Christ himself may be saved from immorality," that is, by "restoring, wherever necessary, the traditional marriage bonds that preserve morality" (pp. 78–79).

Several observations cast doubt on this interpretation, however. First, the motive of "preventing immorality" disappears after 7:2. When Paul subsequently expresses a preference for celibacy, he does not seem worried that sexual immorality will result if these women, or men, pursue celibate lives (in apparent contrast to what he expects from married people).

Second, it isn't clear that Corinthian women have in fact separated or withdrawn sexually from their husbands. That Paul talks about sexual abstinence within marriage (7:5) does not require that the Corinthians were actually practicing it, or had publicly advocated it, or had asked Paul about it.

Third, there is no reason to tie the "immoral acts" (*porneias*) of 7:1–2 to the *porneia* of 5:1. Paul responded to the immorality mentioned in chap. 5 by insisting categorically that the offender be expelled from the congregation (5:2–5). There is no hint there that Paul considers that response insufficient, or in chap. 7, that his advice regarding sexual relationships continues that response. Neither is it evident that his address to the congregation in 5:2–5 is directed primarily to the women who, on Wire's view, bear the brunt of responsibility in chapter 7.

117. Nils Dahl has argued that the tensions in the Corinthian congregation arose because some individuals did not wish to look to Paul for advice ("Paul and the Church of Corinth").

118. Larry Yarbrough cautions that Paul's remark about "boasting" "should not be taken as evidence of a libertine party which takes pride in the man's freedom," but indicts the congregation's "inability to deal with the case of immorality" (*Not Like the Gentiles,* pp. 96–97). I suggest that inability stems from imbalances of power and status within the congregation. See also Chow, *Patronage and Power,* pp. 130–141.

119. Brown, *The Body and Society,* pp. 50–53.

120. John C. Hurd, for example, has argued that the Corinthians' confusion regarding sexual matters resulted from the ambiguity of Paul's own preaching (*The Origin of 1 Corinthians* [New York: Seabury, 1965]).

121. Wire discusses 1 Corinthians 7:1–2 under the heading "argument dissociating principle from practice," and 8–9, 32–34, and 36 under "argument dissociating private from public" (*Corinthian Women Prophets,* pp. 13–23), depending on categories discussed by Perelman and Olbrechts-Tyteca, *The New Rhetoric,* pp. 411–459. There is a dissociative element in Paul's arguments (represented by the adversative conjunctions *de* and *alla*); but Paul's argument is not that practice must be other than what people think, but that practice other than the ideal is nonetheless acceptable.

His argument more closely resembles what rhetorical theorists call the "double hierarchy" argument. In such an argument the speaker is concerned to "show why a particular term"—in this case, sexual relationships within marriage—"should occupy a particular place rather than another. . . . One will introduce a correlation of the terms of the contested hierarchy with those of an accepted hierarchy" (*The New Rhetoric*, pp. 337–345).

122. See A. J. M. Wedderburn, *The Reasons for Romans* (Edinburgh: T. & T. Clark, 1988); Donfried, *The Romans Debate,* 2d ed.; Elliott, *Rhetoric of Romans,* chap. 1.

123. The most important challenges to that premise have come from Gaston, *Paul and the Torah,* Tomson, *Paul and the Jewish Law,* and Campbell, *Paul's Gospel in an Intercultural Context.*

124. Elliott, *Rhetoric of Romans.*

125. Furnish has argued for the paraenetic character of Romans, demonstrating that the letter is structured around the transformation accomplished in baptism (*Theology and Ethics in Paul,* pp. 105–106); see also Bultmann, *Theology,* 1:72–73, 105–106, and Elliott, *Rhetoric of Romans,* pp. 94–104, 277–283.

126. On the contours of anti-Semitism in Rome see Gager, *Origins of Anti-Semitism,* pp. 63–88; for texts, Menachem Stern, ed., *Greek and Latin Authors on Jews and Judaism,* 3 vols. (Jerusalem: Israel Academy of Sciences and Humanities, 1974–84).

127. Pompey carried captured Jews to Rome to serve as slaves; they were eventually released, being considered unserviceable by the Romans, and became the foundation of the Jewish *politeuma* in Rome: Philo, *Embassy to Gaius* 155.

128. On these issues see the discussions in H. J. Leon, *The Jews of Ancient Rome* (Philadelphia: Jewish Publication Society of America, 1960); Mary Smallwood, *The Jews under Roman Rule* (Leiden, Netherlands: E. J. Brill, 1976).

129. Gager speaks of "a semi-official portrait of Judaism in Roman literary circles" (*Origins of Anti-Semitism,* p. 64).

130. The Fulvia episode: Josephus, *Antiquities* 18:81–84; Suetonius, *Tiberius* 36.

131. According to Dio Cassius, *History* 60:6:6. On this reconstruction see Wiefel, "The Jewish Community in Ancient Rome."

132. Daniel Fraikin, "The Rhetorical Function of the Jews in Romans," in *Anti-Judaism in Early Christianity,* vol. 1: *Paul and the Gospels,* ed. Peter Richardson with David Granskou (Waterloo, Ontario: Wilfrid Laurier, 1986), p. 101.

133. For issues involved in the identification of "weak" and "strong" in Romans 14 and 15 see Elliott, *Rhetoric of Romans,* pp. 52–57.

134. Campbell, *Paul's Gospel in an Intercultural Context;* see also my qualifications of this theme at the end of chapter 5, above.

135. J. C. O'Neill, *Paul's Letter to the Romans* (London: Penguin, 1975), p. 209; Stanley Porter, "Romans 13:1–7 as Pauline Political Rhetoric," *Filología Neotestamentaria* 3 (1990), pp. 115–139; Ernst Käsemann, "Principles of the Interpretation of Romans 13," in *New Testament Questions of Today,* pp. 200–207; and Winsome Munro, "Romans 13:1–7: Apartheid's Last Biblical Refuge," *Biblical Theology Bulletin* 20:4 (1990), pp. 161–168.

136. Joseph Klausner, *From Jesus to Paul* (London, 1939), p. 565.

137. James Kallas, "Romans XIII.1–7: An Interpolation," *New Testament Studies* 11 (1965), p. 369.

138. In addition to the essays by Kallas and Munro (see note 155), see Munro's monograph, *Authority in Paul and Peter: The Identification of a Pastoral Stratum in the Pauline Corpus and 1 Peter,* New Testament Studies Monograph Series 45 [Cambridge: Cambridge University Press, 1983]), and Walter Schmithals, *Der Römerbrief als historisches Problem* (Gütersloh: Gütersloher Verlagshaus Gerd Mohn, 1975).

139. There is minor textual disturbance here: the earlier reading of p46, "be subject to all the governing authorities," was changed to an even more universal and timeless formula, "let every soul be subject to the governing authorities," at some point before the great fourth-century codices. But there is no manuscript witness to a text without 13:1–7 in some form. As J. I. H. McDonald concludes, it is doubtful whether the arguments from theological coherence "can be held to shake the evidence of the primary [manuscript] witnesses" ("Romans 13:1–7: A Test Case for New Testament Interpretation," *New Testament Studies* 35:4 [1989], p. 541).

140. Porter, "Romans 13:1–7 as Pauline Political Rhetoric," p. 118. The center of Porter's argument is the contention that the obedience Paul encourages is a matter of "willing submission, with the unstated though clearly understood assumption that this obedience is to be made to a just power and that submission is not to be made to an unjust power." Unfortunately, an exegesis based so fundamentally on what is "unstated though clearly understood" remains dubious, however attractive to modern perceptions.

141. Dunn, *Romans 9–16,* Word Biblical Commentary vol. 38 (Dallas: Word Books, 1988), p. 773. It is particularly surprising that Dunn can speak of a "theology of political power" after insisting that "the discussion in these verses is context-specific," and that Paul "writes with the reality of his readers' political context very much in view" (p. 768); but this perhaps shows the resilience of the generalized conventional reading of this passage.

142. Bammel, "Romans 13," p. 381.

143. Rebecca I. DeNova, "Paul's Letter to the Romans, 13:1–7: The Gentile-Christian Response to Civil Authority," *Encounter* 53:3 (1992), p. 223.

144. Robert H. Stein, for example, can still declare these verses "the clearest passage in the New Testament dealing with the relationship of the Christian to the State" ("The Argument of Romans 13:1–7," *Novum Testamentum* 31:4 [1989], p. 325); regarding these verses, James D. G. Dunn speaks repeatedly of "a theology of the orderly state, of good government" (*Romans 9–16,* p. 771 et passim).

145. Käsemann, *Commentary on Romans,* p. 351.

146. See McDonald's criticisms, "Romans 13:1–7: A Test Case," pp. 544–545.

147. Tacitus, *Annals* 13:50. The taxes in question are "indirect taxes" (*vectigalia*), customs fees and so on imposed on the lower classes within Italy itself, as opposed to the tribute (*tributum*) extracted from the provinces.

148. J. Friedrich, W. Pöhlmann, and P. Stuhlmacher, "Zür historischen Situation und Intention von Röm 13:1–7," *Zeitschrift für Theologie und Kirche* 73 (1976), pp. 131–166.

149. The argument is cited as providing a partial explanation of the passage by Beker, *Paul the Apostle,* p. 362; Victor Paul Furnish, *Moral Teaching of Paul,* 2d ed. (Nashville: Abingdon, 1985), pp. 131–133; Dunn, *Romans 9–16,* p. 766;

and Wedderburn, *Reasons for Romans,* p. 62. McDonald declares it "the most impressive scenario" produced to date ("Romans 13:1–7: A Test Case," p. 547).

150. Porter observes that this reconstruction "lacks necessary historical evidence that such taxation was an issue, but more importantly lacks textual evidence that Paul was aware of and concerned with such taxation in writing to the Romans (v. 6 is slim evidence indeed)" ("Romans 13:1–7 as Pauline Political Rhetoric," p. 116); DeNova calls the hypothesis "speculative at best" ("Paul's Letter to the Romans, 13:1–7," p. 221). Even McDonald, who advocates the proposal, cautions that we are dealing here "with probabilities, not certainties" ("Romans 13:1–7: A Test Case," p. 547).

The same criticisms would apply to Winsome Munro's argument that the taxes in question are to be located more specifically during the reign of Trajan (thus supporting her argument that the passage is a later interpolation: "Romans 13:1–7," pp. 164–165).

151. "The *gar* shows that *teleite* must be taken as an indicative," declares Dunn (*Romans 9–16*, p. 766; also Wengst, *Pax Romana and the Peace of Jesus Christ,* p. 82).

152. Marcus Borg, "A New Context for Romans XIII," *New Testament Studies* 19 (1972–73), pp. 205–218.

153. Borg's arguments concerning "Jewish messianic agitation in Rome, provoked both by the experience of the Roman Jews and sympathy with the contemporaneous aspirations of and outrages suffered by Palestinian Jews," are compelling (ibid., p. 212; so also McDonald, "Romans 13:1–7," pp. 545–546; against the doubts of DeNova, "Paul's Letter to the Romans, 13:1–7," p. 219, and Porter, "Romans 13:1–7 as Pauline Political Rhetoric," p. 116). Others have insisted that Suetonius' reference to "tumults at the instigation of some Chrestus" must refer to specifically Christian agitation, as if the two were mutually exclusive. That is a premise I find no reason to share.

154. Porter, "Romans 13:1–7 as Pauline Political Rhetoric," p. 116; Dunn, *Romans 9–16,* p. 773.

155. McDonald, "Romans 13:1–7: A Test Case," p. 546.

156. Prisca and Aquila are identified as the link through which Paul has become aware of the taxation burden, and as individuals likely to have suffered especially under it, by Friedrich, Pöhlmann, and Stuhlmacher, "Zür historischen Situation," pp. 158–159; and Wedderburn, *Reasons for Romans,* pp. 62–63.

157. Dunn, *Romans 9–16,* p. 761. Despite his certainty of Paul's "knowledge of current affairs in Rome," Dunn nevertheless explains the passage as the expression of Paul's view of "a divinely ordered society," and thus "a theology of political power," Paul's "political realism" (ibid., pp. 759, 763, 773; see also "Romans 13:1–7—A Charter for Political Quietism?" *Ex Auditu* 2 [1986], pp. 55–68).

Similarly, McDonald, who accepts the theory that Paul is responding to extortive taxation in Italy, links Paul's emphasis on "the necessity to submit to the state's requirements" with "the need for spiritual transformation (12:2) and Christian discernment (13:5)," but fails to explain the connection between these ("Romans 13:1–7: A Test Case," p. 546).

158. Borg, "A New Context," pp. 214–216.

159. Ibid., p. 218. James D. G. Dunn is similarly compelled to warn Paul's readers against making "the same mistake as his fellow countrymen had—that of

identifying God's purpose of salvation with one particular nation's well-being and political dominance" (*Romans 9–16*, pp. 773–774). And Alexander Webster argues that in 13:1–7 Paul affirms the Roman congregation in the "confident hope that the secular authorities are actually *on their side* against their enemies," whom he declares "were most likely Roman Jews" ("St. Paul's Political Advice to the Haughty Gentile Christians in Rome," *St. Vladimir's Theological Quarterly* 25:4 [1981], pp. 278–279).

160. Dunn, *Romans 9–16*, pp. 768–769.

161. As Rebecca DeNova insists, "It is not the Jews or Jewish-Christians" of Rome who require "a lesson in government relations"; indeed, "the majority of Jews understood and approved the compromise between 'submission' and 'tolerance.' Paul didn't have to remind them of what the proper attitude toward the government should be" ("Paul's Letter to the Romans, 13:1–7," p. 218). James D. G. Dunn can even characterize Paul's comments here as "a restatement of the long-established Jewish recognition of the reality and character of political power" (*Romans 9–16*, p. 773).

162. Schottroff, " 'Give to Caesar What Belongs to Caesar,' " p. 227.

163. Smallwood, *The Jews under Roman Rule*, p. 234.

164. Gager, *Origins of Anti-Semitism*, chap. 3; Schürer, *History of the Jewish People*, vol. 1, pp. 388–398.

165. Gager, *Origins of Anti-Semitism*, pp. 52, 48.

166. Schürer, *History of the Jewish People*, vol. 3, pp. 76–77.

167. Dunn, *Romans 9–16*, p. 766; on antagonism among the Roman elite, Gager, *Origins of Anti-Semitism*, chap. 3.

168. Schottroff, " 'Give to Caesar What Belongs to Caesar,' " p. 229.

169. Gordon Zerbe, "Paul's Ethic of Nonretaliation and Peace," in Willard M. Swartley, ed., *The Love of Enemy and Nonretaliation in the New Testament* (Louisville: Westminster/John Knox, 1992), pp. 177–222. On the question of the political efficacy of nonviolent witness among the early Christians, see Everett Ferguson, "Early Christian Martyrdom and Civil Disobedience," *Journal of Early Christian Studies* 1:1 (1993), pp. 73–73.

170. See my discussion of this biblical doctrine of world sovereignty, as it appears particularly in Jeremiah and Daniel, in chapter 5 above. The biblical and apocalyptic background for Paul's affirmations here are widely recognized by the commentators.

171. The eschatological character of Paul's thought here is routinely obscured by mistranslations of 13:1 declaring that God has "ordained" or "instituted" or "established" the authorities. That they are *tetagmenai hypo theou* means rather that God has "put them in their place." As John Howard Yoder writes, "God is not said to *create* or *institute* or *ordain* the powers that be, but only to *order* them, to put them in order, sovereignly to tell them where they belong, what is their place" (*The Politics of Jesus* [Grand Rapids: Eerdmans, 1972], pp. 203–204; see also Dunn, *Romans 9–16*, pp. 761–762).

172. Stein, "The Argument of Romans 13:1–7," p. 329.

173. Schottroff, " 'Give to Caesar What Belongs to Caesar,' " p. 242.

174. *Acts of the Scilitan Martyrs*, 37, found in ibid.

175. Ibid., pp. 226, 229; K. H. Schelkle, "Staat und Kirche in der patristischen Auslegung von Röm 13,1–7," *Zeitschrift für die neutestamentlichen Wissenschaft* 44 (1952–53), pp. 223–226.

176. Ferguson points out that even when early Christians recognized that martyrdom had political implications, "the conviction that massive civil disobedience would in fact change the laws," or that "passive resistance was an instrument for political ends," was completely absent ("Early Christian Martyrdom and Civil Disobedience," p. 83).

177. Dunn, "The New Perspective on Paul"; Gager, *Origins of Anti-Semitism,* chapter 12.

178. Ibid., p. 198.

179. Käsemann, "Paul and Israel," in *New Testament Questions of Today,* p. 184; Gaston, *Paul and the Torah,* p. 3.

180. Schüssler Fiorenza, *In Memory of Her,* chap. 3.

181. Nelson-Pallmeyer, *War against the Poor.*

182. Wink, *Engaging the Powers,* chap. 16.

183. Elisabeth Schüssler Fiorenza uses the phrase in *Bread Not Stone,* p. xv.

General Index

Index of Names

Index of Citations of Ancient Literature

OTHER EARLY JEWISH WRITINGS

OTHER EARLY CHRISTIAN LITERATURE

RABBINIC LITERATURE

CLASSICAL GREEK AND LATIN LITERATURE